THE PRESTER QUEST

Nicholas Jubber

BANTAM BOOKS

LONDON • TORONTO • SYDNEY • AUCKLAND • JOHANNESBURG

THE PRESTER QUEST
A BANTAM BOOK : 0 553 81628 4
9780553816280

Originally published in Great Britain by Doubleday,
a division of Transworld Publishers

PRINTING HISTORY
Doubleday edition published 2005
Bantam edition published 2006

1 3 5 7 9 10 8 6 4 2

The author and publishers are grateful for permission to quote from the following
publications: *The Travels of Ibn Jubayr* by R. J. C. Broadhurst, published by Jonathan
Cape, used by permission of The Random House Group Limited.
Extract from *Fuzzy-Wuzzy* by Rudyard Kipling, by permission of A. P. Watt Ltd
on behalf of the National Trust for Places of Historic Interest or Natural Beauty.
Extracts from *The Crusades Through Arab Eyes* by Amin Maalouf printed by permission
of Saqi Books, 26 Westbourne Grove, London W2 5RH.
Extract on page 247 from Jacob R. Marcus, *The Jew in the Medieval World*,
reprinted with permission of the Hebrew Union College Press, Cincinnati.
Prester John's Letter (Appendix 1) from Robert Silverberg, *The Realm of Prester John*
(Ohio University Press, 1999), reprinted with the permission of Ohio University Press,
Athens, Ohio. Extract on page 172 from *The Sea of Precious Virtues*, translated by J. S.
Meisami (Salt Lake City, University of Utah Press, 1991). Extract from *The Penguin Book
of Hebrew Verse*, edited and translated by T. Carmi (Penguin, 1981), copyright © T.
Carmi, 1981; extract from *Parzival* by Wolfram von Eschenbach, translated by A. T.
Hatto (Penguin Books Ltd, 1980), translation copyright © A. T. Hatto, 1980; extract
from *The Conference of Birds* by Farid ud-din Attar, translated by Afkham Darbandi and
Dick Davis (Penguin Classics, 1984), copyright © Afkham Darbandi and Dick Davis,
1984; extract from *Istanbul: The Imperial City* by John Freely (Viking, 1996), copyright
© John Freely, 1996, all used by permission of the Penguin Group (UK).

Set in 10.5/13 pt Sabon by
Falcon Oast Graphic Art Ltd.

Bantam Books are published by Transworld Publishers,
61–63 Uxbridge Road, London W5 5SA,
a division of The Random House Group Ltd,
in Australia by Random House Australia (Pty) Ltd,
20 Alfred Street, Milsons Point, Sydney, NSW 2061, Australia,
in New Zealand by Random House New Zealand Ltd,
18 Poland Road, Glenfield, Auckland 10, New Zealand
and in South Africa by Random House (Pty) Ltd, Isle of Houghton,
Corner of Boundary Road & Carse O'Gowrie, Houghton 2198, South Africa.

Printed and bound in Great Britain by
Cox & Wyman Ltd, Reading, Berkshire.

Papers used by Transworld Publishers are natural, recyclable products made
from wood grown in sustainable forests. The manufacturing processes conform
to the environmental regulations of the country of origin

Nicholas Jubber was educated at Downside School and Oxford University. His travels have taken him through South America, Africa, the Middle East and many parts of Asia, and he has written for the *Tablet*, Boston's *Globe and Mail* and the Lebanese *Daily Star*. *The Prester Quest* is his first book.

Acclaim for Nicholas Jubber's *The Prester Quest* . . .

'Jubber's début is a gloriously entertaining historical romp. His quest for Prester John is one of suspense and high adventure – a heady blend of epic riddle and historical jigsaw that is written with exuberance, confidence and passion'

Giles Milton, author of *Nathaniel's Nutmeg* and *White Gold*

'Having read *The Prester Quest* almost at a single sitting, I think I can say without fear of contradiction or a libel suit that Nicholas Jubber is full of it. But his is the most passionate, exuberant and charming kind of 'it', and his account of his travels in search of – well, in search of something – is a delight . . . It is an engrossing and highly enjoyable read . . . a sumptuous, entertaining and informative historical romp'

Spectator

'Jubber's search for the legendary priest-king Prester John is quixotic to the point of madness. But his is an inspiring madness, bright with medieval fervour for the obscure, yet softened by scepticism and unflagging humour. This contrast, or melding, is crucial to his book's vitality and conviction . . . a discredited, if not moribund, genre, that of the modern mystical travelogue, has here been given new life . . . Beneath the humour and the self-deprecation, Jubber . . . shows a profound love of the Middle East and a steely resolve to do right by its tragically complex conundrums. He loves the people, and he loves learning . . . an ending that justifies the book all on its own' *Independent on Sunday*

'The contemporary travel book requires a conceit – and Nicholas Jubber has chosen an excellent one: to finish Philip's awkward mission and deliver Alexander's letter 828 years late. Of course, it is unlikely, but that merely adds to the adventure. He attacks his task with admirable energy and enthusiasm'   *Sunday Telegraph*

'Jubber's plan was to trace the emissary's route and deliver the letter. The Post Office would be proud of him . . . he jumps to the task with gusto . . . this first book shows ambition and promise'   *Guardian*

'The pages teem with spices and castles, camel herders, monks, troubadours, saints, heroes, and villains, put into historical context and all depicted with great zest and insight. As in the best legends, only Prester John himself remains elusive'   *Good Book Guide* 'Editor's Choice'

'Reads like a historical romp, an exuberant fiction designed to entertain the reader – but it also has the added attraction of being true . . . an eccentric and highly amusing travelogue'   *Birmingham Evening Mail*

'Before starting his journey, Jubber did enough research for the 12th century to be as alive to him as the 21st and, as he covers the ground, he flips between past and present. Both then and now provide such material as the friends travel through one of the world's most fascinating, colourful and disturbed regions . . . this is a significant début from a writer who can deliver both serious historical research and entertaining escapades with credibility and passion. As to whether he locates the great Prester, I leave that to you to find out'
Anthony Sattin, author of *The Gates of Africa*

'Jubber's historical romp takes some beating . . . a cracking idea, and one perfectly suited to Jubber's enthusiastic – if occasionally eccentric – sense of adventure. The result is a glorious mixture of arcane historical facts, intriguing trivia and memorable encounters. I enjoyed it hugely'
Yorkshire Evening Post

'A noble scholarly quest, or a comic *Da Vinci Code*, or a sort of Bill and Ted do the Crusades. Much fun'   *Hampstead & Highgate Express*

To my father

Contents

ACKNOWLEDGEMENTS

Where do I start? I've managed to rack up such a collection of debts that, were I blasted back a century or two, there'd be a strong argument for having me hanged. Since we live in less punitive times, however, I shall try to make amends by issuing my thanks.

To the Frères de la Salle, Maria Khoury and Abouna Iyad Twal, thank you for employing and accommodating Mike and me during our first trip to the Holy Land, for which the help and encouragement provided by David and Nora Hirst (as throughout the course of this venture) was extremely generous and very much appreciated. The priests of the Latin Patriarchate, particularly Abouna Ra'ed Abusahlia, Abouna William Shomali, Abouna Maroun Lahham and His Beatitude Patriarch Michel Sabbah, always made us at home when we found ourselves in Jerusalem; as did the wonderful Father John-Luke Gregory. Particular thanks for hospitality and/or other kindnesses in different corners of our trip to Johnny Van den Bergh, Fr Tekle Mekonnen, Mgr Khaled Akasheh, the Harb family of Byblos, Abdul Rahman and his family in Ghada, Munther Twal, Bishop Selim Sayegh, Fr Michel Awit, His Beatitude Patriarch Nasrallah Sfeir, Dr David Wasserstein, George Hintlian, Diala Sa'adeh, Raymond Stock and Dr Yusuf Fadl Hasan. In Britain, thanks to Michael Adams, William Dalrymple, Jack Arbuthnot, Hratche Koundarjian, Charles Malas and Chris Doyle, and a big nod to Father Henry Wansbrough for help with the translation of Master Philip's letter and for familiarizing us with the Judean desert. Various newspaper and magazine editors helped by commissioning articles and providing encouragement, of whom I would particularly like to thank Philip Lawler in Washington. To my family, especially my mother, thanks for encouragement and support (and apologies for all the worry!). Professor Bernard Hamilton and Arkady Hodge were invaluable advisers on historical matters, and suggested all kinds of incisive revisions to the text, for which I am enormously grateful. Equally invaluable were my agent Maggie Noach, my editor Simon Taylor and Deborah Adams at Transworld, who helped to cull the more verbose and pompous passages, for which you've no idea how grateful you should be. There are dozens of others – people who helped us on the journey or during the writing process – and I apologize to anyone I have failed to mention.

Most of all, as I hope will be apparent from reading this book, I owe an incredible debt to my travelling companion, Mike Hirst. His brio and determination were a tremendous source of strength and without him the journey described in these pages could simply never have been accomplished, nor this book written. Mike – *shukran jazilan, habibi!*

THE PRESTER QUEST

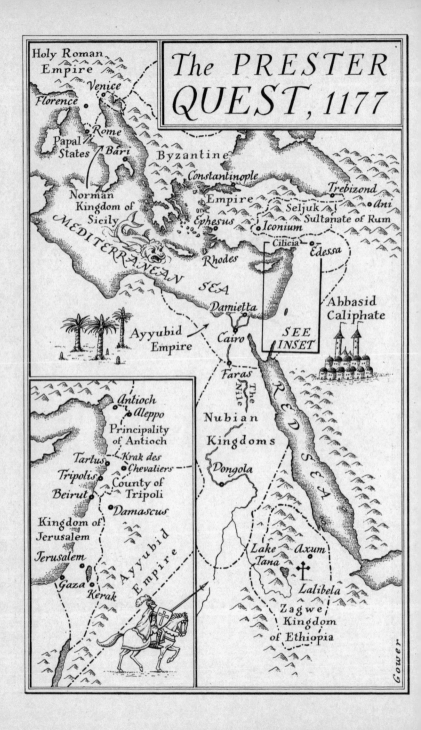

The PRESTER QUEST, 1177

Holy Roman Empire

Florence

Venice

Papal States

Rome

Bari

Norman Kingdom of Sicily

MEDITERRANEAN SEA

Byzantine

Constantinople

Empire

Ephesus

Iconium

Rhodes

Cilicia

Edessa

Trebizond

Ani

Seljuk Sultanate of Rum

Damietta

Cairo

Ayyubid Empire

Faras

The Nile

SEE INSET

Abbasid Caliphate

RED SEA

Antioch

Aleppo

Principality of Antioch

Tartus

Tripolis

Beirut

Krak des Chevaliers

County of Tripoli

Damascus

Kingdom of Jerusalem

Jerusalem

Gaza

Kerak

Ayyubid Empire

Nubian Kingdoms

Dongola

Lake Tana

Axum

Lalibela

Zagwe Kingdom of Ethiopia

Gower

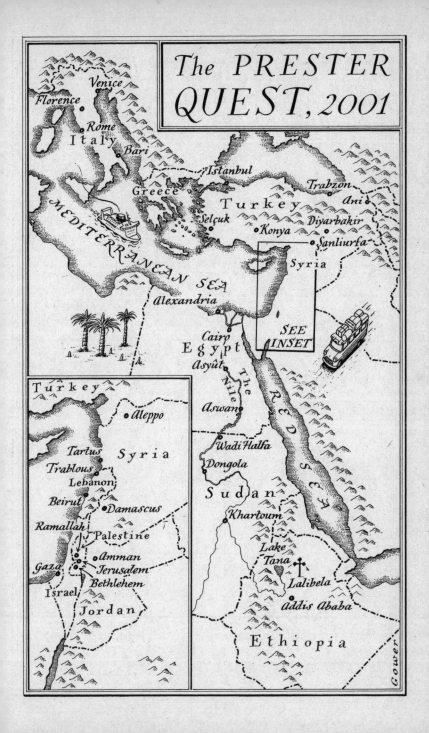

The PRESTER QUEST, 2001

CHAPTER ONE

THE INVISIBLE PHYSICIAN

MY FIRST ENCOUNTER with Prester John – priest-king of the Indies and trustee of the Fountain of Youth – took place in an intifada.

Jerusalem: October 2000. An Ethiopian monk clutches the skirts of his serge cassock and bolts past the chapel of Simon of Cyrene. Two elderly Arabs pack up their backgammon board, the pieces chattering as they tiptoe down a side street. Behind them, sub-machine guns bob above flak jackets as a pair of Israeli settlers swagger between two black tents of Palestinian womanhood. The Via Dolorosa has been stripped to the essential components for a fight: the Israeli army versus the Palestinian youth.

Khaki-suited soldiers file around the chapel: stiff-jawed young men whose boots chime on the bricks; teenage girls biting their lips, weapons dangling from their fingers. Behind shields of reinforced plastic, they huddle under an archway, waiting to be provoked. The Palestinians cluster around the chapel, *gelabiyya*s and leather jackets swelling in front of a pinstriped Armenian hawking 'I got stoned in Jerusalem' T-shirts. No one is interested in his wares: all eyes are on the path to the Wailing Wall.

Sticks, stones, the plywood seat of a chair – the street clatters as they shoot off a rooftop and land under parachutes of dust. Noses and helmets peek out of the archway and into a lull. Noses and helmets retract as a shriek precedes a king-sized thump against the ground. Someone has disposed of a sofa.

'Come on, Nick!'

Mike's hand claps my shoulder as he inches ahead. I tread gingerly beside him – anything he can do – but didn't that *tchk!* come from a safety-catch? A soldier rasps, 'Get back!', a *boooooom!*, and I note (with some relief) that Mike and I are both on the safe side of a horizontally held machine gun.

'Show over!' barks the soldier whose weapon is currently employed as a cordon.

Then the shooting resumes. As do the screams.

Mike and I had arrived in Jerusalem three weeks before the intifada broke out: enough time to get our bearings, see the major sites and find the best place for baklava. Then the city turned into a pinball machine where the pellets were propelled by slingshots, automatic rifles and long-range rocket launchers. Jews rocked in front of the Wailing Wall, while stones flew from al-Aqsa Mosque. Each stone augmented the volume of the Hebrew prayers, and the volume of the Hebrew prayers augmented the quantity of stones. Little boys with slingshots ran in front of tanks and went home on stretchers. Mike and I were teaching some of them in a school in the Old City. They turned up to class with rubber-coated bullets that they'd picked up on the battle sites. They rolled up their trousers and competed for Wound of the Week.

I first aspired to visit the Middle East at the age of ten. For my birthday, I had been given a *Treasury of Children's Literature* – a collection of stories that included several tales from the *Thousand and One Nights*. I fancied turning the peg of the Enchanted Horse, or grasping the wings of Sindbad's Rukh as it swooped through an Oriental updraught. But the horses in Hertfordshire weren't made of ebony and no one I knew had ever fished a genie out of the river Chess. So, when Christmas brought an old door painted like Dr Who's TARDIS, I decided to go to the planet of the Cybermen instead.

Some years later, long after I conceded that there were technical obstacles to my extraterrestrial ambitions, my Oriental interests resurfaced.

I was working as a lackey in a publishing firm, where I spent so much time preparing coffee for my superiors that I wondered if I wasn't turning into a cafetière. Any day, my right arm would grow into a brass handle and my left arm into a spout.

'This isn't what you want to do, is it?' said Mike, fresh from coaching cricket in Bangalore.

To the tune of Teacher's whisky trickling into chipped coffee mugs, a plan was hatched. We would leave London post-haste (slurp), plonk ourselves in Jerusalem (more slurps) and teach English (several more slurps and some hiccups). We would write a few articles (someone open the window) about the final stages of the peace process (oh my God, Nick, you've ruined the flower bed).

We just didn't expect its final stages to be a whizz of stones, religious slogans and dumdum bullets.

Even the school was mayhem. The secret smokers, who emerged from flanks of pastry-coloured brick with red faces and burnt fingers, were at war with the basketball jocks, who detested the recorder players, who kept stumbling over the staircase layabouts, who hated the kids who played intifada. And the kids who played intifada were divided into three mutually antagonistic sects: the 'demonstrators' who threw marbles; the 'ambulance-drivers' who *neenaw-neenaw*ed around the playground; and anyone who was big enough and could get hold of a stick – the 'Israeli soldiers'. It was as irreconcilable and uncontrollable a web of tribal identities as any in the Middle East. Which made teaching akin to an apprenticeship for the UN diplomatic service.

'Can we turn to page forty-three of *Wuthering Heights*?'
Silence.
'Samir! Stop flicking ink at Ahmad. *Wuthering Heights*?'
Silence.
'Jamal, where's your book? Ibrahim, will you give Jamal back his book?'
'Meesta – why we read this story?'
'Ah well, it's, er – Samir!'
But when teacher, now reduced to a quivering lump of exasperation, asks, 'So who thinks Arafat will make a deal with Barak?' – hands shoot, spring, stalk into the air.
'The talking goes nowhere!'
'Why the Arabs doesn't help?'
'Meesta, is true there is monster in the lake of Scotland?'
Very restless and exciting, sure. But all the time? Sometimes, all I wanted was a bit of shush. So, every few days, I stole out of the school and strolled into the Franciscan Library behind the Chapel of the Flagellation. There I certainly found (give or take the scratch of a few pencil sharpeners) plenty of shush. I also found several mythical quests, a couple of wandering poets and a few fair damsels in pelisses of damascened silk. I found the Crusades.

As well as a Templar Knight who turned al-Aqsa Mosque into a toilet; a Syrian prince who, fearing a coup, buried his brother alive; squabbles over the proprietorship of relics; desecration of religious sites; and arguments about the status of Jerusalem. I hadn't left the intifada, I'd just found it in a different costume. The gunships droning over the library marked a change in technology, not mentality.

Even the physical distinctions clinched past to present, since so much of the detail on which modern Western civilization was founded – from the mathematical discoveries that preceded the Industrial Revolution to the silk and brocade that refurnished European wardrobes – could be traced to the Crusades. The medieval and the modern: like trains on circular tracks, truckety-trucking in opposite directions; but, once each circuit, passing side by side, so that a passenger in the brightly lit carriage of one could peer into the misty windows of the other. Yoked together, squeezing out the centuries in connections as thick as blood; as distant and as close as the opposite ends of a family tree:

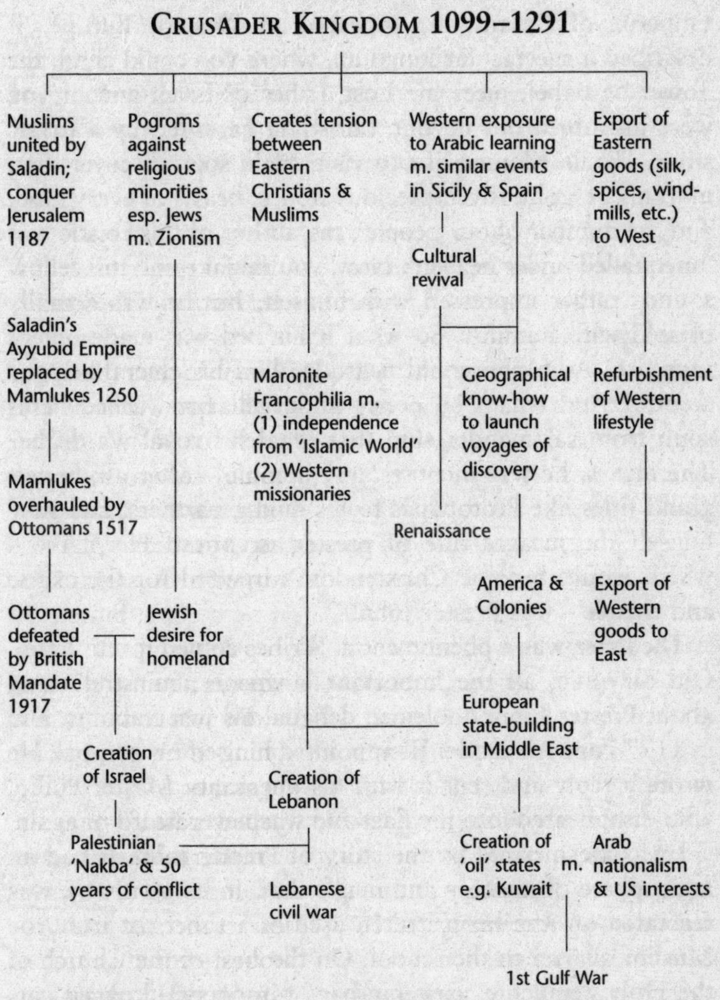

CRUSADER KINGDOM 1099–1291

Muslims united by Saladin; conquer Jerusalem 1187

Pogroms against religious minorities esp. Jews m. Zionism

Creates tension between Eastern Christians & Muslims

Western exposure to Arabic learning m. similar events in Sicily & Spain

Export of Eastern goods (silk, spices, windmills, etc.) to West

Cultural revival

Saladin's Ayyubid Empire replaced by Mamlukes 1250

Maronite Francophilia m.
(1) independence from 'Islamic World'
(2) Western missionaries

Geographical know-how to launch voyages of discovery

Refurbishment of Western lifestyle

Mamlukes overhauled by Ottomans 1517

Renaissance

America & Colonies

Export of Western goods to East

Ottomans defeated by British Mandate 1917

Jewish desire for homeland

European state-building in Middle East

Creation of Israel

Creation of Lebanon

Palestinian 'Nakba' & 50 years of conflict

Lebanese civil war

Creation of 'oil' states e.g. Kuwait

m. Arab nationalism & US interests

1st Gulf War

Figure 1: The Crusader Kingdom family tree.

These links brought the Crusades breathlessly to life. But there were other, stranger stories that occupied the spaces outside the links, and introduced me to a world whose bridge into the present day had, apparently, long since sunk.

In 1165 – sixty-six years after the Crusaders had seized Jerusalem – a letter, addressed to Manuel Comnenos, the Emperor of Byzantium, appeared in Western Europe. It described a spectacular kingdom, where you could climb the Tower of Babel, meet the Lost Tribes of Israel and, if you were an infirm but devout Christian, be cured by a magic stone. Would Manuel like to visit? He'd soon discover that, in terms of 'gold, silver, precious stones, beasts of every kind, and the number of our people', the author of this epistle was 'unequalled under heaven'. Now, you might think this fellow sounds rather impressed with himself, but he was actually blessed with humility. So what if his bed was made out of sapphire? And who could begrudge him his emerald-tipped sceptre? And what's so poncy about the fire-washed items spun from salamander skin that filled his royal wardrobe? The fact is, he was incontestably humble – after all, he left grand titles like Protopapas to his dining partners, and gave himself the meagre title of prester, or priest. His name – which would become Christendom's byword for the exotic and elusive – was Prester John.

The letter was a phenomenon. Scribes copied it into Latin, Old Slavonic, all the important languages; minstrels sang about Prester John, noblemen debated his whereabouts, and in 1177 Pope Alexander III appointed himself his pen-pal. He wrote a reply and sent it with his physician, Master Philip, who disappeared into the East and was never heard of again.

I was mesmerized by the story of Prester John. It had an atmosphere of mystery and magic that, in its own way, was recreated on a rooftop I often used as a short cut from the Muslim quarter to the school. On the roof of the Church of the Holy Sepulchre, past bin-bags full of sun-drugged cats and boys kicking footballs between limestone walls erected under the Ottoman Turks, was the Monastery of the Sultan. An egg-shaped dome stood in the centre of the courtyard, near an olive tree that apparently witnessed Abraham's aborted sacrifice of Isaac. Behind them was a row of mud-brick houses with pockmarked doors and lintels of corrugated iron. Outside one of these houses was a member of the Ethiopian community who lived in the monastery. He wore a white *shemma* shawl and a square black skullcap. In one hand he gripped a walking stick; in the other, a leather-bound book with red-tinted pages.

'Chreestiarn?' he asked, his voice a tinny croak.

I nodded.

'Ortadox?'

'Catholic.'

He shrugged. 'Well-kam,' he said.

It was a restful place, far removed from the ruckus of the intifada. Perched on a step beside the priest, I asked about his homeland. His black cheeks caught white sparkles of sunlight.

'Gon-daar,' he rasped, expressing the word as much with his gleaming eyes as with his parched lips: 'Tana . . . La-*lee*-ba-la.'

I didn't know much about these places. But each had a magical association: fairytale castles; the source of the Blue Nile; the tomb of the great twelfth-century king, Lalibela, in an underground church hewn out of pink tufa rock. The priest fluttered his fingers in the air, then stuck his wrists together, opening and closing his hands like a crocodile's jaws.

'Eetopyar,' he beamed.

Over the four centuries in which the Prester John legend proliferated, his kingdom became ever more fanciful. As scriveners hurried to churn out the latest edition of his letter, his subjects acquired horns, hoofed legs or dogs' heads.

Skiapods (whose feet hooded their heads like a parasol) turned up in his realm, as well as cannibals who dined on their parents, and the odd European traveller. Not that they always appreciated the experience. In the early fourteenth century, a Franciscan friar called Odoric of Pordenone located Prester John fifty days west of Peking.

'Not one hundredth part is true,' he grumbled, 'of what is told of him as if it were undeniable.'

But a contemporary of Odoric begged to differ. Sir John Mandeville, a knight from St Albans, assured his readers that Prester John was every bit as wondrous as he claimed, alive and well in the High Ind. Mandeville should know: he'd been there himself. He'd seen the horned men, drunk from 'the well of youthe', and met maidens who protected their chastity by secreting venomous serpents in a sensitive part of their anatomies. His travelogue remained widly popular until it was discredited by the Victorians.

The discrepancies between Mandeville and his fellow peregrines underlined the most baffling feature of the Prester John story. Where on earth was he? Was he on earth at all? So much of his kingdom – the Fountain of Youth, milk and honey, immunity to lies – recreated the mythical detail of Paradise. One of the rivers in his kingdom even emerged from Paradise. Would the discovery of Prester John reveal Adam and Eve's first home? No one could work it out, and Prester John wasn't particularly generous with geographical detail. He did admit suzerainty over 'the Three Indies', but that could be anywhere from the South China Sea to the Horn of Africa. So the best way to solve the conundrum was by default. India didn't have enough Christians, the Tartary Mongols worshipped the wind, and the Great Khan of China was hardly the same as the priest-king. But Africa ... As knowledge of the others ruled them out, the Prester Questers turned to the rhinoceros horn on the Red Sea. In the 1330s, Friar Jordanus of Severac produced a *Mirabilia* of the East, in which he recorded a Christian land full of precious stones and monsters, and golden mountains guarded by gryphons. Its ruler was 'more potent than any man in the world', and it was called 'Æthiopia'.

But the Ethiopian connection may have been made earlier. Sir Henry Yule, the great Victorian scholar of medieval travel, suggested that Prester John was identified with Ethiopia as early as 1177. Pope Alexander, in his letter to the priest-king, remarked that his physician, Master Philip, had met subjects of Prester John *'in partibus illis'* – 'in those parts'. They had asked for a chapel in Jerusalem. There was, Yule decreed, only one candidate. The Abyssinians, as the Ethiopians were called, were Monophysites under the spiritual control of the Coptic Patriarchate in Alexandria. They had appealed to the Catholic rulers of Jerusalem for help against their overseers, and asked for a chapel. They received both the chapel and the monastery that I had visited on the rooftop of the Church of the Holy Sepulchre. But not from the Pope.

In 1187, most of Outremer – the Crusader kingdom – was spat into the sea after the mighty Muslim warrior Saladin won a decisive battle at the Horns of Hattin and seized Jerusalem three months later. Some time after Saladin's accession (although possibly not until 1250), the Ethiopians were granted their first real estate in the Holy City.

Saladin's rise had coincided with Master Philip's mission – a critical juncture for the Crusaders, when the petty Muslim fiefdoms were uniting and Frankish extremists were sparring with moderates. But why, when the bearers of the Pope's evangelical post-bag were invariably clergymen, honour an obscure physician with such a crucial task? Subsequent Prester Questers were friars like William of Rubruck, dispatched to the Mongols in the thirteenth century; Alberto da Sarteano, who set out from Fiesole nearly two hundred years later; Francisco Alvares, whose *True Account of the Land of Prester John of the Indies* recorded his sixteenth-century mission to Ethiopia. The historical records hardly helped – they didn't even mention Master Philip. The only available clues, it seemed, were tucked inside Pope Alexander's letter.

The Franciscan library was like a labyrinth. But most labyrinths boast a guardian and this one had the sort of figure that a medieval Arab poet would have compared to a carnation stalk. She had swollen red lips and skin like satin and a look in her deep-blue eyes that said STOP GAWPING. With a fingernail shaped like the nib of a fountain pen, she beckoned me into a cavernous storeroom. Facing us was a metal wall, punctuated by a horizontal sequence of wheels. She spun a wheel. The musty smell of spine-cracked manuscripts seeped out as metal gave way to a bay stacked either side with old tomes. At the end of this magical, secret corridor, hidden under gold-leaf lettering and a rustle of paper, was Pope Alexander's epistle to Prester John.

> *Alexander the bishop, the servant of the servants of God, to my dearest son in Christ, the illustrious and magnificent king of the Indies, health and the apostolic blessing.*
>
> *The apostolic see over which, though unworthy, we preside, is the head and mistress of all believers in Christ. The Lord attests this, for he said to blessed Peter (to whom, though unworthy, we are the successor), 'You are Peter, and on this rock I shall build my Church' (Matt. 16). Christ wished this rock to be the foundation of the Church, foretelling that it would not be shaken by any whirlwinds or tempests . . .*

In a nutshell: 'I'm the *Papa*. You're not. Bow to me or you'll go to that part of hell where you get stuck in a fiery stone chest.' Even by the unexacting standards of papal correspondence, it's a dull letter. There are no references to the colourful legends associated with Prester John, although a warning that the king 'should seem less inflated with wealth and power' suggests familiarity with them. Instead, there are Gospel quotes, Ciceronian rhetoric and lots of papal supremacy.

But for all the canonical machismo, the Pope does manage a nod to his emissary. He describes Philip as 'provident and discreet, circumspect and prudent', and exhorts the king to 'receive him with kindly duty and treat him with reverent zeal'. I've never read a diplomatic document that expresses such concern for the welfare of its bearer. But we know nothing about Philip outside the letter: a doctor, knowledgeable about Catholic doctrine, a member of the papal household, he had travelled 'in those parts'. Beyond that is an ocean of speculation as intractable as the journey he was about to undertake.

That evening I sketched a map. I coloured it in with blackboard chalk, wrote down place names in felt tip, doodled a red-crayon dragon into the bottom right-hand corner, and drew a dotted line linking Venice, circuitously, with Ethiopia.

'You want to do what?'

Mike raked his coiling brown hair and tapped the felt-tip cross that marked the medieval Ethiopian capital of Lalibela.

'To deliver Master Philip's letter,' I said grandly. 'It's already eight hundred and twenty-three years late.'

Leaning back on his shoulders, Mike studied the map with the air of a judge.

'What do you think?' I asked.

He slapped the palm of his left hand with the knuckles of his right, as he often did to punctuate a point. Then, with his characteristic disdain for pronouns, he suggested: 'Fancy a visit to Diyarbakir. Don't see the point in this detour to Armenia and Georgia. And – what's this in Sudan? Looks like the logo on a can of Four X.'

'It's a castle.'

Over hours of debate, we snipped, shifted and reshaped the trajectory until, one day in spring, Mike celebrated our arrival at a workable itinerary with a conclusive palm-knuckle slap.

'Awesome,' he said.

If I was a medieval building, I suspect I'd be a clock tower – tall and skinny, head in the clouds. Mike would be a castle. Knights in hauberks would man his castellated shoulders and gobble cockatrice in his belly. Since he's not a medieval building, he had to rely on more subtle skills. Scene: Israeli checkpoint outside Bethlehem. Cast: Mike, myself and a machine-gun-wielding soldier.

SOLDIER: *You cannot go through.*

MIKE: *Why?*

SOLDIER: *The Arabs will shoot on you.*

MIKE: *Rubbish. Going through, or have you up for restricting freedom of religion.*

SOLDIER: *My orders are—*

MIKE: *Blow your orders.* (Pushes past the soldier, then turns round.) *Come on, Jubber!*

I knew that travelling with Mike would be a lot of fun. I also knew that he had a job starting in September; which, since we couldn't set out before May, would make things tight, but not unreasonably so. We had been friends for four years, since the freshers' meeting where Mike had sat noisily munching an apple while I, along with most of my peers, quivered nervously as our elders showed us the ropes. We had fought over who got which room in a shared student house, sparred over puzzle-bubble, the odd romantic interest and (with somewhat less competitive edge) essay writing, swapped translations of

Anglo-Saxon verse and sat up till dawn discussing the onto-logical status of cats and dogs. Now we were wrestling over who should write which sections for the various magazine articles that would, we hoped, fund a journey to Ethiopia.

But there was one thing I needed to clarify, if I was to travel across three continents with him. It was a phenomenon that had struck me time and again in Jerusalem, where his father appeared to have more contacts than the King of Jordan. After the tenth stranger that day had accosted Mike on a stroll through the Old City with enquiries after his father's health, I decided to test my suspicion of a local mafia in which Mike would reveal himself as the heir apparent.

He shrugged, with a smile as boat-shaped as a slice of melon. 'Oh, it's just the Knights.'

'Knights?'

My head spun with visions of his father, jacket replaced by chain mail, swapping his three iron for a Crusader's mace.

'Sure,' he said, 'Knights of the Holy Sepulchre. Dad's head of the branch for England and Wales.'

'They don't actually – fight?'

'Fight? Course not. They're a charity. Dress up in fur-trimmed gowns and build lots of schools.'

Back in London in early 2001, I decided to find out if there was some source of Prester John knowledge that I'd missed. Maybe there was a Society of Master Philip that could tell me everything from the cut of his hose to his favourite trouba-dour? I wrote to a dozen universities and waited for the replies to leak through my letterbox:

'I don't feel my knowledge of the subject can compare with that of others.'

'My colleague so-and-so is a great expert.'

'Very kind of him to say so. Simply not true.'

'Speak to X.'

'I've retired.'

I'd been investigating Master Philip for months. I'd found nothing. Britain's most eminent medievalists could not furnish me with One Solid Fact. I should have been distraught.

It was brilliant! A nonentity sent off to God-knew-where, who disappeared into academic oblivion. Master Philip was as mysterious as Prester John himself. Had he succeeded in his mission (and when he set out, he must have entertained *some* hope of success), he could have been the greatest explorer of his age. Instead he was forgotten. Unloved, unmourned, unrecorded. There was something both modern and mythical about him: the little man lost in the big wide world.

He was a bare canvas on to which I could sketch any details I liked, and there were plenty of sources from which to glean them. Because this was no pedestrian age: this was a Golden Age, a momentary flash when East met West – as enemies, but also (and it is this that makes the age unique) on equal terms. Before the Crusades, Europe was caged in its Dark Age: barely literate, without chivalry, paper mills or table manners. After the Crusaders had been swept back where they came from, the Mongol conquests sank the Arabian peninsula in its own dark age. But, for a brief instant, the Mediterranean world shimmered on every side. Forget the hair shirts and the scarceness of running water. Give it up for the twelfth century! Prester John might well claim to be 'the most glorious over all mortals', but what a ziggurat he'd set himself atop:

See Figure 2 overleaf.

As I was preparing for the trip, many of these names – Chrétien de Troyes, Reynard the Fox – joined the travelling companions I'd decided to pack, tour guides to the world in which Master Philip would have travelled. A rapturous welcome, please, for the roving rabbi Benjamin of Tudela, and the Muslim hajji Ibn Jubayr, who travelled about five years either side of Master Philip. Next in line, the German prester, John of Würzburg, who would join us on our return to

Jerusalem, where William of Tyre remains the most accomplished of political chroniclers. Moving along, the multi-talented Syrian emir, Usamah Ibn Munqidh, who numbered Saladin as a fan of his poetry; and, stretching out temporally, the Arab-Armenian Abu Salih, who located the Ark of the Covenant more than seven centuries before Indiana Jones; the irrepressible Mandeville; and Pero Tafur, a Castilian adventurer from the fifteenth century. Their tales, clunking inside my backpack, turned my thoughts to Master Philip's preparations for his own journey, the everyday normality of his work with the sick interrupted by an unexpected summons . . .

The First Letter of Master Philip
to Roger of Salerno

To THE VENERABLE doctor by the grace of God, Roger of Salerno, Master Philip the Venetian humbly sends greetings.

Today, by the will of God, I received a summons that will alter my life for ever.

I was tending to a goitre-ridden coppersmith in the Ca' d'Oro, and following your own recommendation (I am never without your *Practica Chirurgiae*, as indispensable today as the works of Galen were to the ancients), I applied seaweed to his swollen legs. But, as I was assessing my treatment, there appeared a visitor. His name is Rabbi Jechiel and he is Chief Steward to our master the Holy Father Alexander. He offered his greetings and advised me to accompany him to the Patriarchal Palace. With great hurry did I complete my treatment, before advancing in company with the aforesaid Jew.

Dear Roger, the Bride of the Adriatic is a tiring city for the hurried. A mob was screaming 'Assassin!' at a Florentine, who had broken the law by wearing a false

TOP DOG

Prester John
Most powerful man in the world

AGENTS OF GOD

Pope Alexander III
Spiritual leader of Western Christendom

The Caliph of Baghdad
Spiritual (& nominally political) leader of Sunni Islam

Rabbi Azariah
Damascus-based head of the Academy of the Land of Israel

POTENTATES

Saladin
Sultan of Ayyubid Empire of Egypt and Syria

Manuel Comnenos
Emperor of Byzantium

Frederick Barbarossa
Holy Roman Emperor

Kilidj Arslan II
Turkish Sultan of Rum

MOVERS & SHAKERS

Raymond III of Toulouse
Count of Tripoli & amateur Arabist

Old Man of the Mountain
Head of the Assassins of Syria

Odo of St Amand
Grand Master of the Knights Templar

Hasan Gavras
Kilidj Arslan's Vizier & Byzantine defector

Gumushtekin
Wily governor of Aleppo

CELEBS

Usamah Ibn Munqidh
Polymathic Arab memoirist, conspirator, huntsman & author of a book about the functions of sticks

Dame Maenz of Martignac
Super-beauty who stirred Richard the Lionheart's loins

Andronicus Comnenos
Charismatic Greek cad; seduced Philippa of Antioch & romanced Queen Theodora of Jerusalem around the Muslim East

Eleanor of Aquitaine
Feisty French aristo who put it about in France, England & the Orient

Maria Comnena
Married in & out of Crusader dynasties & conspired for her favourites to do the same

Gog and Magog
Savage races of the apocalypse, currently incarcerated somewhere in the East

ENTERTAINERS

Leoninus	Chrétien de Troyes	Archipoeta	Farid ud-Din Attar	Marie de France	Nizami	Reynard the Fox
Choirmaster of Notre-Dame; composed finest organa of his era	Author of Arthurian romances, including first legend of Holy Grail	German knight who lived off charity of Barbarossa's chancellor & wrote about love, drinking & gambling	Sufi poet & perfumier, wrote 40 books and lived to age of 110	Author of beautiful poetic lays	Persian poet, author of the popular romance of Layla & Majnun	Cheeky philanderer and hero of popular fable-cycle

EGGHEADS

Maimonides	William of Tyre	Gerard of Cremona	John of Salisbury	Roger of Salerno	Hildegarde of Bingen	Averroes	Isaac the Blind
Physician, head of Cairo's Jews, author of influential interpretation of Mishnah, essay to help patron's impotence, & other works	Broad-minded chronicler of Crusades	Greatest translator of his time; works included Aristotle's *Posterior Analytics* & al-Farabi's *On the Syllogism*	Scourge of vice; Becket's friend & Bishop of Chartres; composed such works as *On the Follies of Courtiers* & *the Vestiges of Philosophers*	Celebrated physician; published earliest surgical treatise in the West & recommended seaweed to cure goitre	Visionary nun & author of works on magic & medicine; advised prayer, fasting & flagellation to defeat vice	Arab with a magpie mind; wrote an encyclopedia of medicine & works of logic, physics, psychology, metaphysics, law, theology, astronomy, grammar	Co-author of the Cabbalistic *Book of Light*

HOI POLLOI

Men with long beards that had to be gathered in braids, who drank beer for breakfast & slept on straw	Women who wore wimples, had lots of children & tried not to keep the wattle-and-daub hut too clean because nasty smells can deter the devil	Master Philip

FIGURE 2: WHO'S WHO IN 1177

beard. We passed beside a bakery, where was a great crowd assailing the baker, for he had deceived them by secreting dough through a trapdoor in his kneading-board. When finally we reached the palace, the Holy Father was already in the process of applying his seal to a scroll of parchment. I offered the customary supplications, and attended to his speech. Dearest Roger, I have been blessed with a peculiar but most honourable task.

I am to deliver the parchment to the King of the Indies, commonly known as Prester John. There has been much talk of this great ruler in recent weeks. The situation in Outremer, where our Brothers in Christ are daily harassed by the pagan horde, has stressed the necessity of an ally in the East. The King of the Indies has written himself, both to Manuel the King of the Greeks and to the vanquished tyrant Barbarossa, to offer his support to his fellow Christians. I am to visit him, convert him to the True Church, and purge his people of the heresies that corrupt their liturgy.

But first I must locate this king. When I visited the Holy City some years before now, through God's beneficence I encountered certain of his servants. They appear as blackamoors, but they are devout Christians (although they have some heretical practices, including worship of the Sabbath and prohibition against pork, and during their matins they dance and leap in a way unbecoming worship of the Lord). It is my privilege to alter the ways of these people, and to assess their strength for the fight against the Saracen.

Dear Roger, I commit myself to your grace. There is much to do. I have a berth on a ship bound, God willing, for Constantinople. The devil will attack me with tribulations on my journey, assisted by Turks, Saracens, Persians, Ninevites, Catamites and Simoniacs. I ask only this of you, my friend and mentor: please pray for me.

As Mike and I flew over rural England, my head was spinning with anticipation. We would travel in two time zones, modern and medieval. Rome would be the seat of John-Paul II and Alexander III; the Turkish city of Şanliurfa would double as the Crusader stronghold of Edessa; Ethiopia would also be the kingdom of Prester John. It was this double world that I wanted to taste: Master Philip's on the one hand and, on the other, the stew of recently pacified countries (Turkey, Lebanon, Ethiopia), and one (Sudan – land of razed villages and Kalashnikov-toting lynch mobs) still in the thick of a civil war.

'And if that's not enough,' said Mike, turning from his porthole with a phlegmatic grin, 'there's always the intifada.'

But, whatever the dangers, this was the perfect time to undertake the journey. The border between Ethiopia and Sudan, closed since the mid-1990s, had only recently been reopened; before that, it wasn't possible to reach Israel by land from the east. While we were still travelling, events in New York would drive a wedge between travellers' itineraries and the Middle East. But in the summer of 2001, our worries were confined to passport stamps, mountain roads, men in balaclavas and raw meat. Looking at the chalk-green Master Map, it was hard to know what to expect. The dotted line apparently agreed: it had formed the shape of a question mark.

It was late May when a ferry floated us down Venice's Canal Grande. Buttresses flew and stucco bulged above liquorice-stick moorings and waterlogged chapels. Ahead, I could see the Rialto Bridge, smothered in touts, tourists and knick-knack vendors. Somewhere nearby, Pope Alexander III had written a letter.

I

CHRISTENDOM

CHAPTER TWO

CITY OF THIEVES

IN OUR ORANGE-BRICK hostel in Venice, where vines crept around crumbling, spongy archways, we were given a few droplets of magic.

Our benefactor was a Nebraskan busker called Jed. He was stretched supine on his bed in a pair of combat leggings and a black rollneck, a leather guitar case lying alongside him like a cataleptic lover. In one hand he held a plastic phial; in the other, his goatee. He tossed the phial into a nest of Rizla papers and foreign coins guarded by a West African mask, and started to address a radiator.

'Hey, those your shoes?'

The radiator didn't respond.

'I said, "Those your shoes?"'

'Course they're our shoes,' said Mike.

'Not *those* shoes.' Jed's goatee-stretching arm extended towards a pair of plimsolls mouldering under the radiator. '*Those* shoes.'

Had Mike or I owned such a pair, it's highly unlikely that either of us would have admitted it. Which meant, as Jed triumphantly declared, slipping them on and fiddling with laces as thin as horsehair, 'they must be, like, mine'.

Slumped on our bunks, Mike and I laid out our maps. We

had already covered six hundred miles of sky, but a strip of paper and a scale bar presented us with the prospect of six times that distance, to be tackled in four months, by bus, boat and barouche, train, tractor and pick-up truck. That first day in Venice, Ethiopia looked like the far side of the moon.

'So, where you folks heading?' asked Jed.

We told him. He asked us why. We told him. He blinked.

'This Philip dude – he's dead, yeah?'

'Yeah.'

'So why . . .?' A flicker of curiosity was gobbled up by a shrug. 'Whatever.'

He handed Mike the African mask.

'You know why I travel?' he said. 'To find myself.'

'Course you do,' said Mike, tossing the mask between his hands like a rugby ball. 'Been to Africa?'

'Nah, man. Got this baby in Rome.'

'And the phial?' I asked.

'Medic dude at the college. It's, like, some weird medieval potion.'

'Medieval?'

'It's called *teriaca*.'

He flipped it about in his hand. It was brown; a lavatorial shade of brown.

'What's in it?' I asked.

'Herbs, honey . . . viper's flesh.'

'What?'

'Like, folk used to think it could cure you of *any*thing. Except the plague. Wanna try some?'

It was deeeesgusting. Imagine a solution of liquorice, ammonia and something scatological. But, considering it was invented two thousand years ago, the recipe was holding up well. Just not as well as in Master Philip's day, when it was the wonder drug of Christendom: nowadays viper's flesh isn't so fashionable as a medical constituent.

'Hey, man, why don't you take some?' said Jed. 'Like, if you get ill in the desert.'

He poured a few droplets into an empty ampoule in my medical kit and handed it over with the flourish of an Elizabethan courtier.

'Gonna take that with you?' said Mike.

'Well.' I shrugged. 'You never know.'

'Hmmm. That should sort you out when you get shot.'

I tucked it into the pocket of my chinos, a few drops of Master Philip's world to carry with us as the crowds glued our elbows to our hips and a vaporetto slewed into the waterway. It was a world that reared its column heads and campaniles among the perfect proportions of Renaissance marble and the exuberant foliations inspired by the Arabs. Its triptychs shared the same galleries as Tintoretto and Paolo Veronese, its 'dragon's tooth' (possibly a whale bone) attracted an elderly matriarch's 'Ave Maria' in the Church of San Donato e Maria; and, eschewing sea breeze for slops, it whispered through the fetid alleyway where mud-faced children, T-shirts streaked by a housewife's emptied dustpan, hunted down a rat – a reminder that Venice was like one of her fabled courtesans: under her splendid silks, she was racked with disease.

Master Philip would find modern Venice very odd. He would be scandalized by the nudes in the Doge's Palace, sculpted on to Foscari's archway and painted on to the maps in the Hall of the Shields, where he would be equally perplexed by some strange place called America. Making his way on to St Mark's Square, surrounded by visitors from that place, many of them as underdressed as an African slave, he would marvel at the columned arcades of Sansovino's library and the tuxedoed pianist at the Caffè del Chioggio, and even the Magi who pop out of the clock tower in Ascension Week (although the figures would be familiar – the twelfth-century chronicler Otto of Freising identified Prester John himself as 'a lineal descendant of the Magi'). And what had happened to the cage chained to the tip of the campanile, where starving convicts got to die with a stunning view over the lagoon?

But there is plenty that Philip would recognize. Venice has never altered its fundamental structure – the same waters intersecting the same islets – so that a woman dangling a carpet from her balcony recalls a Canaletto canvas and a visit to St Mark's Square is a trip inside Bellini's 'Procession of the Relic of the True Cross'. The square, in particular, would pique Master Philip's memory: its present shape was laid out by Doge Sebastiano Ziani in 1177. He opened it to the waterfront, linked the houses with arches and stuck a pair of granite columns by the Molo. There might also be something familiar about the polyphonic crowds that coil around the Basilica of St Mark. Philip probably wouldn't recognize the Japanese tourists with their shiny contraptions that flash and click whenever they stand still. And he would raise an eyebrow at the rope-haired Rastafarian maraca-clapper. But the volume of the crowd wouldn't be unfamiliar to anyone who was in Venice in the summer of 1177. Because it was then that the city hosted the most populous gathering that it had ever seen – a gathering that had a direct bearing on Pope Alexander's letter to Prester John.

In 1156, Frederick Barbarossa (or 'Redbeard') – the Roman emperor, whose territory, strictly speaking, didn't actually include Rome – had committed an unforgivable felony. He had neglected to hold the Pope's stirrups. He'd also slaughtered a thousand Romans, but it was the first offence that really grated. The papal chancellor, a celebrated decretalist called Orlando, was dispatched to the imperial court at Besançon to insist that Barbarossa's title (to which the emperor had recently prefixed the adjective 'Holy') was a papal gift. Not so, insisted Barbarossa; his rivalry with Orlando had officially begun.

Four years later, Orlando beat a brigand called Octavian at the papal election. Unfortunately for Orlando, the brigand's unpopularity with the papal curia was more than matched by his popularity with Barbarossa: the emperor declared Octavian the victor, and Octavian accidentally put the papal cope on back to front. God, Orlando decided, must be on his side: it was just a matter of time.

A swift parting of ways. Orlando tramped around Europe, canvassing biddability and bullion from Catholic kings, and Barbarossa strengthened his candidature for the Seventh Circle of Hell. He catapulted children at the walls of Cremona. He razed Milan and stole the bones of the Magi. And he stormed Rome, sprinkling blood like holy water.

Then Divine Favour struck (at least for Orlando). Barbarossa's forces were beset by plague, the incredible alliance of Italy's northern city states, and the entirely credible treachery of the emperor's closest allies. At the battlefield of Legnano, the emperor lost his shield, banner, cross, lance, coffers of silver and gold, and the battle. And the war. Barbarossa (whom German legend would later lock in immortal sleep in a Thuringian cave, and whose name Hitler would affix to his invasion of Russia) had been vanquished: Orlando was secure as Pope Alexander III.

After months of negotiations, a peace ceremony took place in Venice. Doge Ziani collected Barbarossa in his gondola and floated him to his appointment with self-abasement. A crowd of clergymen and locals, and travellers from as far apart as Britain and Byzantium, cheered and jeered them on to the piazza, under dressed windows where householders waved papal flags. Barbarossa, wrote a German eye-witness, 'threw off the red cloak he was wearing and prostrated himself before the Pope, and kissed first his feet and then his knees. But the Pope rose, and taking the head of the Emperor in both his hands he embraced him and kissed him, and made him sit at his right hand, and at last he spoke the words, "Son of the Church, be welcome!" Then he took him by the hand and led him into the Basilica. And the bells rang and the *Te Deum Laudamus* was sung.' The war that had dissected Western Christendom was over.

After the ceremony, Pope Alexander stayed in Venice to consider the direction of his pontificate. He had subjugated the successor of Charlemagne, but there were more prodigal sons to be dealt with. Among the negotiators representing Barbarossa's interests before the ceremony was Christian, the Archbishop of Mainz, rumoured to be the author of a certain letter written around 1165 by one John, Prester.

There was a reason for this rumour: Prester John's utopian realm mirrored the sort of kingdom that Barbarossa envisaged, with the lowest-ranking cleric (a prester in John's case, a deacon in Barbarossa's) lording over bishops, patriarchs and popes in a fusion of church and state that Alexander had personally dismissed in his decretals. The first documented reference to Prester John was by Otto of Freising in 1157, in his *History of the Two Cities*. Otto was no impartial bystander: he was Barbarossa's uncle.

Perhaps papal pride had been stung by Christian of Mainz. Perhaps, as rumour hinted, mysterious emissaries had met the Pope in the Patriarchal Palace. Perhaps he was simply acting on the information of his physician. In any case, Alexander now became the first Western figure to address the ruler of a realm more mysterious than the court of the Tatar Chin or the empire of the Ghaznavids: the puffed-up priest-king of the Orient – Prester John.

The basilica that hosted the Peace of Venice was looking sumptuous in the afternoon sun. Rising in a heap so bright with mother-of-pearl, gold and serpentine that it stings your eyes, St Mark's boasts the colouring of an Oriental pleasure-palace, gables the shape of a Saracen's helmet and, according to Mark Twain, the likeness of 'a vast, warty bug taking a meditative walk'. It's easy to forget that this is a place of worship: the religious narratives shining inside the vaulted porches and the angels floating under cosmic crosses are swallowed by the magic of alabaster plant life and porphyry pillars and the bronze horses that leap out of a madness of pinnacles and amethyst-inlaid arches.

The ostentation makes up for the indignity of St Mark's journey to Venice. In the ninth century, a trio of Venetian merchants swiped his corpse from an Alexandrian church and hid him in a basket of pork. Muslim customs officials were too busy wincing at the stench of infidel meat to ask if they had anything to declare, and before they could interfere, the patron saint of glaziers was swinging between two quarters of pork in the ship's rigging. After a humiliation like that, there's only one way to make amends: you build him the most glorious basilica in Christendom.

Brass doors damascened with angels and prophets sweep you into a shadowy, cross-shaped cave, where fingers of light beam through the domes to point out Eve and the serpent or a couple of headdressed Egyptians or a menagerie of pseudo-beasts that could have been lifted from Prester John's zoo. The sensual, Oriental purée of molten colour solidifies in the golden altar panel – the Pala d'Oro – where miniature seraphs and saints exist in a fantasy as rich in precious stones as the priest-king's palace.

The Pala d'Oro was one of many exhibits shipped from Constantinople. But it had the unusual distinction of being legal. Because, holy as it is, St Mark's isn't the best place to preach against the eighth commandment. It may be the most famous building in Venice, but it's not actually very Venetian. What's not from Constantinople is from the Holy Land, Egypt, Syria, the islands of the Aegean . . . If you've had something stolen in the last nine hundred years, perhaps you'd like to look in St Mark's. Somewhere, between the rock on which Christ preached the Beatitudes (Tyre, 1120; removed by Venetian merchants 'trading' with the Crusaders) and St Stephen's rib (Constantinople, 1204; go nicely with his previously accrued feet); maybe near the body of St Isidore (Chios, 1125; Venetian 'merchants') or the wonder-working Icon of the Madonna of Nicopeia

(Constantinople, 1204 – again),* you might find that missing heirloom.

But what would you expect of a city whose patron saint himself is stolen property? Things are only things, but Venice is one robber's den of other people's things. Isn't that door-knocker in the Campo Sant' Agostin an Alexandrine hoof? And didn't those lions outside the Arsenale (one of which has Nordic runes inscribed on its rump) come from the Aegean? And as for the Armenian monks on the island of San Lazzaro† (as Jed had shown us, you don't need to be Venetian to take an interest in other people's property), well might they clutch the folds of their cassocks and condemn the 'barbarians' – 'Romans, Hittites, Tatars, Arabs, Persians, Turks, Kurds' – who had persecuted their people, but weren't the manuscripts in their library – a crinkly Qu'ran, an eleventh-century *Evangile de Saint Jean*, a slim Persian volume, a seventeenth-century Ethiopian chapbook – as broad a cross-section as the catalogue of their attackers?

And hands up who owns the granite columns standing upright in a puddle of pigeons in the piazzetta near St Mark's? They were pinched from Constantinople, not in 1204 but thirty-three years earlier. The Byzantine emperor Manuel Comnenos had imprisoned ten thousand Venetians

* This being the date when Enrico Dandolo, the nonagenarian doge whose last visit to Constantinople had lost him an eye (courtesy of a curved mirror that concentrated sunlight on his face) and gained him a vendetta, brought the Fourth Crusade under Venetian control and engineered one of the most destructive detours of all time. He led his troops into Constantinople, spreading pillage, rape and plunder, lifting the prized artefacts that would shortly grace St Mark's, and placed a prostitute on the Patriarch's throne.

† Armenians in Venice? Of course! Not long after Master Philip's day, Armenian refugees gravitated from their kingdom in Cilicia, where they had been allied to the Crusader kingdom, and acquired the Calle degli Armeni, which still bears their name. Venice was an appropriate place to go: it was refugees fleeing Attila the Hun in the fifth century who first drove stakes through the mud of the archipelago. It may not look it, but Venice is the world's most glamorous refugee camp.

after an attack on Constantinople's Genoese Quarter, and the Venetian navy had been dispatched to exact revenge. Except they didn't: they rested on the island of Chios, where most of them died of pestilence. It was the city-state's most inglorious moment, from which the columns – one now surmounted by St Theodore, the city's patron saint before the abduction of St Mark, and the other by an agate-eyed Chinese chimera dolled up as the Lion of St Mark – were the only tangible boon. The prize chosen by the Castilian engineer who accomplished the feat of erecting the columns is typical of the local attitude towards the law. Drawing attention to the steps around the columns, 'he requested' (as Pero Tafur, his fifteenth-century compatriot, wrote) 'that if any criminal, whatever his offence, took refuge there, justice should not be executed upon him. And now rogues play there at dice and commit other knaveries, praising the man who secured them such immunity.'

It was an immunity with which Mike and I tried to identify. We positioned ourselves on the steps, among the pigeons who'd sought refuge there from the tourists, and played out our act of wanton knavery: a game of 'paper, scissors, stone'. Sure, the three-thousand-lira stake doesn't sound very glamorous when translated into sterling. And yes, no one actually tried to arrest us; in fact no one even noticed us: they were more interested in the baggy-trousered clown with the silver-star eyes who was juggling under St Theodore. And it was also somewhat unclear who had actually won:

'Awesome – that's three–two to me!'

'Hello? I've won the last four.'

'Rubbish!'

Rather than reviving another medieval tradition by burying each other upside down between the pillars, we agreed to continue our exploration of the city; although agreement on the direction of that exploration proved trickier to achieve.

'I won,' announced Mike, cracking knuckles against palm, 'so it's my decision.'

'Yeah, yeah, of course you did. Anyway, I want to see the Mappa Mundi.'

'I did and you don't. This way!'

'I don't think so. I'm going *this* way.'

And I did. And a few steps that way, I glanced back (not too conspicuously, wouldn't want him to *see* that I'd glanced). Mike was – where was he? I kept going. Nice porticoes with Renaissance statuary. Stuccoed staircase. Plenty of marble. Everything's white, as if it's made out of icing sugar. Now where *is* that Mappa Mundi?

Fra Mauro, the great fifteenth-century Venetian mapmaker, shares plenty in common with the thieves of medieval Venice. He filched stories from the *Arabian Nights*, *The Greek Alexander Romances** and the Bible. But what art isn't indebted to its sources? A travel writer, of all the filchers around, should keep shtum on that score. Any self-respecting medieval wayfarer would consult a map before his journey, and, though composed two centuries post-Philip, none so joyfully scrambled the mythical lore that galvanized the legend of Prester John as Fra Mauro's celebrated Mappa Mundi, or World Map.

The attendant at the top of the staircase responded to my enquiry after its whereabouts by tapping a biro against her lips and screeching at her colleague down the corridor.

'You won't see Mappa Mundi,' said the colleague.

'But it's just a map. I'm not going to steal it.'

She consulted her nails. They were ambivalent.

'Maybe,' she announced. 'You will be escorted to the Biblioteca Marciana. There you may ask to see the Mappa Mundi.'

She delegated me to another colleague, whose heels pattered down the corridor, producing an arpeggio of

---

* The apocryphal legends of Alexander the Great were translated into Latin in the fourth century ad (and later into Hebrew, Magyar and Scots, among other languages) and possibly influenced the Qu'ran.

click-clacks like the suspense tune in a slasher movie. Suits of armour brandished their axes as model boats and egg-timers rose and fell in a wave of medieval artefacts. A spiked ball swelled on a stick and a dragon's head spewed from a hammer. In Venice, even instruments of death look pretty.

Outside a jungle of giant globes and lofty bookshelves flush against dark-stained panelling, Attendant Number Three raised her eyebrows, flourished a wrist at a bushy-moustached curator slumped over a desk, and clicked her way back down the corridor.

'*Scusi?*' I whispered.

The bushy moustache flickered.

'Um, I was wondering—'

'*Che?*'

'Um, *dov'è – il – Mappa Mundi* Fra Mauro?'

A frown curled above the moustache, which emitted a noise halfway between a grunt and a snore, and dragged its owner off the desk with a yelp.

'*Il Ma-ppa Muuun-diii!*' he exclaimed, whisking me past the globes, reeling off the names of the cartographers respon-sible – 'An-toniyo Za-tta! Vin-cenzo Co-ronelli!' – and escorting me into a dark anteroom, where he swept a cordon off its hook, guided me on to a raised platform and opened the shutters.

As the light settled in the room, it illuminated the glass screen in front of me and the parchment behind it. I was looking at a green landmass, beaked at the top and descend-ing into a scraggly heap. It had the shape of a duck and the texture of a cabbage. It didn't look much like the Collins atlas that I used to thumb through as a schoolboy. But my escort sprang forward to offer guidance, twirling his hands like he was spinning a football, then pointing from bottom – '*Nord!*' – to top – '*Sud!*' The map was orientated south–north: Sumatra near the top, Norway clinging to the bottom. It was a weird way of viewing the world: no longer crowned by Europe, which gasped under the axe-shaped threat of Africa.

'*Inghilterra?*' enquired my escort, pointing first to a blob near the bottom of the map and then to me.

'*Sì,*' I muttered. There was something slightly emasculating about my homeland's cartographic irrelevance. He indicated Italy, dangling indecently out of the Alps, and placed a hand across his heart: 'Na-poli! Ro-ma! Ven-ezia!' With the last, he'd shrunk the distance between himself and the map to less than the length of a schoolboy's compass. But, before anything untoward could happen, he remembered that he wasn't alone, and stepped aside to let me study the map.

The parchment was dizzying. Religious, commercial and anecdotal information gleaned from travellers such as Marco Polo was crammed into tiny scrolls. It was also dizzying because the south–north orientation had me screwing my neck like an ostrich. With each new country, another crick. But it was worth it for the intriguing world in front of me: Gog and Magog immured in north-west Asia; Adam's Peak near Saylam; and, bursting out of the Arabian peninsula, meeting my eyes via the intermediary of a stool, the terra incognita of Africa.

There, the Gion (the biblical Nile) wriggled into the city of Amaglerich, where, between two clusters of golden towers and an ice-coloured mountain, Fra Mauro had inserted the legend: 'Here Prester John makes his principal residence.'

Ethiopia, 'Austral' and 'Occidental', or 'Abassia', dominated sub-Saharan Africa. It was full of detail suggesting that Fra Mauro had done his homework. He'd identified the title of the Negus, or emperor, the route of the 'Avasi' or Awash river snaking into modern-day Djibouti, and he knew about the mountain-top 'Ambas' where Ethiopian kings imprisoned their brothers to deter potential coups. Sure, some of the detail was suspect. Beside one of Prester John's islands was a scroll narrating the tale of a stranded crew who met, like Sindbad the Sailor, 'a bird called roc', with wings sixty paces long and the strength to lift an elephant.* And verisimilitude wasn't too conspicuous when it came to scale: Ethiopia took up half of Africa. You'd need impressive management skills to unite a tract of land as big as that (although Prester John made do with a magic mirror to check on his enemies). But it reminded me of an anecdote in Francisco Alvares' *True Account of the Land of Prester John of the Indies*. The Negus has been given a map of the world, which he discusses with the Portuguese ambassador. He is very impressed by the size of Ethiopia. He is less impressed by the 'few lands' of Portugal, which 'would not', he suggests, 'be strong enough to defend the Red Sea from the Turks'. Bristling with indignation, the ambassador snaps back that the reason Ethiopia is so big is because it is 'an unknown thing'.

'So, see your horn-headed monsters?'

Mike's smile was speckled with enough pistachio nuts to imply he'd spent the afternoon in the *gelateria* in which I found him. In fact he'd barely settled, having rushed from Peggy Guggenheim's art collection, via the Arsenale, with a detour to the Renaissance-era customs house. We would often set off in different directions, unable to agree on our route, and determined to outdo each other on reconnaissance.

We did, however, manage to agree on our last stop before catching the train to Florence. We boarded a vaporetto and stepped off at the bridge originally built by the dice-playing engineer who erected the columns on the Piazzetta San Marco. In Master Philip's day the Rialto was the commercial hub of Venice. The first state bank in Europe, the Giro, was located here, as were the merchants peddling goods from the East. Now, most of the merchandise is geared to tourists – Bellini table mats, gondolier T-shirts, La Serenissima baseball

---

* The same bird was located in Prester John's Æthiopia by Friar Jordanus de Severac. The priest-king's empire was a convenient trove for all sorts of mythical treasures.

caps, gondolier calendars, posters of the groin of Michelangelo's 'David', cassettes by the all-dancing, straw-boatered, sailor's-necktied gondolier pop band.

Beyond the bridge, the atmosphere shed a few centuries. Market stalls crowded round shoppers as ladies with larynxes like loudspeakers screamed the prices of rabbits and rose petals, while hen-pecked husbands flashed their teeth over pyramids of cumin and coconut towers. The smell of sea salt squirmed out of baskets of spider crabs and razor-shell clams on beds of fake grass. I imagined Master Philip turning up here before his journey, mingling with merchants who spiced their wares with tales of men with dogs' heads and palaces inlaid with sardonyx. For a good whiff of his destination, there would have been nothing like a good passeggiata along the Rialto.

CHAPTER THREE

MONKS, *MOTORINI* AND THE VIRGIN MARY

THE TRAIN CROSSED the lettuce-coloured plains of Lombardy, flat as *ciappe* bread. On the bench opposite us were two old women in several layers of black cotton. They wrung their hands and squeaked at each other. Occasionally they glanced at us, as if to check we weren't eavesdropping. There was no need to worry. Had they been speaking Italian, we would have struggled. As it was, they were talking in an impenetrable mish-mash – some words sounded French, others Arabic or Greek. I assume it was the little-known dialect of the Veneto. They did, in fact, have some grounds for suspicion: although I couldn't understand a word, I *was* eavesdropping. I was fascinated: was this the dying tongue with which Master Philip had conducted his affairs in Venice? Once – I'd nudged myself a little too close, one ear cocked towards them – they turned their shrewish eyes on me. I smiled and one of them showed me her tooth. Then she said something that sounded very wise. I nodded solemnly and slid back to our end of the carriage.

Mike was deeply engrossed in a biography of Pope John-Paul II. Above his head, the cornfields of northern Italy were slowly replaced by the gorgeous undulations of Tuscany. The landscape was bright and lush, spoilt only by the sprawl of terraced houses and telephone wires. We were approaching Florence.

Because we hadn't booked in advance, it was impossible to find a room. For a couple of hours we wriggled through the promiscuous heat of Italian traffic, leaping out of the way as bonnet clinched bumper and boot embraced bollard, huffing up marble staircases, puffing inside iron lifts that looked like giant birdcages, pulling our hair at the repetition of '*completo*' – full. Whether sympathetic or supercilious, every maître d' in Florence had '*completo*' on their lips. *Completo!* That horrific word thumped like a fist in my ears when we collapsed in a hideaway hostel on the wrong side of the Arno. *Completo!*

'Too many tourists,' announced Mike in the morning.

'And it costs too much,' I added.

The queue for the Uffizi and the extra charges for seats in the cafés quickly bustled us out: fitting Florence into a budget of twenty pounds a day is as tortuous as it must have been for a Crusader to fit into his cuirass after an all-night feast. Besides, Master Philip's world was barely able to raise a whimper: *thees is Firenze*, sneered every piazza, palazzo and ponte, cherub-print apron, da Vinci coffee mug and Donatello ashtray, *we do not a-do the twelfth century he-a!*

Even on the subject of Prester John, the Renaissance was all-powerful: as I realized that morning in the Medici-Riccardi Palace, when I stumbled across a fresco cycle with a link to Prester John that carried Mike and me eight kilometres outside Florence, to a Franciscan monastery in the little town of Fiesole.

Friars sat in the shade of apple orchards or contemplated frescoes of St Francis in the cloisters. The scent of geraniums tautened into the musty aroma of the crypt, where a knife-wielding horseman and ghostly drummers held court among Chinese lanterns and pipes, turquoise pharaohs and an Egyptian sarcophagus, the souvenirs brought back by Fiesolean missionaries from Asia and Africa. Behind the chapel, a spiral staircase led to the friars' cells, where wooden chairs and chests sat in a silence intermittently disrupted by the clink of a visitor's coin.

One of these cells bore the name of a missionary who was also remembered in a plaque outside the friary gates, erected in 1937 when Mussolini wanted to underline his five-year conquest of Abyssinia, as Ethiopia was then called. In 1439, it recorded, Fra Alberto da Sarteano was sent 'to carry the light of Christ' to Ethiopia. That is, to a country where 'the light of Christ' had been burning for more than a millennium. Fra Alberto was the fifteenth century's Master Philip.

His Pope Alexander was Eugenius IV, who, at the Council of Florence that year, had found himself increasingly attracted to the concept of the Union of All Christendom (with himself, *naturalmente*, at its head): the Ethiopians could be one more string to add to the recently Catholicized Armenians and the temporary reconciliation with the Orthodox Greeks. So, off went Fra Alberto, in search of the ever-elusive Prester John.

I had already glimpsed the council. In the Medici-Riccardi Palace, a fantasy of muscular nudes, gold stucco and apple-cheeked cherubs superimposed on to gilt-framed mirrors, I had climbed into Benozzo Gozzoli's magical 'Journey of the Magi'. White leopards snarled and cheetahs skulked among aquamarine trees and raspberry-ripple palaces, between slopes that zigzagged with horses, camels and high society, in hats as diverse as at Ascot – birettas, fezzes, turbans and tiaras. The most exciting aspect of the frescoes also recalled Ascot. Gozzoli depicted the Magi and their retinue with the features of his contemporaries and delegates from the council: the cycle is a Renaissance celebrity-spotter's paradise. Ooh, see the boy in blue – that's Little Lord Lucca. What about the chap on the mahogany horse, inspecting his fingers? Why, that's Cosimo de' Medici. You see his son, Lorenzo? With the gold casket. Frightfully proud, isn't he? Today he's Caspar the Magus.

Another Magus was a portrait of the Byzantine emperor. In his black tabard, embroidered with gold heliotropes, he cut an exotic figure. But what struck me most was his colour. He was as dark as a KitKat. Why portray a Greek with such a hue?* Well, one of the Magi had to be black. In his *History of the Three Holy Kings*, written in the fourteenth century, John of Hildesheim described Caspar as 'a black Ethyopye wythout doubte'. Although there is confusion over which of the Magi receives the designation, it is traditional for one of them to be of African provenance. Looking at Balthasar's beautiful costume, I remembered Prester John's alleged descent from the Magi, and the council's revival of interest in him. Was Gozzoli, I wondered, depicting the priest-king whose support Fra Alberto was sent to secure?

Unfortunately, the initial effect of our enquiries into Fra Alberto in Fiesole was nothing more substantial than incarceration in a cell in the cloisters, by an old friar whose bulldog jowls appeared to have been borrowed from a hoodlum in a Mafia film.

'*Aspetta!*' he exclaimed. 'Wait!'

A conspiratorial wink and he'd shot out of the cell. We could hear the friars chortle and the tap of steps on flagstones. The door shook and gave way to the prior. He had a chest like a pigeon and an anxious squint. His chest swelled as he listened to our enquiry; then he flapped his hands against his belly and retracted like a clockwork cuckoo. Another friar gulped solemnly as I described Fra Alberto's mission in my syntactically mangled version of Italian. Then he fled.

At least Fra Davide, a young novice who accosted us in the cloisters, was more eager to talk to us. His grandmother hailed from Harrogate, so he quizzed Mike for the latest news on Leeds United.

---

* It might simply have been realistic: Manuel Comnenos was so dark that the Venetians mocked him by dressing up an African slave in imperial robes.

'Yes, great, fantastic, but,' I burbled, 'I wonder—'

Mike patted the friar's shoulder. 'Thing is, we're looking for someone who knows about this Fra Alberto.'

'Ah!' Fra Davide's lips lifted promisingly, then sank back into their dimples. 'I do not know this man,' he sighed.

But he did know someone who might.

'There eez someone,' he said. 'He knows everything in historia.'

Fra Vito was his name, the Franciscan convent in Florence his home, and the asphyxiating fumes of antique books our introduction to his archive. He was wrapped in a tatty olive-green cardigan, a pair of horn-rimmed spectacles dancing in a whirligig of wrinkles and corrugations. He might have looked old, but did that friar move! Dust clouds haloed the books as he smacked them on a table, before bustling back to his almanac turrets and bastions of red-edged tomes where markers floated like banners. There were books everywhere – even in a shopping trolley, improbably crammed with manuscripts under the tower of a metal shelf.

'Fra Alberto travelled like an ambassador,' explained Fra Livio, a younger friar who was translating Fra Vito's spitfire splutter. 'He had a splendid horse and stirrups. Not very Franciscan, eh? He goes to Jerusalem – he meets the Ethiopian bishop. The bishop gives him two Ethiopian monks and he sets out for the land of Prester John. But when he reaches Egypt, the Sultan – he finds out about his mission. You know what he says?'

'What?' said Mike, producing a Dictaphone from one of the half-a-dozen pockets of his sleeveless jacket.

'He says, "Eh! You don't go any more distance!" So Fra Alberto goes back to Firenze. But he brings the Ethiopian monks with him. At the council, there is great excitement – here is subjects of Prester John!'

'Did the Ethiopian monks put them straight?' I asked.

'How could they? They speak no Italian.'

Fra Vito's soft hands ran across our palms before disappearing, like the rest of him, in a jungle of dust, paper and animal hide. But Fra Livio, his head shaking as he showed us to the door, belonged to a more practical world.

'It is an irony,' he sighed. 'At the Council of Florence, they sent friars like Fra Alberto to Africa and India. But now, we have few priests and many problems. So it is the priests from Africa and India who are coming to us.'

Italian trains are fast, comfortable, usually on time and an absolute pain if your eardrums are functioning. As Mike and I bedded down on our pull-out benches, two faces peeked through the door to our cabin. One of them belonged to a young lady. She had a hard, straight-angled nose and long black hair that stroked the shoulders of her leather jacket. Beside her was a young man with a bewildered teddy-bear face and perfect symmetry between the curly brown tufts on his head and the repetition of that pattern on his chin. Their names were Natalia and Giacomo. We discovered this despite their decision not to join our cabin. Their faces disappeared as quickly as they arrived, but provided an image to fix to the verbal explosion that, a few minutes later, erupted from next door.

'What the hell's going on?' exclaimed Mike, his head bursting out of his paperback.

It was hard to tell. Giacomo, who spoke in a fierce baritone, had apparently upset Natalia, who had a terrific rasp, like an Italian Bette Davis. '*Testa di cavolo! Stronzo stramaledetto!*' she cried. '*E chi se ne frega?*' Giacomo shot furiously back. An eruption of tears, a basso profundo of '*Porco l'oca!*',* tense whispers, a soft hush, muffled breath. Silence. The star-crossed lovers had reached a reconciliation.

---

* Literally, 'Cabbage-head! Wretched turd!'; 'Who gives a damn?'; 'Pig-goose!'

Which was good. The train was quiet. Which was even better.

As we carried our packs on to the platform of Rome's Stazione Termini in the early evening, we were preceded by Giacomo and Natalia, arms around each other's waist. I watched them trot off to McDonald's, filled with the warm feeling you get at the end of an early Meg Ryan movie. But, as we squeezed through the commuting horde on to the Via Nazionale, squiggled past the giant typewriter of Vittorio Emanuele's Altar of the Fatherland and lost ourselves in the Via del Corso, the city's medieval thoroughfare, the warmth evaporated.

Most capital cities preserve a certain froideur towards the newcomer. Whereas provincial towns greet you with a hug and a column of cut-price hoteliers, a big city like Rome stiffly turns up her nose. Men in Armani suits swing you this way and that with their busy shoulders; ladies in Luca Luca micro-miniskirts and ballet shoes stare through your grimy backpacker's uniform. Rome – a catwalk with churches and cafés. Master Philip would be goggle-eyed: what happened to curly-ended shoes and breeches, and why aren't the women wearing veils? And what on earth happened to the numbers? In Master Philip's day, the same pestilence that put paid to Barbarossa's imperial concupiscence had reduced the population to less than a hundredth of its modern-day mass.

But he could quibble all he liked. He wouldn't even receive a sympathetic grunt from the fat *tabacchi* stallholders with cotton-wool moustaches. They've cigarettes and comic strips to sell, and no, *mi scusi*, they can't show you the way to Via dei Serpenti. So you trudge on, unguided and unloved, arguing over whose stab-in-the-dark at guidebook map-reading is the more promising,* passing the gaunt façades of grey

---

* A toss-up between Mike's *Lonely Planet 2001* and Nick's *Travels of Benjamin of Tudela*, c. 1170.

churches and glass-skinned office blocks. And when you cross the road, you'd better be conscious of your invisibility. The drivers have enough to worry about. They've got bollards to avoid, the tiny gap between the Alfa and Lancia in front to exploit, the model in her pink-fur bikini on the billboards to gawp at, sudden unsignalled turns to make, even crazier drivers to taunt and traffic conductors on precarious mid-carnage platforms to circumvent. The conductors unfurl their arms with the balletic fluency of mime artists, islands of grace in an impetuous sea.

Opposite the café where the young Karol Wojtyla swotted up for his Latin-language tests, in the thick of medieval Rome's red-light district, an intercom crackled and a utilitarian turn-of-the-century apartment block spun us up stone steps intermittently interrupted by potted plants.

'Chaps! Quality!'

A short young man with a floppy fringe was standing in a doorway on the top floor. The towel girdling his waist gave him the air of a dandy at a centurion's feast. He was Johnny, an old university friend now working for the Vatican newspaper, *L'Osservatore Romano*. For the next few days he would be our host.

'In you get,' he said larkily as he escorted us into the sitting room, where his Balthasar-hued flatmate was whispering to the floor.

'Don't worry about Atanas,' said Johnny. 'He's just contacting his voodoo overlords.'

Those three days in Rome, Johnny was a mercurial host. He guided us around the sights that would have filled a medieval pilgrim's itinerary. We gawked at the Colosseum, prayed at St Paul Outside-the-Walls, paid a fee to climb the tower where Nero legendarily watched his subjects burn; he pointed out what was Byzantine or baroque, Renaissance, rococo or art nouveau. But we saw so many churches, fountains, hideous neo-classical statues, Renaissance frescoes in which ancient philosophers doubled as contemporaries of the artist, crypts and Japanese tourists, that in my mind's eye they have all merged into one whisked-up *panna cotta*. Some individual sights stand out. Such as Bernini's 'Fountain of the Four Rivers', where a marble veil dropped over the face of Old Nile, emphasizing the pre-Victorian uncertainty over its source that empowered Prester John to stem its flow. Or an enormous three-thousand-year-old obelisk in the Piazza di Porta Capena, brought from Ethiopia during the Italian occupation. Successive Ethiopian governments clamoured for its return and even printed postage stamps to celebrate its arrival, but it was still rooted in Rome, a relic of Mussolini's adventure in colonialism.

'Looks like Il Duce had quite a thing for Ethiopia,' said Mike, as we strolled out of the piazza.

'So did the Holy See,' said Johnny.

'Apart from Pope Alexander's letter?' I asked.

'Well, there's the college.'

'The college?'

'In the Vatican. There's a bunch of Ethiopian seminarians. Got their own college and church.'

On a cobbled backstreet near Johnny's apartment, the sounds of a Gepetto-like accordionist, whose sense of rhythm was probably excellent around the time of the Italian occupation of Ethiopia, charmed us into Johnny's favourite trattoria. Young ladies polished their eyelids in the glass table-tops, while men with rigid gel-heads nodded solemnly and tugged their ties. We chewed tough chunks of wild hare lubricated in onion sauce – a dish that would have been familiar to Master Philip – while Johnny whispered about career-climbing priests and the difficulty of arranging an audience with the Pope.

'What do the locals think of him?' said Mike.

Johnny took a ruminative gulp of his wine, which tasted like it had been treated to the medieval tradition of thinning by water.

'Love him,' he replied. 'Really. He's an institution. But . . .

he's unquestionable. He made me work on Good Friday –
with no overtime!'

We saw Johnny's boss the next day; along with several thousand fans, in the keyhole-shaped square of St Peter's. Newly
married couples with carnations and clotted-cream gowns
waited for a pontifical blessing in front of a façade that
looked like it had been built out of all the cakes from their
wedding breakfasts. It would have disorientated Master
Philip, who'd have to trudge past Renaissance *pietà*, Peter's
Pence counters and a bronze St Peter before climbing into the
crypt to stoke his familiarity with Constantinian pillars and
the Niche of the Pallia. But the carnival in the piazza would-
n't be alien to a medieval observer. The division of proletariat
from pre-paid seats (by makeshift barricades and cordons),
the crucifix-waving tour groups (photographing each other
with the Pope in the background) and the instruction-spitting
clergymen (albeit spitting into mobile phones rather than
lackeys' ears) added to the hustle-bustle of popular piety. As
did an Indian nun, rattling past us in a tangle of rosary beads
that made her sound like a packet of hundreds-and-
thousands, underlining the Holy See's attraction to Christians
from across the globe – an attraction that galvanized
medieval pilgrims from Ethiopia. The action that her passage
prompted in the man beside me was an even more ancient
tradition (or so I was told that night by a Belgo-German
model living in Rome with a Hungarian faux count, who
happened to be a friend of Johnny's): 'If a monk or a nun
casts a shadow across an Italian's path, the man will touch
his crotch and the woman will touch her breast. They believe
that the shadow of a holy person will make them infertile.'
That explains why (a) people in St Peter's Square seemed to
be very tactile with themselves; and (b) Italy has the lowest
birth rate in Europe.

The focus of the occasion was a stage in front of the
basilica. Under a canopy of red brocade, the Pope hunched in

a glow of white cotton. In front of him, a cardinal in a black, scarlet-trimmed simar trawled a microphone across the stage and identified specially chosen pilgrim parties.

'The Archdiocese of Hertford, North Carolina.'

Squeals.

'The Melkites from Israel.'

Ululations.

'The Buddhist Lao sect of Thailand.'

White handkerchiefs.

The atmosphere was pure pantomime. Any moment now, the cardinal would surely pluck out a white rabbit from under his skullcap. But when the Pope read out the psalm in a muffled croak that articulated the rumours of Parkinson's disease, the hullabaloo was snuffed into silence.

When you find yourself a few hundred worshippers and some Swiss Guards away from the so-called 'conqueror of Communism', former Gestapo prisoner, survivor of two assassination attempts (one by a mad priest with a bayonet, and more famously by a Turk who later believed, as did the Pope, that his bullet was distracted by the 'motherly hand' of the Virgin Mary), you want him to reproduce the scale of his biography by towering several feet over everyone else. But the Pope looked like you could knock him over with a small crucifix. How did this man stand up in the Umayyad Mosque in Damascus only a few weeks earlier? His commitment to inter-religious dialogue, something of a departure from the policies of many of his predecessors, had turned a frail octogenarian's body into an extraordinary vessel of diplomacy: the flesh might be weak, but the spirit was still willing.

'These visits are so important,' said Monsignor Khaled Akasheh, the Vatican's Jordanian spokesman on Christian–Muslim relations, in an office whose bookshelves appeared to be a testament to how many styles of dust jacket you could design for the Qu'ran. 'It remains God's wish to unite people of different nations and beliefs.'

Mike's forehead squinnied into a bar code of frowns. 'But

religion is often the cause of the divisions, particularly in the Middle East.'

'It is the misuse of religion that complicates the situation,' said Akasheh. 'If Muslims are true to the Islamic law of "salaam" and Christians are true to the commandment of loving their neighbour as themselves, there will be less confrontation.'

Within the hour, Akasheh's office had melted into the squillion narrow steps coiling to the top of Michelangelo's dome. Pigeons excreted over the blanket of red tiles, doing to the Leonine City what their ancestors were doing in Master Philip's day. Except that now they had Renaissance chapels and telecom towers to splatter.

'Got to get in there,' said Mike, swivelling my shoulders until down below me – an emerald trapezium of fountains and foliage – was the forbidden zone of Vatican City. A hundred sculpted acres as alluring as the Garden of Pleasure, where William de Lorris's lover wanders between allegories of the virtues in the *Romance of the Rose*, one of the most popular poems of the Middle Ages. Except, instead of Beauty and Courtesy, we saw the Lego-sized ecclesiarchs of the Inner Sanctum. It was irresistible, and we were instantly seized by an Alice-like desire to step across its herbaceous borders.

But slipping into the sacred statelet is no mean feat. You can argue an appointment with Johnny in his office at *L'Osservatore Romano*, creep past the Vatican supermarket (where Rome's cheapest alcohol and tobacco is sold) and scrutinize a map of the Vatican's innards. And you can bound past the papal post office, the gardens only as far away as the radius of a sprinkler. But when your path is blocked by the halberd of a Swiss Guard in the blue-and-yellow uniform legendarily designed by Michelangelo, there isn't much to say.

'Identification?' he asked.

'Ah,' said Mike.

'Er—,' I added.

We'd had a taste of the Vatican. We wanted more.

Across the Tiber, the frail figure of John-Paul II was replaced by a stern face with an aquiline nose. We were standing in front of a monument to Pope Alexander III in the Cathedral of St John Lateran, the home of the papacy until the four-teenth century.* Statues of Christ and a column of saints carrying trademark props (John the Evangelist† had the goblet that nearly poisoned him, while John the Baptist car-ried what looked like a TV aerial) towered over the entablature on a double-storeyed portico. In the nave, coats of arms and cross-keys bulged over a rare Gothic baldachin.

Pope Alexander's face was incised into a black marble slab on the back of a pillar, above a eulogy to 'the Father of his City and of the World'. It's rather more genteel than the immediate response to his death: a volley of stones from a mob. Not that Alexander would have expected anything more. It was outside Rome that he canvassed support against Barbarossa, and it was outside Rome that he received his best notices, from men like Voltaire, who applauded him as the greatest of medieval men – for abolishing slavery, overcom-ing Barbarossa and bringing Henry II of England to book over the murder of Thomas à Becket. He stabilized the pro-cedure that still decides papal elections, and championed education and the poor. And, in an age that relished pogroms

* An anonymous twelfth-century tract describes the visit to the Lateran Palace, in 1122, of 'the Patriarch of the Indians'. The Patriarch was called John. He met Pope Calixtus II and described the capital city of his kingdom. Only good Christians lived there: if an 'infidel' approached the city, he either 'comes to his senses or falls by sudden chance into mortal sickness'. Although there is doubt over the credentials of the Patriarch in question, the tract shows that, early in the twelfth century, rumour was already spreading of a Christian kingdom in the East.

† Whose partnership with the Baptist as the cathedral's co-dedicatee was established only in the twelfth century, when his popularity, as we would discover in Greece, was bolstered by his mystical associations.

against Jews (usually by Crusader knights warming up for the Middle East), he was surprisingly tolerant. When Master Philip's Jewish contemporary, Benjamin of Tudela, visited Rome in the 1170s, he commented on the 'honourable position' of the city's Jews, who 'pay no tribute, amongst them are officials of the Pope Alexander'.

'Don't care how awesome you think he was,' said Mike, as the colours and loose clothing favoured in the Renaissance vaulted over us on the other side of the road from the Lateran. 'Can't see him getting up these.'

Ahead of us was a marble staircase, plated in walnut-wood, reputedly once located between Christ's cell and Pontius Pilate's courtroom, and known as the Scala Santa. Assuming that Jesus used them while the judge dithered, pilgrims pay tribute by ascending the steps on their knees. Each step supported several pious middle-aged women dressed in black. They laid down their shopping bags, hauled themselves up to the next level, and clapped their hands in prayers enunciated with all the grace of a price-bawling greengrocer in the Porta Portese. Whether the mood was self-abasement or self-aggrandizement, the motive was established by a sign at the foot of the steps:

> *The following indulgences may be received, in accord with the usual conditions:*
> *Plenary indulgence: on all Fridays of Lent, and once more each year on an occasion of one's choice.*
> *Partial indulgence: on all other days of the year, as long as one is sincerely repentant of one's sins . . .*

It was at moments like these that I felt close to Master Philip – reading similar legislation, preparing to emulate him with a bend of the knees: eight centuries compressed, like wind in an accordion, by a shared ritual.

'Don't you think so, Mike?'

He was already halfway up the stairs. It was an obstacle

race: him against the shopping-bag-bearing mother who started at the same time (albeit encumbered by the weight of her shopping and her own . . . well, let's just say she was no ballerina). She didn't have a chance: in the seconds that it took Mike to reach the top, he must have broken the course record.

If Mike was Formula One, I was more like an also-ran in the egg-and-spoon race. Each step crippled my knees, so I decided to ascend at a nice, leisurely pace. A sightseeing pace. I was full of admiration for the po-faced signoras who dragged themselves up one wince-inducing step after another, assisted only by the cacophony of Ave Marias that they left in their wake. They deserved their indulgences: the steps were as knobbly as a bar of hazelnut-speckled *torrone*.

The balloon of black corset floating behind me suffered from no such affliction. A tap of my feet, a flick of her wrist, a command – '*Avanti!*' – and she launched herself up three steps in quick succession. But, just when she looked like she had Mike's record in her sights, she stopped and turned to the woman beside her. They waved their arms at each other and chattered away. I don't think they were reciting the Lord's Prayer.

It was a far cry from the Scala Santa that the fifteenth-century Castilian traveller Pero Tafur visited, where women were forbidden access to the chapel because 'a woman once uttered such things that she burst asunder.' With that in mind, I thought I'd better sneak quietly around them, without unsettling their shopping bags. But I didn't have long before they were panting down my neck.

There was a reward at the top. After shaking the tingle out of my legs, I looked through a waffle grille at a triptych depicting Christ enthroned. Alexander III considered it so holy that he covered it in silk. Innocent III went a step further, protecting it with a plate of hammered silver. It's called the *acheiropoeton*: 'not done by human hands'. Apparently, the artist was an angel.

*

'The thing is,' said Johnny, 'if you want to see the Vatican gardens, you need to *know* somebody.'

Mike flicked through Johnny's Vatican directory, looking rather glum. 'But we don't know anyone.'

'Isn't there some secret underground passage we could use?' I pleaded, as I picked at a plate of lasagne.

Johnny shook his fringe.

I was comforting myself with the thought that lasagne was mentioned in the fourth-century treatise of Apicius (as *laganae*) and would therefore have been available to Master Philip, when a fist struck the table, so hard that Atanas was momentarily distracted from his conference with a floor tile.

'The Ethiopians,' bellowed Mike, running to the telephone. 'We'll interview the Ethiopians!'

Our mouths still numb from the next morning's double espresso, we stood under a pair of travertine eagles at the Porta Sant' Anna. Beside us, a Swiss Guard, wielding a three-pronged halberd, kept the Vatican free of unwanted proles. His face muscles appeared to be as immobile as the eagles, because none of them moved when we strode past him and into the Forbidden City. In the *Romance of the Rose*, the lover is admitted through the Garden of Pleasure's tiny gateway by an allegory of Idleness. We, on the other hand, were accompanied by Father Tekle Mekonnen, rector of the Ethiopian seminary, a tall, tidy figure in his neatly creased black-and-white suit. Past the Vatican Bank, beyond a courtyard of golden office blocks, freshly cut grass and honeysuckle perfumed the rump of St Peter's and escorted us into the tidiest garden in the world.

The Church of St Stephen was requisitioned in 1481, forty-two years after the Council of Florence, to house the increasing numbers of Ethiopian pilgrims. The locals attributed them to the empire of Prester John; the pilgrims themselves, unable to speak Italian and unwilling to jeopardize the hospitality they were receiving, did little to contradict this view.* Lambs gambolled between foliage on the pastry-coloured façade, a pastoral complement to the simple darkness inside. The smell of dust and mould wound thick and pungent behind the stone altar, into a cavernous underground gallery that split into tiny stone cells once inhabited by pilgrims. Each cell was small and airless, and suggested an ascetic lifestyle at odds with the opulence of the lawns. Pilgrims' names crawled around the nave in stiff Latin spokes or the looping characters of Amharic.

'The monks,' said Father Tekle, leading us past the Palace of the Governorate and up the manicured hill towards the college, 'would eat, sleep and pray in this church.'

'Was it healthy?' I asked.

'No. Many of them died of pneumonia soon after they arrived. But after the college was built in 1919, they had greater comfort.'

The college was a bulwark of sharp-cut brick on stalks of pillared stone, as modern and sophisticated as St Stephen's was archaic. But its sterile plaster cloaked the survival of traditions like the wooden tablet (or 'tabot') in the chapel's sanctuary: a replica of the Ark of the Covenant.

'When you go to Ethiopia,' said Father Tekle with a smile, 'they will tell you they have the Ark. But they will not let you see it.'

'You don't believe they have it?' asked Mike, as the priest eased into the swivel chair in his office.

'You have to remember,' he said, 'that Ethiopia has been surrounded by Muslim countries for centuries. She is isolated. So many ideas and beliefs have developed that have not

* This was an issue that I raised with an Ethiopologist several weeks later at the Hebrew University in Jerusalem. 'When the Ebo of Nigeria claimed they were the lost tribe of Ephraim,' said Dr Steven Kaplan, 'that doesn't mean they were. And if Ethiopians were telling people where they were from and they just drew a blank, but when they said, "Prester John's land," people understood, then I think that explains why they said, "We're from Prester John's land."'

been accepted in other parts of the world. And many ideas developed around her, like the Prester John story that you talk about.'

His mahogany desk was carbuncled with modern para-phernalia – papers, pens, lever-arch files. But above Father Tekle's head, a painting glowed with the circular heads and coloured cloaks that had enchanted me in the Ethiopian chapels of Jerusalem.

'Although Ethiopia was isolated,' continued Father Tekle, 'she had a lot of trouble from outsiders. The Copts of Egypt always controlled the Church. Sometimes they didn't install a bishop, so it fell into chaos. There were no bishops when the Italians invaded in 1935, and of course they attacked the country with mustard gas.'

'Bet that soured relations with the Catholic Church,' said Mike.

'Not really. You see, relations were already bad.' Father Tekle shrugged. 'When the Muslims invaded Ethiopia in the sixteenth century, the Portuguese king sent the Jesuits. They came with a big army, but they weren't coming to rescue Ethiopia. They were coming to change her: the alphabet, the culture, everything. They even converted the king. But the people revolted and from that moment there was a historical hatred of Catholics. When missionaries arrived in the eighteenth century, they were hanged.'

More recent Western visitors, whether evangelists or aid workers, had attracted as much aggravation as appreciation. We were heading, Father Tekle assured us, to a country torn apart by war, famine and governmental malpractice: a rather less optimistic appraisal than would have been offered to Master Philip.

The interview over, Father Tekle's gloom was blown away by cherry blossom.

'Right,' announced Mike, slapping his right hand in his left palm, 'we're not leaving till we've found the Pope's heliport.'

We passed a flower bed sculpted into the papal coat of

arms, and nearly reached the papal petrol pump before a shrill whistle pierced the air.

'That'll be the guards.'

Mike turned slowly, to face a walkie-talkie-bearing harlequin.

'Where are you going?' asked the guard.

'On an – architectural mission,' ventured Mike. 'St Stephen's – to investigate – tabernacle – very important –'

The guard nodded. 'You have seen St Stephen.'

'We have? Oops. Must have slipped the old retention system.'

'The exit is behind you and to your left.'

'It is? Ah. *Grazie!*'

One of the frustrations of any trip is the number of exciting possibilities that have to be ruled out. On our last afternoon in Rome, I suggested spending several more days in Italy. I wanted to visit the bones of St Thomas (popularly associated with Indian legends of Prester John) in Ortona di Mare, to travel to Palermo, the capital of the Norman kingdom that ruled southern Italy in Master Philip's day, to penetrate the Vatican's secret archives.

'NCD,' said Mike, as a waiter carried over cups of coffee with hats of bitter cocoa.

'What's that mean?'

'No can do. Haven't got all year. Anyway, you'll get the Normans in Bari and Tom crops up in south-east Turkey, doesn't he? Got to push on to Greece, DWI.'

'DWI?'

'Deal with it.'

So we DWI'd to Bari, via a train that woke us up with a midnight caterwaul.

'What the—?' Mike bolted upright and rubbed his eyes. No lovers' tiff this time; instead, an even noisier party of nuns, chanting their rosary with the same devotion that had their medieval counterparts flocking around visionaries like Elizabeth of Thuringia, whose nipples were sequestered by her followers and kept as sacred relics. Which, while we're on the subject of female devotion, brings us to the great love affair that rang through Master Philip's Christendom.

Throughout this era, one woman had men on their knees. The same woman who would peer, tessellated, frescoed or carved in relief, in Istanbul, Cairo and outside the Ethiopian Patriarchate of Jerusalem. The woman to whose presence we would be invited in Upper Egypt, and whose pennant would form a crucial component of our mission to Ethiopia.

'Here you go,' Johnny had said the previous evening, as he placed an almond-shaped piece of tin in the palm of my hand.

It had an image of the Madonna and an inscription: 'O Mary conceived without sin, pray for us all who have recourse to thee.'

'It's to keep you and your quest,' said Johnny, with a knowing nod, 'under Our Lady's mantle.'

It was an appropriate keepsake. The cult of Mary, thrice-blessed virgin inviolate (and just you wait for what the Copts have to say about her), was at its meridian in Master Philip's day. She was carved into the cloisters of Romanesque churches, moulded into Black Madonnas and encoded in cryptic rosettes. The rediscovery of classical texts such as Ovid's *The Art of Love* inspired new codes of chivalry, and Mary became the Queen of Heaven, celebrated in the lyrics of the troubadours, the pop stars of medieval Christendom. Master Philip would probably have carried his own Marian talisman, a source of solace in times of trouble.

The nuns' chant had been swallowed by the soothing chug-chug of the train, which trundled us into Apulia.

'What are you reading?' said Mike.

I showed him my anthology of tales about the James Bond of twelfth-century literature – Reynard the Fox.

'Reynard's just disguised himself as a doctor and recommended that his arch-foe Isegrin the Wolf should be flayed so his skin can be used to cure Noble the Lion. How about you?'

'Robert Fisk, Lebanese civil war. Talking about an old man who got beheaded by the fin of a Katyusha rocket.'

'*Bariiiiiiiii!*'

We were in a land of pine woods, sand dunes scuffed by heather, and bent-double depressives with bulging eye sacs who gravitated towards the dingiest dive in town – a seaside haunt of stained coffee cups and tables encrusted with rock-hard ravioli – the Titty Tuister.

Its owner had gone to great lengths to live up to its name: he wore a string vest and baggy trousers, and had a bushy moustache and itching fingers gummed to his armpits. His clientele, without exception, had big red noses and mottled skin that looked like it had been scraped off dead people. The hair that should have been on their heads was dispersed in terrific displays across their backs and over the rims of their vests, framed in colourful tattoos depicting 'danger' motifs like motorbikes and snakes. We watched them chattering among themselves and making strange gestures with their hands. One of them held his thumb between his middle and index fingers, indicating (in jest, I think) that his friend should 'take a walk'. There were other, more esoteric gestures, involving rapid manipulation of wrists and digits. What were they referring to? The rise of fascism? The menu's lack of white meat? The girl in a micro-skirt crossing the road in front of them? The owner's body language was the most transparent of all. He was looking towards the port, his face screwed into a tight scowl.

Good point. In Master Philip's day, Bari was one of the gateways for traffic from the East. Persian carpets, Levantine pottery and Indian spices travelled to the capital of Apulia. Now, most of the traffic is the human cargo of Albanians, Kurds and Iraqis. As we walked around the port looking for the Aegean Lines ticket office, I saw families in faded shawls huddled around crates and boxes packed, I imagined, with either their worldly possessions or contraband items that smugglers had forced them to carry. Wan-faced mothers rocked their babies, while fathers glared across the port and children squiggled the dust with their fingers.

The lugubrious atmosphere was thrown aside in the Old City. A troop of young men perched on their mopeds, armed with tight T-shirts and tufts of greasy hair that they coiffed in their side-mirrors. They vroomed around the Saracenic town square, an army of noise that filled every corner with the clamour of their engines: *vroom vroo vroo-vrooo vroooom*. When eventually the revving died, it was replaced, not by silence, but by HECKLING housewives, old grannies in tattered cardigans SCREECHING the price of tomatoes, ghetto-blasters TRILLING arabesque love ditties, and SCREAMING football-kicking children. This must be the noisiest place in Italy. And Italy's a noisy country. Bari's ear-splitting decibels made Rome sound like an uncomfortable pause in the conversation.

In the thick of the mayhem, there were four weddings. Middle-aged men with handlebar moustaches bustled outside the Cathedral of San Sabino, debating which way to lay the red carpet. Ferocious mothers-in-law shook their fans, waved their arms like tic-tac men and pushed up the netting on their hats. Guests preened on the red carpet: ladies in lipstick-coloured shawls and stilettos; men in jacket-and-tie-and-shades, puffing cigars or nodding piously while eyeing up the *bellissime*. At the end of the carpet, three little boys peered into the velour upholstery of the open-top bridal car, hands held politely behind their backs. The band picked up the tune, a couple of moped drivers attempted wheelies, two boys tried to maim each other with sticks, a crowd rushed around the steps, and the happy couple was lost in a tempest of confetti.

The Romanesque cathedral defied such vitality. A chorus line of grey gargoyles squinted at a gloomy icon of the Virgin, her mood wrecked by a party of chubby cherubs who arched her like some camp chat-show host's ghastly back-up team.

Even grimmer was the crypt, where the smell of stale incense and the opaque half-light cast a medieval aura around caskets filled with the tibiae and fibulae of saints such as Theodore and John the Baptist. It was the storage of such relics that transformed Bari into a commercial hub in the eleventh century, when the Sicilian Normans established the city as the capital of their territory on the southern Italian mainland. Their penchant for eccentric architectural embellishments was expressed in the sculptures attached to the cathedral. One particular corbel not only boasted crouching bears but also a bearded gnome.

Pandemonium ricocheted across the streets, bouncing between huge bedsheets above our heads that spread a smell of soap. At eye level, windowsills were cluttered with flowers, some of them transformed into shrines where the faithful had left their devotions in little wax candles. A fruit-bearing van groaned on the cobbles and passed a shop selling religious paraphernalia. Among the crosses, rosary beads and holy figurines were Greek Orthodox icons and – surprisingly – a basket of brass menorahs.

'Jewish?' asked Mike.

A lady with a giantess's bosom and a handkerchief wrapped round her head took hold of the candles.

'Is all religious,' she purred. '*Ortodossi, cattolici, giudei, mussulman.*'

'*Mussulman?*' I exclaimed.

Behind a column of icons were some luminous lime-green Muslim prayer beads and a Christian rosary. Seeing these devotion props, physically so similar, reminded me of their shared heritage. It was during the Crusades that the Franks adopted the rosary from the Saracens and introduced it into Europe; the Muslims had borrowed it themselves, from the beads used by Buddhists.

More Asian acquisitions wafted across the road. Artichokes and aubergines – first encountered in Europe during the Crusades – breathed their smells out of a restaurant whose owner cranked his pasta machine, producing the staple of Italian diet that was, extraordinarily, introduced to the country by Arabs in the twelfth century. The corkscrewing, vaulted-arched streets also whispered of the East, as they guided us under an Angevin fleur-de-lis to the Basilica of San Nicola.

It was the saint's corpse (stolen from Arab territory in 1087), more than any other relic, that established Bari as a place of pilgrimage. Encased in a silver reliquary, it is still reported to exude a holy liquid as pure as spring water. On the façade of the basilica, garlands of fruit entwined fierce leonine faces and a flock of live pigeons sat on a sphinx. Norman Crusaders swung their swords in a relief around the corner, recalling their short-lived expedition to Alexandria in 1174, when the approach of Saladin's army sent them scuttling back to their boats.

There were more eccentric sculptures in the Norman castle. Although there was a fortress on this site in Master Philip's day, the present building dates from the thirteenth century. Its predecessor had been the victim as much of Barese impetuosity as of the Normans' one-dimensional foreign policy: hatred of Greek Byzantium. This was rather unfortunate for Bari, because her population in the twelfth century was predominantly Greek. Even now, there is a Hellenic aura to the capital of Byzantine Italy, expressed by the icons in San Nicola, where Mary is *panaghia* rather than Madonna. The Baresi certainly felt Greek enough to welcome a Byzantine army in 1156 and, as a show of their support, raze the castle to the ground. Which had the not particularly beneficial effect of provoking the Normans, once the invaders had been expelled, to do the same to most of the city.

Behind a phalanx of beige brick hunching over the castle's moat, a Greek harpy menaced a Gothic portal. Eagles were incarcerated in pillars that ran towards plaster casts of medieval statuary. A rosette-winged gryphon swooped near a flappy-eared elephant dangling its trunk over sharp incisors.

The menagerie was thrillingly diverse, a fitting symbol for a patchwork kingdom where Arabs, Greeks, Latins, Normans and Jews enjoyed legal parity, half the army was Moorish, most of the naval commanders were Byzantines and the archbishop was an Englishman. It was a similar eclecticism that invigorated the letter of Prester John: Greek myths like the tales of Alexander the Great, the apocryphal Syriac Acts of Thomas, the Hebrew legends of the Lost Tribes, Nordic grail myths and Latin tracts such as the story of the Patriarch of the Indians were stuffed together like rice and pepper in the vine leaves of a Greek dolma. Just as the twelfth-century cultural revival served up Arabic and Greek translations in Palermo and Bari, so too it cooked up the legend that propelled poor Master Philip into the unknown.

After exploring the castle, we followed Philip's invisible footsteps and boarded the Aegean Lines Superfast II to Greece.

The Second Letter of Master Philip to Roger of Salerno

MASTER PHILIP THE Venetian by the grace of God to his illustrious friend Roger the Salernitan, greetings and sincere affection.

Many have told of the terrors of the sea, and now, through the clemency of the Most High, I inform you of such things through the eye of experience.

The wind was soft and favourable for the first ten days of the voyage. We dropped anchor at Bari, where, though unworthy, my devotion to the reliquary of St Nicholas was honoured by the emission of holy liquid. I must tell you, dear Roger, about the conditions below deck. Each of us was allocated a place some six feet long and two feet wide, marked by lines of chalk, in which to guard our chests and mattresses. Beside me in the hold was a merchant, Guglielmo of Palermo, a pious man and a great traveller. He had visited the most illustrious cities of the world. Imagine my delight as he described the lighthouse of Alexandria, on which a magic mirror provides forewarning of the approach of enemies, and the mountain of Ararat, where Noah's Ark is guarded by fiery dragons. But our conversation was distracted by the many applications for my assistance. My supply of groundsel was exhausted by requests to ward off scurvy, although I had no curative for the troubles that would later afflict us.

Another traveller there was, an English knight, with whom I passed many a diverting hour in debate. This man had some strange and marvellous ideas. For example, he held that Jerusalem is not situated at the centre of the earth. His argument was soundly defeated when Guglielmo narrated an experiment that took place before his eyes in Jerusalem. A man suspended a log on the mountain of the Temple of the Lord. At the summer solstice, the shadow was directly under the log and circular in shape, proof that Jerusalem is indeed the centre of the earth. But the knight was determined to prove his superior knowledge, and he gathered a great audience to listen to his tales. He had travelled to the High Ind, he claimed, and met there many strange folk. These included people with long ears like donkeys, headless men with eyes in their stomachs, and folk that shade themselves from the heat by lying on their backs and holding up a single large foot over their heads. But such people, I explained, could not possibly exist, for they were not included in Noah's Ark.

We travelled like this for many days, but a black cloud darkened the sky on a terrible Sunday, soon after the priest had administered the Holy Eucharist. High winds buffeted the roaring waves, and the steersman plunged to his death. Near to us was a mighty trireme, carrying petraries and mangonels and all such engines as are needed for the taking of great cities. Her strength, in good weather a virtue, was transformed into a curse. We watched as she was thrown about by the waves and dashed against the rocky crags near the homeland of Odysseus. Many of our number, Jews as well as Christians, fell to their knees at this sight and submitted to the mercy of God.

The storm continued through the night. The boat filled with foam, and terror took possession of our hearts. I remember a woman with a child in her arms. Her hair and clothes ran with water as she held out her child and screamed. I could do nothing for her, because her child had already drowned. I saw men toss themselves into the sea to anticipate their fates. Others made rafts of the rigging, hopeful to enhance their chances of survival. I watched the English knight slip off the side of the boat, pressing his chest against a plank and disappearing under a torrent of water.

Dear Roger, these were frightening times. Waves towered over us like mountains of sulphur, thrashing the boat and tearing my companions off the deck. I tried to tend to the injured, but the storm was too violent and my medicine was soaked. I ran back and forth along the deck, staring into the cauldron of the sea, as cursed and discoloured as a witch's oils, and in my frenzied mind I saw things that I scarcely dare repeat. I saw burning trees with tortured sinners hanging from them by their tongues and a fiery wheel turned by an angel with flaming horns and a devil extracting the soul of a sinner from its body. And then I saw Guglielmo and – by God's mercy! – he was thinking better than I. He cut a rope holding a great wooden tub, and he pushed me inside and rolled the tub over the edge and bestrode it and turned his feet to paddles.

Dear Roger, I have spent a week in convalescence. I am in a small house inhabited by Greeks. They found us on the shore and carried us to their home, and they have taken nothing from us. Instead, they have fed us goat meat and wine, and they attend to our needs. They show especial favour to me, because they found on me a letter. It is the correspondence that I am carrying from my Lord Alexander to Emanuel, the King of the Greeks. And though this letter is in poor condition, the details and the holy seal are intact. Other letters also have remained with me, so that I do not worry about the loss of my chest. Most important of these is the letter to the King of the Indies, which I intend to carry to that distant land, if God spares me from greater danger. I must hurry – a boy is waiting to take this epistle to a consignment for Corinth, and I hope that it will speedily find you in good health. My Greek hosts have prepared mules to carry Guglielmo and me to the Via Egnatia, where, God willing, we will connect with the caravans to Constantinople. Dear Roger, I ask you to remember me in your prayers.

CHAPTER FOUR

MYSTICS OF BYZANTIUM

IT'S HARD TO empathize with the medieval seafarer from the distance of the modern Greek ferry. Of course there would have been no flexi-chairs to recline in as you watched a 1970s American cop show, no rubbery pasta and chocolate bars served in the canteen, no square-jawed foreign-exchange man flicking out drachmae like an over-heated fruit machine. And what was all the fuss about the Aegean? Shorn of Homeric sea monsters and medieval Saracenic pirates, its turquoise waters were as quiet as Medusa's house-guests. The only danger, in fact, was in the bar.

A silver mirrorball revolved above smoky cauldrons of table, conspiring with the glint of beer glasses to expose the hairy chests and bulbous stomachs of clinically inebriated truckers. Beer waterfalled off their lips and swelled in table-top puddles, before plunging its victims into a riot of pelvis-wiggling and beer-belly-wobbling on the dance floor. The route to the bar hurtled between the Scylla of flailing elbows and the Charybdis of boulder-sized backsides.

When the entertainment had disintegrated into the sort of noises that people only allow themselves to make when they're no longer aware that they're making them, I strolled on to the deck. Around me was a big expanse of black. A few hours earlier, a pink fuzz had bloomed over the sugar-lump houses and ice-cube factories peeking between the peach-coloured cliffs of the mainland. Offshore islands had seemed to be swimming, like schools of medieval sea-monsters, in a cobalt-blue sea whose white fringe washed against golden beaches and rugged headlands covered in scrub.

Now there was nothing to see. It was dark and quiet. As I breathed the air that swept over the gunwales with a sprinkle of salt water, I felt that we were on our way. We had entered Byzantine waters: the empire of Manuel Comnenos, the addressee of Prester John's letter.

Gradually, as dawn sucked up the last inky spots of night, an island shaped like an arrowhead jutted out of the sea. Fruit fields and elevated hills glanced over a medieval city knuckled with bastions and rippling with crenellations. Catamarans and short-distance fishing boats chased us towards the Arsenal Gate, while hydrofoils peeled off to Mandraki Harbour. Sun-worshippers scuttled over the gangways, the smell of their lotion bottles as powerful as the massive forearms and stomachs of the beer-belly-wobblers whom they were racing in a battle of elbows, backpack-clips and cameras that crashed against a bulwark of touts.

They flung themselves at us – portly men in suits, young men with eyebrow rings, ladies with too much mascara. They all promised Holiday Heaven, with sun, sand, lots to drink and lots of sex. A dark, lizard-shaped man called Michaelis promised none of these. He promised a small room and a patio, and showed us a clipboard on which he'd sellotaped photographs of his toilet, his laundry room and his vegetable garden. It was the cheapest offer we could find, so we got into his car.

In Master Philip's day, Rhodes was a stopover en route to the Byzantine mainland and a centre of theological research. It wasn't until the early fourteenth century that the island entered her most illustrious period, under the Knights of St John. The Hospitallers, as they were also known, were founded in the 1070s in Jerusalem, where they established a hospital. It became the most important institute of its kind in the Christian East, pampering Muslims and Jews as well as Christians with feather mattresses and fresh meat. During the early decades of the twelfth century, the Hospitallers were Outremer's most philanthropic organization. They clothed the poor, looked after orphans and set up makeshift battle-site infirmaries to tend to wounded soldiers. But somewhere along the murky trajectory to mid-century, chasuble was replaced by hauberk: praying was all very well, but you can't kill Saracens by kneeling in a pew. The Hospitallers joined the Knights Templar as the heart of the Crusader forces, acquiring land, tithes and castles, becoming the wealthiest of the military orders, securing a seat at the High Court of Jerusalem and generally playing the 'Latin barbarian' that revolted the Byzantine chronicler Anna Comnena: 'At one and the same time he communicates the body and blood of God, and looks murderously and becomes a "man of blood".'Although they continued their hospital work, so far had it fallen in their priorities that, soon after the Peace of Venice, Pope Alexander III warned their Grand Master against compromising their 'care for the poor'. Increasingly a law unto themselves, the Hospitallers squabbled with the Templars, refused to pay church taxes, and magnified the disunity that enabled Saladin to capture most of the Holy Land in 1187.

After that defeat the Hospitallers kept a few toeholds, such as the castle of Krak des Chevaliers and their palace at Acre. But in 1291 the Mamlukes booted them out of the Levant for good. They clattered around the Mediterranean in search of a suitable stomping ground and, after an interlude in Cyprus, seized Rhodes from a band of Genoese pirates. Around the same time, the Templars were being burned at the stake on drummed-up charges of homosexuality and worship of cats' heads, so it was crucial that the Hospitallers prove themselves to be good Catholics. That meant building the most macho fortifications (and a few churches), battling with the nearby Turks, and even enquiring after the whereabouts of Prester John. But, after more than two centuries on Rhodes, the Hospitallers were unable to resist the army of Suleiman the Magnificent. In 1522, against a quarter of a million well-trained Turks, the knights could offer only a few hundred fighters and a herd of goats. The Turks let them leave with dignity, and they established themselves on Malta. But their prime had passed.

In Acre a few months earlier, I had witnessed that prime in the vaulted hallways of the Grand Masters' Palace. Now, the chivalric coats of arms carved on to the thick, honey-coloured walls of medieval Rhodes reintroduced the muscular architecture of the Hospitallers, pregnant with the power of militant Christianity. There was a stark contrast between the puissant walls and the little men in string vests on the quay, reeling in hauls of sea bream and mullet. It seemed to capture the historical disaffection between the Hospitallers and the natives of Rhodes.

'Why you come to Rhodes?' asked Michaelis. He peered through the iconostasis of his windscreen, all glittering crucifixes and plastic Christs, as if he was struggling to tell where the road ended and the walls of the Old City began.

'We're on our way to Ethiopia,' said Mike.

'You crazy? This is a million kilometres from here!'

'Yes,' I said, 'but we're here for the Knights of St John.'

I heard a long, bitter groan. 'Everyone,' growled Michaelis, scrutinizing his rear-view mirror as if apprehensive of a stray Hospitaller, 'he come to Rhodes, he say "Knights of John, Knights of John".'

'Bet you're glad the Knights have closed down,' said Mike.

'Closed down? No, you make mistake. The Knights is not closed down. We have visitors – they are Knights of John.

They come, they say, "We are the great-great-grandchildren of the Knights of St John."'

'Where are they from?' I asked.

'Belgium.'

The modern Knights of St John are more in the spirit of the original Hospitallers than the militant order that they became. Their projects include an ophthalmic hospital in Jerusalem, work with the handicapped in Lourdes, and the St John's Ambulance Service.

They might have abandoned their broadswords (and Rhodes for that matter), but we did meet one active order of knights on the island. We called them the Newky Brown Knights. They wore matching yellow tunics that ended in crenellations around their knees. They wielded bottles of ale and held court outside Charlie's Dutch-Belgian Café, where they chanted war cries like 'Coom 'n' 'ave a goo if yu think yer 'ard anoof.' And, in the spirit of the knights of old, they offered their protection to damsels-in-undress. Whoever said chivalry was dead?

Eschewing diesel for the smells of animals and axle grease with which Master Philip would have been familiar, Rhodes is the largest inhabited medieval city in the Mediterranean. Boys shoulder wooden carts packed with cut-price icons down the Street of the Knights, while a caricaturist sets up under a plane tree flanking the pastel-pink Suleiman Mosque. The old city plays out an elaborate debate – between the chunks of medieval stone and the mass-produced frippery of miniature Colossi, coffee-table books on classical eroticism, tattooists, body-piercers and purveyors of all the other ancient arts of Greece. On one side of the street, a fish restaurant thrums to the tune of a bouzouki classic; on the other, a cut-price haberdashery to the warble of a singing Barbie doll.

We spent the afternoon in the Palace of the Knights. Inside a brawny pair of circular towers, limp-wristed cloak-huggers preened in vaulted niches. Poems and philosophical treatises crinkled among sketches of the Colossus and pottery shards pointing to life before the Hospitallers; cross-spangled twelfth-century monks wilted on the walls. The collection was eclectic, racing through the gamut of Rhodiote history, but it was the building itself – huge, proud, stamped with the escutcheons of its Crusading rulers – that left the mightiest impression. Except that a plaque near the forecourt indicated another influence. It was dedicated to Vittorio Emanuele III, Mussolini's puppet-king and 'Imperatore di Etiopia'. When the Italians assumed control of Rhodes in 1912, the palace was in a parlous state. Later, the Fascists renovated it as Mussolini's summer palace. The Blackshirts of colonial Italy and the militant Knights of Jerusalem: Il Duce certainly saw a parallel.

As did Michaelis.

A conveyor belt of medieval masonry – domes, steeples, minarets (and, in the gardens of whitewashed houses, broken shopping trolleys) carried us towards our All-Knowing Hotelier in his palikari vest. His wife wielded her rolling pin in a tempest of flour, butter, cheese and Michaelis' mother gabbling on the spot as if in imitation of the stove-pot. If you stepped too close, you'd be temporarily blinded by onions. This is the Mediterranean, where the kitchen is the woman's castle.

Cicadas chirped in the grass and a hibiscus tree hung over our table. Hanging even closer, and checking any temptation to Elysian comparisons, were Michaelis' armpits.

'You like Knights' Palace?' he asked, dipping his fingers into a dish of black olives. 'You think the Knights is good?'

'Well . . .' I began.

'Everyone,' said Michaelis, spitting out a pip, 'think the Knights is good.'

'Which means he doesn't,' groaned Mike. The ashtray that Michaelis held up with one hand became 'the Knights', a bottle of Steamwhistle Pilsner 'the Arabs'; and so began

The History of the Knights in Rhodes
by Michaelis the Rhodiote

Pilsner/Arabs clink against Ashtray/Knights.
'The Knights they lose to the Arabs.'
Ashtray/Knights are placed in Napkin Basket/Cyprus.
'They go to Cyprus. But Cyprus no will have them.'
*Ashtray/Knights are removed from Napkin
Basket/Cyprus.*
'They look for place near Holy Land.'
*Plates of lamb, seasoned with marjoram and spit-roasted
in the Byzantine manner, rattle above the table.
Ashtray/Knights hover tensely, above the plates.*
'Where this will be?'
It will be a Backgammon Board, doubling as Rhodes.
'The Knights they are building castles and walls and
Rhodes become the most protected town in the world.'
*It certainly becomes the most protected board game in
the world, surrounded by a salt pot, a plate of feta cheese
and a basket of mastic-flavoured bread.*
'But in sixteenth century, the Turks come for attack.'
*Which they proceed to do with toothpicks, backgammon
chips and, briefly, my fork.*
'And the Turks win.'
*Ashtray/Knights are removed from Backgammon Board
and begin their ignominious flight to Olive Bowl/Malta.*
'And the Knights no more have the power.'
*Hence Ashtray/Knights are laid beside Olive Bowl/Malta,
and the narrator's hangdog head is buried in his hands.*

The expression on his face was one with which the forth-
coming weeks would breed increasing familiarity: that of the
Mediterranean man for whom the last thousand years are as
fresh and bitter as a drink squeezed from the local lemons.

'Were the knights good for Rhodes?' I asked, as Michaelis'
wife turned up with a tray and took away his props.

'Were good?' His brown eyes bulged with indignation. 'When Cattolic and Orttodox together, always is problem. You remember 1204? The Cattolic destroy Constantinople, so is easy for the Turks to conquer. These Cattolics the same as Knights of John – are fascist. Like Mussolini!'

'How about the Turks?' asked Mike.

Michaelis peered studiously at the onions on our plates.

'I tell you a story,' he said. 'My grandfather live in the Turkey. Ha! Now they call it the Turkey. But eight hundred years before, there no is Turks. Is because of the wars – the Crusades, the conquest of Constantinople, the War of the World – we lose this land to the Turks. The Greeks from the Turkey come to Greece and the Turks from Greece come to the Turkey. My grandfather he is coming from the Turkey and the Turks is cutting up the Greeks with their swords. There are American and British ships, and what they do? Nothing!'

'Yes, all right,' said Mike, 'but did your grandfather survive?'

'Ha! The Turks they want to cut him in pieces. But the people from Rhodes come in their boats. They save all the Greek people and take them back. We never have help from the Allies, only from the Greeks. Why do the West always supports the Turks? They are evil and they want to conquer all the Europe.'

An evening of political diatribe was unfolding before us; and I've no doubt that Michaelis would have sat there expatiating at us until the early hours had his wife not intervened. To us she gave hazelnut biscuits (probably not much different from the 'delicate biscuit' that William of Rubruck found in thirteenth-century Constantinople) and to Michaelis a shriek.

'So I go,' he said. 'You leave tomorrow?'

'Yep,' said Mike.

'Where you go?'

'Turkey.'

Michaelis had turned Turkey into a terrifying prospect. But after the hovercraft delivered us to the Anatolian mainland, it seemed that something was up. A mountain of hornbeam and alder trees arched round our bus as we were swallowed into a world of women in black wimples and men in peaked caps like golfers in P. G. Wodehouse. Instead of the Seljuk Turk's iron cuirass, the men wore tweed jackets; instead of scimitars, they carried clay pipes. The landscape was less rocky, ostensibly more fertile than Greece: a hiccup in our progress towards Oriental stereotypes. But the greatest shock was the excessive, often ponderous, civility. The customs official who patted our backpacks and wished us 'good time in my country'; the Sarap Bir Bardek wine served to the strains of Chopin in the Hospitaller castle in Bodrum; the man in Selçuk who, his attempt to sell us tea, carpets or a room in his uncle's hotel having been rebuffed by Mike's most exquisite assumption of authority (knuckles slapping palm as he declared: 'Don't want your tea, don't want your carpets, and certainly don't want your hotel'), not only wished us 'good time in my country' but also offered to show us the way to the hotel at which we wished to stay; and the manager of that hotel, who planted us on camel-hair cushions, played gentle Sufi music and crammed us with meat-filled dolmas – all these belonged to a different genre from the Gothic breviary of Michaelis' mind.

Perhaps the killing fields would have to wait until we'd ventured further east. After all, if the Holy Land is where people rise from the dead, Anatolia is where they don't even die. Underneath the textbook-grey battlements of Selçuk's Ottoman castle, marble slabs poked out of tussocks of untended grass and littered the ruins of a nave. Cubic capitals and undulating piles of red brick offered a mere rumour of the six-domed cruciform basilica built in the sixth century by the emperor Justinian over the disputed tomb of St John.

Disputed not because of uncertainty over *where* he died, but *whether*.

St John came to Anatolia soon after the first Pentecost. He governed the Church of Asia, composed his Gospel and inspired a series of botched murder attempts by the pagan emperor, Domitian. First the emperor offered the evangelist a drink. It was poisoned, but since the goblet turned into a snake and slithered away, Domitian decided to forget about the formalities and simply plunged St John into a cauldron of boiling oil. To this the evangelist proved frustratingly immune, so the persevering emperor exiled him to the island of Patmos. Which wasn't much good either, since it was there that John composed his masterpiece – the Book of Revelation – before returning to end his days in Selçuk.

Except, after he'd cheated death twice, written the most mysterious text in the New Testament, and inspired a Gospel rumour 'that this disciple would not die' (John 21: 23), it wasn't terribly clear whether his days had actually ended. He was – or so decreed the folklorists who have a monopoly on such matters – worthy to join Elijah and Enoch in the ranks of the Earthly Immortals (to be joined later by Finn MacCool, the Wandering Jew, Barbarossa, Elvis Presley and Bobby Ewing from *Dallas*). Discrepancies over authorship of texts attributed to him, and his identification as Christ's 'beloved', didn't matter a jot: John became a Byzantine Elvis, destined to roam the earth, spotted by cranks and embellished by wags. But where, asked his more inquisitive fans, had he gone?

His Graceland was Selçuk. But its only image of the saint, a pale fresco painted on to a rough face of rock, was locked inside a wooden shed. I headed towards the tomb, but my solemn search for a clue was suddenly interrupted by a stern baritone thundering down what was left of the nave.

'I want you to do it yourself.'

Mike had made a friend. Rather an old friend from the looks of it. Rather an old tortoise, to be strictly biological. It was trying to crawl to the top of an iron ramp. Each time it approached its target, the ramp tottered and sent the tortoise back to square one. And each time, the tortoise picked itself up and started again: creep-crawl-slink-totter-crash. This could have gone on for ever, had Mike not decided to play the deus ex machina. He lifted up the hapless reptile by its shell and placed it at the top of the ramp. Clearly accustomed to the local prevalence of divine intervention, it didn't even blink: nonchalantly and creakily, it crawled towards the tomb.

The resting place of the saint who reputedly didn't rest was marked by a large marble square, flanked by four serpentine columns. Geometric patterns mingled in nearby mosaics. According to legend, when the tomb was opened, all that was found was dust. In the absence of a body, the dust acquired magical attributes and inspired Christendom's infirm of limb to visit the tomb in search of a cure. One able-bodied visitor, ever on the lookout for the outlandish, was the fourteenth-century English knight Sir John Mandeville:

> And in the tomb of St John is nought but Manna, that is clept Angels' meat; for his body was translated into Paradise . . . And ye shall understand, that St. John let make his grave there in his life, and laid himself therein all quick; and therefore some men say, that he died not, but that he resteth there till the day of doom. And, forsooth, there is a great marvel; for men may see there the earth of the tomb apertly many times stir and move, as there were quick things under.

Mike was now prostrate on top of the tomb, squinting through one of two grilles that locked us out of the holes channelling deep underground.

'Can you hear anything?' I asked.

'Nothing.'

'Hmm. According to Friar Jordanus of Severac, we should be able to hear the sound of a man snoring.'

'Well, we can't.'

'How about holy dust?'

'Can't see any.'

'Well, according to Abbot Daniel – a twelfth-century Russian – it only rises on St John's anniversary. Which would mean waiting until just after Christmas.'

Mike stood up, brushed the dust – a distinctly secular form – off his beach shorts, and fitted a panama hat on his head.

'Yeah, maybe it *would* – but it won't.'

St John's body has never been found. All sorts of theories have suggested its whereabouts. One latched on to two New Testament epistles attributed to him. The writer styles himself 'John the Presbyter'. The terms 'Presbyter' and 'Prester' were interchangeable. Where was John the Divine, immortal until the Second Coming? Had he established himself as the omnipotent ruler of a faraway land? The Italian poet Ludovico Ariosto located him in a mountain in the land of Prester John. John of Hildesheim, the fourteenth-century author of the *History of the Three Holy Kings*, suggested that Prester John was named after the saint, 'the most speciyall chosen and loved of God almyghty'. St John's Revelation mixes heavenly images with hellish creatures like Gog and Magog; Prester John's kingdom mixes heavenly images with hellish creatures like Gog and Magog. In the medieval imagination, the author of the Apocalypse and the priest-king of terra incognita were inextricably linked.

Some snapshots. A bus to Yalova, travelling through thickly wooded ridges. A cone of deliciously stretchy doldurma ice cream, eaten amid a crowd of excited children who squealed as they identified themselves in the digital screen of Mike's Milex camera, and insisted on holding our hands. (Considering that we were in 'the country round Nicaea', where Anna Comnena reported that Western Christians 'dismembered some of the children and fixed others on wooden posts and roasted them at the fire', I thought they were very brave.) A ferry across the Marmara. On one side, European mountains bustled towards Bulgaria. On the other, Asia slid – via the scrap-built dwellings of recently urbanized country folk – towards the Trojan plains. A conversation with an old *hoja* in the first *gelabiyya* I'd seen since Jerusalem, about the merits of Galatasaray and 'Mansheesta United'. Ahead of us, Istanbul rose as a black pencil-holder on a glass table-top. Detail slowly coloured the silhouette: pen-shaped minarets, the triangular towers of the Topkapi Palace, the cupolas of Haghia Sophia, the flags of foreign consulates, office blocks, high-rise hotels, chimneys, cars, mobile snack-carts, people. A hoot like an elephant, the battle for the gangplanks, the smell of dead fish and diesel, the squawk of seagulls, a little man in a neat yellow suit: 'Well-com in Istanbul.'

When Odo of Deuil accompanied King Louis VII of France in 1147 to 'Constantinople, the glory of the Greeks, rich in renown and richer still in possessions', he was wonder-struck. He marvelled at the great church of Haghia Sophia and Byzantine Emperor Manuel Comnenos' palace of Blachernae, whose 'interior surpasses anything that I can say about it'. Then he let off some green-eyed steam: 'Constantinople is arrogant in her wealth, treacherous in her practices, corrupt in her faith, just as she fears everyone on account of her wealth, she is dreaded by everyone because of her treachery and faithlessness.'

In the twelfth century, there was no love lost between Byzantium and Western Christendom. Odo accused Manuel Comnenos of providing inadequate provisions for the Crusaders and conspiring with the Turks, and saddled him with the failure of the Second Crusade (a fiasco, organized in the immediate aftermath of Prester John's introduction to the West, that petered out near Damascus, when its leaders ran out of water). Odo's attitude was typical of the unwritten rule of mutual recrimination: *it can't be my fault, so it must be yours*.

A typical example of this mutual contempt was the aborted engagement, in 1160, between Manuel Comnenos and Melisende of Tripoli. It was a match much favoured by her brother, Count Raymond, who prepared a fabulous trousseau of anklets, bracelets and gold tiaras, and waited for confirmation. And waited for a year. And sent a knight to Constantinople. And wasn't best pleased when it turned out that Manuel's roving eye had settled elsewhere. So displeased was Raymond that he hired a gang of desperadoes to pillage Byzantine land. 'On all sides,' wrote the Crusader chronicler William of Tyre, 'they plundered, burned, and massacred.' Not that it did much for Melisende. She locked herself away and became an international icon for broken hearts.

Had the rival poles of Christendom co-operated more closely, more of Byzantine Constantinople might have survived.

'Thought you said there'd be lions and bears,' protested Mike, as we strolled across the Hippodrome.

'Ah, well,' I said with a shrug, 'that was according to Benjamin of Tudela.'

Shoeshine boys and snack salesmen were circling pock-marked obelisks in a slow-motion parody of Byzantine horse races. The tens of thousands of Byzantine supporters screaming for their favourite charioteer were replaced by women in hijab, gossiping under the chestnut trees; and students – leather-jacketed and miniskirted, mobile phones hinged to their ears.

They probably weren't Greek.

Because, among thirteen million Istanbulites, the Greeks represent 0.02 per cent. Some were nudged out by the Turkish Sultan Mehmet's conquest of Constantinople in 1453, the city's subsequent Islamization and the Christians' reduction to second-class *dhimmi*tude.* Many more were evicted when the Ottoman Empire was torn apart in the First World War. Although Constantinople was briefly wrested out of Turkish hands, it was wrested right back by the army of Mustafa Kemal Atatürk, leading to the transfer of 1.5 million Greeks, including Michaelis' grandfather. And those who still hadn't been persuaded that continued cohabitation with the Turks wasn't for them were given a rude awakening one night in 1955, when a mob of thousands ransacked their property, incinerated their priests and raped their wives. Istanbul's Greeks were now on the verge of extinction.

That much, once we had penetrated the barbed wire and airport-style metal detector fortifying the Greek Orthodox Patriarchate, became as clear as the chandeliers that dangled plum-sized pendants over the comic faces smiling or scowling from the arms of velvet-seated pews in the Church of St George. The scraggly-bearded priests on the esplanade were rather less expressive: they swivelled round and scuttled away, shooing us towards Panyotos, a camp layman in a pin-stripe suit.

'You want you ask me question?' His hands fluttered in front of his face, as if they'd mistaken themselves for doves.

'I'd rather speak to a Metropolitan,' said Mike.

'But no!' Panyotos beamed, his body quivering in a rhapsody of extraneous gestures. 'Very they are beezy!'

'Busy? But . . .' Mike glanced at a black-robed Merlin hurrying into his office. 'What about that one?'

'He is Metropolitan of Ephesus.'

'And he's busy?'

'Very beezy.'

'But . . .' Mike removed a pair of wasp's-eye sunglasses

---

* The *dhimmis* were religious minorities in the Dar al-Islam, who were protected by legislation but barred from certain privileges, such as public worship, and subject to a *jizya* (head tax) and a *kharaj* (property tax). A similar system was operated in the Crusader kingdom, where Muslim subjects were liable for a *dime*, or tithe.

from his face and peered suspiciously after the disappearing Metropolitan. 'How many parishioners are there in Ephesus?'

'None.'

Panyotos wasn't all that keen on hanging about himself. His wife was pregnant and he was unsure about bringing up a child in a city where resources for Greeks – particularly schools – were so weak.

'No many Greek in Istanbul!' He sighed, hands twittering over a ziggurat of papers in an office complex that buzzed, whirred and beeped to the tune of telephones, fax machines and CCTV. 'The young they saying, "Greece good democracy drachma wooosh! Europe all family." Understanding?'

Certainly. But what about the other Christian denominations? Didn't they all band together?

'Mixing I am!' chirped Panyotos. 'Mother Polish Cattolic, father Greek, father's mother Bulgarian Orttodox, wife Armenian and grandmother Muslim Kurd. Understanding? Mixing I am many belief in Istanbul. Example: today grandfather celebrate a vest.'

'A vest?' I frowned.

'Yes, yes! The vest of Antony of Padua.'

'Oh – you mean a feast?'

'Yes! My grandfather Cattolic. Understanding?'

'You don't celebrate the feast?'

'Orttodox I am! Always we different from Cattolic.'

It seemed odd that, reduced to such small numbers, the Christian sects didn't share the fellowship that was celebrated in Panyotos' bloodstream. Rocking on his chair under a giltframed print of Christ's crowded entry to Jerusalem, the Catholic bishop complained about accusatory Greeks, uncommunicative 'others', and the lack of a common language.

'Constantinople is important,' he said, gabling his fingers under his lips, 'even if there are no Christians, because she is the first city of the Christian empire.'

But the Christian population, bolstered in Master Philip's

day by Italian merchants, was still being bolstered. In Taksim, where churches were hidden behind iron gates to avoid offending 'Islamic sensitivities' and the only Italian merchant was an ex-hippy hawking pastel prints outside the Church of St Mary Draperis, we did manage to meet some 'local' Christians. Just not of the Byzantine variety.

'We from Nigeria,' said Desmond, their leader, after they'd completed a rendition of 'Bind Us Together' in an underground church hall. 'We are here for transit. Tis da easiest way ta Europe.'

They were in Istanbul, whispered the priest looking after them, against the law.

'Their papers,' he said, 'are not right, so they will find it difficult to get out.'

Despite his dog collar, this particular padre was somewhat ambivalent about Christians. He liked Sufis, because they reminded him of King David ('they like to dance'), and he brushed off any hint of Christian difficulties. The bomb that exploded in his church the previous Christmas, he insisted, 'was small and it did not cause much damage'. What really concerned him was 'Muslims who want to become Christian. I cut them short. I make it seem impossible. Because we are not allowed to evangelize, and if the government think we do this, we have big problem.'

It was rather different from Manuel Comnenos' time, when the emperor removed the anathema against Muhammad, traditionally expected of converts, in order to facilitate Muslim conversion and strengthen Christianity in the territories of the Seljuk Turks.

Fra Fidelio, who introduced us to another group of immigrants in the Catholic Cathedral, was equally disgruntled.

'They are-a refugees.' He shrugged. 'From Ee-raq.'

'They're the best behaved schoolchildren I've ever seen,' said Mike. They sat neat and tidy in their pew, eyes locked fiercely on the altar, as if any movement might return them to the nightmare from which they had come.

'We escaped the torture,' said Fawzi, their teacher. 'We want to go to Europe.' He raised his eyebrows and puffed out his cheeks. 'Inshallah.' God willing.

It was, Fra Fidelio grumbled as we climbed into the gallery, a 'difficult situation'.

'The refugees need bread. So we give them bread. But eez not easy. The economy eez a mess. But Istanbul eez where Asia and Europe meet – we have Arabs, Africans and Filipinos, people from Europe and America. We are very diverse in Istanbul.'

That was certainly true in Master Philip's day. Benjamin of Tudela identified 'all sorts of merchants' in Constantinople: 'From the land of Babylon, from the land of Shinar, from Persia, Media, and all the sovereignty of the land of Egypt, from the land of Canaan, and the empire of Russia, from Hungaria, Patzinakia, Khazaria, and the land of Lombardy and Sepharad.' But now, Fra Fidelio's claim rang hollow. Istanbul is no longer a meeting place between East and West. It's a caravanserai where the East prepares its papers so it can move to the West.

This confusion – this sense of in-betweenness – exemplified by Digenes Akrites, the hero of a popular twelfth-century Byzantine literary cycle, born of a Muslim emir and a Greek noblewoman – is more common in Istanbul than the immediate cloud-piercing thrust of her minarets suggests. Greece and Turkey met across the dining table, where okra, yoghurt, halva and aubergine supported a culinary collusion barely separated by semantics. Greeks and Turks munched dolmades or dolmas and pitta or *pide* bread, basted their spit-roasted lamb with lemon juice and left a froth of *lakia* or *kaymak* on their demitasses of thick coffee. It was the same cultural seesaw that enabled Kilidj Arslan II, the Seljuk sultan who was Manuel Comnenos' chief rival, to hire a Christian chancellor, and the Ottoman sultans to convert the churches of Constantinople, with little trouble, into mosques.

In a district of top-heavy wooden houses, where long-lashed eyes peeked through fretted window frames, Mike and I found the great monastery complex of St Saviour Pantocrator, built by the Comneni but Turk-formed into a mosque. In the prayer hall, a pockmarked restoration worker with a beard as big as that of Sultan Beyazit II peeled back a carpet to expose a Byzantine mosaic inlaid with opus sectile figures and showed us crosses carved into a *mimbar*. 'Comneni,' he said.

We moved to examine a wooden pit. 'Comneni,' he repeated.

'Comneni who?' asked Mike.

'Comneni John. Comneni Irene. Comneni Manuel.'

He shuffled his forearms and swung his hands across his shoulders. The pit was empty: Manuel's bones were as obsolete as Prester John's.

St Saviour was one of many mosque-churches in Istanbul, architectural hermaphrodites neutered by their double history. Yet their most famous member, Haghia Sophia, is still virile with the fascination of Christian architecture's most ethereal space. You do first have to penetrate its ghastly exterior, a pale-pink egg carton sinking under minarets and plane trees. That achieved, you shuffle into a spiritual soufflé where sunlight seeps through Islamic calligraphy and washes the hem of Mary's cloak, and a marble muezzin's lodge looms over the coloured circles of the Byzantine *omphalion*. Inserting themselves into this inter-creed fantasy are the tour guides, gaggling and barking and slapping their tummies to the tune of legendary epigrams ('Mehmet to his soldiers: "The gold is thine, the building mine!" '), statistics ('thirty million tiles, dome one eight three feet, inauguration five three seven') or implausible errors ('This Aya Sofa, meesta, builded by the Seljuk Turks. Meesta want tour?'). Meesta expressed a firm negative, and followed the tunnel that rolled into a gallery above the nave, in search of a pair of twelfth-century mosaics.

In one, the eleventh-century empress Zoe stood beside her third husband, Constantine, who had been mosaicked over his predecessors. She was a vivacious empress. She didn't lose her virginity until her sixth decade, but after that there was no stopping her. Prester John, who had rather old-fashioned views on women (his wives, though abundant and beautiful, 'approach us only four times a year and then solely for the procreation of sons'), would have widened his eyes in disgust. The Zoe here was more dignified: mosaics were the Byzantine propaganda poster, like the images of Turkish politicians plastered on to Istanbul's walls or the personalized billboards that we would encounter further east. Zoe and Constantine wore colourful chequered garments, gem-studded crowns and haloes. They held gifts in their hands – a small sack and a scroll – in offering to Christ. Theirs was a typical representation of the relationship between royalty and divinity. It resembled the beautiful mosaic downstairs, in which Justinian and the first Constantine offered the church and the city to Mary and Child. In both cases, donors bowed to the divine, with humble expressions.

The next mosaic was different. It depicted Manuel Comnenos' father, John, the empress Irene and their son Alexios. Between them stood Mary and Child. Again, generous helpings of gold, coloured stones and haloes. Like Constantine, John held a sack. But there the comparison ended. His head was not bowed. He was not turned towards Mary and Christ. Nor was his wife. They stood straight, looking outwards, the same height as the holy figures. This was more than just an artistic detail: it was a political statement. Whereas Constantine was Christ's servant, John was his peer. According to the chronicler Niketas Choniates, John wished 'to ascend the mountain of the Lord, as the psalmist puts it, and to stand in his holy place; justified by the law of war to drive away the encircling enemy, who have often seized the Sepulchre of our Lord'. The similarity with Prester John's designs on Jerusalem suggests that they share more than the same Christian name. But it was upon John's son, Manuel, that Prester John's letter would pour scorn.

Sitting on silk pouffes in our hotel's salon, hankies tied round their heads and rolled cigarettes tucked between their fingers, an army of backpackers locked their anecdotes in battle. An American who'd just emerged from a submarine near Odessa sparred with an Australian who'd entered Tibet clasping the belly of an elephant. A Swiss cyclist's stoning in Iran fell to the mightier volume of a New Zealander who was checking the acoustics of the churches of Asia by singing in every classical amphitheatre she could find. Somewhat ruthlessly, I left Mike trapped by the piercing soprano of this latter-day troubadour and ventured into the Grand Bazaar.

Pyramids of nutmeg, ziggurats of nougat blocks and copper troughs of aromatic sauces yielded to clothes lines of khaki trousers and angora goat-hair rugs. Beyond the outer labyrinth of the Covered Market – jewellers, embroiderers, men in Ottoman uniform banging their copper jugs of *sahlep* (fox's testicles), men offering carpets, cumin or sisters, toothpick stores, handbag stalls, cafés serving Soup of Sheep's Feet – through the Street of the Calpac-Makers and the Gate of the Fez-Makers, past the second-hand mobile-phone salesmen and black-market foreign-exchange merchants behind the Beyazit Mosque, there emerged a whorl of stalls under the tentacles of willow trees: the Sahaflar Jarshishi. In Master Philip's day it was the Chartoprateia – Byzantium's Book and Paper Market: a place of magic, at a time when Constantinople offered Western scholars their first glimpses of Aristotle and St Augustine. Stacks of comic books and encyclopaedias dispensed a musty scent that wafted past calligraphic masterpieces like a rowing boat fashioned out of the Arabic letter for 'W'. Ink paintings celebrated topics – such as the Flood or the paradise of the Old Man of the Mountain – that would have been equally popular in Manuel Comnenos' city.

The books themselves were stacked in eclectic piles. *The Last Caravan of the Silk Road* gathered the same dust as Trixie Belden's teenage detective work and a worm-eaten Turkish *David Copperfield*. A copy of *Anatomie Vétérinaire* peeked between Jacques Pervititich's *Insurance Maps of Istanbul* and the collected sayings of the medieval Turkish wit Nosreddin Hoça, a little man with a cotton-wool beard surrounded by bubble trees and fluffy animals.* Others were more homogeneous, particularly the piles of crumpled romances. Beautiful black-haired women reclined on their covers, while big-bearded men brandished their scimitars at the world.

In Master Philip's day, Byzantine literature was at a zenith, thanks to the *theatra*, or literary salons, where Maecenas figures like Manuel Comnenos' sister-in-law Eirene gathered such luminaries as Theodore Podromos – fabulist, scholar, panegyricist – or John Tzetzes, a miserable man of letters who railed against his home town's artistic vulgarity in a letter to a sausage-maker. 'For now,' he wrote, 'every disgusting and thrice-accursed wretch like you only has to put on a monastic habit, or hang bells from his penis . . . in short, to dress himself up to look self-effacing in an ostentatious and highly calculated air of artless simplicity.' Tzetzes' fulminations against a city where 'the rogue is publicly feted as a saint' do seem justified. Because, for all Constantinople's literary talent, the principal use to which it was put was not one with which modern commentators have much truck: that oldest of literary forms, the hagiography.

Outside one of the smaller shops was a fat bookseller with

---

* An example of one of his stories, translated for me by a local browser: 'Nosreddin says, "Yesterday I quarrel with my wife. So we make a bet. No more talkings. The first who talks is the loser. So I take care I win this bet. I say nothing. Then a burglar come in the house. I say *nothing*. The burglar take all my possessions. I say *nothing*. Then my wife come in. My wife say, 'What happened?' and other such things. I say, 'Ha! You lose bet!' I am so happy."'

a golfer's cap on his head and a pipe between his teeth. Fellow pipe-smokers crowded him, forming their own *theatra* as they listened to his anecdotes. I browsed inside for references to Manuel Comnenos. Theodore Podromos hailed him as the 'Purple-born third sebastokrator ... cub of the mighty lion, chick of the golden peacock'. Michael Italikos, teacher of the Gospel, addressed Manuel as 'a living and moving statue of the King above who made you king'. They reminded me of the opening salvo of Prester John's letter. After saluting Manuel as 'governor of the Greeks', he pours scorn on the emperor: 'Your little Greeks regard you as a god; still we know that you are mortal, and subject to human weakness.' Here is one of the letter's possible motivations: to satirize the pomp of the Byzantine court.

A glance at the hagiography by John Kinnamos suggests that there was good call for this. Kinnamos makes no pretension of impartiality. His book is called *Summary of the Successes of the Late Emperor and Porphyrogennetos Lord John Comnenos and Description of the Deeds of his Renowned Son the Emperor and Porphyrogennetos Lord Manuel Comnenos*. Two conclusions can immediately be drawn from the *Summary*: a) Manuel had a big ego, and b) Kinnamos was a shameless sycophant. In fact, the *Summary* is the textbook for sycophants. If you need to learn to simper, crawl and lick someone's butt-cheeks, read it. It's not so much a biography as a fallen bureaucrat's desperate bid for advancement.

Manuel, as far as Kinnamos was concerned, could do no wrong. He slew a monstrous leopard-lion hybrid, received supernatural visions predicting his glory and attracted the universal love of his subjects. He was also an expert physician. When King Baldwin of Jerusalem broke his arm on the Syrian hunt, Manuel applied the bandages and 'surpassed many who had been occupied in the physicians' art throughout their life'. Master Philip would surely have been thrilled to meet him – after all (in Kinnamos' no doubt non-partisan account), the emperor had himself 'contributed much to the healers' science which had remained unknown to it for all time'. In my mind, I locked them in the imperial laboratory for a heart-to-heart on Oriental ointments and lancing methods, Manuel pledging Philip to let him know if he found any decent curatives in the empire of Prester John.

One occasion, above all others, squeezed every last drop from the unctuousness of Kinnamos' stylus. In 1162, the Seljuk sultan, Kilidj Arslan II, arrived in Constantinople for a meeting with Manuel. The emperor 'received him with magnificent banquets . . . charmed him with horse races . . . set alight some boats and skiffs with liquid fire, and absolutely gorged the man with spectacles in the hippodrome'. Filling his golden throne 'with the magnitude of his well-proportioned body', Manuel is lost in a rhapsody of bijouterie that turns him into a human diadem, before the Pamperer of the Imperial Posterior mocks the astonished sultan on his low stool, 'very humble alongside the lofty throne'.

Poor Kilidj Arslan: trapped beside the pompous emperor, at risk of being blinded by the dazzle of the imperial costume or choking on his own vomit. It would be fourteen years until he could deliver his riposte; but on that occasion, at the battlefield of Myriocephalum, Manuel would walk straight into it . . .

The owner had shuffled back into the shop. As I turned round, he shot me a quizzical look.

'Er – Prester John?' I asked.

He tamped his pipe. Would he reveal some obscure manuscript containing the secrets of the priest-king bound in Byzantine calfskin? He spread out his arms, waved them towards the shelves and announced:

'Book!'

'It's this way.'

'Hello? Who's got the map?'

'You're not big, you're not clever. It's this way.'

'Keep going that way and we'll reach the Golden Horn.'

With Mike detached from his bucket of *doldurma* ice cream and the Antipodean chorister, our attempt to pay homage on Master Philip's behalf at the court of the Comneni quickly disintegrated into a competition for control of direction. Narrow, hilly lanes lost us among cracked walls and muddy windows, boys socking sagging footballs, and a marketplace where tents of black burkas shrieked at whiskery prayer-bead-clutchers. We were rescued by a student called Ali, who escorted us along the Byzantine land-wall, where stones fortified by Manuel Comnenos were crumbling like feta cheese, and bowed as he deposited us beside a kiosk outside the Palace of the Porphyrogennetos, the best-preserved part of the Great Palace of Blachernae.

'See?' said Mike. 'Knew it was this way.'

'Ditto.'

Inside the kiosk was a portly security guard, who shook off his siesta and blew on a whistle. But Mike was already halfway up the wall, and I quickly scrambled after him, marching up a dirt track that wound into the upper gallery.

My first impression was that the palace had fallen to rack and ruin. The columns of silver and gold, battle scenes and magic throne reported by Benjamin of Tudela were dulled into a three-storey façade whose nether parts were sunk in a tangle of nettles and grass. Byzantium's grandeur had been squeezed into a smattering of details – the banded voussoirs winding geometrically round the windows or the daisy-cloaked plinths squatting under screens of marble and brick – while the courtly intrigue that made 'Byzantine' synonymous with subterfuge was turned into the figure of my travelling companion, spying on the security guard through an arrow-slit window.

'Is he coming?' I said.

'Hovering by the wall. Looks too fat to climb over. No – he's moving forward. Go on, my son!'

'What if he finds us?'

103

'Well, there's a decent-looking stick over there. No worries. Hey, guard! Bring it on!'

While Mike kept a keen watch, I followed a bumpy dirt track that shot into a fire-blackened tunnel full of dust and cobwebs. I tried to imagine Manuel scribbling his *pittakion* in defence of astrology or tasting the recently discovered delicacy of caviar rustled up for him by a local abbot when he decided to hold an impromptu marriage feast. Or (because Manuel, like many powerful men, had a weakness for pretty girls) seducing his niece. I wondered what his reaction would have been if Prester John's letter had reached him.* The owner of an *Oracle of the Erythrean Sibyl*, commissioner of treatises on alchemy and fan of magical tracts such as the *Kiranides of Kiranus*,† Manuel would have been entranced by Prester John's tales of strange peoples and medicinal miracles like the Fountain of Youth. He would have been less entranced by the priest-king's boast of omnipotence. As his treatment of Kilidj Arslan suggested, Manuel liked to be top dog.

At the end of the tunnel, stones cluttered an uneven chamber and tongues of sunlight flickered through loopholes. Outside these openings, houses were leaning against each other like exhausted friends, under an umbrella of washing

---

* In his essay 'Prester John: Legend and History', the Russian scholar Alexander Vasiliev quoted a response by Manuel, written in Slavonic. Although its authenticity is dubious, it probably isn't far from the sort of epistle that the emperor might have composed, being full of hyperbole and self-glorification: 'Thou vauntest of gold,' he exclaims, 'and I do vaunt of all the Saints, both of the angels and monks, bishops and holy men, as well as all the holy relics I have.' He has, he insists, twenty-one subject kingdoms, 'the paradise of Adam' and the 'crown-stemma which was given me from God to reign on the earth'. And if Prester John would come and 'bowest to me', then Manuel would be happy to 'give thee as many relics as thou needest'. Touché.

† Which offers much useful advice; for example, in order to close the tongue of one's enemies, one should wear the dried tongue of a weasel inside one's socks.

lines and TV aerials. On one of the rooftops, a lady in hijab dusted down a carpet while her children ripped up a cardboard box. An old man in a tartan jacket smoked a cigarette as he gazed across the Golden Horn. Closer to me, under the window, the security guard was back in his shack: he had resumed his siesta.

As we scuttled past him on our way out, Mike stayed me with a grip of my shoulder: 'Listen.' Caiques were sliding across the Bosphoros, wraith-like in mists that rose towards the city and mixed with the smoke of its chimneypots. A soft, plaintive moan seemed to be crawling towards us.

'It's coming from the sea,' I said.

Mike cocked an ear. 'No, it's coming from the other side.'

'Well, it's certainly coming from below us.'

'I think you'll find it's behind us.'

'It is – it's down there.'

'You think so, do you? Well, I'm *sure* you're right.'

It was coming, in fact, from everywhere: cries, caws, calls, whines and whispers, screams and stammers – as if the sky itself was unleashing an adagio. A taxi swept us into a tooting ramshackle of houses and cars and a square where pigeons squawked around Eastern motifs: an ashen-haired musician plucking the strings of his *saz*, a tower of *gelabiyya* and beard laying out bottles of mineral water on a tatty rug, a group of black-clad women like a flock of crows, and the cries, still audible, luring us to Konya – a presage of the Dar al-Islam:

'*Allaaaaaah-u akbaaar!*'

II

ORIENT

CHAPTER FIVE

SUFIS, SEX AND PARADISE

WHEN MASTER PHILIP'S contemporaries imagined the journey to heaven, it was all spiritual ladders with seraphim and cherubim, or (if your faith was of the croissant rather than the hot-cross-bun variety) Muhammad's winged horse. But in the modern age we need to update the transport to paradise, and I think I've found just the thing. Reader – there's *nothing* like a Turkish bus.

The attendant brushes down his waistcoat and gestures to your seat. You set the recliner, lie back and watch the snack salesmen through newly polished windows. The attendant apologizes for disturbing you, but would you be interested in a sponge cake? Crumbs are still trickling down your shirt when he's back with plastic cups of Pepsi. A reflex of your eyebrows summons mineral water, biscuits, napkins – all flourished with a diligence that smooths out the bumps of the road and sees you off in a spray of rosewater, an ear-to-ear smile and a 'Good time in Turkey, sir!'

Anatolia itself was less genial.

There were grudging gestures at fertility – a farmstead, wrapped in whitewashed mud-brick; a clump of trees that housed a herdsman and several yellow-fleeced goats. Otherwise, we were wrapped in a dusty cloud of bone-dry, sick-coloured scrubland. The eateries that broke up the journey were no jollier. Early on, we bought chocolate bars and Diet Coke in enormous glass-and-billboard resthouses that looked like mid-steppe supermarkets. As we ventured deeper into Anatolia, these were replaced by Stygian shacks that reeked of stale kebab, where we queued for dishes of un-identifiable sludge and sat at tottering wooden tables with old men who scratched themselves and sneered across the plains. One of them growled when I sat at his table. Sensing hostility, I offered him a cigarette. Another growl: 'Grngeunggg.' He pointed at the bench. I lifted my bottom and discovered that I'd sat on a very old aubergine.

It was even worse for Manuel Comnenos. In 1176, pro-voked by the mischievous Ghazis, the holy Muslim warriors who picked at Byzantine watch-posts, God's Viceroy on Earth decided to do away with the Sultanate of Rum once and for all. So he marched towards the city of Konya with a great fanfare and an even greater baggage train, and, near Myriocephalum, rather unadvisedly hedged his army into a defile. The Byzantines tangled themselves in their equipment, while Seljuk archers snipped at their fringes. The Byzantines pursued a party of Turks. The Turks retreated. The Byzantines followed. Then hordes of Kilidj Arslan's finest burst out of nowhere and cut the Byzantines to bits.

Manuel's mind was slightly addled, but he knew what to do. He fled. He took his best bodyguards and left everyone else to die. Only the diplomatic skills of his rearguard com-mander persuaded him to stitch his army back together. The battlefield had turned into a feast of Greek corpses, kebabbed on Turkish daggers, arrows poking out of their chests like cocktail sticks, many of them stripped and deprived of phys-ical as well as material endowments. When Arslan, rising triumphant out of the massacre, offered the terms of peace, it was more than Manuel could have gleaned from his most favourable *oneiricriticon*. He was allowed to depart, with full dignity, a splinter of the True Cross and the negligible onus of flattening a couple of fortresses. But his all-conquering image had been irreparably shattered.

He shuffled back to Constantinople, 'so oppressed', according to William of Tyre, 'that never again did he enjoy peace of mind'. Western Christendom's need for a stronger ally in the war with Islam had been reinforced: Prester John's market value had risen.

As had Kilidj Arslan's. He had cemented the Turkish presence in Anatolia (as well as annexing the Danishmend territories, thereby asserting the Seljuks as Anatolia's single Turkish power), so that the dispute was no longer over the existence of his sultanate, but its size. He imposed control over the Ghazis, minted silver coins and linked his lands with caravanserais. Mosques and madrasas sprouted in Anatolia. Books and brains were uprooted from the old Islamic centres of Khorasan and Baghdad and transplanted to the court of Kilidj. It's no wonder that, in the 1920s, Atatürk compared his regime to that of the Seljuks: theirs was a golden age that lasted until the mid-thirteenth century, when the Mongols replaced the minarets with the towers they raised from their victims' skulls.

The Seljuks' founder was a Central Asian warrior who, after dreaming of urinating fire over the world, selected a career in world domination. Very macho, sure – but the greatest legacy of the Seljuk era was comparatively genteel. Its exponents wore wool, preached detachment from worldly things, aspired to union with God, and acquired such influence that they reputedly inspired Kilidj Arslan to abdicate in 1187. The Sufis were at their peak in the twelfth and thirteenth centuries, led by masters such as Philip's contemporary, Farid ud-Din Attar (a.k.a. 'Pearl of the Faith Pharmacist'), who wrote 200,000 lines of poetry and was beheaded by a Mongol at the age of a hundred and ten. Before he died, Attar was credited with blessing the greatest of all Sufis, the child who would become Konya's most famous son: the author of the *Mathnawi-i Ma'nawi* (which marries the lyricism of Shakespeare's sonnets to the exuberance of *The Canterbury Tales*) and the founder of the Whirling Dervishes – Jalal ad-Din Rumi.

My first encounter with the Whirling Dervishes was in a Sufi lodge in Istanbul. Inside a ring of Sufi knick-knacks – portraits of masters, manuscripts and musical instruments – a pair of high heels click-clacked on to an octagonal wooden stage.

'If you dip a cup into the sea,' announced a rhetorical soprano, 'how much can you get?'

Members of a tour group from Burnham-on-Sea decided to confer.

'Only enough for one day,' explained the soprano.

Members of the tour group from Burnham-on-Sea nodded wisely: just as they thought.

The dervishes, coiled in black cloaks and hatted in cone-shaped camel-hair *sikke*s, girdled the stage. Flute whistled and cymbal clashed. Their master, swaying on a rug, nodded to the arpeggio of their chant. There was a silence as the dervishes concentrated. Then, from behind a screen on a balcony overlooking the stage, a scream: a full-throated, stomach-churning yowl.

Slow, deliberate steps drummed the stage, which filled with fallen cloaks. The ladies were brightly coloured, the men in white with coloured cummerbunds. And around all of them, rising and expanding and floating as they turned, were bell-shaped folds of skirt. Right feet looped in the air, spinning them around the pivot of the left, serene expressions on their faces – breeze fanning from a kaleidoscope of molten features. 'In these ecstasied and abstracted states,' wrote Master Philip's Muslim contemporary, Ibn Jubayr, 'the world forsakes them, such is their rapture and transport.'

It was a four-part ecstasy of equilibrium, spinning the dervishes up the thermal towards God, each sally achieving such speed that the entire company vanished in an exhilarating white blur banded with colour. For the final movement, the previously inert master joined in. He rotated in centre-stage (with slightly less poise than his protégés), and closed the ceremony with a strange series of drones. The response was a second contribution from the stomach-churning yowler on the balcony: 'Yaeuuuchhhaaaaaghhh!'

Rising out of the Phrygian plains, book-ended to the West by the Pisidian mountains, Konya spread in a lake of red roof-tiles dissected by crocodiles of lorries and buses. Rising rather less impressively, off a stool outside his hotel, was Galip Bey. I say hotel; a more accurate description would be prefab sewer with sullied bedsheets and things that extravasated on the walls. So this was the Fabled East: the land of spices, sun and bed-lice.

I empathized with Galip Bey. After a night of wriggling in the mid-mattress tureen of my bedstead, flicking insects off my face and dreaming of sleep, I couldn't claim to be any less listless than him. But no one looked the part like Galip Bey. He was like a medieval allegory: a statue of Somnolence. Rheumy eyes and sunken jowls paralysed a face as crumpled as his bedsheets. When Mike and I approached him for a room, he padded into the foyer and dawdled his eyes across a clipboard. We filled out our names and occupations (sooth-sayer and snail-farmer respectively) safe from the prospect of scrutiny. He was already sinking into his sofa as he handed over the keys to our room. When we came back down, he was curled up like a cat.

At first glance, Konya didn't seem much brighter. Men in Adidas T-shirts scuffed their shoes in a column of pay phones or spat pistachio shells outside their fathers' carpet shops. The only exotica were the ladies with Ray-Bans perched over their head-shawls and a man who ran across our path with an androgynous wooden mannequin.

We tottered on the wooden stools of a *kebabhane*. Above a greasy apron, onion sauce dripped off a bushy moustache. Pink, fleshy slices were sawn off a whirling stump of chicken and dropped in metal bowls. The smells were broiled meat and pepper-seasoned pilav – the same smells that penetrated Sultan Ala ad-Din's massive moustache at a banquet in 1237. At the table beside us, two crescent-eyed policemen whispered surreptitiously, as if there was clearly something fishy about Mike's panama hat. Personally, I'd have recommended an inspection of the yoghurt-soup drinkers behind us. They had weaselly faces and leather jackets, and they sniggered deviously when Mike asked them what there was to do in Konya. All but one advised us to go to their cousin Kilic's bathhouse. The other one pointed at himself and said, somewhat obscurely, 'Australia.'

'So,' said Mike, with the customary knuckle-palm slap, 'Cousin Kilic's *hammam* it is.'

Cousin Kilic tipped his cap, mumbled nervously and pointed us to our cubicles. We took off our clothes and put on wooden clogs and tiny cloths that we gripped round our waists, using our hands as safety pins to preserve our dignity. As we sat on the belly-stone, a thigh-freezing roundel of marble, the sweat and energy was reeled out of our pores. Cracking joints and the groans of overstretched stomachs and a surprisingly high-pitched skirl from Mike, who had preceded me into the steam room, cast a sinister pall over the imminent 'massage'. Several minutes later, I was met by a man with a chest like a shag-pile carpet and a bucket of scalding water. Having attempted to boil me, he rubbed, pinched and stretched my limbs until my epidermis was as malleable as blancmange, scraped a Brillo pad across my back, extracted pistol shots from the gaps between my bones, flipped me over, and tried to knot my arms. Then he boiled me again, before pulling me up and offering his hand, as if that made it all right.

'It's not supposed to be like *this*,' moaned Mike through the curtain of his cubicle, as we slumped on wooden seats in post-scalding convalescence. 'Feeling more knackered now than I did when we got here.'

Chains of water-beads were dribbling down my chest.

'Let's get a cup of tea,' I said.

The bath had turned us into acolytes of Galip Bey. We wandered round Konya with barely more energy than the corpses who inhabited the City of Brass, from *çayhane* (for tea) to *beerhane* (for bottles of lager sipped in a black vault with full-volume music), and then tried to animate ourselves at a *cavehane* (with demitasses of acrid coffee only a small portion of which was liquid). Everywhere we went, we were watched. By black, rakish eyes that twinkled under bushy eyebrows. By bright button eyes that skipped in little faces. By furtive glances under long eyelashes beneath silk head-shawls. Everywhere except our hotel: Galip Bey's eyes were clamped shut.

That night we both lost the battle with the bed-lice. Our early-morning jaws were as stiff as if they'd turned overnight into steel, while our eyes were clogged with sleep. But Konya was wide awake. Boys ran with tea trays to the shops, whose owners cried out prices to ladies with arms full of shopping bags and babies, who dodged the yellow saloons that threaded in and out to the screeching feedback of honk-skid-curse. Young men tugged our shirtsleeves and laboured under the illusion that our wallets shared a destiny with the tills of their fathers' carpet shops. One of them stuffed a furry snake down Mike's back, coerced us inside with an offer of tea, and trapped us in a basement where all the furniture was made out of textiles (saddlebag sofas, an ikat chest, a coffee table composed from several layers of kilim). Our escape was engineered by Mike, employing a technique that I – dazzled by the variety of carpet-ware, the apple-flavoured scent of the teapot resting on the kilim coffee table and the anaconda-eyed salesman's pitch – hadn't considered. That is, he got up and walked out.

On the street was a crowd of men who could have done with some carpets of their own. They were prostrating themselves on the pavements, kneeling in front of a traffic light, kissing the road and holding up the angry-looking motorists. The mosque was too small for its faithful: traffic flow was the first casualty of the call to prayer.

We were in Konya's most devout quarter, the area around the burial place of Jalal ad-Din Rumi. Women in buttoned greatcoats and men with sewn-on elbow patches coiled round a fortress that looked like it had been baked out of butterscotch. Rumi wrote: 'A tomb with domes and turrets is unpleasant to followers of the Truth.' So, while you or I might be rather flattered by the superfetation of domes – upturned silver dishes and an enormous turquoise flute – were the great coupleteer to pass by, he'd have a bone to pick with the commemorators of his bones. And if he wanted to storm the compound, rending his woollen gown and screaming parables about the transience of worldly things, he'd have a job on his hands. He'd have to push through the enormous queue, prodded by elbow patches, jabbed by arms snaking out of burkas, pronged by prayer-bead-clutching hands, before being swept under an archway as if there was some mysterious magnetism between himself and the ticket booth. And once he'd reached the open-air courtyard, if he didn't collapse from the heat (which he probably wouldn't, Sufis being quite familiar with physical discomfort), he'd find it hard going to distract the dreamy-eyed men washing their calves at the ablutions fountain.

But I imagine that Rumi's indignation would be unsustainable once he'd entered the mausoleum. His *Mathnawi* is a whirlpool of the surreal and the cerebral: merchants converse with parrots, an envoy searches unsuccessfully for the Tree of Life. There are contentions on the arts of painting and picturing, a discussion of the inner meaning of rain, the tale of a horse that goes backwards. It is the same spirit of medieval jouissance that breathes life into the letter of Prester John, a spirit exhaling from the exhibits: a silver casket containing most of Muhammad's beard; medieval castanets and flutes and curved walnut bellows; two prayer chains containing 990 beads each; Qu'rans as big as a chest or as short as a thumb; a shirt decorated in a chessboard of squares crammed with writing that seemed to assign its wearer – apparently Rumi himself – an aura of omniscience. So, once Rumi had squeezed past the ululating linen funnels in front of his tomb – a velvet-coated mountain in a landscape of wall-painted fruit trees and flowers – avoiding knockout from shaking folds of arm or raspberry-flavoured unguents, I suspect that he would have been mollified.

However, the strict sheikhs who condemned the Sufis for distorting the Prophet's teaching mightn't be so easily placated. They wouldn't take kindly to the paintings of the *Sem'a*, or to the lions bursting out of a folding Indo-Arabic Qu'ran stand. As for the bronze April bowl in which rain-water used to be collected – not only was it a riot of graven slave girls, warriors and musicians (images that would have equally infuriated the Christian iconoclasts of twelfth-century Byzantium), but, in a mutation of pagan ritual, invalids (dipping Rumi's turban in its depths) attributed to it the same magical powers granted to the dust of St John's tomb in Selçuk.

The relationship between the Sufis and Orthodox Islam has never run smooth. When the tenth-century Baghdadi Sufi Ibn Mansur publicly declared, 'I am God,' it wasn't the sort of conviction that ever endears one (or One) to a strict religious community. Ibn Mansur was flogged, maimed, hung on a gibbet, crucified, beheaded and incinerated. As far as Rumi was concerned, the authorities got it wrong: 'The one who mounted the scaffold,' he wrote, 'was not Mansur.' God Himself had got the chop. 'In things spiritual,' wrote the poet, 'there is no partition, no number, no individuals.' All created matter is conflated through the creator: if you kill a Sufi, a king or an ant, you kill God.

Rumi himself, who once bowed thirty-seven times to a Byzantine monk and wrote, 'I am neither Christian, nor Jew, nor Gabr,* nor Muslim,' had an equally difficult relationship with the orthodox authorities. Sitting on some steps beside a pond where steam-ironed pilgrims dipped their fingers, I remembered reading about his popularity in medieval Christian circles. Rumi, Farid ud-Din Attar and many other Sufi poets, like their Christian contemporaries, enjoyed quest tales, allegory and anthropomorphism: Attar's *Conference of the Birds* (composed around the same time as Master Philip's mission), in which the birds of the world set out over seven valleys to find their king, shares the quest structure with the Grail legends that were being written at the same time by Chrétien de Troyes (of whom more later). The great Dante, like Rumi, transfigured his beloved into a compass for his metaphysical journey to God – in his case Beatrice, in Rumi's a mysterious dervish from Tabriz – and reputedly belonged to a secret order of Sufis. What this suggests is that, culturally, the barrier between medieval Christianity and Islam was not as thick as we tend to think. Once the faiths have been stripped of their domes and turrets, they are as inter-fluent as the rivers that straddle national frontiers.

While I was scribbling these thoughts into my diary, a young lady sat on the steps beside me. Her face was visible through a gap in her hijab that could have been cut around a saucer. It was a costume that would have bred less discomfort in Master Philip, who came from a society where women were expected to wear foot-length robes and veils, than it did in me. I wanted to speak to her, but I felt uncomfortable: she could see me, but I couldn't even tell the shape of her ears.

'Ha!' shouted Mike, his rope-soled sandals slapping the ground. 'Found yourself a girlfriend?'

The young lady's forehead subtly arranged itself into a frown.

'She might understand English,' I whispered.

'Course she doesn't.'

* Zoroastrian.

'Excuse me,' she said, in pitch-perfect English, 'you want to speak?'

Silence. Long. Painful. As if it had tumbled out of a tomb and we were waiting for the undertakers to put it back in.

'Er . . . Rumi,' I eventually mumbled. 'Very nice building, important to you?'

She nodded wisely. 'He is very important, and when people pray here, they say their prayers mean more than in an ordinary mosque.'

'Yeah,' said Mike, 'but Rumi's not popular with all Muslims, is he?'

'I think every Muslim see the truth in the Sufi.'

Her name was Rüya. She was studying to become a teacher, and she wanted to travel to London to see the Big Clock and the Queen. Women, she said, were not badly treated in Turkey – they could vote, and there were women in positions of political power – but there was a stronger sense of family, so that women were expected to fulfil functions that had been forgotten in the West.

'I think,' she said, 'that you see the hijab and you think that—'

A shadow clouded her sentence. I looked up to see a face like a camel-hair cushion and a pair of arms as thick as tree trunks.

'This,' announced Rüya, 'is my father.'

He nodded perfunctorily. He shook our hands slowly. Then he led his daughter away. There would be no union with this young lady.

At the top of the Acropolis hill, Kilidj Arslan's citadel rolled under a tea-garden. At least, what remained of it: a rumple of stone where his palace once stood, like a giant's amputated thigh, and the Ala ad-Din Mosque, dedicated to his kebab-chomping grandson.

Inside a hypostyle jungle of Byzantine columns, an elderly man in a patchwork *gelabiyya* scratched his head and peered

119

at the strange foreigners studying Kilidj Arslan's mihrab, the niche indicating the direction of Mecca. Blue and black lines danced through turquoise tortoise-shells, drawing us to a single rhythm, interlacing and rimming the cupola with stars and geometric and cruciform patterns. They radiated harmony: the confidence of a triumphant culture.

Through the main doorway, a gang of schoolboys lured Mike towards their football and quickly enveloped his battle cries in their squeals. The other door led out into a two-tiered courtyard, where I climbed on to a small platform in front of a domed *türbe* – a Seljuk mausoleum. Behind a grimy sheet of glass, one of eight, headstoned with turbans and draped in green velvet, was the body of Manuel Comnenos' nemesis – Kilidj Arslan II himself. Three elderly men joined me on the platform. Two of them wore tweeds; all of them wore skull-tight woollen caps – navy, white, brown. Navy shook his arms in the air. White shook his prayer beads. Navy murmured mysteriously. Brown lectured the window. Navy's murmur turned into a tuneful incantation. Brown shrieked and flattened his palms beside his ears. Feeling somewhat in the way, I retreated to watch them from the esplanade. It was there that I met Orhan.

His chequered shirt was tucked into his corduroys, providing unnecessary definition to his pot belly. He had bright black eyes and a fat, onion-shaped nose that rested on what looked like a dead gerbil.

'They pray to the dead sultans,' he explained.

'But,' I said, 'I thought Muslims only pray to Allah?'

'Ha! You are Chreestian?'

I nodded.

'But interesting in Islaam?'

'Very much.'

'Like to be Muslim?'

He didn't give me a chance to consider.

'Islaam the best religion. We have all your prophets, all the Jewish prophets, and some from our own.'

'I could never give up alcohol and bacon.'

'Ha! You think Islaam – cover your womans, no drinking!'

'I thought Turkey prided itself on being secular?'

'Is true. After Atatürk. Actually, I drink raki and I love for beautiful womans! You say I am bad Muslim?'

He leaned towards me. I could smell the bristles of his gerbil.

'Didn't Atatürk want to mirror the Seljuks?' I asked, as we sat down on a ledge, facing the *türbe*.

'The Seljuk like trade and education,' said Orhan. 'But the difference between the Seljuk and Atatürk – the Seljuk is the good time of the Sufi, but Atatürk say, "No Sufi".'*

Orhan was a newspaper salesman. He liked *The Times*, but it wasn't a patch on *Milliyet*. He had travelled to Europe once, to a 'conference' in Finland. He didn't enjoy it. It was cold, and everyone kept to themselves. 'No one know anyone in Europe,' he had concluded, and decided never to go back.

I found my own activities harder to explain.

'You go Ethiopia,' he exclaimed, nearly slipping off his ledge, 'to find a man who die eight hundred years before now?'

'Well, I'm not actually expecting to *find* him.'

He smiled. 'You are like the Sufi,' he said. 'Rumi say all Sufi must travel so they never grow close with any place in the world.'

'That's rather a negative reason to travel.'

We crossed the forecourt. Navy and Brown had finished their prayers and shuffled back inside the mosque.

'This is gift you have time for travelling,' said Orhan. 'What are you?'

It was rather an intimidating question.

'Well, um – I *was* a teacher. In Jerusalem.'

---

* In 1925, Atatürk abolished the Sufi orders in Turkey and appropriated their property. He saw them as backward and out of synch with the modern Republic of Turkey.

'The Holy City. And now what are you?'

'Ah, I – er . . .' I'd expected him to ask about Jerusalem. Mentioning Jerusalem was often a convenient way to avoid too penetrating an analysis of my own activities. 'Well,' I finally said, 'I suppose I'm hoping to be a writer.'

'Ha! You know Ibn Shakir? He is writer.'

'When?'

'He live in Baghdad, at time of Mongol conquest.'

'Isn't that over seven hundred years ago?'

'He think his books live for the end of time. But the Mongols come and they throw his books in Tigris river. After that, he is great artist, but he never write again.'

On that enigmatic and slightly dispiriting note, Orhan clasped my hand and padded towards the mihrab to pray. Through the mouth of the porch, I could see a panama hat bobbing above a tornado of children.

'*Dawid Beg-ham!*'

'Aha!' called Mike. 'Want to show them *your* skills?'

'*Hasan Saş!*'

'Oh,' I replied, 'I'm sure I couldn't possibly emulate yours.'

'*Mikal Uwan!*'

Mike scooped the ball into the hands of a boy in a Tweety Pie T-shirt and patted his head.

'Come on!' he beamed. 'Let's bus it to Trabzon.'

Meeting Orhan underlined the feeling that, somewhere between Istanbul and Konya, a frontier had been crossed. We might have left what classical Islam termed the Dar al-Harb, or House of War, for the Dar al-Islam, or House of Islam, when we touched the Turkish mainland. But it was in Konya that Master Philip's world turned Muslim, and it was here that the tokens of its expression became all-pervasive. The men started to trade jeans for *gelabiyya*s, the women skirts for hijab; the muezzins drowned the traffic, the butchers turned halal and every shop owner offered us tea. On a more practical level, it was starting to get very hot. Master Philip, I imagined, would have felt much the same. Like us, he'd had a prior taste of the East: but probably, like us, that had been in Jerusalem, which is a law unto itself. It was in Konya that, alongside Master Philip, we slipped through the gateway into the Orient.

But, before the further confabulation of Oriental motifs, a diversion: eastern Anatolia's correlatives for heaven and hell.

The Third Letter of Master Philip to Roger of Salerno

TO ROGER, BY THE grace of God, most glorious doctor of Salerno, Master Philip the Venetian sends greetings.

At times this strange journey of mine recalls to me the words of Job: 'My life passes like the swiftest boat, as fast as an eagle swooping down on a rabbit.' Certainly, my heart was filled with terror on the sixteenth day on the Imperial Road to Antioch. The journey had been pleasant, excepting the heat, because there was amusing company: merchants and scholars of divers nations, including a poet from the land of Barbarossa, who calls himself Archipoeta. He sings ribald songs throughout our journey, from a Book of Roisterers. He sings about nothing but feasting and fornication, and his morals are as wretched as his mantle is rich in fur. Worse still, he applauds his master Barbarossa, calling him King of the Christians and damning his enemies as godless Titans. I tell you, dear Roger, we exchanged many sharp words on this matter.

With these I passed the ride, until our horizon was darkened by the fearsome spectre of Turkish horsemen. They wore iron corselets and headdresses decorated with falcons' wings, and they carried double-bladed swords. Their horses, which are known to mate with the wind, were as swift as hinds. Their leader removed his headdress, exposing a moustache that he knotted around his head, and a lack of nose, but rather two holes through which to breathe. He informed us that he was a soldier of the sultan Kilidj Arslan, and would escort us to the sultan's court. We wished to decline, and should have done so, had he not unsheathed his sword. We would, he informed us, travel directly to a caravanserai, to repair till morning.

Dear Roger, you must think me peculiar that I use such strange words. Let me explain the caravanserai. A splendid gateway, patterned like a honeycomb, yielded to a grand courtyard. Turks in gowns and turbans kissed the ground and prayed to their god, or washed their feet at an elaborate well. Elsewhere, merchants sat on enormous rugs and rubbed their hands around the fires. Servants carried steaming trays of rice and goat's milk or fruit and cakes and set them on brass table-tops, or washed the horses and camels. The captain of the soldiers informed us that we were free men within the confines of the caravanserai, and invited us to sit. We were joined by a great crowd, consisting of every pernicious creed on God's earth – a Jew, a Kharijiite, a Manichean, a Sabaean, an Assyrian heretic and numberless Muslims. Roger, we think of these people as one, but truly they are divided. For, just as we have Catholics and heretics, so they have Sunnis, who follow the teachings of the camel-driver of Mecca, and Shiites, who venerate a warrior called Ali. They showed us their holy book, and I shivered to look at it. It is called Alcoran, and it is as devious as a woman arrayed in silk and paint. As such a woman conceals her vices behind her beauty, so the perfidious teachings of the pagans are hidden behind lacquer binding as delicate as a spider's web. But they were kindly towards us, and invited us to eat their meat and drink their milk, so that we were enchanted into forgetfulness that we were prisoners.

And we were entertained by the strange music of these peoples. Their chief instrument, which they call *saz*, is like the harp, though laid across the lap. But, dear Roger, this was no plainchant! They sang manifoldly, in many manners and notes, so that as many songs were sung as singers were seen. Their music delighted the German poet, who let fall his veille and took hold of the *saz*, and sang damnable songs from his mischievous book.

But even stranger was the next day, when we rode to Konya, a great city with many towers and a place of pagan worship that looks as beautiful from outside as it is ugly in their souls. Mosaics adorn the porch and the halls are roofed with beams that unite in a sharp point. Everywhere in this town there is the smell of ambergris, for the Turks fill the air with pleasant scents to distract the people from the perfidy of their teachings. We were welcomed into the palace, which was decorated with brocade hangings and turquoise tiles depicting the sultan and his women and strange beasts like the Sphinx of Babylon.

This sultan is very wealthy, for a year before now he defeated the emperor of the Greeks in battle at Myriocephalum, and went away with great riches. He sits on an elevated throne and wears a large turban and a signet ring. And he surrounds himself with astrologers and oneiromancers, those pernicious readers of dreams. He invited us to be seated, and asked me about the Holy Father and the trade in Venice and the teachings of Christ. He told me that he praises the Messiah, but he does not consider him God, and he invited me to betray my faith. I wished to say that I would rather eat my own flesh. But I thanked him for his kindness and said nothing. He introduced me to his chamberlain, a Greek man called Gavras, who has converted to the pagan faith for the sake of worldly gain. I felt sorrowful for him, for he will be buried in an acrid well sealed with seven seals, and he will not be remembered in the sight of the Lord. But he talked pleasantly and poured me a bitter drink of lemon and sugar from a sardonyx vase.

It was a splendid feast, enhanced by the sultan's merry conversation. He boasted that he was king of the Romans. I suggested that Rome is far from his domains. He slapped my thighs, and told me that he debated this point with the emperor of the Greeks, who believes that he is truly king of the Romans. And what of my lord Alexander, I said, who is truly master of Rome? Or, added Gavras the Apostate, Barbarossa, who believes himself the king of Rome?

And this sultan claimed much for his empire. He esteemed it the best in the world for mathematics and medicine. For in the hospitals, Turks bathe and listen to music, and they say that this makes them well. When he had boasted his fill, he clapped his hands, and a group of Sufis – which is like our monks, except that they eat the flesh of snakes and wander like the nomads – entered the hall.

They fell about, making strange noises and weeping, and the sultan considered this to be good. Then they made way for a sorcerer, who carried a dead goat. He cut it open at the sultan's feet, and tore out its entrails, and laid them on a silver salver. Then he danced for joy and kissed the sultan's knees. For he had seen, Gavras informed me, a turban spinning in the air, and two arms growing out of it; one pointing to God, the other to Tartarus. I asked what this meant, and Gavras explained that a great man would come to Konya, and so illustrious would be his works that the city would endure everlasting fame. And the sultan smiled at this, but when he turned to the sorcerer, his aspect grew sombre. For the sorcerer was beating his breast and tearing his clothes. And he screamed in a terrible voice. He had seen another vision. It was a monstrous horde of warriors, carrying knives and bows and cutting up infants.

Anxious words spread through the hall. Some clamoured in terror of a foreign aggressor, and Gavras whispered to me that he had heard of a warrior people near the High Ind. Dear Roger, how I struggled to keep myself from smiling – for surely this is the king of the Indies, and he will come to destroy the pagans and unite with us Christians!

Dear Roger, I must discontinue this missive, which I will send when I return to the Imperial Road. The sultan has provided us with new horses and servants to accompany us to Antioch. I have been surprised by his kindness. But I will rejoice when I return to Christian land, for I worry that the air is full of devils in league with Mahomet.

'What the hell brought us here?' said Mike.

Hell being the operative word.

If Jerusalem is the world's navel, then Trabzon is its armpit. Once capital of the Byzantine Empire (for eight years after the Turks captured Constantinople) – or, more precisely, its last resort – Trabzon was now the ugliest town on our itinerary.

Feet squelch through lanes pockmarked with potholes and puddles of splattered fruit. Mud dribbles down walls scrawled in graffiti, and rusty panes flap over gutters swollen with shattered roof-tiles. The people aren't exactly pulling out the stops to mend the atmosphere. Miserable Russians peddle second-rate black-market goods under an equally grim sky, while men in tweeds chain-smoke and shuffle cards in cadaverous *çayhane*s.

Our hotel was a deliciously decrepit old mansion, with ash-coloured walls and ash-coloured windows, and an ashen-haired owner slumped over his bureau in front of a bust of Atatürk and a certificate for Best Hotel Management 1973. Having reached the pinnacle of his profession, he apparently decided not to change a thing. Not even fuses, pipes or light bulbs. Our room was a shrine to un-management: it locked only from outside, once you turned the water on you couldn't turn it off, and a whiff of incontinence seeped under the woodworm-infested door.

The rest of Trabzon shared the same atmosphere of decay – even the Byzantine churches, now locked up, derelict or long since Islamized. But in the evening we stumbled across Trabzon's pulse: in a tenuously lit *kebabhane*, a waiter in a string vest dangled a cigarette between his lips, which peppered our dishes in lieu of pepper, and passed round the same basket of bread to any table that needed it. Gurgling beside us was an extremely filthy man whose nose appeared to be communicating with his knee.

'Hey, chap,' said Mike, 'where's a good place for a drink?'

A nod, a grunt, a spit on the floor. The man leered at us. 'Want to fuck?'

His name was Mehmet and he had a habit of scratching his most personal parts whenever he bared his piano keyboard of black-and-white teeth. Who better to show us around?

Down an alleyway of black tenements, men in tuxedoes leaned out of plastic-curtained doorways that reminded me of butchers' shops. Which was appropriate. Through a door padded with deep-buttoned leather, candlelight flickered on linen-dressed tables. Secretive voices were drowned by the pop of wine corks and the rustle of tights. Metallic miniskirts rubbed against our legs and skewer-heeled feet clacked against the steps that spiralled down, down towards the tongues of strobe-light licking the jackets of rabbit-eyed men gorged on a buffet of female flesh. We had entered a meat market.

It may not have been as obvious as in Master Philip's day, when prostitutes were uniformed and prohibited from wearing certain jewellery, but we were clearly in the company of *les grandes horizontales*. That much was clear from a glance at the dance floor. Oh, sure – the lover sees Helen's beauty in a brow of Egypt, and a sense of humour or a fat wallet go a long way – but I refuse to believe that the besuited lump on the dance floor, gangly limbs jerking out of the muddle of his central nervous system, was linked romantically to the glacier of frosted lipstick and snowmelt chignon whose eyes drooped as he engaged her in a face-lock.

You had to pity the prostitutes. In the days of the sultanate, the denizens of the harem were selected from the same hinterlands of Turkey – Georgia, Bulgaria, Armenia, Russia – as now provide the prostitutes. A leggy blonde, sliding her silk trousers from under a peach-coloured tablecloth and accepting the arm of her temporary sugar-daddy, was unable to conceal the scowl of disappointment. She might have bagged a shipping executive or a small-time racketeer, but she knew he was no sultan.

'Well,' I said, as we strolled towards our hotel in the early hours. 'I suppose it was nice of Mehmet to take us there.'

'Nice?' Mike's eyebrows were emigrating up his forehead. 'Nick, he was a pimp.'

'No?'

'There you were admiring the ambience, our friend Mehmet's asking me how much we want to spend. And he wasn't talking about bar snacks. Well, not exactly. Now I've had enough of Trabzon. I vote we get out of here first thing in the morning.'

It was time to visit paradise.

The bus out of Trabzon was a slob. The attendant was dour and monosyllabic and, unlike his predecessors, he didn't ask us if we wanted rosewater; he simply sprayed it in our faces, wielding his bottle like a Seljuk wielded his double-bladed sword and smiling sadistically as we wiped the glutinous liquid off our noses.* When Saladin heard of his nephew's

---

* Master Philip might have been more excited to discover this new substance, renowned as a cure for 'hot' fevers.

untimely death, he used rosewater to wash his tears. In the hands of this psychopath, it was more likely to induce them.

To make matters worse, my stomach was harrumphing over the sour beer it had been forced to host in the brothel. I glared at the ash-coloured cityscape and fell asleep in a haze of eau de cologne and self-pity. But negative thoughts were hard to sustain. As I moved to stop the side of my head rattling against the window, a blur of green and blue clarified into velvet hills studded with sycamore trees and sliced by streams. Fields of lavender and poppy squiggled into woolly hills gilded by the alchemy of the sun. Ridges of birch soared towards rocky boulders that turned blue and grey as they punctured the sky with craggy, snow-capped ramparts – a natural line of defence under purple-tinted cotton-wool clouds. The mountain dived into humps, veered towards monstrous spears and swirled into ice-capped buttresses and wisps of cloud. We were entering historical Armenia, the land that Byron identified with the Garden of Eden. It was the most extraordinary landscape I had seen, undermined only by a history of destruction as intense as its beauty.

The Armenians are one of history's unluckiest races. Throughout the centuries, the dazzle of their homeland has stimulated their neighbours' most rapacious instincts. We were hoping to visit their greatest medieval city – Ani, the 'Pompey of the East', legendary metropolis of a thousand and one churches, famous for its scientific academies and scriptoria, which produced some of the region's most sophisticated psalters and illuminated manuscripts. It was also linked to a candidate for the origin of the Prester John legend.

But Ani was a tragic city, a symbol of a tragic people. Over the years, she had been sold to, conquered or levelled by Byzantines, Arabs, Seljuks, Kurds, Georgians, Mongols, the Black Sheep Turkomen, Tamburlaine the Great, the Ottoman Turks and the Russians. As we drove towards Kars, the launch pad for any trip to Ani, I remembered my meeting a few months earlier with a 95-year-old Armenian who had lived in one of the villages in this area. I had been writing a magazine article about the death of up to 1.5 million Anatolian Armenians in 1915–23 and, hoping for a first-hand slant, took the Tube to a house in Ealing to sip tea with Yervan Shekerdemian.

'I was only a boy when I left Hadjin, my home town,' he said, 'in 1920.'

His cup rattled on his saucer as he began to tell the same sort of story that Armenians have been telling for centuries.

'The Turkish *chetés* were near. An army of six hundred residents was drawn up. I was an errand boy. I delivered letters among the leaders of the resistance. Oh, the sound of the cannons and the machine guns – it was terrifying! But we held on to Hadjin for eight months. Then our defences crumbled.'

He glanced at a tapestry of Mount Ararat, hanging above his mantelpiece.

'What happened?'

'Many people fled to the mountains or escaped to Adana. Everyone else was shot or hacked to death. I was in a group of twelve. The other eleven were beaten to death. I thought they would do the same to me. But I shouted the names of important Turks my father worked with – they didn't touch me. They took me to their leader, Yousef. He said, "Ah! I know your father. He was a good man who helped me out." So Yousef took me to his house and told his family to look after me. As soon as he'd gone and his family found out I was Armenian, they turned on me. There were three wives and thirteen children. They beat me, they made me work all the time, they never let me sleep. I was like a bad slave.'

He put down his cup and fixed me with swollen, watery eyes.

'My brother had escaped to Adana, where he tried to find out what happened to me. He met a Turkish peasant called Kazim, who was good at finding things out. Kazim made enquiries and, one night, he tiptoed into Yousef's house. He hid me in his carriage, under the food and goods, and drove me to Adana. I was so joyful to be reunited with my brother. But we didn't have long before the Turks were attacking Adana and we had to escape again. We took a boat to Cyprus, where we found our sisters. We were lucky. But our parents, uncles, cousins, most of our friends – we never found any trace of them.'

An olive-green river spun between vertical cliffs pierced with pins of shiny rock. Scruffy goats bleated over a bridge, whipped across by an even scruffier boy, beneath a cattle army grazing among barley fields. We passed the 'Welcome-Goodbye' hotel and an out-of-place petrol station. Man-made constructions seemed an affront to the impeccable achievement of nature.

Turning round to see what Mike thought of it, I was surprised to see that he had disappeared from his seat. Down the aisle, I saw a corner of his jacket: he was talking to another traveller, a blond man with a goatee who made drawstring trousers look so smart that he could only be French. He was a Parisian nobleman called François, and he spoke (or rather, proclaimed) the sort of English that you would too if you lived in a chateau.

'Michael has apprised me of your intentions,' he announced, stroking his carefully groomed beard.

'Intentions?' I repeated uncertainly.

'You must beware the bandits of Ethiopia! They shall attempt to assail you, but keep your head down and you should be preserved.'

'Thanks for the tip.'

'Not in the least. Now, enlighten me. What carpets have you purchased?'

'We haven't,' said Mike.

François gasped, and fiddled with his 24-carat necklace.

'This is folly. I flew into Istanbul last Tuesday. Already I have purchased thirty-six. They will collect a fine tariff in Paris. If I send back fifty, I shall accrue thousands of dollars.'

It was inevitable that our experience of Kars would be filtered through François' aristocratic leadership skills. Even Mike, not normally retiring, found himself chattelled by our new companion's extraordinary self-assurance.

'Suits me,' he whispered. 'François can wangle all the permits.'

Access to Ani required the acquisition of three separate passes; 'a bit complex', as I put it.

'Clearly,' said François with a sniff, 'you never attempted to traverse the landmines of Nagorno-Karabagh.'

The Kars through which we were whisked, a grey spread of prefabricated housing and a typical frontier marketplace – dodgy toasters and smuggled liquor sold by men in stolen overcoats – is mashed up in my memory with the smells of its offices. Tourist office, police station and museum return in a flammable cocktail of vodka and bad breath, through which I can see men with hairy cheekbones staggering to their filing cabinets and thumping stamp to chit. When, arms full of forms, we finally emerged in the marketplace, it was like coming up for air.

'Let's get some food,' said Mike.

'You have ten minutes,' replied François. 'Then we shall reconvene outside that *kebabhane*.'

'Where are you going?' I asked.

'I shall purchase kilims.'

The menu offered *börek* and *pilav*, with side orders of Albanian liver and sautéed brains. We dug into our steamy dishes, while a man called Jejy kindly studied them for worms. Jejy was a taxi-driver, who'd clung to us like a limpet ever since we arrived in Kars. He seemed to think he'd be driving us to Ani. I don't remember a deal being discussed: it was, apparently, a local rite of passage. You come to Kars, Jejy drives you to Ani. Jejy also eats half your meal, persuades you to buy him a mint tea, and when you decide to make him useful and ask about the Armenians, insists that none ever existed in Turkey and those that didn't exist were working for Tsarist Russia.

*

The drive from Kars was as extraordinary as the approach. Streams ran between bubble-shaped trees, carving up alpine meadows bright with flowers, cogent arguments both for the attachment of Armenians and for the jealous grip of the Turks. With a couple more cows, it could have been the wrapper of a Swiss chocolate bar. The sheen of the fields was churned into soil and crumbling mud-brick huts guarded by squawking children and chickens. Two bulging dun-coloured towers hove into view ahead of us, held back by a double-layered archway.

'Let's DWI,' yelled Mike, as he ran like an all-action movie hero, inside the spongy ramparts, several yards ahead of François and myself, and straight into the wall of a rifle-bearing soldier.

He was standing in front of a metal board-map that depicted churches and palaces inside the dotted lines of a ravine. Using a cane, he tapped out our itinerary, rapping the map at the 'forbidden' points.

'This church is good, and here is OK, but if you go there –' Tap. 'Or there –' Tap. 'You may be shot.' Tap. 'And no photographs in that direction.'

'That direction is Armenia,' whispered François.

'Exactly,' barked the soldier. 'We do not want no pictures of Ermenia.'

Tap.

Now, we all know that a double negative equals a positive, so when we scuttled on to the heath we proceeded to photograph Armenia, and put the loud military whistles down to soldierly merriment.

We were knee-deep in overgrown grass that melted into scarves of mist winding round lumpy walls and rocket-shaped steeples. Wrapped about the site like a picture frame was the shimmering Arpatchai river. In the sky, a black wool-pack struck a note of foreboding that mixed with the pressure of the breeze and the scent of cold air. On the far river bank, buttresses of rock pegged down a yellow no-man's-land that slipped into a settlement of barbed wire and concrete: the Russian military base.

Most of Ani's buildings were in a shoddy state, thanks to the site's politically precarious location, as well as the drilling of a nearby Armenian quarry, botched Turkish 'restorations' and Field-Marshal Nature. The polygonal Church of the Redeemer was dissected by a thunderstorm in 1957, exposing its insides like a broken eggshell. Faded evangelists frowned over lone plinths and knocked-about slabs that lay where the rest of the church once stood, inscribed in the mysterious lettering of medieval Armenian. *Khatchar*s and a winged angel clung to the exterior, under a chessboard drum and the mound remnant of a roof. The church oozed a fragile, apocalyptic aura that fitted its benefactor: an Armenian general who returned to Constantinople in 1035 with a fragment of the Holy Cross, and demanded that services take place every night until the Second Coming.

Down a glissade of hill, splodges of grass burst out of grey tiles that slipped around the funnel-like drum of the Church of Tigran Honents. Stone rosettes wound round ruddy portals, while angels and eagles nestled in the spandrels between blind arcades. There was an energetic atmosphere, bolstered by the tumbledown appearance. Inside, fading treats survived from vandalized frescoes: a *tetromorph* guarding a heavenly gate; a panel of winged dragons; St John, standing beside Christ at the Crucifixion. There was a cycle dedicated to Gregory the Illuminator, the fourth-century saint who made Armenia the first state to adopt Christianity. One of the scenes depicted Gregory baptizing King Trdat, ahead of a queue of local rulers, including the King of Georgia.

The Georgian presence was linked to the church's foundation in 1215 by a Georgian merchant, when Ani was enjoying a period of Georgian rule that could be traced to an unexpected victory associated with the legend of Prester John.

For the best part of a century, Georgia's rulers had been playing ping-pong with the city against the bats of Kurd and

Seljuk, ever since John Orbelian captured Ani for Georgia in 1124. It was a famous triumph, with an impact that rippled through Christendom, accompanied by rumours of a great Christian king east of the Tigris. Was Orbelian, asked the nineteenth-century scholar Philip Bruun, the prototype for Prester John? When Otto of Freising introduced Prester John to the West, he may have confused the Persian city of Ekbatana, the site of Prester John's victory over 'the brother kings of the Persians and Medes, called Samiardi', with Ani, since he wrote that Ekbatana was 'called in their own tongue Hani'. But, if Prester John's prototype was Georgian, he surely held a loftier status than that of a mere general.

Orbelian's boss, King David the Builder, shared much with the priest-king. He united church and state, purged Georgia's towns and *eilags* of its Turkish hordes and cancelled the tribute his predecessors paid to the Seljuk Sultan of Persia. In 1121, around the same time as the Prester John legend was first starting to emerge, he defeated a united Muslim army nearly seven times the size of his own, assisted by a thousand European Crusaders. The Frankish preceptor Ansellus credited him with 'dominion over the Caspian port where Gog and Magog [the savage races legendarily trapped in Prester John's empire] were arrested'. And, according to a Crusader knight, like Prester John he intended 'to deliver the Holy Land of Jerusalem and subjugate all the heathen territories'. In 1219, a rumour reached the Crusader forces in Damietta of the imminent arrival of Prester John's son, a king called David. Jacques de Vitry, Bishop of Acre, traced the king to the same victory over the Turks enjoyed by King David and the Orbelians.*

---

* Further evidence to link Georgia with Prester John is offered by the thirteenth-century chronicler Ernoul, according to whom Georgia was widely known as 'the land of Feminie', because of its single-breasted women warriors – like the Amazons of Prester John's kingdom. More credibly, Jacques de Vitry announced that 'There is also in the East another Christian people, who are very warlike, and valiant in battle, being strong in body, and powerful in the countless number of their warriors' – the Georgians.

Yet, despite all the Georgian influence, the Church of Tigran Honents was solidly Armenian. It was dedicated, after all, to the patron saint of Armenia; its structure, especially the drum, was Armenian, as were its inscriptions. Rather than being conquered by the Georgians, Ani had assimilated them.

'Come on, team – let's hit that flag!'

Mike was itching for adventure.

'We will ascend the citadel,' announced François.

We clambered around scattered stretches of wall to the Turkish flag that crowned the hillock. There, we spotted the Kizkale – a crumbling castle of red and grey at the peak of a promontory that lunged over the Arpatchai like some sea-beast, all grey and green with dagger-shaped scales. The cliff slid into a track that scurried between the beaten remains of an archway and plunged into a gorge full of water's sensuous sound and smell. In front of us rose a magical jumble of mist-shrouded rock and solitude; behind us pealed the whistles of the soldiers.

By the time we reached the entrance gates, covered in soil and scratches, their guns were shaking like a race-starter's flag.

'Ermenia dangerooz!'

'If you cross the river – Ermeni mines!'

Mike patted the soldier's back and we squeezed into Jejy's car, where we were joined by an elderly shepherd. He had a battered crook and a face that slopped over his skull like kneaded dough.

'Armenia?' I said, as the walls of Ani shrank behind us.

He grunted. 'Turkiyem.'

CHAPTER SIX

THE FOUNTAIN OF YOUTH

THEY WERE BUSTLING out of their mud-thatch home-steads in hilltop villages; women carrying buckets to the water-pumps, men busy around their hayricks. At the sight of soldiers, the women hid their faces behind red calico and hurried their children inside. The men, bushy-bearded with baggy shalwar trousers, chewed twigs and knotted their arms in defiant crosses.

'They will have many hard questions,' whispered a school-teacher called Selim, leaning over my backrest in the bus.

'Are they Kurds?' I asked.

He nodded.

'Are they badly treated?'

He shrugged. 'They are not allowed even their language. What are you without your language?'

The scenes through the window seemed like a drama on a TV screen, but military checkpoints reminded us that we weren't in a cocoon. Hawk-eyed soldiers stamped down the carriage, forcing the attendant to juggle his sponge cakes. More than once, we were ordered to disembark. A groan rippled through the bus – the sound of an unpopular ritual, like the response to an Engineering Works announcement on the London Underground.

'Terrorist problem,' said an old man in a dusty shift.

'Kurdish?' I asked.

'Kurdiyem. Turkiyem. Always is problem.'

We had said goodbye to François that morning (he was heading west to accrue further thousands of dollars in carpets) and boarded the bus for Diyarbakir. More Kurdish villages swam past the window, and more checkpoints, before the landscape parched itself into urban sprawl – clusters of concrete, petrol stations and apartment blocks hung with drying bedsheets. As the sun dissolved over the basalt Byzantine walls that encircled a jumble of mud-brick and metal – flats and businesses, workshops and *kebabhane*s – we arrived in the old city of Diyarbakir.

We stayed at the Hotel Palas, where the only quality that could conceivably be described as palatial was the courtesy of its owner. So keen was Ramazan for our custom that he opened the door of our taxi before it had stopped and unfurled his arms as if he was auditioning for the part of Haroun al-Rashid's chief vizier. He shouldered our backpacks and, shalwar trousers sagging between his legs, hustled us down a side street to a jagged aperture surmounted by a cobwebbed sign:

HO   L   P L S

'Well-com!'

A proud hand gestured across the scene, as if he was a king surveying his capital. Except Ramazan was surveying, left to right, a set of swivel chairs that no longer swivelled, a rusty safe, a couple of broken beds pierced by springs; and, above us, a balcony that teetered off the upper storey like an indecisive suicide. Elsewhere, the whiff of the washrooms – rusty, grime-smothered plugless sinks and flushless drop-loos – spiralled into a cavernous staircase and made itself comfortable in the guest rooms. Ramazan knocked open the tottering door to our suite, stabbed helplessly at a light switch and beamed towards the beds: wooden planks with straw-filled cushions and coverlets that could have been chiselled out of pumice. Something slimy was growing on the wall. We winced. Ramazan clasped his hands and watched us with the doe eyes of the desperate.

'Hmm.' Mike turned to me with a theatrical wag of his chin. 'Just what we wanted, don't you think?'

In the morning, we carried our insect bites and backaches to a coffee house.

'I am Kurd!' announced the curly-haired waiter, baring an infectious smile that was conspicuously more endearing than the fossilized *gözleme* bread in his hands.

'The government makes it very hard for Kurds,' he whispered. 'He call us Turks of Mountain. But we know who we are. We are living here in Kurdistan many years before the Turk. The Turk are only here for one thousand years.'

Indeed, Kurdish origins are swamped in the misty bogs of ancient history.* One Islamic tradition ascribes their birth to the time of King Solomon. A rather randy Solomon, who sent five hundred envoys to Europe to find him the five hundred most beautiful women across the Med. But, before we cast judgement on the great king's motives, we should bear in mind that he never had the chance to put them into practice. By the time the ladies turned up, he'd died, leaving five hundred men at a loss for what to do with their beautiful female charges. Nine months later, five hundred half-European newly born babies signalled the arrival of the Kurds.

Their greatest flowering was in medieval times. In the tenth and eleventh centuries, the Merwanid Kurdish court of Diyarbakir was said to rival Damascus and Cairo. An irony that is lost on the governments of Turkey and Iran, which refuse to acknowledge the existence of Kurds, and on Arabs who use the name Kurd as a pejorative, is that Saladin, who

---

* As you would expect of a people whose calendar dates from the defeat of the Assyrians by the Medes in the seventh century BC.

would have won most popularity polls among Master Philip's Muslim contemporaries, was himself a Kurd. But most Kurds are unaware of a parallel irony: the idea of Kurdistan was invented in the twelfth century by Sultan Sanjar, a Seljuk Turk.

The Kurds weren't Diyarbakir's only anguished minority. The Suriani Christians at the Church of Meryemana traced their faith to King Abgar of Edessa, who once wrote to Jesus, offering him free board in his 'little city' if he cured him of lameness. Jesus was rather busy (lots of evil spirits to cast out and parables to narrate) but he sent Thaddeus, who established the Antiochian rite.

'Welcome,' said a bushy-bearded Suriani as he beckoned us across the flagstones of the church and poured tea into small china cups. 'This is Aramaisch,' he said, noticing that Mike and I were looking at an inscription above the church portal. 'It is the language of our liturgy and of Jesus the Lord. You see! We are the first Church of the world!'

The priest, a bearded man in a skullcap called Father Yusuf, had recently been imprisoned for 'crimes against public order' under Article 312, Book 2, Section 5, of the Turkish Penal Code. His offence? He had intimated to undercover reporters that the Young Turk government might have had something to do with the massacre of Armenians, Syriac Christians and Greeks in the 1920s. The present-day government disagreed and it was only an international outcry that secured his release.

Father Yusuf's experience reflected the difficult circumstances faced by the Suriani, whose ancestors so expertly squeezed between Catholic Crusaders and a hostile mosaic of competing sects, and acted as the principal agents of translation between ancient Greek and medieval Arabic learning. When the Turks captured Edessa in 1144, it was a Suriani, Abu al-Faraj, who negotiated terms for the locals. After the initial mayhem, 'everything was taken from the Franj', while the Suriani 'returned to their homes safe and sound'.

'Is no persecution,' said a female student when we asked about the present-day condition of the Suriani, 'but our problem is another. The Armenian, they have different problem, but they have land. We have no land. And look.' She pointed to the inscription. 'You see?' She sighed. 'I am Suriani, this is my language, but I do not know this, because we have nowhere to teach me. Our problem is a question of identity.'

The difficulties endured by minorities such as the Suriani and the Kurds were emphasized by a wander round the Old City, where every twist unfurled another gun-toting soldier, and every turn another scowling shopkeeper. Inside the black belly of the keep, visions of bookworms' beard-ends brushing against crinkled papyrus in the famous medieval library were scotched by tense soldiers polishing their machine guns. One of them stopped us beside a barricade and ushered us into an old mosque now functioning as an administrative centre.

'Give us camera and passport,' barked his commanding officer. As we handed them over, I assumed my meekest smile and Mike pressed his panama hat piously against his chest.

'You must be very careful in this town,' the commanding officer continued.

Mike and I glanced apprehensively at each other, doing to our eyebrows what grannies do to bundles of wool. Surely we wouldn't be targets of Kurdish militants? I remember shivering as a huddle of shifts, grimaces barely discernible inside their enormous beards, was escorted up a dark basalt staircase.

'Why?' said Mike.

As the commanding officer took the panama and placed it on Mike's head, his sombre expression was lit up by a twinkle.

'The sun is very hot,' he boomed, letting out a laugh like a coffee-grinder.

We were escorted round the keep by Ahmet, a skeletal conscript who particularly loved tourists.

'They mean for me the cigarette break!' He beamed, and led us on to a patio behind the old museum. He told us the grimacing men were prisoners. When I asked if they were Kurds, he dipped his head and exhaled a cauliflower of smoke.

'I am a Kurd myself,' he said. 'But I do not want the terror, so I'm in the army. I hate it. I want to go to Bodrum and be a tour guide.'

Underneath us was one of the four rivers of paradise, the river that (or so the twelfth-century chronicler Otto of Freising assures us) Prester John attempted to cross en route to abetting his fellow Christians in Jerusalem, and 'tarried there for several years', hoping that it might freeze. It was a scrawny slip of a river that nosed across a rugged hill where banners of smoke ('Many terrorist over there,' whispered Ahmet. 'They make the plans.') blasted from shiny terraced houses.

'This,' said Ahmet, 'is the best part of Diyarbakir.'

'This?' Mike's nose scrunched as he winced at the vista.

'You should see the rest of the town.'

It was no oil painting. Alleyways streamed between tottering brick piles, awash with litter and urchins. But there was a kind of beauty to Diyarbakir – the beauty that is available only if you don't have to live there. Round the corner from the keep, wrapped-up women sifted bundles of mint in their laps, beside a twelfth-century mosque. Children skipped around us with chocolates, while cross-legged old men uttered their prayers on the flagstones. It was an oil painting after all – a David Roberts, full of the sweaty bustle and mystique of the East.

The children were ubiquitous. They offered us jelly beans and prayer beads, screamed 'Ha-llo!' and 'Meesta!', and seeped around a grocery truck parked to wall them off. Big matriarchs marched shopping bags and offspring past tea houses where old men slammed cards under canopies that sheltered them from the heat. A girl in calico let her veil drop from her cheeks as she smacked a dusty carpet against a doorstep and watched the children who ran over the rubble to enlist in our army, leaving behind the torn shirts they'd turned into skipping ropes and swarming about us all the way to the HO L P L S. But they were scattered by Ramazan, brandishing his broom like a Saracen's mace.

'Come back soon?' he pleaded, as he carried our bags to the *dolmuş* taxi that would take us to the bus stop.

'Maybe.'

'Next week?'

'Might be tricky.'

He nodded stoically, one hand clinging to his prayer beads, the other windmilling us away. As we reached the city gates, I felt a twinge as I watched a solitary, sack-legged figure waddling back to his hotel.

But I was happy. The bus journey out of Diyarbakir included the mandatory sponge cakes and around us, like characters in a medieval woodcut, men were hoeing vegetables and plucking grapes in vineyards. Ahead lay Şanliurfa, formerly Edessa, one of the most important cities in Prester John folklore. I opened a copy of Chrétien de Troyes' *Conte du Graal* (or *Story of the Grail*, recently perfumed by the sun lotion that had exploded in my backpack); Mike, thrilling at our increasing proximity to the trouble spots that had first drawn him to the Middle East, dug into a history of the Hizbollah.

We reached Şanliurfa around teatime, to be met by a little boy with extremely dirty hands. He uttered a couple of shrieks and frogmarched us to the Hotel Gumbay. It was a world away from the Hotel Palas. It had a working shower, mattresses and fresh air. We had rooms on the flat rooftop, where Muslim pilgrims slept on bed-frames, stroked by the cool night air.

Sitting on the edge of the roof, dangling their legs above the calico wraps and cotton gowns that floated between fruit carts and revolving kebab-machines, were the dirty little boy and his equally dirty friend. Their trousers were held up by string and their toes peeped out of their leather sandals. They looked like they'd just escaped from the workhouse in *Oliver*

Twist. As we emerged from our room, local curiosities were cast aside. This was much more intriguing: two strangers with faces the colour of chalk and leather belts with shiny buckles. First they circled us, hands behind their backs, like we were made out of plaster-of-Paris. Then, with a cry of 'Clin-büts!', they rattled their wooden boxes and opened them up to show us brushes and tins of shoe polish.

I'd met a few shoeshine boys by now. In Istanbul, four feet of pluck had chased me around the Theodosian obelisk in the Hippodrome. I didn't fancy a chase this time – rooftops are not ideal for such activities – so I decided to turn the tables. Beckoning for one of the boxes, I took out the tin and offered to polish the shoes of its owner. Since they were open-toe sandals, there wasn't much to polish. They were also his cleanest component. But anything to keep him from shining my own shoes. Soon he was giggling, baring discoloured teeth and, despite the role reversal, shuffling his fingers for payment. This boy wasn't leaving till he'd got what he came for. So I gave in.

'Sultana Elizabeth,' I declared, presenting a five-pence piece with as much importance as I could muster – and asked him his name.

'Farouk,' he squealed.

The only Farouk I'd ever heard of was the King of Egypt in the 1950s. So I named him 'Malik Farouk' – King Farouk – and he in turn addressed me as 'Sultana Elizabeth'.

There was still a chase. His friend, sniffing money, pursued his accomplice across the rooftop with a cry that would have done credit to the army of Kilidj Arslan.

'Here you go, Mr Battleaxe.' Laughing, Mike placated him with another 'Sultana Elizabeth' coin. We left them squabbling over their gifts, to explore the city that once called itself Edessa.

Cavehanes, where men expectorated at TV sets, and mosques had replaced the churches of the Crusader city. The Orthodox Cathedral was long ago converted into the Ulu Jamii, its Christian past hidden in the octagonal minaret, once a steeple, and a couple of Byzantine capitals. Children leapfrogged these Christian remnants, hurdled men lying on mattresses outside the medieval prayer hall and skipped through the cemetery, where faceless widows wrung their hands in front of elegantly inscribed headstones.

Edessa used to be famous for her relics. Her inventory included the arm that baptized Christ, the bones of St Thomas and the enigmatic Mandylion. Some scholars believe that the Mandylion was a portrait of Christ, taken by a court artist of the lame King Abgar. Others argue that it was Christ's baptismal towel, or a cloth that wiped His face before the Crucifixion. Whether work of art or repository of the Messiah's sweat, it attracted the Byzantines enough to inspire a siege in 943. The city's Arab rulers agreed to swap the spurious artefact for several hundred Muslim prisoners and twelve thousand pieces of silver. But local Christians insisted that the Byzantines had been given only a copy, and the original remained in Edessa.

The bones of Doubting Thomas have had an equally mysterious history. After their Edessa phase they did a stint on the Greek island of Chios, before turning up at the Italian coastal town of Ortona di Mare. Their brief presence in Edessa may have contributed to the city's association with Prester John. One of the most popular features of the priest-king's letter was St Thomas's tendency to rise from the dead and preach in Prester John's palace, which had been built according to the design of a palace constructed by Thomas for King Gundafor of India.* In the fourteenth century,

* According to the legend, Gundafor provided Thomas with a stupendous budget, which the saint proceeded to distribute among the poor. The king wasn't amused. He had Thomas beaten and imprisoned. His brother Gad was even less amused, and died of grief. But on his journey to heaven, Gad saw a beautiful palace. When he asked about it, he was told that it had been built by Thomas for Gundafor. He returned to India (in those days you could pick a postponement option on death) and related this to Gundafor, who immediately asked to be baptized. In this way, Christianity was introduced to India.

Joannes de Hese claimed that Prester John's capital was four days' journey from 'Edissa'. Another tract from the same period, the *Travels of the Infante Dom Pedro*, identified the Prester in 'Edicia'. It was an intriguing link that, many weeks later, would become more pronounced through Edessa's linguistic connection with an African candidate for Prester John's capital.

But the city's most specific link with Prester John is her capture from the Crusaders by the local Seljuk bigwig Imad ad-Din Zengi in 1144. Despairing of the setback, the Crusaders sent Bishop Hugh of Gabala to the papal court at Viterbo to urge a new crusade. It was then that Bishop Hugh related the story of Prester John that became famous through the chronicle of Otto of Freising.

The siege of Edessa was a bloody affair – Michael the Syrian suggested that it led to the city's infestation by jackals and vampires, while Abu al-Faraj more credibly described the Turks' immolation of the walls with wood, sulphur and animal fat:

> *Women, children, and young people fled to the upper citadel to escape the massacre. They found the gate barred – the fault of the bishop of the Franj, who had told the guards, 'Do not open the gate unless you see my face!' Groups of people climbed up in succession, trampling one another. It was a lamentable and horrifying spectacle. About five thousand people, perhaps more, died atrociously, twisted, suffocating, pressed together into a single, compact mass.*

Yet the citadel remained intact. We found it at the top of a hill where local shepherds grazed their goats: a bulk of sandstone lunging above buttresses of grey rock. A cavernous passageway snaked to a scorching esplanade, where women top-to-toe in black milled around two columns from which Nimrod the Hunter-King legendarily catapulted the prophet

Abraham into a burning furnace. Except God – that champion of unlikely escape routes – turned the furnace into a sacred pond with a safety raft made out of fish.

Tumbling down from the citadel was a magic carpet's view of mulberry and cypress trees entwining the domes, arcades and minarets that crowded about a rectangle of water. The Birket Ibrahim swarmed with children, their after-school hours taken up, as they were for children across the medieval world, with work. Some hawked keffiyehs (Arabic headdresses), some clip-on butterflies, but the real entrepreneurs were heaping up their lira by selling sachets of herbs that pious Muslims fed to the carp. The descendants of Abraham's lifeboat service clashed in gilt-brown storms, as if the siege of Edessa was being re-enacted in the sacred pond. Hypnotized by their carping, I barely heard the patter of small feet that preceded a tug at my shirtsleeves.

'Sultana Elizabeth!'

A little, nail-bitten hand stretched towards me and shook my fingers. Standing beside me, now bereft of his shoeshine box, was Malik Farouk. He strolled by my side as I circled the pond, stopped when I stopped and peered intelligently into the water. He had apparently made an important decision: I looked in dire need of protection and he was the best man for the job.

We found Mike in a tea garden behind the pond, shaded under a tamarisk tree. Malik Farouk sat down beside me and, when we ordered him a drink, cupped his hands around it, as if to shelter it from the cruelty of the outside world. Then, slowly, his bright, brown eyes lifted mischievously:

'*Lokanta?*' Restaurant?

It didn't take long for Farouk's accomplice, Ahmet, to swagger alongside us. 'Ah, Mr Battleaxe!' exclaimed Mike. Within minutes their jaws were munching through cabbage dolmas. They taught us Turkish numbers, drew a map of Urfa with the contents of the salad bowl, and laid out our napkins for us with exaggerated attentiveness. Then, once they were full, they shook our hands with hockey-stick swings and marched off into the night.

'So,' said Mike, back on the rooftop of our hotel, his head briefly parallel with my knees, 'what's all this about the Fisher King?'

'Ah, well . . .' I leaned forward on my bedstead, but his head had already dipped to the floor.

'Forty,' said Mike.

'You see, there's the lame King Abgar, the fishponds, the Mandylion – a sort of hotchpotch of folklore all in one city.'

His head had disappeared again. A puddle of sweat was forming on the floor.

'You see—' I continued.

'Forty-five,' he said.

'—Edessa was as close as Master Philip's world—'

'Forty-seven.'

'—had to a real-life landscape for the castle of the—'

'Forty-nine.'

'—Fisher King and therefore for the home of the—'

'Fifty.'

'—Holy Grail.'

Mike rolled on to his back and flicked a towel over his head. Tonight's press-up regime was complete.

Master Philip's contemporaries liked a good yarn – whether the tales of love-lorn troubadours or the classic *chansons de geste* – such adventures as *The Song of Roland* or *Bert with the Large Feet*. In 1175, Chrétien de Troyes delivered a new masterpiece at the court of Mary of Champagne. His *Story of the Grail* would become one of the most influential of all medieval poems and revolutionize the European chivalric narrative.

Chrétien's hero breaks the contemporary mould. Forget your conventional virtuous beefcake: at the outset, this yokel-boy from the Waste Forest can't even remember his name. His manners are so bad that he steals a ring, a goblet of wine, one and a half venison pies and a kiss from a maiden who is subsequently consigned by the Haughty Knight of the Heath to trudge in a dress of which 'not a palm's breadth was intact'. He stumbles through a series of comic misadventures (like accidentally knocking off King Arthur's cap) before cobbling together an impressive portfolio of rescued damsels, vanquished knights and succoured cities, guessing his name as Perceval and happening upon the Holy Grail. In the castle of the Fisher King, he eats Alexandrian gingerbread and pomegranates at an ivory-topped trestle table that blends Oriental snacks with venison and claret. A beautiful maiden carries the Grail before his eyes, but he commits the moral error of failing to ask a single question. Rebuked by a weeping damsel and a hunchback with the lips of an ass, Perceval loses centre stage to Sir Gawain. As for the Grail – it remains elusive, not because of further chivalric shortcomings but because Chrétien apparently died before his champions could complete their quest.

The Crusader knights fondly identified with such stories. Like the Round Table swashbucklers, seeking out sacred artefacts and saving pointy-hatted damsels, the Frankish knights prided themselves on their codes of honour (in dealing with fellow Catholics) and perceived the Crusade as a divine quest. They even discovered a few artefacts of their own: most famously during the First Crusade, when the penniless hermit Peter Bartholomew uncovered the lance that pierced Christ's side (and also caused the legendary illness of the Fisher King) in Antioch.

But few artefacts matched the Grail. The Cistercians linked it with Mary – the vessel containing the Holy Blood of Christ. The troubadours addressed her as the 'Grail of the World'. Chrétien made it a particularly valuable item of the Fisher King's crockery, 'that supports his life in full vigour'. Later legends linked the Grail with the Ark of the Covenant, that other elusive biblical artefact. They were a handy pair of knick-knacks: the Ark made its owner invincible; the Grail gave him eternal life. If you had both of them, you could hardly lose.

The most famous early Grail account was *Parsival*, written by the German poet Wolfram von Eschenbach in the early thirteenth century. A mongrel text spawned from the work of a Provençal minstrel, an Arabic manuscript, a Jewish astronomer and Chrétien's *Conte*, *Parsival* is a masterpiece of beasts, battles and sexual cross-pollination, in which the Grail is recast as a stone: 'however ill a mortal may be, from that day on which he sees the Stone he cannot die for that week, nor does he lose his colour . . . Such powers does the Stone confer on mortal men that their flesh and bones are soon made young again.'

Prester John also had a magic stone, 'of incredible medical virtue, which cures Christians or would-be Christians of whatever ailments afflict them'. It had a mussel-shaped cavity filled with water and was guarded by two holy men. But, in its effect, Wolfram's Grail-stone had more in common with another of Prester John's treasures: the Fountain of Youth. 'Anyone who tastes three times of this fountain, while fasting,' related the priest-king's letter, 'will suffer no infirmity thereafter, but remains as if of the age of thirty-two years as long as he lives.'

It was natural that there should be links between Prester John, the elusive king, and the elusive Grail. Like Prester John, the Fisher King is also a priest living in a mysterious castle, sought by the leaders of Christendom. In the Grail legend, Arthurian knights travel to the Heavenly City of the East. Prester John, 'most glorious over mortals', ruling as far as the rising sun, was believed to have his own heavenly city in the East. The link wasn't missed by Wolfram.

In *Parsival*, a Christian knight woos the black heathen queen of Zazamanc, before excusing himself on the grounds that he has military glory to acquire. The fruit of their brief liaison takes after both his parents: his skin is black with white spots. An odd complexion, sure, but not entirely unattractive to the ladies – if this mulatto's success with the purest maiden of all, the Bearer of the Grail, is a suitable measurement. Their son, who becomes the Grail's guardian, is called 'Prester John'.

In the morning, our return to the sacred pond unveiled a new set of satraps. Mehmet Ali, Mustafa and Ma'bud were a few years older than Malik Farouk and spoke slightly more English. They were disappointed to learn that we were not Muslims, but that could easily be remedied.

'Maybe,' said Mehmet Ali, 'if you spend the day with us, you will decide is wise to be Muslim.'

Then, with a cry of 'Sultana Elizabeth!', Malik Farouk and Ahmet joined our new platoon and it was Malik Farouk – his eleven-year-old arm stuck out like a general's cane – who would be dictating our activities.

It was a wonderful day, as mosque melted into madrasa and museum (where a musical archaeologist played on a Bronze Age pipe) into souk, and we ate when we liked (which meant a lot), sharing out mouthfuls of meat-filled *manti* pastry like Central Asian Turks in a pre-medieval tent.

But being ordered around by an eleven-year-old wasn't quite Mike's cuppa *çay*.

'Going to the souk,' he announced, as he detached Mustafa and Ma'bud from the army and made up for his lack of local knowledge with generous helpings of self-assurance. A mutiny! Farouk fixed me with the steely eyes of a grand sultan. Was I too planning a schism? I didn't dare.

At the Ibrahimi Mosque, elderly worshippers risked hernias on their prayer mats or pressed hands to hearts and chatted under the trees in the forecourt. Others, palms inscribed by prayer beads and foreheads embossed by prayer bumps, drank or washed away their sweat at a sputtering tap.

'You drink holy water?' asked Mehmet Ali, filling up a metal bowl. 'It come from Prophet Ibrahimi birth-cave. You know Ibrahimi was born in Şanliurfa? Drink, is good for you!'

Before entering the cave, Farouk gestured for me to remove my shoes. He gripped them earnestly and turned himself into a statue.

Inside was a cavernous chamber where men slurped from a stone well. Most of their faces were stiff with piety, but one flushed ecstatic seemed to be drinking a different kind of liquid. Pulling himself away from the well, he clawed my shoulder blades and insisted that my happiness depended on a drink.

'Some people,' said Mehmet Ali with a chuckle, 'they come here every day for drink the water. They think it give them the life always!'

It was sounding rather like Prester John's Fountain of Youth. I drained a tepid mouthful, but unlike Sir John Mandeville I didn't 'thinketh I fare the better'.

My movements, once he'd tied up my shoelaces, were governed outside the cave by Malik Farouk. Carpet dust billowed like censer smoke as we entered the bazaar. Malik Farouk was squinting for trouble. It came in the form of a boy with butterfly clips. When the boy pressed his trinkets against my chest, his nose received the full force of my guardian's fist. Malik Farouk's methods of protection were becoming decidedly unchivalrous.

We were brushed by Arab gowns and Kurdish pantaloons and the robes of Iranians with the stony beards of an Assyrian frieze. The clang of copper-etching yammered from medieval niches where old men hunched like the marginalia of a life-size breviary. The pungent breath of kebab grills tussled with the odour of too-many-bodies/too-little-space, and picked up a scent of syrupy tea from where men dressed for a Seljuk caravanserai gabbled and gurgled under a sky-framing balcony that sagged beneath a sewing circle of conservatively dressed women. I could hear hints of different languages – reedy, rattling, rasping, roaring. For the first time since we'd left Jerusalem in January, I could hear Arabic. But now my elbow was being yanked out of the bazaar: Farouk had decided to grant us a rest. Within moments I could hear a rather more familiar brogue.

'Get over here!' yelled Mike, bound to a table near the sacred pond by the protective cordon of Mustafa and Ma'bud.

'Awful lot of children here,' he whispered, glancing at the hordes of midget butterfly-clip merchants prancing around the garden.

Logic suggested high birth rate, but my romantic instincts wondered if there was another explanation.

'Perhaps,' I said, 'they're not actually children. After all, if that water is the Fountain of Youth . . .'

Mike showed me one of his less indulgent frowns, so I turned to Mehmet Ali.

'How old are you?' I asked.

'I,' he replied, 'am very religious.'

'I see, but that doesn't tell me—'

'I like for go madrasa,' he continued, 'study Qu'ran. I will be imam and dedicate my life to God.'

'Well, you're clearly older than your years.'

No time for further investigation into the Fountain of Youth: we had a bus to catch, for Antioch, once home to Master Philip's most deliciously unpleasant contemporary. Farouk and Ahmet shook our hands stoically and bade us goodbye, while the teenagers called us a taxi.

'Good journeys!' shouted Ma'bud, opening the door.

'Call us when you are next in Şanliurfa,' exclaimed Mustafa.

'May God make your journey safe and prosperous,' declared Mehmet Ali.

'Let's get our hair cut,' announced Mike – a more pragmatic sentiment – as we reached the bus stop.

Hair was cascading off creaky flexi-chairs, on to a tiled floor smothered in the cosmopolitan locks of a frontier town: thin Iranian strands, thick Arab mats and Yuruk pigtails, Turkish wisps, the greasy quiff of an Aleppan exhibitionist. This dusty composite of different ethnic types seemed to express Urfa's habit of jumbling the unlikely together. I gulped on soap-scent and gel-whiff and wondered if it was this talent for fusion that made Edessa a centre of Grail interest. Holy fishes and life-giving waters intrigued the merchants, from East and West, whose far-flung tales met in Urfa's salad bowl.

By the time my turn came, we had about ten minutes. I gestured to the barber to be quick. He rammed my head into the sink, yanked it back to shear the crown, shredded away like he was trying to put out a fire and saturated my throat with hibiscus tea. Finally, with seconds to go, he swept the towel from my neck, and brushed me down like I'd just emerged from a collapsed building.

'Finish!' he panted.

We still nearly missed the bus. It was sweeping away from the bus stop, careening on to the motorway, deaf to our screams.

'Balls!' yelled Mike, at such volume that a man nearby sprinted across the esplanade, leaped on to an expressway bridge and flagged the bus to a halt. As he bowed, with the gentle civility so common among Turks, we backed into the carriage on a volley of thank yous – 'Teşekürler'. He stood rigid, a hand on his heart, as the plain that links the Lebanon Mountains and the foothills of the Taurus lulled us towards Antioch.

A dreadful night! Antioch's silhouette spun in three-quarter-closed eyes at four in the morning. The odd straggler staggered out of a *beerhane* to shatter the steam-chilled silence with burps. Most of the hotels, locked tight, were impervious to Mike's most fearsome rat-a-tat-tat-tat-tat-tat-tat. But a lopsided 'welcome' sign lured us up a creaking staircase, and once we'd woken an old grouch in stripy pyjamas from his kitchen sofa there was nothing he could do to keep us out. With a twinkle in his otherwise bleary eyes, he attempted to extract a mighty price for his interrupted beauty sleep. So we convened around his kitchen table and negotiated. On his side, he had the room, and we wanted it. On our side, he wanted to go back to bed and we knew it. We reached an agreement. By the time we slumped on to concave beds with cushions as stiff as alabaster, we didn't like him, and judging from his grumbles as he stamped back to his sofa, he didn't think much of us.

Not enough hours later, we wandered the daylight streets in search of Antioch's Crusader past. Boys japed beside saddled horses while their wrapped-up sisters haggled for watermelons. Under the vine-wreathed balconies of Ottoman villas, their fathers sat on milk crates and smoked in front of TV sets perched on car bonnets.

It often happens that the cities with the most exciting stories are the ones with the least to show. But the whitewash of Antioch's Crusader era was a particular shame. Had we made it here eight hundred years earlier, we would have found the Church of St Peter, where Peter Bartholomew discovered Longinus' lance, rather than scuffing across a lorry park. We could have practised archery on the Plain of Issus, where the first Crusaders encamped in 1097, instead of scowling at a compost of flat-roofed concrete. And we could have cavorted in the banqueting halls with the dissipated Franks who turned Antioch into an Oriental Sybaris. Antioch, after all, is where Eleanor of Aquitaine (future mother of Chrétien de Troyes' patroness and Richard the Lionheart) learned all the latest fashions and dances and turned herself into the Princess Diana of her day. Rumour crowed that she'd copped off with her uncle Count Raymond, and even (one minstrel suggested) had one foot in Saladin's boat before King Louis caught up with her. Here the Count of Flanders* and his retinue turned up looking for marriage alliances and, grumbled the chronicler William of Tyre, 'spent their time at the baths and at banquets and indulged in drunken debauches and other pleasures of the flesh'. And the prince of this city was once the Grand Dastard of Outremer himself – plenty of boos and rotten tomatoes please, as we hiss the arrival of Reynald de Chatillon.

Reynald's problem was poverty: he was one of the chancers who travelled to the East to make his fortune. He had no family money to speak of, but in 1156 a solution erupted in the cesspit of his mind: an invasion of Cyprus. His lack of funds posed a small problem, but once he'd approached the Patriarch of Antioch, and treated the patriarch's refusal by thrashing him, smearing his wounds in honey and leaving him outside in the insect-buzzing heat, that was solved. Monasteries were ransacked, virgins interfered with, children murdered. Reynald was delighted. Manuel Comnenos, suzerain of Cyprus, was not. He marched towards Antioch and issued a demand for submission. A less cunning individual would have panicked, but Reynald had a plan. He donned a woollen tunic, shaved his head, tied a rope round his neck and threw himself at the emperor's feet, with water in his eyes and cries of contrition. Having grovelled sufficiently, he held Manuel's stirrups in the Imperial Procession and turned what should have been a humiliation into a personal triumph. Manuel was able to revel in his ego, and Reynald was able to return to his troublesome ways. Little did he know he had only a year before his luck would run out . . .

One still extant antique building – or cave, to be precise – lies on the outskirts of Antioch. A taxi drove us past pack-saddled

---

* Who gave to Chrétien de Troyes the book that inspired the *Conte du Graal*.

donkeys and mulberry groves to the grotto where St Peter founded the first Christian community. Tents were dotted down the decline, erected for refugees after a recent flood. As Mike and I charged past a toothless old man hunched over 'authendic arkeelogic find' – featureless figurines hacked out of shards – a wiry teenager in a tracksuit scampered beside us. His name, he said, was Christopher.

The blancmange façade melted into a cavern where Greek letters and Ionian whorls were anchored to the atmosphere of underwater. Mike had become the focus of a shoeshine boy, who chased him round the forecourt until, with Mikely vigour, he coerced the boy into escorting him to a rock engraved with an image of the Virgin Mary. I was alone, in a narrow recess where water dribbled into a cool basin of rock, with Christopher.

'Water from mountain,' he said. 'Is holy for Christian. You Christian?'

'I think so.'

'My religion we think this place holy. Mother Mary very important.'

'You're Christian too?'

'I am Alawite.'

'Al-a—?'

This sounded like the sect that Syria's ruling family, the Assads, belonged to.* But I'd always assumed it was a branch of Islam. So had the Syrian constitution, which requires its president to be a Muslim. Intrigued, I sat beside Christopher in a corner of the church.

CHRISTOPHER: *I am thinking my family, in Amareeka.*

ME: *You have family in America?*

---

* Otherwise known as Ansariya or Nosairi – in the Middle East, if you want your creed to be taken seriously, you need at least a couple of synonyms.

CHRISTOPHER: *I have grandchildren in Amareeka.*

ME: *Grandchildren?*

CHRISTOPHER: *In previous life.*

ME: *You had a previous life?*

CHRISTOPHER: *I have many powerful friend in previous life.*

ME: *Like who?*

CHRISTOPHER: *John F. Kennedy.*

ME: *?*

CHRISTOPHER: *I am soldier in US army. I fight Hitler.*

ME: *That was brave.*

CHRISTOPHER: *You have previous life?*

ME: *Not as far as I can remember.*

CHRISTOPHER: (Peers around the church, then leans forward, pressing his face against my ear.) *I hate Eastern country.*

ME: (Detaching my ear.) *That's a shame.*

CHRISTOPHER: *I have mission. Must destroy Turkish civilization. Europa compatriot little time. Necessary I destroy Turkish.*

ME: *Now you're talking like a Dalek. Look, I'd better be off.*

CHRISTOPHER: *You will help me?*

ME: *Er – why don't you try the Kennedys?*
               Bye.

CHRISTOPHER: *Is important for destroy Turkish!*

'So how was our man Christopher?' asked Mike, as our taxi drove towards the bus stop.

'He thinks he knew John F. Kennedy.'

'As in *the* John F. Kennedy?'

'In a previous life.'

Mike crooked an elbow over the half-open window and glanced across the neat line of market stalls standing side by side like schoolboys lined up for a photograph.

'Know what?' he said. 'A previous life could be awesome.'

'What sort of life would you like to have had?'

'Hmmm. Wouldn't mind being one of those British officers in the Raj.'

'I'd like to have been Master Philip.'

'Live in a palace, with black-tie balls and hunting expeditions.'

'Then I'd know what happened to this damned letter.'

'And my own private army of elephants.'

'Although I'm not sure if I'd remember what happened to him – do you think you can remember your own death?'

'Coffee?'

In a dingy café, a couple of old men were playing back-gammon. One sat upright, placing his counters with mathematical precision, brow creased in concentration. The other was slumped across the table, scratching his walrus moustache and dismissing the dice across the board. I was fascinated by their asymmetry, and wondered if it had a geographical source: the courtesy of the Turk against the brashness of the Arab, whose lands lay only a few kilometres away.

But first there was customs. A bus dropped us beside a hall full of men in *gelabiyya*s and ladies in hijab. Officials stamped our passports and flung them back at us, with the same disdain that distinguished the walrus's backgammon. I scanned the walls, papered in hagiography to the Assads as pompous as the Comnenian mosaics of Constantinople.

'This is Hafez Al-Assad, our great leader,' explained my Syrian neighbour. 'He sadly no more.'

'Ha!' snorted Mike. 'Didn't he raze the city of Hama because some of its citizens didn't support him?'

'He kind, gentle man.'

'Course he was.'

'Now that's Bashar, isn't it?' I asked.

'Bashar new leader, mighty man.'

Not that he looked it, with his long neck and nervous moustache.

'Everyone can say no bad word for him,' my neighbour added.

'No, I don't suppose they can.'

There was a third icon, in military get-up with big black shades. He looked like a character from *Top Gun*.

'He dead,' said my neighbour. 'He Basil, son for Assad. They say he for leader, but no longer. Allah take him in quick wheelie.'

Basil, it turned out, had a penchant for fast cars. He was on his way to a skiing holiday when he lost control of one such car, and died.

Our passports checked, we strolled back to the bus and unloaded our bags for inspection. A pair of officials in white suits with colourful epaulettes marched towards us. With what might they take issue? Mike's Swiss army knife? My insect repellent? Mike's Milex camera? Perhaps they would take umbrage over one of my books? Maybe they would see Rabbi Benjamin of Tudela as an ambassador for Zionism, the most hated -ism on the Arabian peninsula? But they were already occupied: they had cigarettes and fat to smoke and chew. They stood near us, watching out for their superior officer, then marched back into the compound when sufficient time had elapsed.

Back in the bus, we watched the landscape shed its last scraps of fertility. Our fellow passengers' lips curled delightedly as our surroundings turned into an ochre-coloured scrub, and their shoulders juggled to their song:

'*Ya'al-laaaa ha-beeee-bi!*' Let's gooooo, my deeeee-ar!

'Oh yes,' chuckled Mike, 'back in the Arab world!'

CHAPTER SEVEN

APOLOGIES IN OUTREMER

WE'D REACHED THE 'Arab world'. At least, we'd crossed the north-east frontier of a land mass of 5.25 million square miles of desert, marsh, mountain and metropolis. A region that would offer us carpets, cakes, a coterie of lethal explosives, and several sisters. But was it really one homogeneous bloc?

One of the men *ya'allaaaa*-ing in the bus was Armenian. At a café en route to Aleppo we sat beside a Kurd. It's more like:

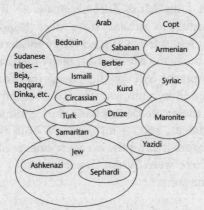

Figure 3: The 'Arab world'.

Demographic preconceptions didn't last much beyond our arrival in Aleppo.

Under the vermicelli scaffolding of the Great Mosque's octagonal minaret, a wooden board cranked beneath my feet and wrinkled worshippers rocked in a walled eighth-century quadrangle. Ahead of me, glowing in a dust-coloured cavern, was a luminous green cage that claims to be the resting place of John the Baptist's father. A Jew from the Christian New Testament in a Muslim shrine: I should have sensed that strange things were afoot.

To be precise, Athliat – gangly, hawk-nosed and clutching a paperback – was afoot.

'It is under restoration,' he explained.

'But you still have your services here?'

'I am not Muslim.'

In that case he must be a Christian? No? Nor a Jew? Aha – already had this one. An Alawite?

'No.'

Heavens above, had I come across Syria's only atheist?

'I follow the faith,' he said, 'of the prophet Zartusht.'

The prophet who?

'He live a hundred years before Muhammad. He preach goodness and equality and purity of light and fire.'

A Zoroastrian! The faith that dominated pre-Islamic Persia, whose most famous alumni were the Magi, reputed ancestors of Prester John. Most Zoroastrians were absorbed by Islam but, according to Athliat, there were 'hundreds of thousands' of them left. Medieval (and many modern) commentators branded them fire-worshipping dualists, and abhorred their custom of leaving their dead on 'Towers of Silence' to be devoured by vultures. The Zoroastrians themselves pointed out their creed's emphasis on cleanliness and the natural environment, and its influence on both the Jews of the Babylonian captivity and the early exponents of Islam.

'I didn't know there were *Syrian* Zoroastrians,' I said, as Athliat led me to the souk.

'I am not Syrian.'

'Should I say Arab?'

'I am Kurd.'

I hadn't expected this.

'I'm sorry,' I said. 'The Middle East is very confusing.'

Athliat frowned.

'I don't understand,' he said, 'why you say this "Middle East". We are hundred kilometre from Cyprus, but Cyprus is in Europe. So, if this is Middle East, where is Near East? In the sea?'

I apologized.

'You Westerners,' said Athliat, 'you think everything here is so simple.'

I apologized again. But I felt rather cheated when I noticed the title of his book: J. M. Roberts's *A Concise History of the World*.

I'd been caught out simplifying the (forgive the simplification) Middle East. But, in my defence, many of its citizens do that too. In Ramallah, a few months earlier, an English-speaking Palestinian friend introduced me to another man who, I presumed, also spoke English.

'Pleased to meet you,' I said, to a stern elevation of eyebrows.

'We are in Palestine,' he said. 'Palestine is in the Arab world. In the Arab world, we speak Arabic.'

The concept of an Arab world – as Nasser's attempt to form a United Arab Republic in the 1950s showed – is as strong inside it as outside. But to bracket together the inhabitants of all Arab countries is to ignore the region's celebration of mankind's impulse to splinter. A Zoroastrian in Aleppo may be an exception, but there are plenty of exceptions. Take the non-Arab Christian sects: Copts have their own liturgical language; many Maronites speak French; both claim a presence in their respective countries that pre-dates the Arabs. One of the sources of the Lebanese Civil War was the Maronites' difficulty with Arab identification. But it was a Maronite, Butrus al-Bustani, who spearheaded the Arabic literary renaissance in the nineteenth century, by publishing an Arabic dictionary and encyclopaedia in 1881. It's not just Christians – the Middle East is sprinkled with idiosyncratic complications of its 'Arab' identification, like the 'devil-worshipping' Yazidi, the Druze, and the Sabaeans of Iraq, who believe that John the Baptist was the real Messiah. As we travelled around the 'Arab world', I sensed that this was important: that the tragedy of the modern 'Middle East' (and not only the 'Arab world') is tangled with the tendency to reduce its people to labels that they don't want. Kurds in south-east Turkey resented the name 'Mountain Turks'; Palestinians abhorred the incorporation of their territories – linguistic as well as military – into 'Israel'; Bedouin in Sinai detached themselves from the Arab Republic of Egypt. Master Philip's might have been the Golden Age of Labels, when inanimate qualities received statues or national identities (e.g. effeminate = Greek). But terms like Crusader (applied to fighters against pagan Balts, Mongols, Muslims in Andalusia, North Africa and the Middle East, Christian Cathars, Orthodox Greeks and Russians – and applied now by the likes of Osama Bin Laden not only to America but also to the state of Israel) were used to construct the same 'them' and 'us' equations that unite and divide disparate groups today.

But some things were common to every 'Arab' country we visited: souks, sunshine, black-and-white banding on mosque brickwork . . . and, as we discovered on arrival in Aleppo, raucous taxi-drivers.

A whiskery, ferret-like face popped through the door of the bus.

'Welcom in Seeria! You like taxi?'

No, we insisted, we had two legs each and were happy to use them; which inspired the even firmer insistence, 'Taxi very good price, meesta.' Not just one but an absolute horde of them: the cheapest lift in Aleppo, Amareeka's favourite chauffeur, the four-dollar leather-jacketed man, the big-bearded, squint-eyed five-hundred-Seerian-pound man; a mob of taxi-drivers as diverse in dress sense, shaving customs and physique as they were united in their hunger for our fare.

The sequential nature of conventional prose can't do them justice. Their voices were too jumbled:

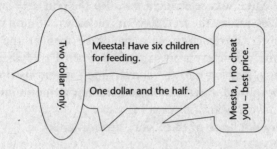

'Right,' I said, anchoring myself to Ferret while Mike sliced through half a dozen of Ferret's colleagues to retrieve our back-packs, 'we'll go with you for one dollar or we won't go at all.'

Ferret nodded, bundled our packs into his boot, leaped behind the steering wheel, and got lost in the (in his defence) complicated streets of (to his shame) his home town.

'*Ya*, Sharia Al-Ma'ari – sure I know it, inshallah. Maybe I just stop and ask someone to advice.'

In the evenings, Aleppo is a seedy place. Under the kung fu film posters flapping against the walls, men stand by steamy braziers, spitting meat-fat into the gutter. The smell of deca-dence and grease spills around aproned restaurateurs demanding that you eat in their establishment ('You know Mr Peter? He like very much my lamb kofta!') and seeps up narrow staircases where nightclub hosts lure their clients into the arms of Caucasian prostitutes.

One of the problems is that the streets are empty of women. They come out in force during the day, but as the light fades they scuttle back to their houses, to watch the after-work world through the crack of a shutter. The restau-rants are full of men, bantering over plates of hummus and tabbouleh salad, sharing *nargileh*s,* waving white hankies to their favourite folk tunes and salaaming newly arrived Western visitors to the Parliament of the People, where your voice is beaten to a whimper as your shoulders sink under the history of your nation.

While Mike was selecting a *nargileh* (he had very specific preferences among the fruit flavours on offer), I found myself drawn into conversation with the three men at the table behind me. Their eyebrows twitched when I told them my nationality. Fearing that the conversation would be brought to an abrupt end, I made a brazen attempt at ingratiation.

'You have a beautiful town,' I said.

'We are not,' one of them said, 'from Aleppo.'

'No?'

'I am from Baghdad.'

'Oh,' I said, 'how are – things – there?'

'We are bombed by the Amareekans and the British. Why you bomb us?'

'I – well, I don't know.'

'I am Armenian,' said his companion. 'Why does your country refuse to acknowledge the genocide of 1915 against my people?'

I fiddled with the vinegar bottle and contemplated the table.

'Um, well . . .'

The shashlik kebabs and baked aubergine were sunk in a mattress of rocket.

'And I am from Jordan,' said the other.

A dish of hummus appeared, paved with minced pistachios.

'But I was born in Palestine.'

Ingredients introduced to 'the West' by medieval Arabs.

* The importance of an item to a particular culture can often be gauged by the fertility of its vocabulary: the Yup'ik Eskimos, for example, have twenty-four words for snow. By that yardstick, one of the most important items in the 'Arab world' is the water-pipe that men smoke in the coffee houses. They call it a *nargileh*, *qalun*, *sheesha*, *chiboux*, or even, Arabizing an Anglicization for an Arabic item – *al-Hubbly-Bubbly*.

'Yes,' I said, 'I think I know what's—'

As if the table was making a point.

'Why,' he continued, 'Britain sold Palestine to the Jews?'

'Um,' I mumbled, through a mouthful of lettuce (at least that's a neutral ingredient), 'sorry.'

There was a great clank of movement behind me. At a corner of the table, a waiter had placed a contraption of gleaming brass and azure-tinted glass, with a dish on which he was stoking the charcoal with a pair of tongs.

'So,' said Mike, puffing on the *nargileh* and exuding an apple-flavoured floret of smoke, 'who are our new friends?'

By day, Aleppo was more amicable. Crocodiles of late-afternoon shoppers multi-sected the streets, streaming into a sticky soup of sweat and bustle, where every shop sign, traffic direction and T-shirt curled to the exotic dance of the Arabic script. Temporarily dislocated from Mike by our mutual inability to agree on our direction, I popped out of the crowd like a cork from a bottle, and popped into the Great Mosque. When I emerged, Athliat holding my elbow, a sea of all-black baboushka dolls* washed us – to the twang

---

* The question of female dress provokes more comment from Western observers than any tenet of Islamic doctrine. When I raised the issue with an Aleppan called Ahmet, he remarked that his wife always wore a 'beautiful shawl' in public. 'It make good her face,' he said. 'She no go cover up in black. This I hate: is selfish and is not religion.' However, a few weeks later, I was given a different perspective by Amina, the wife of my Palestinian friend Ghassan. When I met her, Amina was dressed in a sleeveless blouse and a pair of tight black jeans. But she informed me that, in public, she always wore hijab. 'This allows me to go about my business,' she said, 'and there is no hassle. People in the West see us in our hijab, they say we are mistreated. These people come from a place where women make themselves sick so they can be thin and they go to nightclubs where they are drugged and raped. We have hijab, you have rape. I know which one I prefer.' Interestingly, even in Master Philip's day – when women were hardly emancipated in Europe – Jacques de Vitry, Bishop of Acre, saw fit to sneer at the 'Saracen fashion', in which men 'shut up their wives' and 'wrap up both of them and their daughters with cloths, that they may not be seen'.

and trill of Aline Khalaf, the Lebanese pop princess whose kohl-eyed image smouldered on posters, calendars and café TV screens – towards the souk.

It was an extraordinary place – an Orientalist's fantasy, mixing the slatternliness of Jerome Golmard's silk-mercers with the sumptuousness of the *Thousand and One Nights*. 'These markets,' wrote Master Philip's Muslim contemporary Ibn Jubayr, 'are all roofed with wood, so that their occupants enjoy an ample shade, and all hold the gaze from their beauty, and halt in wonder those who are hurrying by.' The description still held true. Hunchbacks dragged sacks of cardamom past fat pasha figures who invited us in for tea, while bartering with minaret-shaped odalisques over pieces of muslin, the material that first reached 'the West' through 'the Crusaders'. Each street was dedicated to a particular trade – tin-smiths, glass-blowers, silk-weavers – a feature with which Master Philip would have been more familiar from his experience of Europe than I was from mine. I stopped to marvel at the colours in the Street of the Spice-Sellers: the rusty red of Aleppo pepper, golden pyramids of turmeric, purple fingers of aubergine. The air was thick with the spices' sharp and tangy scents. What would they have meant to Master Philip? He lived in the Age of Spices, when they dominated international trade as oil does now; and, like oil, they were primarily found in the East. They were fundamental to food preservation and useful for medicinal purposes – Master Philip would have known that ginger helps digestion and clove comforts the sinews, that nutmeg is good for the spleen and mace helps colic. They were passed round on silver platters, sprinkled in beer and boiled with wine, paid out in lieu of gold, bequeathed as heirlooms, used to cover up the taste of foul food, and presented as diplomatic gifts: in 1194, Richard the Lionheart demonstrated his magnanimity to the visiting King of Scotland by a daily provision of pepper and cinnamon. But their greatest virtue? Spices (so went popular opinion) were the very breath of paradise.

Europe's craze for spices outlasted the Crusades and became the principal catalyst behind the voyages of discovery, galvanizing such breakthroughs as Vasco da Gama's sea route to India. But, with the realization that terra incognita wasn't as magical as wags had promised, spices lost their value. Around the same time as Europe discarded the quest for Prester John, its tastes veered away from spices and towards native aromatic herbs. Both promised terrestrial paradise; both declined when the search for terrestrial paradise was abandoned.

In the souk, the smells of the spices and the surreal lighting of the square hatches that shot sunlight through the roof, spotlighting random shop staff in dust-mote shafts like some celestial advertising ploy – a scrawny matchstick-seller illuminated rather than a *nargileh*-puffing plastic-cow salesman ('Seeria much farmland!'), a snub-nosed shoeshine boy given precedence over a merchant with a mutton-chop moustache; these, welded to the corkscrew structure, the din of the marketplace, the fetishistic flash of a hijabed lady's ankle, contributed to the multi-layered, madcap atmosphere.

Moments flash through my memory. Mr Mutton-chop Moustache resting one hand on my shoulder as he fills my nostrils with the smell of his lunch. His other hand holds a scabbard embossed with an image of the Virgin Mary.

'No business this many weeks,' he moans, 'because the war with the Eezra'eel!' drawing out the name of his nation's enemy with the ugly pronunciation that perfectly conveys the Arabs' attitude towards it.

Another moment, Athliat clasps my elbow as he narrates his childhood in the mountains – 'we must hide because we follow the faith of the prophet Zartusht'. Suddenly he folds himself inside his shoulders when he decides that the chickpea-seller eyeing him from his dust-shaft must be a member of the *mukhabarat* – the secret police.

Later, an effete teenager whose elbows are hinged to his sides whisks me into a trinket shop, where Mike sits under tinkling lamp-holders and a poster of Oscar Wilde, rubbing his stomach as he sips his tea. Hovering over him, patting his throat as he opines that 'the only way for to rid of temptation is to yield to', is a self-proclaimed aesthete called Sebastian. His T-shirt might display an Arabic logo, and his buffed complexion might imply a Levantine pedigree, but Sebastian knows where his heart belongs.

'It is simple, my dear,' he purrs, one hand flat on the lid of his lacquered pot as he trickles mint tea into china cups. 'Oscar is one of my lovers.'

And then the rush of oxygen as we emerge from the must and fruit-flavoured tobacco and the whiff of dozens of spice sacks; and Mike, who's been looking slightly queasy since I found him, celebrates our arrival at the citadel by – in front of an audience of two taxi-drivers and a man on a donkey – reproducing last night's shashlik kebab on its steps.

Out of his mouth stumble the words 'need' and 'bed'.

Once Mike was tucked in at the hotel, I returned for a proper look round the place that, for fifteen years, was home to the Gargamel of Outremer.

Reynald de Chatillon, only recently reprieved by Manuel Comnenos after his anarchic invasion of Cyprus, had learned nothing. When, one day in 1160, he spotted a band of unarmed herdsmen in the Euphrates Valley, he couldn't resist. He swept out, made away with their cattle and crashed into a group of Saracen soldiers alerted by the herdsmen. Reynald was bound to the back of a camel, carried to the citadel and consigned to the dungeon. Deep, dark, wet: as fitting a home as he'd ever have. No one made much effort to ransom him, until, fifteen years later, Aleppo's ruler feared conquest by Saladin. Governor Gumushtekin appealed to Prince Raymond of Tripoli. As payment, he offered Reynald. Which is rather like giving your mother a coronary thrombosis for Christmas.

The citadel hunches high over Aleppo, 'like a round table rising from the ground', as Ibn Jubayr put it; wrapped in stout walls and gates decorated with mythical beasts, flourishing inscriptions and great corbels that look like giants' fists. The cobbles dog-leg between inner gates and odd curiosities – among them a tomb, draped in green velvet, adorned with framed calligraphy and an image of the Kaba'a of Mecca.

'Al-Khadir,' announced its gap-toothed guardian. He clutched my arm and pointed reverently towards the tomb.

Al-Khadir? I'd heard of al-Khadir before, 'the Green One', who drank from the Fountain of Youth and tested Moses in the ways of God.* But my last encounter with him suggested a surprising tradition. That afternoon, in al-Jdeida, Aleppo's Pimlico, where our nostrils filled with the scent of flower boxes and newly applied paint, a gangly-limbed deacon had dragged Mike and me into the Greek Catholic Church. Much of the church's iconography appeared to be dedicated to the same saint: duelling with a knight, groaning under a wheel, gripping a dragon by the neck as he protected a princess.

'Al-Khadir,' said the deacon.

'St George surely,' retorted Mike.

Could there be a link? How could the Roman-soldier-turned-Christian-martyr be linked to the heavenly guide of Islamic lore? But the Green One, like St George, was also credited with the redemption of a sacrificial maiden from a rapacious dragon. Separate Christian and Muslim traditions

* In a Qu'ranic passage that also includes mention of Gog and Magog. Some apocryphal Muslim texts located al-Khadir in an earthly paradise called Yuh, ruling over saints and angels; others placed him on a green carpet in the heart of the sea. Some believe that he can be reached through the Bir al-Waraqa in Jerusalem. A man once descended from this point in a bucket and was shown the Garden of Paradise by al-Khadir. He was also linked with Alexander the Great, who failed to discover the Fountain of Youth in the same mission that gave al-Khadir his immortality.

had severed them, but here in Aleppo they were sutured back together.*

Cupolas and yellow-grassed terraces proved stepping stones to the top of the citadel. Underneath me, concrete and sandstone and the odd construction site spread towards the cotton fields and olive groves of the Syrian littoral. Beyond them would be the grimy port of Latakia, the next day's first destination. We had allocated ourselves two days to reach Lebanon, via three Crusader castles, a fortress built by a sect that was neither Crusader nor Saracen, and the Crusader town of Tartus. This wasn't only the 'Arab world'. It was also, as it had once been for young T. E. Lawrence, the world of the Crusades. The world whose fragile state injected urgency into Master Philip's mission. The world that would carry us all the way to Egypt and the Nile, the river that swam into the heart of Prester John's putative empire.

But, as we staggered to Aleppo's bus station the next morning to start our sojourn in Crusaderana, the omens were – well, dreadful. Mike was still suffering from something he'd eaten; I felt like I had been eaten, by the bedbugs that had tucked into me as soon as I'd tucked myself in.

And then there were the taxi-drivers. They filled the port town of Latakia, typing extortion into their pocket calculators, each insisting that he – and he alone – could (at great personal cost, he did this only as a favour to us, his special friends) magic us to the castle of Sayhoune. There was, they each assured us, no cheaper way. What about the microbus, we asked. Ha! You've more chance of finding an Eezra'eelee embassy.

* In fact, the Green One is common to all three of the great monotheistic faiths. A Jewish legend credits him with bringing a sack of coins to the Jews of Hebron to pay an unjust tax imposed by an Ottoman pasha. Like his former pupil, Moses, he is a testament to the shared heritage of Christians, Muslims and Jews.

But there *was* a cheaper way. There was the microbus. As we negotiated with its driver, a crowd of children and entrepreneurs swamped us with fruit, drinks and shoe polish, only to be swept aside by the driver's lackey, who pushed us inside and swung the door shut.

It was a beautiful landscape, where fudge-coloured pathways sliced through lemon-and-lime fields and ran between flat-roofed lumps of Turkish delight. From posts in the street hung the ubiquitous Holy Trinity of Syrian propaganda: the Assad *deisis*. Earnest, swan-necked Bashar and Action Man Basil, in beret and shades, gazed across the peasant population. Between them was Hafez, in jacket and tie and fake favourite-uncle smile.

We gripped the seats in front as the road twisted about, no more reliable than the taxi-drivers – bending one way, then the other, before doubling up on itself, swooping up a precipice and plunging into a seventy-five-foot ravine. At the top of a shaggy, conifer-spiked spur was a grey-brick horseshoe, 'a well-fortified and strong castle', as Saladin's secretary, Beha ad-Din, admitted. Slices of cliff darted towards a straw-strewn stairwell that disappeared into a thicket of firs. Here was Sayhoune, T. E. Lawrence's 'splendid keep, of semi-Norman style, perfect in all respects'.

Behind the brattices we turned into knights, marching up steps, down tunnels, between boulder-shaped columns, among collections of rubble where pieces of plinth and the edges of capitals sat like chunks of meat in a sloppy stew. Mike (because yesterday's illness should not be interpreted as a Sign of Weakness) made sure that he was the first to the top: 'See, al-Jub,' he said, using the nickname that he gave me throughout the 'Arab world', 'just a temporary blip.'

We leaned over the machicolations that were used to pour boiling oil on to would-be usurpers, and gazed across the canyon. Like the most fanciful Arabic calligraphy, brambles and bushes spindled towards the Mediterranean, a sapphire necklace hanging in the cleavage of the mountains. Behind us loomed the summit that Saladin used to conquer the fortress in 1188. His men knocked out the Franks by tossing boulders into the keep, then swept inside to fill not just their booty-bags but also their bellies. Beha ad-Din watched his co-religionists seize 'cooking-pots, in which food had just been prepared, and eat while battling against the castle'. The medieval warrior's version of the office sandwich.

Looking across Sayhoune – and, later that afternoon, scrambling up pitch-black stairwells and tiptoeing across the crenellated ramparts of al-Marqab, a bulwark of black basalt that perched, like a bird of prey, on an olive-green hilltop – I felt a frisson of Master Philip's world.

Under al-Marqab's muscular round towers, 'which seem rather to sustain the sky than to provide defence', as Wilbrand of Oldenburg suggested in 1212, a carpet of brambles crackled towards a vaulted dining hall. The smell of bats' droppings cloyed where newly discovered ingredients once smoked from the chimney-shaped ovens.

'Wouldn't mind being a knight!' Mike pounced from a stone screen that looked like it had been constructed for the sole purpose of eavesdropping.

'Let's climb up here,' he said, spiralling to the top of a cob-webbed tower. It was the sort of place you'd expect to find some medieval damsel, tears rolling down her cheeks and a fountain of hair bound inside a pointy hat.

'*Salam-u aleykum,*' announced Mike.

Who was he addressing? I scrambled to the top. He'd made himself comfy on a metal bedstead under posters of the Assads. But he hadn't found Melisende of Tripoli. Hovering over a tin kettle was a hairy man in a string vest and a pair of ripped jeans.

'*Ahlain,*' he said. Welcome.

We managed to work out that he was fitting telephone cables. Why, or for whom, we couldn't fathom. He poured us glasses of mint tea, sat down beside us and fingered his prayer beads. Tea with a Saracen! Reynald de Chatillon would be appalled.

That evening, the sun hitched up its pink petticoats to expose night over the old Crusader port of Tartus. Steam from our tea glasses warmed our chins while the gusts from the sea tugged at our spines. From gurgling *nargileh*s and the mouths of sloth-eyed men came thick swirls of smoke, screening the daughters who fiddled with fibrils of luxuriant hair. Children glided scooters past the youths playing 'Who's got the toughest scowl?' in men-only cafés, and pedalled into the medieval city, where vaulted arches loomed over them, balconies peeked out at them and bedsheets stroked their heads. There were rats and goat droppings, open drains and buckets full of soapy water and the callused hands of washerwomen.

We found two bits of Crusaderana in Tartus. One of them was the cathedral, whose grey and cream-coloured façade shouldered out from the ribbed arches that lidded its doors and windows. Its sides bulged with buttresses and loopholes pierced its towers: it looked more like a fortress than a church, capturing the medieval confusion between piety and pugnacity. Inside, Greek sparred with Persian for mastery of a triapsidal Gothic structure. The former's tessellated Poseidon, winged Athena swelling on a sarcophagus, and the curling leaves of its Corinthian column-heads vividly expressed the absorption of Greek culture into medieval Christendom; the same interest that contributed such elements as Alexander the Great's 'Letter to Aristotle' to the legend of Prester John.

The other evidence of Crusader occupation could be found tucked under silk shawls, stubbling swarthy chins, trimmed over a clipboard in our hotel:

'This town,' said Mike as we paid our bill in the morning, 'has got a lot of redheads.'

George, our red-haired hotelier, agreed. 'They say it's the Crusaders.'

'Seriously?'

'Why you are surprised? They was here a long time. And the Arab womans are beautiful, no?'

It was a good day for Arab womans. Muhammad, my neighbour on the microbus to Masyaf, gave them a ringing endorsement. But then, Muhammad gave womans of all nations a ringing endorsement. We had abandoned Outremer for the sinister world of a sect that would have haunted Master Philip's journey through northern Syria: the knife-thrusting Assassins – reputed Inhalers of Hemp and precursors to the modern-day suicide bomber – as famous for their unusual brand of terrorism as for the reputed liberality of their morals.

But first, a meeting with Muhammad's morals. He had the faintest rumour of a moustache, which he stroked proudly, as if it was as thick as a Syriac priest's.

'You like Arab womans?' he asked me, as an ice-breaker.

'Very nice,' I said.

'You like make with Arab womans?'

'I'm sorry?'

'You go Homs, I have friend her name Aisha. You give her fifteen dollars, she make with you. Or you like Armeni, Georgi, Rooossi?'

Muhammad was the national expert on the art of 'making with'. He had apparently 'made with' a member of every nation that ever passed through Syria. The 'best womans' of all were the Czechs, the measure of 'best womans' being the contours that he traced through the air, kneading the female body part that men in the East often liken to pomegranates. But maybe Baritanya could outclass even the great Bohemian bulges? An address was scribbled and before Muhammad gave me back my wrist I had weakly agreed to help him build up his harem.

There was a hint of more liberality as the arched peak of

the Assassins' castle followed our progress between the clumpy stone-built houses – not so much square-cut sugar cubes as misshapen lumps of barley sugar – that sank into underground trenches.

'Well-com,' said a shopkeeper, handing us bottles of Coke.

He wished us the grace of God and asked us what we were doing here. I remembered the Arabic for Assassins – '*Al-Hashishiyyin.*'

'Hashish!'

His eyes twinkled like a cavalier's as he tweezered his fingers around an imaginary joint.

'Hmm, you go for it,' said Mike. 'Smoke hash here and they'll lock you up.'

'No.' The shopkeeper chuckled, slapping a hand against Mike's shoulder. 'Here – cocaine!'

The Hashishiyyin gave Europe two words – assassin and hash: someone who wastes people, and a way to get wasted. They first emerged in the Persian wilderness – a heretics' playground, a hangout for Zoroastrians and Gnostic Christians, both of whom contributed to the Hashishiyyin's eccentric Ismaelite brand of Islam. It's no wonder the Sunni and Shiite authorities disapproved: the Ismaelis rejected traditional Islamic rituals, insisted that Muhammad's revelation wasn't God's final word, and developed obsessive personality cults around their leaders. More practically, the Hashishiyyin had a habit of knocking off public figures: viziers, muftis and emirs were felled in mosque, harem or rose garden, by *fedayeen* disguised as students and Sufis. The Crusaders were delighted by the murder of Muslim notables. They were somewhat less delighted when the Hashishiyyin killed important Franks such as Raymond II of Tripoli.

After Raymond's murder, in 1152, the Templars descended on Assassin territory, forcing a twenty-year tribute that was concluded by a surprising meeting between the Syrian Assassin leader Rashid ad-Din Sinan and King Amalric of

Jerusalem. According to William of Tyre, Sinan offered to convert to Christianity.

Sinan, known to the Crusaders as the 'Old Man of the Mountain' for the mythic powers that enabled him to rule the Ismaeli territories of central Syria for three invincible decades, was at his peak in 1177. In that year, the Muslim historian Kamal ad-Din grumbled, 'men and women mingled in drinking sessions, no man abstained from his sister or daughter, the women wore men's clothes and one of them declared that Sinan was his god.' Two years earlier, Barbarossa's envoy, Gerhard of Strasbourg, marvelled at the Old Man's potency. 'This prince,' he wrote, 'possesses in the mountain numerous and most beautiful palaces' where 'he has many of the sons of his peasants brought up'. They were taught that the prince, Sinan himself, 'has power over all living gods' and 'will give them the joys of paradise' so that, when their training had been completed, 'the prince gives each of them a golden dagger and sends them out to kill whichever prince he has marked down.'

In 1176, Sinan's power was demonstrated by his victory over no less a leader than Saladin. When one of Sinan's *fedayeen* struck Saladin's chain mail, the great warrior hurtled his siege-engines to Masyaf, his enemy's stronghold. The Old Man of the Mountain couldn't possibly overpower the Defender of the Faith. But, after just a week, the siege had been lifted.

Rumour, inevitably, spilt through the souks. Saladin, it was claimed, had woken up one morning to find, beside his bed, a poisoned hemp-cake and a letter from Sinan. How his bodyguard had been penetrated, or why he hadn't been killed, was less important than the realization that the Assassins weren't to be messed with. Instead they became partners, and Saladin used the Assassins in his decisive victory over the Crusaders at the Horns of Hattin.

Masyaf doesn't look like the impregnable fortress that defied Saladin. It seems too small. But it has an atmosphere that larger castles have lost, erupting out of jagged rocks like a gigantic digestive biscuit moulded by Mary Shelley. Its square towers and crumbling walls sputter as the tentacles of fruitless trees wind out of the earth and threaten to choke them.

Up a steep stairwell, a cavernous hall was cluttered with scaffolding, architectural sketches and a bushy-bearded misanthrope.

'You no want to see castle?' He watched us warily, as if such an aspiration might bring down the sky.

'We've come an incredible distance,' I said.

'Just to see this castle,' added Mike.

'I am working.'

'Oh, *habibi* – my dear,' said Mike, 'pleeeease!'

'I am working.'

'You know,' I said, hands piously clasped like a choirboy, 'how the *fedayeen* used to throw themselves off the battlements? If you don't let us in, we'll be reduced to such despair we might do something similar.'

He shook his head like we'd really let him down. 'Ten minutes,' he muttered.

A wooden bridge carried us to a bumpy rock face that slipped into the gravelly gallery cloaking the cisterns, where we poked around subterranean catacombs and squeezed through jagged openings like dragons' maws. There was a stout turret that sneered across yellow fields full of fat-tailed sheep, and tiny cells, once bedrooms to the *fedayeen*, and light passageways where ladders and scaffolding disrupted the Hammer Horror atmosphere. As if to compensate for the lack of tension, the wind made a terrific, howling effort that temporarily estranged Mike from his hat and blasted me into an open-ended corridor so long that its heart was black. Standing in that airless, lightless vacuum, I had my Hashishiyyin moment. I imagined daggers plunging between the folds of *fedayeen* cloaks, and when I heard a scuttle I think I jumped. A lizard shot out from a pile of stones. Then I heard Mike's voice in the distance, and we wandered back across the wooden bridge.

It was time to leave Syria. Tripoli, our first target in Lebanon, was not only closer to Masyaf than Damascus but also in the same Crusader state – the County of Tripoli – as castles such as al-Marqab. The tattooist and body-builder of a mountain-top monastery and the mobile-phone rings of a Damascene storyteller's salon would have to wait. As – judging from the gang of villainous-looking taxi-drivers in the industrial sprawl of Homs – would Lebanon.

They weren't taxi-drivers, after all – despite their owner-ship of several taxis, they were in fact professional backgammon players. Even when, finally, one of them admitted to a weakness for commerce, nudging us into his Mercedes with fork-prong fingers, his price quickly nudged us out.

'That's it,' announced Mike, positioning himself in their midst and defiantly planting his legs. Within seconds, hubbly-bubblies and backgammon chips had been abandoned. The entire taxi-driving community peered, their expressions ranging from amusement to consternation (and one of them even looking quite impressed), as he sang out the Coldplay hit 'Yellow'.

'This,' said a driver called Abu Ibrahim, who wore a denim waistcoat over his *gelabiyya* and had a thickly stubbled face the shape of a cinder block, 'Western muzika?'

Mike nodded eagerly. Abu Ibrahim nodded, less eagerly, and drove us towards the Lebanese mountains. Rust-coloured tanks overflowed with ant-like soldiers, before the scorched firing ranges coloured into the hills' palettes of green and brown. We approached towers of blue rock, matted woodland and then – squatting in the cleft of the mountains, surveying its surroundings like a pasha in his harem – a symmetrical vision of semicircular towers bursting out of white ramparts: the Krak des Chevaliers. Behind the castle, emphasizing its ideal location for control of medieval trade, an eye of silver sea peeked through a curtain of cliffs, hinting at the commerce that boosted the coffers of the Hospitallers. Sunlight shot arrowheads between a medley of pillars or haloed from ogival windows in the cloisters. Near a pea-green moat, carved lions recalled the English 'Lionheart' known to the Arabs as 'Malik Rik'. It was the most sophisticated of all the castles and took us two hours to explore. Which meant that, as we scrambled down the zigzag corridor that weaved out of the lower bailey, recalling the citadel of Aleppo, Abu Ibrahim was having a fit.

'I say one hour,' he screamed, 'you take two!'

'Oh, Abu Ibrahim,' said Mike soothingly, 'don't be angry.'

Abu Ibrahim glared: his face had turned beetroot, as if all the blood in his body was having an emergency meeting in his face.

'Here you go,' said Mike, offering him a tape.

'No Western muzika!' he snapped, and turned up the volume to music that was more to his taste. A chanteuse vibrated her vowels in a tonsil-rattling cluster. Her voice was high and theatrical, more opera than pop. She was replaced by a Syrian boy-band: a male chorus, chanting to a martial downbeat with deep, angry voices. I couldn't decipher the lyrics but I guessed, from my experience of Palestinian music the previous year, that we were listening to the two strands to which we'd managed to reduce modern Arabic music: the *habibi* 'my dear' song; and the *harb* 'war' song.

Abu Ibrahim's music, like the tunes that played in the Syrian souks, was very different from Western tunes, despite the latter's debt to the former. Before the Crusades, European sounds were sacred and monophonic, but the harp-wielding troubadours came back with lutes, psalters and a musical revolution.* European castles and town squares resonated to harmony and instrumental accompaniment; the sound of entertainment changed for ever. It's stretching things to suggest that, without Arabic music, the Beatles would have been a quartet of monophonic harpists; but not by much.

Abu Ibrahim dropped us at the Lebanese border, where Syrian workers, anxious for employment in Lebanon, formed a queue as thick and unwieldy as some of their beards. Lebanon, Lebanon, I thought, with a certain apprehension: the land where corpses were tied to taxis like bunting is to wedding cars and bombs were planted in florists' plastic rocks or dialled up by mobile phone.

'Right,' said Mike, braced for the third degree, 'we're just tourists, want to see a few castles and churches. Never heard of Hizbollah.'

When we reached our turn, the officer handed us some forms, asked for the entrance tax and smiled.

'Well-com in Lebanon,' he said.

At once, we were enveloped in class: avenues of plane trees either side of our taxi, and a typical Lebanese couple either side of us. She was absolutely gorgeous, with long black hair,

---

* Some of them didn't come back. Jaufre Rudel shot to fame with the love ditties that he sent to the Countess of Tripoli, the same Melisende who was rejected by Manuel Comnenos. When the Second Crusade was announced, Jaufre followed his poems across the sea, fell ill en route and died in the arms of his beloved. Melisende gave him a grand burial and, grimly accepting that she was not destined to be lucky in love, ensconced herself in a nunnery. The story is typical of the troubadours – the pop stars of the medieval Mediterranean, whose romantic dalliances and exotic adventures turned them into cult figures. It had been suggested to me that Master Philip was a troubadour. I rather liked the idea of him plucking a lute and composing his *canzoni* to his oriental sweetheart. But it was impossible: the troubadours' principal base was heretical Provence. A troubadour was as likely a papal ambassador as Mick Jagger.

perfect skin and teeth, and a scent like crushed flowers; he was fat and stank of arak, but he had a gold watch.

When the Crusaders captured Tripoli in 1109, it took a seven-year siege; after which they slew as many civilians as they could find, and burnt a hundred thousand volumes of Arabic, Persian and Greek learning in the library of Banu Ammar. Our arrival was much less fraught. *Gelabiyya*-clad, slipper-shod men filled the dusk with shrieks and whistles as they shunted their vegetable barrels or mobile cupboards splashing with fruit juice. Our taxi dropped us under an Ottoman clock tower and, before we could even close its doors, they had us surrounded.

'Do you know where Rue Tall is?' asked Mike.

'Amareeka?'

'Inglizi. Rue Tall?'

'I like Amareeka.'

'Aha. You know Rue Tall?'

'Amareeka good, much money.'

'Great. Rue Tall?'

'Y'all right, mate?'

An unmistakably antipodean accent emerged from an old man in a *gelabiyya*. He was the most unlikely Aussie I'll ever meet. He escorted us to Rue Tall, chattering about rugby, cricket and the Olympics, before running off to the evening prayers.

The Hôtel des Cedres offered the cheapest rooms in town. Which meant it was pitch-black, you could hear the rustle of rats on the three flights of steps, and the vestibule had lost its floor to a swamp. The manager handed us a couple of candles and introduced us to our room. It stank, sounded of cockroaches, and once we'd unpeeled our covers we could discern the precise shapes of our predecessors.

'Only one way we'll get any sleep tonight,' said Mike grimly. His voice and shadow faded, I heard the rattle of distant footsteps and, minutes later, he returned with a bottle of arak procured from a nearby kebab-vendor. It performed its function with aplomb: within an hour I had passed out, numbed to my hyperactive bedmates, and was floating dreamily into the more salubrious Tripoli that Master Philip would have visited . . .

The Fourth Letter of Master Philip to Roger of Salerno

To Roger, by the grace of God most glorious doctor of Salerno, his most dear friend, Master Philip of Venice, sends greetings.

Truly does Outremer testify the beneficence of God towards his faithful. For the city of Tripolis boasts lush gardens and elegant villas with running water. Tumblers and minstrels perform in every corner, unsettling the market stalls where burgesses trade such goods as silk cloths and glass and sugar. There are four thousand looms for the silk, which is purchased at great expense to cover the ladies, who spend all their labour on their garments and gild their veils with gold thread and cover their faces in paint.

The people play dice and go to the baths and frolic in the gardens with no distinction of gender, nor of sects. For the city is overrun with Assyrians and Armenians and Greeks, also Ninevites and Saracens and Bedouins and Khorazmians and Turcomans. And Tripolis is controlled by the Provençals, so that much heresy is practised, for they preach the teachings of Persian priests and refuse to swear oaths. But I do not fear overly for Tripolis, because the city throngs with knights and the children play at being knights. They jump on each other's shoulders and wield sticks and cry out the phrases that they have heard on the lists.

The count of the city is a Toulousian called Raymond, of eagle-like features and swarthy complexion. He bedecks himself in silk and muslin and eats from copper plates incised with ungodly patterns by Saracen craftsmen. He entertained me in the citadel, where the food included doves stuffed with chestnuts and subtleties fashioned from sugar and almond-paste. Truly, dear Roger, they eat well in these parts! This count is a serious man of great knowledge, which he learned in captivity in Aleppo. He speaks the language of the Saracens, which enables him to apprehend their plots. And he believes that Outremer depends on this: namely, that the Christians must trade and converse with the Saracens, and treat them as their brothers. I asked him if he wished to spread the apostolic creed among the heretics in his dominion. And he replied in a strange manner. For he said that not only will he not impose his faith on others, but he welcomes that the different communities have their own law courts and their elders are like little princes in his county. And he says that this is important, because there are but two hundred and fifty thousand Latins in Outremer, and there are five times as many of other creeds, both heretics and pagans, as well as the numberless horde in the desert. And so he even hires a heretic for his physick. But there is one creed that – O wondrous event! – is seeking to return to the True Church: these people had followed the heretical doctrines of a certain Maro, from whom they took the name of Maronites. And they are many in number, and a stalwart and valiant people, of great service to the count, for they understand the terrain and the wiles of the pagans. But while these people seek to unite with us Latins, there are divisions that cause great concern.

Even within the walls of the citadel I witnessed this, for a fight erupted between two knights. One wore a black mantle embroidered with a white cross, and he was of the Order of the Hospital. The other wore a red cross on the left breast of his surcoat, for he was of the Order of the Temple. And the count demanded that they return their baselards to their sheaths. The knight of the Temple marched to the portcullis and made much mention of the devil, as Franks are wont to do. But the knight of the Hospital greeted us and called himself Sir Guido. And when the count enquired after the cause of the dispute, Sir Guido explained that it was a little thing. But he escorted me to a tavern, and he told me that he blamed the Templars for the divisions at the High Court of Jerusalem, and that the Master of the Temple is in league with the Count of Oultrejourdain to inspire trouble and strife.

The tavern was in the Genoese commune, a house of many floors with a flat roof and a storehouse, where stood manifold jars filled with sugar. In a courtyard inside, men sat on floors paved with mosaics, among tapestries and silk. Dishes were formed from flat bread, and there were many kinds of drink, both sugared lemon and barley beer made with wheat, rice and walnuts. Perhaps, dear Roger, you think this was verily paradise, but if so I shall keep my feet on God's earth, for the noise was great in this tavern. Not only from the music played by troubadours. One sang of Floire and Blanchfleur, but the greater applause was reserved for him who sang of lechery. And there were Saracen dancing girls who displayed their flesh and intoxicated the men with their jewellery and their strange smells. This caused great distress among the Christian harlots, so that there was much scraping of fingernails and a Saracen girl lost one of her eyes. Nor was this all, for a Pisan accused a Venetian of stealing a crier's stone, and the crowd baited him to exact vengeance with his knife, and furthermore among my own company was a great tempest in the form of the Templar. He accosted Sir Guido and blood rose in their cheeks, and would have spilt from their veins had not this contest been disrupted by the remonstrations of an old priest. For he threw himself between their swords, tore his hair and clothes, and burst forth: 'Truly, the kingdom of Christ is in peril. For whereas our forefathers were religious men fearful of God, in their places has grown a generation of sinners and falsifiers, who run the course of all unlawful things without discrimination.' And after this speech, Sir Guido and the Templar made a pact and Sir Guido bade me farewell.

But I was eager to hear the words of this Templar, so I sat with him, and he told me that he was aggrieved by Sir Guido's taunts, for he considered his order to be responsible for the redemption of Outremer. For not three months before now, the Saracens attempted to seize the Holy City. And because the compact between the Franks and the Greeks had fallen to disarray, and the Count of Flanders had occupied himself chiefly at the banquet table, Saladin besieged the king in Ascalon. But though the pagan horde was great, it was undone by its wickedness, for as the Saracens were pillaging the land, the Templars arrived at the hill of Montgisard, zealous for the fray. He described to me the sight of rocks hurled from trebuchets and the clash of mace and baselard. It was terrifying in the telling, yet he never doubted victory. For he saw St George fighting alongside him. And therefore the Saracens fled, hiding their breastplates and ironshod boots in the march, and perishing from the rains that God sent down to afflict them.

Dear Roger, I must leave off this letter. Does all go well in Salerno? I often imagine us together in the academy, comparing waters and studying the recommendations of Archimatheus. Such thoughts are great comfort during a difficult journey. I wish you well and remember you in my prayers.

Tripoli is a city of two halves. There is dirty Tripoli, a spider's web of crumbling alleyways that trap the scent of rotten fruit and exhale it over the children running coat hangers along the earthen streets. And there is chic Tripoli, a city of French-style parks, Lancôme perfumeries and the Banque du Liban et Outremer. The two cities meet when a lady in a gabardine trouser suit buys *Paris Match* from the same street corner that provides a woman in dowdy hijab with soggy lamb shawarma in torn paper bags. Combining Syrian scruffiness with Lebanese Francophilia, Tripoli captures the problem of Lebanon. Does it belong to the 'Arab world' or is it – the only country in the Middle East with a Christian head of state – the last bastion of the Crusades?

The most conspicuous Crusader relic is the old citadel, built by the House of Toulouse. Beyond a stepped street full of clutter – empty tins, fruit skins, goat detritus – a polychrome block of limestone and basalt loomed over the tombs of an Islamic cemetery. Inside a gateway framed in black-and-white bands and an Arabic inscription, narrow staircases spiralled into wet-smelling cells curdled with lichen. Blades of sunlight skewered through slit windows and guided us up to the esplanade that glanced across the vista: a mountain of apartments, teeming with balustrades and bedsheets and drying underwear, looming over a grey lowland of cube-shaped houses.

In Master Philip's day, the citadel was home to one of Outremer's most important leaders. Raymond III of Toulouse was just twelve when his father's assassination thrust the title of count before his name. He hadn't even mastered those crucial arts of hawking, jousting and Latin; as soon as he had, he was captured in battle and locked in a dungeon in Aleppo with a copy of the Qu'ran and Reynald de Chatillon. Judging from his fluency in Arabic and his later animosity towards Reynald, the book was his preferred jail-mate.

Eight years and a fifty-thousand-dinar ransom later, Raymond's return to public life saw him instated as regent to the child-king Baldwin IV and an inevitable target of the

Frankish hawks. The likes of Reynald and Odo of St Amand, Master of the Templars, couldn't stand him: his beard, his *gelabiyya*, his habit of signing independent treaties with Saladin, his weakness for Muslim masons and physicians. When he escaped the thrashing at the Horns of Hattin, gossip inevitably cast him as Saladin's bosom buddy and had him prostrating himself towards Mecca.

But Raymond was far from the only Crusader to take an interest in all things Eastern. Long before Richard Burton started wandering Sindh in native disguise and Eugène Delacroix erected his easel in front of Moroccan prostitutes, Orientalism enjoyed its first flowering. Men who came to the East to subjugate its citizens were conquered by its customs. Men like the Antiochene Frank who pops up in the memoirs of the twelfth-century emir Usamah Ibn Munqidh: 'Eat, be of good cheer! I never eat Frankish dishes, but I have Egyptian women cooks and never eat except their cooking.'

Christians and Muslims were getting together in banking, in the surgery, in the souk, even in the marriage bed (which is just about as together as you can get). The letter of Prester John, with its wide range of source material, celebrates the cultural interaction accidentally triggered by the Crusades. As the chronicler Fulcher of Chartres marvelled, 'we who were Occidentals now have been made Orientals.'

A few corners from the citadel, the Orientalist-Crusaders' flair for accommodation with the enemy was recreated in that modern-day shrine to cultural crossover – an internet café.

'Why you come in Lebanon?' asked the miserable manager, as he doodled despairingly on a sheet of paper.

'For tourism,' said Mike.

'Is a bad country. I want to go to Eezra'eel and marry a woman there.'

'But I thought Arabs hated Israel?' I said.

'In Eezra'eel is work, is money. Here, is nothing.'

Well, there wasn't strictly nothing. There were, after all, the cakes. In fact, Tripoli – and this is no mean feat – is the Middle East's official capital city of cakes.

Near the (very French) public park, the click of teacups and the scratch of slicers welcomed us into a sweet tooth's paradise. There were walnut-filled, syrup-soaked turnovers, cinnamon-sprinkled, nut-filled triangles, coffins of lacquer-latticed cheeses, almond-nippled domes of baked dough, an eternity of orange-blossomed baklava fresh in their baking pans, and an awful lot of calorifically enlarged men with cream-capped fingers. Not that we were there just to indulge ourselves. Good God, no! No, you see – well, sugar first started rotting European teeth during the Crusades. We were simply partaking of the same pleasures that inspired a Mamluke poet called Ibn Sudun to declare: 'Praise be to God the Almighty, Who bestowed upon His servants various niceties . . . He made the kernels of pistachio nuts, having been cracked, whole. He made streams of sugar syrup descend from the firmly anchored mountains of sugar, down into the bellies of the wadis of syrups.' But to any medieval pilgrim, a diet of tea and cakes could never be adequate. And so it was that I found myself attending the Great Debate.

In the Khan of the Tailors, beyond the haberdasheries where belly dancers' brassieres hung beside cotton burkas, a Lombard campanile communicated the Great Mosque's previous incarnation as a Crusader church. While Mike wandered through the prayer hall, I sat in the arcaded cloisters to scribble in my diary, watching the men washing their calves at the ablutions fountain and soaking up the Peace of Islam.

'May God,' announced a young man's voice, 'bless you with fruitful offspring and bounteous health.'

I fumbled for a reply: 'Er . . . God for you . . . a tree . . . of beautiful.'

He wore cotton pantaloons and a loose shirt. His hair was

shaven, except for a thick tuft on the crown, spared – according to Islamic tradition – so he could be lifted to heaven. He was bent over a Qu'ran, a beautifully calligraphed vellum-bound copy with gold-leaf titles.

'Mussulman?' he asked.

'*Massihi*' – Christian.

I said it apologetically, sensing his disappointment. But he clutched my hand, and introduced himself as 'Jihad'.

'Why you say Jesus Christ is God?' he asked. His eyes were calf-like, gentle and endearing.

'Well . . .' I began.

'Because,' boomed Mike, marching out of the prayer hall, 'we believe in the Holy Trinity.'

And so began *The Great Debate*:

On the left-hand side, speaking for Islam –	On the right-hand side, speaking for Christianity –
JIHAD	MIKE
'How you have *three* people in charge of *one* religion? And how God have child?'	
	'Because *nothing* is beyond God.'
'God is God, not human.'	
	'But he made man in his own image.'
(*Frowns as he struggles for the words.*) 'You think God has – how I say this?' (*Pointing to – of all places! – his crotch.*) 'For make baby?'	

193

'We think that God – is *equipped* – to do anything he wants.'*

'You think that God make love to a woman?'

'It's more complicated. Jesus isn't an ordinary human.'

'Now Jesus is not human. My friend, what *is* he?'

'Well, he's human *and* God.'

'So he is like the horse and the donkey – how you say?'

NICK: '*Mule?*'

'This is so.'

'It isn't *so* at all.'

'So Jesus is from God?'

'Yes.'

'So is Adam. This means Adam and Jesus is the same.'

'No. God created Adam, but Jesus *is* God.'

'So Mary is wife of God?'

'Not wife.'

'So Jesus is bastard?'

* This issue has always divided Muslim and Christian theologians. One of Saladin's favourite books was *The Sea of Precious Virtues*, whose author cautions that 'anyone who believes that his God came out of woman's privates is quite mad; he should not be spoken to, and he has neither intelligence nor faith.' (Mind you, the same author also counsels against sitting on swings and suggests that elephants who participate in jihad deserve a greater reward than camels.)

194

'No.'

'So Mary is wife of God and
mother of God also?'
(*Shakes a disapproving head.*)
'In our society this is not good.'

Mike, declaring himself victorious, marched towards the gateway. Before I could join him, Jihad, declaring himself equally victorious, grabbed my sleeve.

'I think you like to be Mussulman,' he said.

'I'll take that as a compliment.'

'I can make you Mussulman today.'

'Well, I'm not sure if—'

'You can marry my sister.'

'And I'm sure she's very nice, but—'

'Why not?'

I declined. I followed Mike, very quickly, out of the courtyard, en route to the bus to Byblos. There would be no *walima* for me.

CHAPTER EIGHT

THE MONK IN THE
COFFEE CUP

I WAS SQUEEZED between two young men with slick black hair and sinewy forearms that bulged out of their sleeveless T-shirts. One of them rustled in a plastic bag, ripped open discs of pitta bread, smeared them with hummus and offered them round like he was a prophet dispensing manna.

Butros, my neighbour on the bus to Byblos, was the first Maronite I met. A gold cross hung from his bovine neck and polygonal rings shone on his pudgy fingers, as if a weightlifter had inherited Manuel Comnenos' jewellery box.

'You are Christian?' he asked.

'Yes.'

'Where you go?'

'Byblos.'

'You like Byblos. Christian city. You are Catholic?'

'Yes.'

'You like Lebanon. Christian country.'

'What about the Muslims and Druze?'

'They are nothing. This is Christian land for many years. All the rich people in Lebanon is Christian. Excuse me – you say you go Byblos?'

'Yes.'

'We pass Byblos.'

A screeeech as the driver stopped. Our backpacks were tossed through a side window and ahead of us lay five kilometres of seafront, past grids of apartment blocks with wide balconies and French windows, and a beach that stretched along the coast as seductively as an odalisque on her divan. The light was fading, so we climbed down a pebbled slope and searched for a hotel. They were all too expensive – beach resorts for fat Russians, who sat in the bars, swigging vodka and stroking the shoulders of their rent-a-girlfriends.

'My backpack,' I announced, 'is killing me.'

Back in England, I had approached the job of packing as if, like King David the Builder of Georgia, I could be accompanied by a travelling library.

'Don't know what you're grumbling about,' said Mike. 'My backpack's fine.'

'That's just what I want to hear.'

'Well, DWI.'

I wheezed behind him, as bowed down as a conservative Muslim housewife following her husband. I had been millstoned by my injudicious grasp of weight distribution:

Figure 4: My backpack.

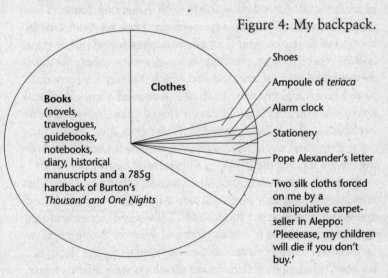

Shoes

Ampoule of *teriaca*

Alarm clock

Stationery

Pope Alexander's letter

Two silk cloths forced on me by a manipulative carpet-seller in Aleppo: 'Pleeeease, my children will die if you don't buy.'

Clothes

Books
(novels, travelogues, guidebooks, notebooks, diary, historical manuscripts and a 785g hardback of Burton's *Thousand and One Nights*

I was regretting all the books I'd packed. Did I really need all three volumes of Naguib Mahfouz's *Cairo Trilogy*? Why hadn't I found a paperback *Thousand and One Nights*? And what on earth possessed me to bring Job Ludolphus' *A New History of Ethiopia: Being a Full and Accurate Description of the Kingdom of Abessinia, vulgarly, though Erroneously, called the Empire of Prester John*?

Having swiftly abandoned the resort hotels as too expensive for our budget, we plunged into a nightmare where shadows leaped out from drainpipes, the air goosebumped our necks and my shoulder blades were surely about to snap. The sea growled and the seagulls squawked, as if by noise alone they could sink a small church on a promontory that was already half submerged. Perhaps we could sleep in its nave. Or on the porch. Mike ran up the steps. (Ran! I could barely hobble.) I followed, fuelled by curses. I cursed the cold, I cursed my books, I cursed Mike for waving so cheerfully from the esplanade. Why on earth was his face stamped with such a massive grin?

There were about twenty of them: young men and women in shorts and skirts and T-shirts with American logos. They were all good-looking and fresh-faced. They all wore crosses around their necks. And they all, once they found out that we had nowhere to stay, wanted us to stay with them. We had, through the sort of fortune for which Master Philip would have known exactly who to thank, stumbled across the local Maronite youth group. The men flexed their brawn on our backpacks; the ladies giggled and swished their hair, chins resting on their shoulders as their eyelashes flickered, crowding round us like the black-eyed houris of heaven.

'You will come with me,' said Manale, the group leader, an attractive young lady (weren't they all?) with wavy black hair and highly pronounced cheekbones. Mike and I instantly closed the gaping portholes of our mouths and assumed the appropriate air of laissez-faire explorers as two boys led us up the slope, our backpacks hanging off their broad shoulders with offensive ease.

'You like football?' asked one. 'I love Mansheesta United.'

'My team!' said Mike with a grin.

'You no like Liver-poo?' gasped another. He looked crestfallen.

'Course I do,' said Mike diplomatically. 'Michael Owen *sadiqni*!' – my friend.

A ponytail swung inches from my nose as my sleeve was grabbed by a girl whose outsize T-shirt billowed over her knee-length skirt.

'You are from London?' she asked, in a voice like an oud.

'Yep.'

Her lips, temporarily pursed as if she was about to suck a straw, were suddenly clamped by a shunt from her friend.

'Have you been to Paris?' she said.

'Several times.'

A gasp. 'This is my dream! I want to go to Paris and London.'

Her friend snorted. 'She wants to be a go-go girl in Moulin Rouge.'

Like its neighbours, Manale's house was a whitewashed villa bisected by a patio balcony that fanned into a windbreak of cypress. Standing in the doorway, a cigarette dangling from her lips and a pair of beach shorts hitched halfway up her thighs, was a large woman who looked as Oriental as the baseball cap perched on her head.

'This,' said Manale, 'is my mom.'

A chorus of 'Well-com!' ushered us inside. Manale's chain-smoking father yanked our hands, her brother Rami high-fived our palms and her sister Layale consolidated our welcome with lips the red of sealing wax. It was a dizzying introduction to Lebanese hospitality.

They couldn't do enough for us. They cleared out one of the rooms and ran about looking for fresh bedsheets. They plied us with clean towels and shampoo. They dragged our backpacks to the washing machine and laundered our clothes. And then, when they had us smelling more fragrant than at any time since we'd left England, they led us on to the balcony and pumped us up with a feast.

There were quails' eggs and foie gras, coriander-sprinkled kofta and *kibbeh*,* bowls of Pringles and platters of fish and chips: a *meze* that mixed dishes familiar to the medieval Levantine with the sort of ingredients you would find in a Home Counties kitchen. We must consider this our home, insisted Manale, as her father handed round glasses of arak; we must look on them as family; if we needed anything – more food? drink? cigarettes? – we had only to ask. We must have loukoumia and coffee. And we must see a miracle.

'It's the miracle of St Charbel,' said Manale. 'He is the great saint of Byblos.'

'He make many miracle,' added Layale, spreading a biscuit with Boursin as shawls of sleek black hair dusted her shoulders. 'There is a woman nearby. She couldn't walk. Then St Charbel made her walk, and now she bleeds from the neck.'

'She must be losing a lot of blood,' I said.

'Ha! I see you are a silly boy. She only bleeds on the twenty-second day of every month.'

While Layale turned her attention to Mike, Manale spread a set of photos across the table. They all depicted nothing more sensational than a coffee cup. At least, *I* thought it was a coffee cup.

'It's St Charbel,'† said Manale.

It looked like a coffee cup to me.

'Look carefully,' said Manale. 'St Charbel – he is *in* the cup.'

In the middle of a triangle of dregs was a white blob.

'You see?' Manale smiled, pointing to the blob. 'This is St Charbel's beard!'

It was possible, with some imagination, to discern a human figure in the dregs. But I didn't expect it of two girls the same age as us. Medieval hermits, sure, but young ladies with

---

* Grilled meatballs made with ice-cold water, originating from the Maronites' historical habitation around the icy streams of Mount Lebanon.
† A nineteenth-century Maronite who spent twenty-three years as a hermit on Mount Annaya. His corpse apparently sweated blood in the 1950s, and he has been credited with many posthumous miracles.

access to TV and the internet? Their clothes and the trappings of their house – the American videotapes scattered across the sitting room, the washing machine and the Pringles – suggested a Western orientation; but these Maronites were as prepared to credit a miracle as the Crusader knights who saw St George on the battlefield of Montgisard in 1177. They hadn't forsaken the faith of their ancestors.

Nor their customs. An offer to help with the dishes was met with an offended glare, as if I'd said something disgusting.

'You are in the Middle East,' snapped Manale. 'No man helps with the dishes in the Middle East.'

I sat down and, looking across to Mike, let my mouth expand into the great gaping cavity of the ludicrously fortunate. His smile, even more than mine, had become a thing of extraordinary size. I'd never seen him looking so happy. Beside him was Layale, and between them was a cluster of grapes, which she was hand-feeding into his mouth. Each handful made his smile bigger, so that it swelled to absurd proportions. You could have fitted a saucer inside it.

'*Oh my God!*' he exclaimed. 'Think we've just found paradise!'

Why were they so hospitable?

'We are Lebanese,' said Manale with a shrug.

It was significant that she hadn't said 'Arab'. Although it is Arabs who are famous for their hospitality, it was not as Arabs that Manale's family were offering theirs. This much was clarified by Rami, snapping me out of the post-prandial warmth of my wicker chair.

'Where you came from today?' he asked.

'Trablous.'

'Aaah!'

His neck stiffened and his head shot skywards. I thought he'd swallowed a fishbone.

'Trablous?' he repeated. 'But is – is full of –' his cheeks had screwed up to his eyes, which shone with hatred – 'is full of Mussulmans!'

'Well, we were in Syria before—'

'Syria? More Mussulmans!'

'You don't like Mussulmans?'

'We like the Christian. The Orthodox, the Suriani. We are Maronite Catholic, so we especially like the Catholics. But the Mussulman? Lebanon is for the Christians. We are the Phoenicians. The Arabs come later.'

'So you don't consider yourselves Arabs?' I asked.

'We hate Arabs!'

The love affair between the Maronites and the West began in Master Philip's era, when 'a race of Syrians in the province of Phoenicia', as William of Tyre reported, 'were restored to their right minds and abandoned their heresy.' After centuries of isolation in the rugged passes of Mount Lebanon, anathematized not only by Muslims but also by the Orthodox and Monophysite Churches, the Maronites relished their role as the Franks' Best Friend, providing the Crusaders with guides, archers and wives. When the French returned in 1920, the Maronites – whose exposure to modernization, organizational skills and expanding population had turned them into the Mount's most powerful community – put in a successful bid for their own state. But economic viability (and, some argued, French desire to retain Maronite vassalage) required that the Republic of Greater Lebanon incorporate Sunni Muslim cities such as Tripoli, the Shiite regions of South Lebanon and the Bekaa Valley, and the Chouf, homeland of the mysterious Druze.*

---

* This esoteric sect, neither Arab nor Muslim (although they accept the teaching of Muhammad and speak Arabic), dominates the Jebel Druze and the Lebanese Chouf. They believe that the last divine messenger was the eleventh-century Caliph of Egypt, al-Hakim, an eccentric ruler who ordered the destruction of the Church of the Holy Sepulchre (one of the motivations for the First Crusade), proclaimed himself divine and prohibited honey. His servant Durazi, sent to proselytize in Syria, made such a strong impression that his converts established a new religion whose beliefs were kept secret

The Muslims wanted to be part of Syria, the Maronites part of France. At a National Pact in 1943, a compromise was agreed: the Maronites could have the presidency, but the Sunnis must supply the prime minister, the Shiites the speaker of the Chamber of Deputies, and Lebanon must be defined as an 'Arab' state. And, had demography remained as consistent as the Arabs' fondness for cutting their cakes into lozenges, all would have been well and good. But demography is a slippery beast, and it likes nothing better than a good shake-up: an exploding birth rate here, a dash of emigration there, and suddenly the Muslims were clamouring for constitutional change. The Maronites could have agreed; but the only time Muslims and Maronites ever agreed was when they stood together against Ottoman Turks or the French. Lack of a common enemy can be a fatal faultline for a hotchpotch state.

Suddenly, with the fertility of the Bekaa Valley's opium plantations, Lebanon became a breeding ground for militias. The Maronite factions gave themselves names like the Knights of the Virgin, stuck Christian icons to their rifles and, as if obeying Pope Urban II's advice to the first Crusaders, sowed crosses on to their uniforms. Then a tense situation became a catastrophe.

In 1971, Yassir Arafat, having infuriated King Hussein of Jordan by attracting Israeli reprisals to PLO hijackings and guerrilla raids launched from Jordan, scuttled across the border to Lebanon disguised in a burka. Pitched battles gutted the streets of Beirut, as the Maronites turned their icon-plastered rifles on the Palestinians. The Syrians rolled in,

from the common people. Benjamin of Tudela reported of them in the 1170s, spinning out the usual accusations: 'They are steeped in vice, brothers marrying their sisters, and fathers their daughters.' But he also acknowledged the tenet that distinguishes them from their monotheistic neighbours: 'They say that at the time when the soul leaves the body it passes in the case of a good man into the body of a newborn child, and in the case of a bad man into the body of a dog or an ass.'

followed by the Americans and the Israelis. Vicious acts were carried out with such brutality that a US secretary of state compared the country to 'a plague-infested place of the Middle Ages'. This was the modern Middle East's most tragic correlative to the militant melting pot that scalded the region in the pre-Saladin twelfth century. Where once there was:

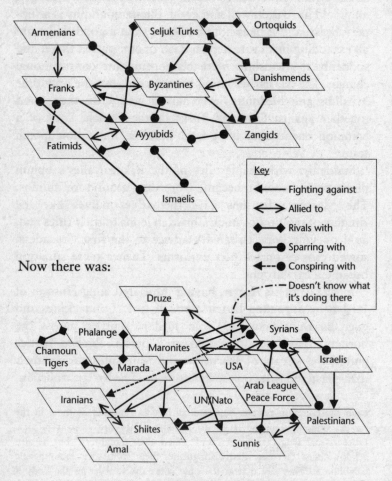

Now there was:

Figure 5: Militant melting pots.

*

When God's on your side, you can get away with the lot. Palestinians can massacre the Christians of Damour, Christians can massacre the Palestinians of Tel al-Za'atar, Druze can pour boiling water over Christians in Beit Eddine, Christians can cut out Druze tongues near Deir al-Qamar, Israelis can fling phosphorus shells into West Beirut on the off-chance they might strike a 'terrorist'. The assassination of the Maronite president, Bashir Gemayel, in September 1982 was compared by the Superior of the Maronite Order of Monks to the Crucifixion of Christ. What happened next would be less familiar to the early Church fathers than to the Crusaders who ate the grilled flesh of Muslim children in the Syrian town of Ma'ara in 1098. Israel's defence minister (one Ariel Sharon) allowed the Christian Phalange to enter the Palestinian refugee camps of Sabra and Shatila. The ensuing carnage, in which roughly a thousand refugees had their throats pulled out, their breasts sliced open, their brains blown out and crosses slashed into their chests, became the public image of the Middle East's most vicious cycle of destruction. And yet – picnics still took place in the Chouf; sunbathers still oiled themselves in Jounieh: Lebanon had become a cross between a medieval apocalyptic tract and a James Bond movie.

The first Maronite church that I saw was the Crusader-built, triapsidal Cathedral of St John, small and rather sweet, built in 1115. Rose bushes and blossom crawled behind the church and mingled their scents with the freshly cut grass. The only martial token was a pair of lions carved above the chevroned columns supporting the bell tower. Inside, the congregation was a sea of swaying arms surrounded by sandstone pillars and a golden glow that washed through the stained-glass windows. Some dried their eyes or hugged their mothers. Others petitioned a yellow-and-maroon St Charbel, who met their prayers with a laconic smile. On the porch, the mysticism was replaced by mobile phones. Men in suits lit cigarettes and conducted frantic business transactions, before returning to throw out their arms and ululate in the nave.

On our tour of Byblos, Mike and I were escorted by Layale and her equally gem-eyed friend Hinud. Perhaps our recent drought of female company released a certain competitive streak, because it wasn't a tour at all: it was a full-on, day-long tournament.

'I *will* win,' declared my travelling companion, leading the way up a Crusader watchtower at the port. Stone crumbled on to my nose as I saw a pair of rope-soled sandals dancing beside a Lebanese tricolour. The medieval streets fanned towards the souk and linked up in the ruins of ancient Byblos, where colonnades and pillars and a Roman nymphaeum marked a civilization that sold cedarwood to the Pharaohs and invented the Phoenician alphabet. Standing behind the ruins, built out of classical blocks and cushioned in hollyhocks, was the limestone citadel built by the Knights of the Cross (a sobriquet eerily echoed by the Maronite factions of the Civil War).

Mike's elbow secured him an early victory as he bounded up the stairwell. His manoeuvres around the scaffolding that cobwebbed the dank, mildew-smeared chambers earned him a peal of laughter and a round of applause.

'I win,' he declared, repeating this observation several times before offering an arm to Layale and leading us all to an Ammonite quarry, where a rendition of 'As Time Goes By' sealed his triumph. His prize was to have the dust on his shorts brushed off by Layale.

'Oh, they are so dirty!' she squealed, lifting her lashes for a mutual gaze, as if their pupils were linked by a cord. Turning round, I was rather gratified when Hinud presented me with a purple-petalled hollyhock.

'C'est une herbe médicinale,' she said. 'C'est bien pour le ventre.'

Which was, I suspect, less a romantic gesture than a comment on the perceived state of my health.

We sat on a Roman plinth and I asked Hinud about her use of French.

'Many of us Maronites,' she said, as she dropped holly-hock petals in the lap of her black trousers, 'prefer to speak French rather than Arabic.'

'We liked the French,' said Layale, 'they were good to us. But the Mussulmans hated them.'

She smiled, picking a fly out of Mike's hair, before locking her arm in his and leading us back to her house.

On the beach, ladies in bikinis as insubstantial as flotsam flicked back their hair (in Lebanon, ladies like to flick their hair) and roasted on imported towels, to be massaged by the oily hands of hairy lotharios with crucifix necklaces. Coins of white sunlight shone on their shoulders and sun-creamed bars sparkled down their spines. After the concealment of Syria, this sudden surfeit of flesh was disorientating, like turning from a bookcase marked 'Orientalism' to the fashion magazine rack.

The only bare flesh that evening belonged to the chicken on our plates. There was a power cut so we ate in the dark, candlelight flickering across our faces.

'You must be careful in Beirut,' said Rami. 'There are many Mussulmans. You will know they are Mussulmans because they stink and they try to take your moneys.'

'I think we'll be safe,' I said. 'It's not like the civil war's still on.'

'You think the war is over?' Rami's chiselled cheekbones grew in the candlelight, as grim as a scythe-bearing reaper in a medieval Book of Hours. 'Between Mussulman and Christian is never peace.'

This was not Ibn Jubayr's Lebanon, where 'the Christians . . . when they see any Muslim hermits, bring them food and treat them kindly, saying that these men are dedicated to Great and Glorious God and that they should therefore share with them.'

As Rami spoke, his hair was lightening, his T-shirt stiffening into a cuirass, a helmet clanking with the coif that had coiled round his neck: he had become a knight of the Crusades.

Our departure in the morning assumed the grand proportions of a royal ceremony. Our backpacks, scrubbed and refitted with distant cousins of the smelly items that had squelched out of them, were gently moulded to our backs. We were hugged and kissed and hand-shaken and high-fived. Our arms were filled with crisps, Pepsi cans and La Vache Qui Rit cheese. Eternal friendship was pledged and, as she removed her arms from Mike's neck, Layale's cheek was smudged by a tear. We strolled down the hill, the cries of valediction swallowed by the rumble of the bus to Beirut.

'And then she started pulling off my shirt and next thing I know she's rubbing oil on my back!'

No detail was spared as Mike described the vigorous massage Layale had provided yesterday evening after he'd been stung by a jellyfish at the beach. It was a memory that he was determined to share, not only with me but also with the tubby local on the other side of the aisle.

'Go Bay-woot?' he said. He was built like an oil tanker, into which his hair looked like it had been dipped. 'Go Pizza Hut! Sports Café for Test Match! Like dance? Club Seventy Unplugged!'

'Is there anything . . . Lebanese?'

'Leba-niss?'

Not a word with which he professed much familiarity.

The busty go-go girls smouldering on flashing nightclub billboards hardly contradicted him. Nor the electronic hoarding that swapped Marlboro cigarettes for a giant shopping trolley housing a tube of Pringles and a bottle of Persil Automatic. Not only the details, the ambition also smacked of Americana: high-rise apartment blocks soared into the sky – ludicrously high, great Towers of Babel whose architects seemed to have been competing with the peaks of Mount Lebanon.

And when the bus had nosed past concrete bunkers where nailed plastic sheeting took the place of doors, and a taxi had deposited us on a street of couturiers, jewellers and hairdressers amid shopfronts with Indian and Armenian scripts, the setting became even more ludicrous.

Fifty years earlier, we would have heard, like the ambassadors, foreign correspondents, bon viveurs and even my grandfather, the peal of lounge-singers in red-roofed French Mandate mansions and the clink of champagne flutes in porticoed Ottoman palaces. Three decades later, we would have heard the kaboom of bomb and bullet. Now, the latter had cancelled out the former.

Not that Beirut was silent: there was plenty of noise.

The noise of jackhammers and pneumatic drills and cement-grinders. The noise of about-to-be-born office blocks and high-rise apartments, rising out of the bulldozers and scaffolding and orange pyramids of sand that resembled mounds of turmeric, tended by men with utility belts and pencils behind their ears. And, away from the hubbub of the city centre, the clang of tills in Vodaphone shops and the crunch of pretzels and the rhythm of R'n'B in a Virgin Megastore, where it competed with the click-clack slingbacks of ladies with Gucci handbags. But also, at the lookout posts or red-and-white barricades slung across the streets, the occasional bawl of protesters demonstrating against the Syrian soldiers whose presence in Lebanon they considered an illegal occupation.

The noise that Master Philip would have heard, however – the gush of water from a marble dragon in one of Outremer's most celebrated palaces, where Frankish spurs stepped on mosaic paving – had long been mute.

But architectural dissolution doesn't cancel Crusaderana. When, in 1110, the Franks 'descended on Beirut', wrote the nineteenth-century Maronite historian Tannus ash-Shidyaq, they 'tightened its siege, and took it by the sword . . . On the second day Baldwin brought all the prisoners outside the city and had them beheaded.' The same ruthlessness was manifested by the Phalange on Black Saturday, 1975, when, in reprisal for the shooting of four Christians, they slit the throats of the first three hundred Muslim men to arrive at specially erected roadblocks.

They did that here? In Beirut? Where now the women with the world's duskiest eyes (not because they're naturally the duskiest but because they've been darkened by so much kohl) – chiffon-sheathed and satin-slippered – catwalk the Corniche in a marching band of tinkling jewellery? No way, man! Where now men in as much leather and hair gel as their contemporaries in Italy zyroom-zyroom in open-top Chryslers, rendering one-way systems, no-entry signs and central reservations obsolete and never – but *never* – stopping for the traffic lights (because the little red man is the Arch Emasculator)? No way, man! To Anglo-Saxon severity such emphases might speak of small minds; but not for the Beiruti. The Beiruti's dollar-sign brooches and diamond rings, hipsters and hair extensions, navel studs and nose rings, perms, personalized number plates and platinum watches, are a defiant two fingers at fate: *Ha! You rained F-15s on me. You attacked me with rocket grenade launchers. You tried to tear out my innards with phosphorus gas. Well,* coos achto! *I'm driving a Ford Mustang, I got a Rolex on my wrist, a babe on my arm, and she's wearing a gold necklace that you never even scratched. So you can kiss my . . .* The Beiruti has survived, to cling to his possessions and dance till dawn, tearing away the city's scars like peel-off stickers. Beirut has a rare gift: the gift of forgetting.

It was outside Beirut, when Mike and I took a bus south to the former Crusader port of Sidon, that I met someone who didn't want to forget.

In the medieval quarter, sandstone walls with the texture of a palimpsest leaned towards each other, trapping the smell of onions chopped by a kerchiefed matriarch, the waft of hot bread oozing out of a bakery where men smoked before a black-and-white TV, the rich scent of the soap bars towering like a Druidic burial mound in a converted Ottoman coffee house, the miasma of dustbin bags manned by malachite-eyed cats. While Mike, choking on the eclectic selection of Sidon's aromas, enlisted a boy in a Bugs Bunny sweatshirt to escort him to the Great Mosque, another boy – this one in stern military combat gear – ordered me over an iron-girded gangplank and shooed me across the stone bridge of the Crusader castle.

The upper walls were spotted like a Garibaldi biscuit, but with rusted cannon-heads rather than squashed currants; lower down, the sea had mottled them to the texture of a slice of Ryvita. They reminded me of some of Beirut's more run-down districts, where Swiss-cheesed apartment blocks still wore bullet holes from the war. On the esplanade at the back of the castle, I sat on a marble slab, sniffing the salty air and jotting in my diary. Across the harbour, men were unbuckling lobster cages and boys were kicking squashed Pepsi cans between strategically placed tins. There was a gentle silence, compromised only by the cooing of seagulls and the nudge of the waves. And the soft patter of two pairs of footsteps, swiftly followed by the announcement:

'My name Muhammad.' His round, friendly face beamed over a white T-shirt with an Arabic logo.

'Pleased to meet you,' I said.

'This my love-girl.'

His arm was locked around her waist. She was dressed in an ankle-length cotton skirt and a rollneck top. She had curly brown hair and beautiful china-blue eyes. Her chin rested on his shoulder. They struck an oddly romantic appearance, like Pre-Raphaelite lovers superimposed on to a David Roberts print.

'Are you from Sidon?' I asked.

'We are from Falasteen,' said Muhammad.

'Palestine? Whereabouts?'

'Haifa.'

'When did you move to Lebanon?'

'I am born in Libnan. I live Sidon all my life.'

A lifetime in Lebanon. But he still considered himself Palestinian. Partly because of Lebanon's ambivalence towards refugees: barred from decent jobs, state schools, property and Lebanese ID. But primarily because he shared the nationalist devotion that is common to nearly every Palestinian I have met. He identified himself by a city in Israel. A city that, almost stripped of its Arabs, had long lost its Palestinian identification. But, as far as Muhammad was concerned, Haifa was his home town: Forever Palestine, the dream of the refugee.

'Would you like to live in Palestine?' I asked.

'We go back Falasteen when Falasteen is ours.'

I resisted a quip about what the Israelis might say and stood beside them, looking out at the sea.

'You know this place built by the Franj,' said Muhammad. 'They try for take Falasteen, but they fail.'

He bit his lip and scrunched his nose. 'So they make Eezra'eel.'

It was an extraordinarily apt connection. We were standing in the building to which Templar Knights had flocked after the collapse of Acre in 1291; where, nearly seven centuries later, the Israeli army had taken control as they rolled through South Lebanon in 1982. It was an advance whisper of the connections between Israel and the Crusades that, less than a fortnight away, would assail me in the Holy Land.

'Always,' said Muhammad bitterly, 'people from the West for conquer Falasteen.'

'I guess,' I said, 'some terrible things must have happened.'

Muhammad's eyebrows lifted in faint agreement.

'My grandfather is in his shop. Near here. He is having his hubbly-bubbly. Twenty years before now. The Eezra'eel tank: they explode him.'

'I'm so sorry.'

And I did feel sorry. The look he gave me; those sharp, shrunken eyes: I couldn't but feel sorry. Because he was looking at me as if I – the One from the West – was responsible.

I left them looking at the sea. She, I imagined, was thinking of marriage and when will he speak to my father. He was thinking of war and retribution.

High in the cedar-ridged mountains above the Casino du Liban is a vast stronghold with a flagstoned forecourt and an audience hall lined with an army of velvet-seated chairs. There, the successor of the bishop whose overtures to Rome so thrilled William of Tyre asked us how much sugar we'd like in our coffee.

'We are in a crisis point,' said Patriarch Nasrallah Sfeir, dropping barley lumps into small china cups. 'Since the war, maybe one million have left. And most are Christians.'

A surprisingly slight man, the Maronites' Patriarch of Antioch and All the East was swathed in a black cassock, which folded neatly around his lap. Above him hung portraits of himself and Pope John-Paul II, a symbol of the union forged in a period when, as Master Philip's mission suggests, the Catholic Church was desperate for Christian allies in the East.

'Over the last five years,' he continued, 'there has been reduced Israeli bombing. But the Syrians exploit Israeli attacks as an excuse to maintain their presence as a protectorate force. As the Lebanese, we have no real power. If this continues, we will be emptied of Christians.'

It was a significant fear, which would strip the Levant of the only ally of the Crusaders still extant, a sect less populous now in Lebanon than in Brazil. But it was a remarkable turnaround.

When the Syrians rolled into Lebanon in 1976, they were greeted by a Maronite hail of rosewater and rice. Their ostensible intention was to prop up the Maronite government. But now it was the Maronites who wanted them out.

'It is more difficult for the Muslims,' said the Patriarch. 'The Syrians are their co-religionists. But in the depths of their hearts, I think they feel they too are Lebanese.'

He lingered over the word 'Lebanese'. It was a term that Maronites used to keep for themselves. But now it was to their benefit to daub their Muslim compatriots with the same brush.

'We are in good relations with Muslims,' Sfeir insisted. 'And we have been living here since the dawn of Christianity and the dawn of Islam. Any community that has not felt at ease where they were, came to Lebanon to find peace.'

Peace? In Lebanon?

The Patriarch's comments belonged to a re-evaluation of Lebanese history, a Maronite acknowledgement that, as the Patriarch said, 'The interest of the Christians is to witness to the Christian faith in a country that is not fully Christian.'

Having grudgingly made its peace with such former enemies as the Palestinians and the Hizbollah (Sfeir spoke warmly of the latter as a 'liberation' movement and the former's need for a state), the Maronite establishment had been forced into a compromise. But it was a compromise inside which Sfeir was still able to glean the kernel of victory.

'The Muslims,' he said, 'now have only one wife. And two or three children, as opposed to eight or nine. They are educated at Christian universities and they go to work with Christians.'

His words trailed away as he sipped his coffee. Here was the old Middle Eastern talent – the ability to claim victory regardless of the circumstances: as long as you maintain your flexibility with language, you can always win.

'Wonder what *his* religion is,' said Mike, as a taxi-driver invited us to sizzle on his plastic-covered seats. Prayer beads, a couple of feathers and an Arabic prayer dangled over his dashboard.

'From where, my friends?' he boomed.

Normally Mike and I would say 'Britain'. Often it was fun to listen to the vitriol heaped on our motherland, apologize or engage in debate with men for whom such activities tended to follow the form of monologue. But this time we opted for another nationality, because, both being half somewhere else, we could.

'Ireland,' we said.

The charnel house of teeth that greeted this information, or the manner in which, one hand on his wheel, he reached out with the other to manacle our hands in his, should have alerted us to his likely reaction.

'You have military occupation in Ireland?' he asked.

'Oh yes,' said Mike. 'Like the Palestinians.'

'The Inglizi,' said the driver.

'They are our Israelis,' I said.

'You want to get rid of the Inglizi?'

'Oh yes.'

'You do?'

He grinned, his eyes fixed on ours, rather than on the approaching bend in the road.

'You want bombs?' he said.

'What?'

He let go of the steering wheel and pumped his fists in the air like a psychopath.

'I,' he announced, in the most operatic of voices, 'am Hiz-bo-llah.'

'Well, that's awesome,' said Mike, 'but if you don't do something about that truck – *heywatchout*!'

Traffic absorbed the driver's concentration for a few minutes, but he clearly found the opportunity to abet some Irish militants much more exciting. He watched us through the mirror, his eyes burning like the wick of an amateur explosive.

'You want dynamite?' he said. 'I get you dynamite. TNT? C-4? We go my friend you want—?'

215

'No, really . . .'
'Gun, mortar, plastique. Rocket grenade launcher?'
'No, *really*. Just drop us off in Achrafieh, please.'

Achrafieh was equally intense, though a Hizbollahi would hardly have felt at home there. After the silence of Syrian nightlife, rarely louder than the gurgle of a *nargileh*, there was something fantastical – in the sense that the City of Brass is fantastical – about the neon streets of East Beirut.

The crowd sluiced down a marble staircase into an underground cavern where coloured blades of spotlight sliced boulders of cigar smoke. The salty smell of sweat and the hyper-real lighting, the slurp of beer, the tendrils of freshly showered hair and the myriad of immaculately glossed mouths sprinkled the nightclub with the atmosphere of an underwater pleasure palace. *Nargilehs* bubbled as men fluted their lips like fish on their fipples. A party of miniskirted she-devils with red-horned hairbands licked salt off their hands and drained shots of tequila while gel-head sharks eyed them from the bar, clutching their shoulders and testing the extent to which their arm muscles could expand. Stilettos and steel toecaps clicked against a laminated floor as slippery as ice, their owners intertwining in a fluid tapestry of movement centred around biceps and breasts; their form, colouring and poise inscribed with some secret code that didn't require the libido of Solomon to attract a second glance.

Girls would float past us, scrutinizing us fleetingly before deciding to anchor themselves elsewhere. I thought of Usamah Ibn Munqidh's tales of liberal Frankish men sleeping with each other's wives and bringing their daughters to the *hammam*. Modern Lebanon is as close as there is to an updated Outremer – a Westernized Christian culture mixed with a proclivity for armed militias and an attitude to nightlife of which Reynald de Chatillon (who liked playing host when he wasn't marauding among the Muslims) would have approved. From the perspective of sexual politics,

Outremer stood in relation to its Muslim neighbours much as Lebanon in the modern Levant. Sure, a lot of women wore veils – to preserve their complexions. But many of them, like their modern Lebanese counterparts, also favoured hair extensions. The prospect of contact with Prester John would no doubt have thrilled them, since it would have increased the availability of precious stones with which to decorate themselves. The soap operas that filled Outremer's *chroniques scandaleuses* certainly suggest that its citizens would have been more comfortable in Achrafieh than a conservative modern-day citizen from Ba'albek. I noted the cruciform ornamentation: the cross on the throat of a girl in a marine-coloured tankini or embedded in the chest hair of a medallioned pelvis-swinger, the cross-shaped earrings of a girl in a very little black dress. In the Middle East, these items really matter – every detail has a political context, even earrings, miniskirts, bikinis. They enable the Maronites to distinguish themselves from their Muslim neighbours and to stress their links with Europe. In Achrafieh, Lebanon declares itself to be Mediterranean rather than Middle Eastern, and proclaims – with red-horned hairbands and marine-coloured tankinis – that it is *not* Syria.

But would Master Philip have enjoyed it? The music alternated wildly between Orient and Occident, so that the same couple who had swayed to Aline Khalaf's 'Lali Lay' were next to be seen 'Spinning Around' to Kylie Minogue. Master Philip, from the more conservative society of medieval Europe, would probably have been shocked; but for Mike and me, the conflation of Eastern and Western music was as seductive as the ambience on the dance floor.

'Man, it's not that cool,' grumbled Mo.

He was sitting at our table, as disgruntled as a sea lion on a (feather-filled) rock. He came from Beirut, thought Achrafieh was so-so, didn't understand why we liked it so much.

'It's awesome,' said Mike, slapping the palm of his hand. 'Ever seen so many beautiful people in one place?'

'Actually,' said Mo, 'I have.'

'Where?'

'Egham.'

Mo had recently finished his studies at the Royal Holloway University in Surrey. There was, he assured us, nowhere quite like Egham.

'Ohhh, man,' he sighed, with a little too much gravitas, 'I should never a-left.'

Across the table, a dozen pairs of lips were being puckered in Mike's direction, their owners competing for the best come-hither look. He got up, shot them his laser grin, and disappeared in an octopod of chiffon and whelk-shaped earrings. I was alone with Mo. And a trayload of cocktails that had mysteriously appeared at our table.

'Down in one!' screamed Mo.

I obeyed both Mo and Abu Nuwas, the medieval Arab poet who decreed that 'the life of a proper young fellow consists in drunkenness after drunkenness.' One. Mo prattled about Egham. Two. His panegyric became a blur. Three. I was beginning to feel very drunk, very head floating up up up hit the ceiling almost – whoosh! – there goes a flying *nargileh* and the dance floor's tipping like a sinking ship and—

'Hey, al-Jub! Y'allah! – *come on*. Let's get back to the hotel.'

'Shure. Goodbye, Mo. Goodbye, byooowteeyful peeepull.'

I remember staggering into the street, cool air rushing at my sweat-glistened neck, the taste of cherries and vodka rich on my tongue. And, as I groaned myself to life in the morning, the suspicion that my head had been replaced by a cement-grinder.

'Come on, Grandpa.'

While Mike sympathetically coaxed me to the bus stop, my hangover performed intricate scientific experiments inside my head.

'What's keeping you? Forgotten how to walk? Come on, one foot forward, then the next – there you go!'

When the microbus-driver's lackey asked where we wanted to go, I said, 'Euaeuaaaaaaeoogh,' and made myself familiar with a nearby wheelie-bin. Mike, more helpfully, said, 'Ba'albek.'

As I slumped beside him in the bus, I would happily have accepted the sort of curative prescribed in medieval leech-books: 'Take half a dishful of barley, one handful of herbs, and boil together, then wrap in a cloth and lay to the sick head.' There was, of course, my ampoule of *teriaca*, but that was only for absolute emergencies.

'You'd better get better,' said Mike, 'or you're not going to appreciate tonight's show.'

But there *was* a curative, more wholesome than anything Master Philip could have prescribed.

Whenever I felt unwell, I could always trust the landscape to help. Bekaa means 'place of stagnated water'. But the Bekaa Valley was far from stagnant. It was a pastoral of pea-green valleys sprung with mulberry trees and running streams. Peasants in wimples and shifts cut stalks of corn with their sickles, silhouetted against the ruby slopes of the mountains. It was stunning, a delightful polyptych that washed out the chaos in my cerebellum.

In the villages, children ran between beech trees and made games out of old shoes and dustbin bags. Women in hijab were hobbling past posters of Jerusalem's Dome of the Rock. Men with moustacheless beards dusted down their *gelabiyya*s as they walked to the mosque. We were back in the world of Islam. The hoardings, dedicated along the coast to household goods and hosiery, were now ideological. In every town and village, we saw a giant, bushy-bearded face with a kindly smile. We were travelling under the watchful beneficence of Sheikh Hassan Sa'id Nasrallah, Secretary-General of the Hizbollah. Sometimes he was joined by the Sunni prime minister, Rafiq Hariri; sometimes by an Iranian mullah. Often, in a reminder of Lebanon's vassalage to Syria, he rubbed shoulders with avuncular Hafez al-Assad. Occasionally he was accompanied by a fifteen-foot bottle of aftershave or a giant Pepsi can. Or a Kalashnikov-wielding *fida'i*, one of his devoted protégés. The Bekaa Valley was plastered in the cult of his personality. He reminded me of the Old Man of the Mountain. Swap assassinations for abductions, and the Hizbollah had a lot in common with the Hashishiyyin: the cult-like secrecy, the isolation from Sunni Islam. And their prime hunting ground was famous for a product associated with the Hashishiyyin.

Behind us in the microbus, a soldier lifted his chin off his rifle and offered us olives.

'You like Lebanon?' he asked.

'Love Beirut,' said Mike. 'Awesome nightlife.'

The soldier smiled. 'You know,' he whispered, 'here is good things also.' He waved towards the fields. 'Here is the land of the hashish.'

The Bekaa Valley's most lucrative industry; which, like the Hizbollah, is popular with locals and loathed by foreign governments. Between them, the Hizbollah and hashish provided the housing, welfare institutions and jobs that the government was unable to offer. Like the Old Man of the Mountain, Sheikh Nasrallah was operating his own state-within-a-state.

That night in Ba'albek, the Temple of Jupiter was the place to be. The sun, seeping through a gauze of silver poplars, streaked sensuous peach-coloured blocks – so chunky that legend ascribed their construction to the wrath of Cain or Solomon in love with Astarte – in dazzling lattices of golden light. Its rays darted around the monumental staircase, smeared an orgy of sculpted monsters and leaf-throttled capitals, and plunged into the shrine of Jupiter Heliopolitan.

But the temple's radiance was undercut by the presence, across the road, of a russet-coloured tank. A soldier emerged from the hatch with a pair of binoculars. Was this a stand-off between classicism and modern militarism? Or did it have something to do with the crowd swarming into the temple, handing over their Gucci handbags and sheepskin overcoats to be searched by the soldiers guarding the temple? We had arrived on the second night of *al-Mutannabi*, a new musical play and the opening production of the annual Ba'albek Festival. Among the guests on the previous night was the prime minister. Tonight, judging by the silver cufflinks and chokers, there would be more VIPs in the audience.

'What are you checking for?' I asked, as the officer frisked my pockets.

'We make sure no terror.'

'Hizbollah?'

'Thank you, sir.'

Inside the temple, we milled among the glitterati. Women with blow-dry bouffants pressed their gowns against marble slabs, while their pinstriped consorts collected G & Ts from mobile kiosks wedged between the columns. Ladies who shared both Eleanor of Aquitaine's fondness for silk and her hauteur crunched the gravel with their spiky heels, spilling olives and Pringles as they sidled up to Armani men with expressions as adamantine as the reliefs. Cigar smoke and laughter climbed up double-tiered pedimented niches where the Roman gods once preened, surmounting the smell of lemon and gin and *la grande toilette*.

The auditorium was packed, a pixelated sea of human heads that sloped into the pit, where the lighting crew scattered coloured lights on to the multi-tiered stage. We squeezed into our seats, between businessmen screaming into their mobile phones, ladies screaming at other ladies' frocks, children screaming for crisps. The light dimmed, the pillars rising out of the stage turned a sickly shade of green, crimsoned, went blue and green. On the band's first strike, the audience rose, soaring like some lumberous beast, uniting in the cacophony of the national anthem. This was much more boisterous than the Proms. It was the full-on tribal self-expression of a football crowd: sectarian nuances soldered together by song.

What should have been a conventional spectacle – showstopping musical numbers, alarums and excursions, huge rolling backdrops, smoke – was transformed, by the audience, into an unlikely spawn of the Theatre of the Absurd. Women waved white hankies at the red-liveried knights, and when they turned their scimitars into dancing canes an elderly man in the next row did the same with his walking stick. The fat man beside me grumbled irritably whenever the sword-swishing villain appeared. A few rows in front of us, a gin-boosted party of Maronites turned the ballad of a chain of actresses in black hijab into their own karaoke show. When the knights juggled helmets and shields, the Maronites emulated them with cigarette packets and Zippos. But no one had it worked out like the hippo-shaped lady in front of us. Whenever anyone sang, cheered or juggled, you could count on her to croon, cry, wave her cigarette, sprinkle the row in front with popcorn and provide a running commentary to her mobile phone. When the fat wazir maypoled his *nargileh* around a belly dancer, she clambered on to her seat and ululated the refrain, and she bewailed the departure of a giant sphinx with a fluttering hanky and such agonized mumblings that it sounded like the death of Lear.

I tried to connect the action with what I knew of al-Mutannabi, the tenth-century Iraqi satirist whose outspoken wit forced him into a traveller's lifestyle as he fled from the various Muslim courts whose masters he had offended. Both his bombastic literary style and the picaresque nature of his biography were sumptuously reproduced in the show's spectacle and variety-show structure. But what did the modern Lebanese think of al-Mutannabi? His great dream had been to revive the unity of 'the Arab Nation', making him a provocative subject for the Muslim Lebanese playwright Mansour Rahbani. I cursed the simplicity of my Arabic, unequal to the nuances of the dialogue. Was there a sophisticated political skin beneath the make-up of flashing lights and rolling backdrops? And if so, what did the Maronites think of it?

An answer of sorts was provided in the interval, when the cross of a young Maronite's necklace swung towards me as I queued at a drinks kiosk.

'Hey, man,' he shouted, in American, 'you dig the show?'

'Great.'

'Yu think?'

'Don't you?'

'No way, man – *next* week's gonna be cool!'

'Why?'

'There's gonna be a Sting concert.'

Typical. You get yourself all excited over the 'native' theatre, and what does the 'native' want? An ageing British rock star.

CHAPTER NINE

PICTURES IN THE DESERT

Mar Musa: 8 July

I AM WRITING – watermelon in one hand, pen in the other – on a tatty Persian carpet under a tarpaulin canopy. In front of me, black rocks and brambles tumble into a wasteland of golden hills, diversified only by the play of light; a place for ancient prophets and thunderstruck catamites. Only a slither of asphalt, at the foot of the cliff, indicates the era and our means of arrival. Behind me is a stork's nest of honey-coloured masonry. From dormitories vine-wreathed stairwells sweep down and slip into kitchens and cells and a chapel that contains the only extant fresco cycle in Syria. We have reached the monastery of Mar Musa al-Habashi.

It came after a journey out of hell: ten of us squeezed into an oven-on-wheels whose driver was so loyal to the philosophy of 'the more the merrier' that he gave up his own seat for an extra passenger and squatted over his gearstick. Back on the Syrian side of the border, we were collected by an amateur opera singer with four yellow teeth. A road, recently built as a presidential gift to the reluctant community, corkscrewed towards the Smoking Mountain. Wheezing under our backpacks, we panted up the gully.

We were welcomed through the wicket by a goatherd called George. He took charge of our backpacks, while a monk bustled us past a wooden door studded with iron nails and through a cavernous tunnel. Young men surrounded us on the esplanade, plying us with watermelons and geniality, their baseball caps and T-shirts masking the ancient tradition of hospitality that was their natural inheritance. The same attitude and the same lifestyle would have succoured Master Philip as he trudged through the Levant: chickens and goats skittering across limestone paths as monks in black cassocks hauled buckets of water from pulleys that snaked into a well at the base of the cliff. Inside the sixth-century church he would have found the same aura of timeless ritual, as potent as the smell of incense.

We take off our shoes, push aside the shroud that over-hangs the portal, and bow as we burrow between sandstone walls and a screen of double arches that conjures an illusion of intricacy. Cushions pamper our knees as we bend in front of a wooden iconostasis and stands bearing silver Bibles encrusted with crosses. Either side of me are Malik, a charis-matic local helper who wears a keffiyeh cowboy-style around his neck, and his friend Hakim, whose forearms, gabled piously under his chin, are tattooed with 'Mother Mary' and 'Metallica'.

To the murmur of Arabic, two monks sweep towards the iconostasis, half hidden by genies of incense spotlit by the clerestory window. They kneel in the chancel, nodding to the fading frescoes of the apse, sliding their heads to the floor, prostrating themselves towards the tabernacle, mumbling to God as their lips touch the ground. It seems extraordinary – the transposition of a Muslim ritual to a Christian ceremony. But the ritual hasn't been transposed. It is an expression of Middle Eastern culture, and a reminder of the link, that Lebanon tempted me to forget, between Christianity and Islam.

'You see the iconostasis?' said Emma, the local English archaeological guru, who took charge of us after the service. Blond, prim, 'frightfully busy', she was a cross between Miss

Moneypenny and Howard Carter. 'It's a replica of the original,' she said, 'which was burned by the local Bedouin tribesmen.'

'Was it a religious dispute?' I asked.

'Don't be silly. They needed wood for their fires. They were hunters and fugitives – you see, the monastery was deserted. They came here for shelter.'

Had their actions been influenced by religion, they would probably have tampered with the fresco cycle on the facing wall. But the cycle, composed around 1192, only a few years after Saladin's conquest of Jerusalem,* was in impressive condition. On the side of paradise, angels, evangelists and Old Testament patriarchs swirled in reds, whites and blues, along with black-cowled Syrian Orthodox monks. So, no prizes for guessing which sect painted the cycle. On the other side of the *hetoimasia*, slightly better off than the naked fornicators with serpents attached to their naughty bits but still utterly damned, were Muslims, Jews and Catholics.

'It's ironic,' said Emma, 'because the head of the community here is a Jesuit Catholic.'

The monks who painted the frescoes would have been shocked: Mar Musa's community had become an ecumenical salad bowl. In the more rigid age of the Crusades, when even Prester John was considered a heretic, such flexibility wouldn't have been possible. The president's road represented more than just ease of access: it had stripped the monastery of the isolation cherished by its founders. While the Hospitallers and their ilk acted as soldiers, policemen and bankers, the Arab Christians clung to the purity of monasticism and distanced themselves from other creeds. The same dynamic was expressed by the contrast between mighty Crusader castles and hidden-away Mar Musa, clinging to its mountaintop like a shy schoolboy to his mother's skirt. Mar Musa had no

---

* At a time when, according to the author Erica Cruikshank Dodd, Mar Musa became a sanctuary for Christian refugees fleeing the recently re-Islamized Holy Land.

interest in the outside world – its walls looked in on themselves, introverted from its surroundings.

This exclusivity made the monastery's dedication all the stranger.

'It's named after St Moses the Abyssinian,' said Emma. 'According to the legend, he was the son of the Ethiopian king, and he fled across the Levant on his wedding night because he didn't want to be king.* He was killed by the Byzantines, but his finger stuck out of the sand – I've actually seen it.'

'His finger?' exclaimed Mike.

'In a church in An-Nabk. Well, you know how these things turn up.'

'Why didn't he want to be king?' I asked.

'He wanted to lead a religious life, which isn't really possible if you're a head of state.'

'Prester John managed it.'

'Prester John?' She twitched her lips. 'Now I've heard of him somewhere . . .'

'He was—'

'No, no, no time for that. Come on, let's eat.'

Crushing each other's hips around a wooden table, we dug shovel-heads of bread into tubs of icky vegetable sauces. I squeezed between Malik and Hakim, while Mike was invited to join a tall, spindly monk with an incense-scented beard shaped like a poster tube.

'My name,' he announced, 'is Father Jihad.'

'That mean holy war?' asked Mike.

'The real war,' Father Jihad grandly replied, 'is inside you.'

'So you're not into bombs and stuff?'

'If I am, you think I will admit this?'

---

* Another legend casts him as an African gangster who terrorized the Egyptian frontier in the fourth century. When he was sheltered in the desert by Christian hermits, he embraced their way of life and converted his kinsmen.

Father Jihad chuckled heartily and passed a platter of goat's cheese to Hakim, who was showing me his tattoos, while Malik explained his fitness regimen.

'Meesta Neek,' Malik announced, 'I am doing much yoga.'

'That's nice.'

'And the one on my wrist,' said Hakim, 'is baby Jesus.'

'I am also doing karate,' added Malik.

'You must be very fit,' I said.

'And this one,' continued Hakim, exposing half his chest, 'is the Angel Gabriel.'

'And I climb the mountains,' Malik said, 'very height, for see from top.'

'You're a real powerhouse.'

'Meesta Neek, it is not for body I do this. Here is holy place: for body and also for heart. When I am climb the mountain I am close to the God.'

'And this,' continued Hakim, rolling up his shirt to expose his back, 'is the Lord of Destruction.'

Despite his keep-fit regimen, Malik wasn't averse to a puff or two, as his call for 'smokee' implied. I joined him on a sandstone ledge outside our dormitory, inside which Mike was fending off Hakim's tenacious efforts to turn him into an advertisement for Guns N' Roses. We blew cigarette smoke at the stars while Malik documented his voracious reading of English literature and explained who were 'the three big writers of Ingiltera':

'Shagspeare, of course, he is the king. Then there is Charles Deeckons.'

'Aha.'

'And after him is Colin Wilson.'

'Right.'

I hadn't slept in a monastery for five years, not since my incarceration in a boarding school in Somerset. Listening to the dog-growls and goat-bleats of Mar Musa, chattering in secretive whispers and stubbing out our cigarettes with frantic haste when the aeolian bluster mimicked an angry monk,

I felt like I was back puffing away behind the cricket pavilion. It was a wonderfully cosy sensation.

The Fifth Letter of Master Philip to
Roger of Salerno

To ROGER, BY the grace of God most glorious of physicians, his most dear friend, Master Philip of Venice, sends greetings.

The grace of divine inspiration chose to test me greatly on my journey to Damascus. For I struggled with my she-mule when a frightening voice was heard in the sky. My dragomanus, an idle-witted Bedouin, screamed aloud and warned that we would be eaten by the Gruul. This is a phantom of the desert. They say it has arms like chicken's wings and the body of a camel. My heart likewise was seized by this fear, for particles of sand swirled through the air like dense fog, and terrible were the visions in our heads as we lay clinging to the ground, not daring to open our eyes or mouths, our hands pressed into the sand as far as possible. When finally the whirlwind subsided, we discovered that the palfrey of my dragomanus had suffered injury. The dragomanus unclasped an amulet from his breast and, reading songs of sorcery, danced around the beast. But I begged him to give me leave, and cauterized the animal's wound. Nor was this the end of our troubles. For, when the Bedouin dropped his stick not ten miles outside Damascus, he threw himself to the ground and tore his clothes. It was only with great patience that I gleaned that he believed himself cuckolded, for so these people conclude when they drop their sticks.

Damascus is a fair city of large extent, with a hundred and twenty thousand gardens and a hundred public baths, extending over fifteen miles on each side. And the people dress in gossamer and silk. All the men have beards, and many carry swords with round pommels. The women wear on their heads a cotton mantle, and nothing can be seen of them except the eyes. If they pass their husbands a hundred times a day, the men would never recognize them, so that the women are free to give themselves to all manner of mischief. And in Damascus is a tower where Paul was brought forth by the angel, but the Saracens do not attempt to close it up: saying that if they close it one night, they find it open again in the morning.

The Count of Tripolis favoured me with a fine letter, so that I entered Damascus without trouble, for he is on good terms with Saladin. And I was escorted by a fellow physician, Zedekiah the Jew. He showed me the chief hospital of this city, which is a fine building where they cure the mad, who have lost their minds on account of the heat. And here many strange practices take place. Before they administer the physick, often they drug the patient with hemp, so that he is ignorant of what is being done to him. And they make much use of music, for they say that it empowers the beat of the heart. And they deride Frankish physicians with great cruelty. They told me of a Frank who treated a patient with an abscess by chopping off his leg. And they considered this to be typical of our medicine, for they think that all from the West are Franks. But I said that we have great physicians and, dear Roger, I spoke proudly of your work in Salerno.

Zedekiah the Jew took me out from this place, for I wished to converse with the wise men of the city. And so we crossed the Street that they call Straight, where folk sell mutton and lentils and sweet-tasting drinks. And as we went, there was a great crowd. In their hands were sweetmeats and rice, for there was a grand procession. And we stood in the door of a fruiterer's shop. And voices cried out, with great passion. 'Hail,' they said, 'the raiser of the banner of justice and benevolence.' And the fruiterer cried out, 'This is the source whose water is not exhausted by the great number of drinkers.' And many cheered him, and threw their food at the ground, to be trampled by the richly caparisoned destriers in the procession. And the cause of this excitement was a short, stout fellow with one eye, the man they call Saladin, for he was marching through the city. I thought that my ears would burst, dear Roger, for people screamed like the howling of hell. And even Zedekiah, though a Jew, said much praise of Saladin. For he told me that this man is compassionate and merciful, and one day when a Frankish woman bewailed in his tent the loss of her child, who had been taken by pagan slave-traders, so sorely did this affect Saladin that he wept and ordered his guard to go to the market and buy back the child. And so the guard returned with the child on his shoulder. And the woman besmirched her face with earth and gave praise to Saladin, though she was Christian.

The wise men of the city were gathered together in the house of a nobleman called Usamah the Son of Moonkeeth. He never ceased to speak of the high-born folk of his acquaintance, and he says he enjoys the favour of the Sultan, and he claims even the Knights of the Temple as his friends. We sat in the courtyard, on couches of juniper wood set with pearls as big as filberts. There, I was quite suffocated by the smells of spices and burning aloe-wood, while a similar affliction seized my companions on the appearance of a dancing girl. She wore a silk dress purfled with gold, and they compared her beauty to the moon. And one told how she belonged to the Prince of Aleppo, but fled his harem for the arms of al-Jawzi the woodcutter. He carved her likeness from wood, and so was her death feigned and her liberty secured.

Many there were in our company, men of learning

who had studied the great books that fill the academies in these parts. And there was much talk of the procession, for in this city they all speak with great admiration of Saladin. And they tell me that he has a pleasant wit, and he has studied the wonders and rarities of this world, so that anyone who conversed with him could gain knowledge of things that could be heard from no one else.

And they have much scorn of the West, for they say that we are dirty and unschooled, and know nothing of justice. And Usamah told of a Muslim man who was accused of practising ruses against Christian pilgrims. He was tied with a rope around his shoulder and dropped into a cask of sour wine. And he did not sink, so he was judged guilty and his eyeballs were pierced with red-hot awls. They considered this to be unjust. But I spoke out and said that we in the West have much trade and great cities such as Venice and Paris. But they say that all our wealth comes from here, and that this is why we have a love of silk and sugar and bathhouses.

Zedekiah introduced me to another guest, a Nestorian merchant conversant with distant lands. And I asked him if he knew of Prester John. And he cried out, 'This man is most glorious above all others, for whenever he rides out, he has thirteen crosses, and seven kings serve his bread. And he has giants nine cubits tall and a race of Christians, with one foot and one leg and their privy parts in the middle of their bodies.' And I was greatly excited by this news, and more so when he unrolled a parchment. It was a mappa mundi, designed by a Saracen in Palermo. My heart throbbed as the Nestorian pointed to the land of Prester John, for this is a great land of large extent, and surely its lord is among the mightiest of men.

Dear Roger, you must think that I have suffered from too much heat. But remember, this is the land of

Christ, and things happen here that would not be believed in other parts. Do you wonder how you receive this letter? In Damascus, they attach their letters to the legs of pigeons and let them fly from the roofs of their houses, and so clever are these pigeons that they deliver the letters wheresoever they have been instructed. And so I send this letter to Acre, whence I hope it will be transported to Salerno. Raise your hands with me, dear Roger, for when I write these letters I think that we are not divided by land and sea, but it is as if we are together. And let us both praise God whose ways we cannot know, me in writing these words and you when you read them.

When the Prophet Muhammad approached Damascus, he was dazzled. He thought it was a mirage in the desert and, anxious not to forfeit his right to celestial paradise, refused to enter. When you're on a microbus with several dozen locals, their boxes and buckets, two chickens and a goat, you're not at liberty to make such a decision. But I agreed with the Prophet in one respect: after a jeep-ride had taken us from Mar Musa to the nearest town, and the highway was chased by the same gold sands and black rock that spread across the Smoking Mountain, Damascus emerged in a dazzle. OK, it was the dazzle of glass-coated tower blocks and electrical hoardings. But it was still a dazzle.

What most impressed (and alarmed) Muhammad was the sudden explosion of fertility. The same quality inspired some of Ibn Jubayr's most beautiful prose: 'its rivulets twist like serpents every way, and the perfumed zephyrs of its flower gardens breathe life to the soul,' he wrote; 'by Allah, they spoke truth who said, "If Paradise is on the earth then Damascus without a doubt is in it."'

The same fertility was celebrated in our hotel, where vines trellised up tiled walls, crawling around a lemon tree and an

233

azalea, intertwining with the trees that acted as a parasol to a marble fountain mumbling like a man at prayer. But, once we'd abandoned our hotel's horticultural luxury, fertility was replaced by dust.

We squeezed between child tea-tray bearers and vegetable trucks too wide for the road. Yellow saloons, lorries and motorbikes interlaced their tracks on a thoroughfare of flashing taillights and fierce wind, flanked, to the west, by tower-block hotels and fairy-lit restaurants, and to the east by a curtain of black basalt. Ahead of us, guarding the Old City, was the man whose military genius prodded Europe's search for Prester John in the late twelfth century. His mantle flowing behind him as spear-brandishing warriors encircled his horned steed, Saladin glared with righteous indignation towards the Syrian Grand Hotel. But the hotel was older than the statue, which was unveiled by Hafez al-Assad in 1993.

Throughout the twentieth century, Arab leaders basked in Saladin's reflected glory. Nasser's triumph in the Suez crisis and his successor Sadat's treaty with Israel were presented in terms, respectively, of Saladin's martial prowess and his diplomatic skills. Arafat was preparing to install Saladin's pulpit on the always-imminent day when he would march victorious into the Dome of the Rock, while Assad had Saladin's statue surrounded with sycophantic writings that linked him to his medieval predecessor. Not that this gesture had much impact on the traffic: taxis and trucks skidded, swerved and zigzagged down the highway, oblivious to the great man in their midst.

Behind the walls, we clambered round handcarts and market stalls that pressed against the ramparts of Saladin's citadel. Men in aprons packed up kebab spits or fruit-filled nets; women hatted with laundry baskets marched down the Street they call Straight, damascened in the dirt of the daily grind – paper and plastic, crushed falafel, roasted aubergines sunk in puddles of *baba ghanoush* – and turned into an alley that squiggled between coffee houses where men played backgammon on wooden tables. A red melon-shaped dome hovered over a chessboard-tiled courtyard scented with jasmine. Inside a chamber inlaid with marine-coloured tiles stood a walnut-wood coffin cloaked in green velvet: the resting-place, built in 1193, of Saladin.

Like it's ever that simple.

Beside the coffin was a chunk of white marble, a gift from Kaiser Wilhelm, donated when he was courting the Ottoman Empire in 1898. It looked like a slice of pavlova. We were joined by a man with large brown pupils like chocolate buttons and a mop of treacly hair, wearing a chequered shirt that took a sudden right angle on acquaintance with his belly. Aptly enough, he didn't pay the slightest attention to the wooden coffin, but raised his hands instead to the pavlova.

'Salah ad-Din,' he whispered, knowingly.

'Is he not that one?' I suggested, pointing to the walnut-wood coffin.

'No! This one!'

A mortified stub of finger shook at the pavlova, before his hand rested agreeably on his belly. Perhaps he would confirm my suspicion by taking out a spoon and tucking in.

'But that one was only built in the last century,' I protested. I was feeling very protective about the location of Saladin's bones.

He shrugged. 'So they moved Salah ad-Din.'

I wanted to scream, *You can't bury Saladin in a cake! This is the most honourable figure of the twelfth century and you've turned him into a slice of Sara Lee. He should be encased in walnut wood and Ayyubid motifs and draped in the colours of Islam.*

'Nick,' said Mike, patting my shoulder sympathetically, 'DWI.'

So we compromised. Mike and I stood before the wooden tomb, while the local paid his respects to the cake.

Whichever was the correct tomb, we were standing near the body of, to quote his secretary Beha ad-Din, 'our Lord the

Sultan al-Malik al-Nasir, the uniter of Islam, the suppressor of the worshippers of the cross, the standard bearer of justice and fairness, Salah al-Dunya wa'l Din, sultan of Islam and the Muslims, deliverer of Jerusalem from the hands of the polytheists, the servant of the Two Noble Sanctuaries, Abu'l Muzaffar Yusuf Ibn Ayyub Ibn Shadi (may God moisten his resting-place with the dew of his good pleasure and let him taste at the seat of his mercy the sweet reward of faith)'.

It is hard not to admire Saladin. He died peacefully, smiling at the holy words of a sheikh, surrounded by his seventeen bickering sons. They can't have been arguing over his estate: he left only forty dirhams and a Tyrian gold piece. Everything else had been given away. Usamah Ibn Munqidh praised him for his 'abundant munificence', 'overflowing generosity' (and, Usamah not being impartial to a little social climbing, his 'good opinion of me'). Beha ad-Din, who couldn't exalt him enough, also identified his deep knowledge and 'pleasant wit'. Even Frankish William of Tyre praised his 'keen and rigorous mind' and 'extremely generous disposition'.

But the hagiographers overlooked the more steely qualities essential to military success. It was Saladin's ruthlessness, as much as his chivalry, that sealed his reputation; qualities that were magnified in his most triumphant hour – the aftermath of his victory over the Crusaders in 1187 at the Horns of Hattin.

King Guy of Jerusalem and Reynald de Chatillon had been brought as prisoners to Saladin's tent. Guy complained of thirst, and Saladin gave him a glass of sherbet. When Guy passed the glass to Reynald, Saladin stressed that he wasn't extending his hospitality. Ever since Reynald had orchestrated the pillage of Mecca-bound caravans in Oultrejourdain and the sinking of a Muslim pilgrim ship in the Red Sea, Saladin had sworn revenge. He offered Reynald a choice: he could convert to Islam or he could die. Reynald, in one last hurrah, replied with a torrent of abuse, and

Saladin cut him in half. While the quivering Guy tried to stop his teeth from chattering, Saladin pointed out that the king had received his hospitality; so, according to chivalric code, his life must be spared. 'But this man,' he added, as Reynald's remains were tossed outside his tent, 'had transgressed his limits.'

The next morning, just a kick of their ball away from the scrum of the souk, children were footling between the pillars of the Roman temple that succeeded an Aramaean shrine that preceded the Byzantine Basilica of St John, that was transformed in the eighth century into the most beautiful mosque in the 'Arab world'. At the end of a lane full of soft-drinks vendors, splattered shawarma and a couple of mendicants was a carved bronze gate. Inside it, framed like a cinema screen, the coloured spots of celluloid translated into sparkling tesserae, was the spectacular face of the Umayyad Mosque. Inside the gate, a porticoed cloister shielded us from the sun. Three men in shifts and golden caps sat on a horse-cart sipping cups of water. Floating past them went a cloud of black cotton that on second glance appeared to consist of several small girls. They were led by a man in jeans, a T-shirt and aviator shades: an Arab Tom Cruise in a sea of pepperpots.

Across the esplanade, Benjamin of Tudela had promised me a crystal sundial and walls of glass, a giant's rib and a 'gigantic head' that could serve as a bathtub. Here was a painful lesson: however good medieval travelogues might be for orientating you towards the fire-breathing dragons, they're not so hot on solid fact. It was a disappointment with which I could cope: the Umayyad Mosque was both the most extravagant and the most graceful mosque that we saw on the trip. But out there on the forecourt, it didn't feel like a mosque.

The kiblah of the prayer hall glimmered in gold and seaweed-green, a legacy of the Umayyad Caliph al-Walid's

determination to exceed the achievements of Islamic architecture past, present and future, and of the belief entertained
by the artists – master craftsmen from Persia, India, Africa,
and even Syrian and Greek Christians – that Damascus was
the Garden of Eden. Glistening streams of stone fused in evo-
cation of the Rivers of Paradise, merging under a pastiche of
columns and porticoes, watering the vines that wreathed
between gable-roofed mansions and multi-tiered pavilion
towers and the sinuous trees glimmering between sharp-
angled fairytale fortresses. There were no people or animals,
their depiction being an offence to Orthodox Islam; had there
been, I would have expected them to be mythological – the
mosaics depict a landscape suitable for sylphs and satyrs, the
sort of supernatural citizens who might pop up in the empire
of Prester John or the terrestrial paradise that frightened
Muhammad.

The mosaics turned the mosque into a paradise fantasy, but
the children who filled the forecourt with their unholy
screeching dragged it back to terra firma. They were everywhere. They screamed like maniacs as they turned ablution
wells into climbing frames, ducked between their fathers' legs
and leaped around the columns that hoist the House of
Treasure (less, nowadays, a trove for gold than for pigeon
droppings); then, feet clapping against marble tiles, they skidded across the courtyard, barricading themselves around the
Dome of the Clocks, before sliding into the weeping Shiite
mothers emerging from obeisance before the caged head of
the martyr Husayn.

The playground spirit gallivanted through the prayer hall,
where the pillars are ideal for hide-and-seek. Cross-legged
worshippers make brilliant obstacles, their upper bodies
rocking up and down as the children leapfrog them. There, in
Muslim Syria's holiest space, it's an ear-thumping racket:
shrieks of joy from hyperactive toddlers hiding behind
ancient columns; shrieks of excitement from children caught
by their playmates; shrieks of mortification from mothers

reaching out to catch their offspring. And, in a corner of the mosque, gathered together like a church choir, deep, low, long- drawn-out shrieks from a band of apprentice muezzins: '*Al-laaaaaa-hu-wak-baaaar*.'

But somehow the prayer hall sustains a spiritual atmosphere. A group of men and women sing inside a wooden fence, eyes raised to the massive Dome of the Eagle, where the names of God, prophets and caliphs are jumbled into a calligraphic puzzle. Others prostrate themselves towards the mihrab, an explosion of gold and gemstones and geometric patterns. Or they gather round a marble dome-capped box, inserting banknotes and petitions as they stretch out their arms to the prophet Yahya. I pray beside them, my breath condensing on the luminous green windows. Some of them turn to look at my odd clothes, my pasty complexion and my strange custom of clasping my hands and bowing my head. But no one suggests that I shouldn't be here. They know that I'm a Massihi, and they know that Yahya is also holy to me. Only a couple of months ago the most famous Massihi of all, the Pope, stood here beside the Grand Mufti of Damascus and prayed to the Prophet Yahya too, in the form with which Christians are familiar – as John the Baptist.*

Damascus might claim to be the oldest inhabited city in the world, but that hasn't stopped its citizens from touching it up. In the metropolis through which Master Philip would have shuffled, Turkish khans have popped up alongside the neo-classical palaces of fantastically turbanned pashas; French bullets have stippled the corrugated roofs of the souks, while modern glass and metal have boxed up traditional Damascene trades. But the papal physician would have experienced much the same city, its gaunt façades doing to its

---

* Although, in accordance with local tradition – the Conundrum of Cadavers – the remains might be those of John's father Zakariah, ostensibly interred in Aleppo; or even St John of Damascus.

fountains what nylon grilles do to voluptuous lips and smouldering brown eyes. Copper-etchers squiggle their trays with elaborate inlay and streams of damask wave across the laps of needle-dancing seamstresses; clapper-tongued touts rattle down the prices of salvers with mythical origins, and (for the price of a Lion bar in London) cuisiniers stack cardboard boxes with subtleties as rich in almond and sugar as the concoctions that Hasan the Bassorite served for his unknown son in the tale of Scheherazade. Sunlight still filters between timber beams and plastered brick on to streets perfumed by spices and sweat, squeezing out your breath like you're stuck between a pair of giant rolling pins. And in the arboreal forecourts of converted mansions, you can still patch together the sort of meal that would have been recommended by the author of an early thirteenth-century Baghdadi cookbook, who advises aspiring chefs to keep their nails constantly trimmed, use stone or earthenware cooking pots and wash their utensils with brick dust:

Meze	meatballs with spinach and chickpeas, artichoke bottoms stuffed with meat and pine nuts, vine leaves stuffed with rice
Rutabiya	lamb slices mixed with almonds and spices, minced and rolled, garnished with dates and sprinkled with camphor and rosewater
Qata'if	deep-fried pancakes filled with nuts and cheese, washed down with an anachronistic thimble of muddy coffee

One morning, while Mike was catching up on his diary in our hotel, I wandered through the Old City in search of another relic from Master Philip's day – the building that, of all Damascus' treasures, would most have excited him. In the thick of the souk, behind a jungle of Damascene brocade and a mountain of primary-coloured pants, was the legacy of Nur ad-Din, Saladin's predecessor – a gentle soul who didn't have the heart to punish a wit who placed him at the top of a List of Fools, but also a puritan who banned the flute. The Bimaristan, raised in 1160 on the ransom of a Crusader prince, is a testament to Nur ad-Din's philanthropism. It was the greatest hospital in the medieval Levant, and provided free treatment for three hundred years.

Forget the characterless modern infirmary, all white lino and disinfectant; the Bimaristan was as splendid and shrub-filled as a Damascene villa. Inside the gateway, beyond a pair of peacocks pouting under a calligraphic band, *iwan*s girdled a scorched, paved forecourt. Inside each of these cavernous chambers was a little world of esoterica: pharmacopiae full of exotic herbs and drugs – a basketball-shaped purgative, a leaf of diarrhoea-destroying myrrh; a sinister pair of scissors with sharp spikes. '*L'Islam*,' read the legend, '*recommende de circoncire les garçons*.'

These were the sort of artefacts one might expect in a medieval Arabic hospital. But no institution preceded by the adjectives 'medieval' and 'Arabic' could possibly conform to a monochrome palette. This was the age of polymaths (or, in modern speak, multi-taskers): men like al-Idrisi, whose upside-down map would have provided Master Philip with the most up-to-date assessment of the physical world, in which Africa bends around Arabia to form a lemon-and-lime lump lunging at India. What use it would have been for an invalid is questionable. It appeared in the *Book of Roger*, a cocktail of anatomical, geological, philosophical and geographical learning, produced at the court of King Roger of Sicily, whose successor was pictured on his sickbed with tur-banned physicians scrutinizing his urine and studying an astrolabe. Like the placards proclaiming '*Les Arabes furent les fondateurs de la chimie moderne*' and the busts of famous physicians such as the not-actually-Arabic-but-of-Iranian-stock Avicenna, author of a million-word 'Canon of Medicine' that became the most important medical text in the world, the painting emphasized the medieval superiority of

Islamic medicine. For Master Philip, Damascus – a city where Sir John Mandeville claimed that saints Paul and Luke practised as physicians – would have been as eye-opening as Ibn Haitham's insights into ophthalmology. He would have learned Al-Razi's analysis of infectious diseases, and discovered rare herbs used to treat sexual diseases and nervous ailments. The range of ideas he could carry back to the West would have been thrilling.

Particularly when many travellers were carrying back scurvy and smallpox. The Middle Ages was the era of epidemics, when those who could cure were second only to the ruler: Christ the Healer to Christ the King. In the West, there was Roger of Salerno, the most famous contemporary physician and Master Philip's compatriot, whose *Practica Chirurgiae* was the first surgical treatise in Europe. Or Rabbi Solomon Hamitari, Manuel Comnenos' physician, 'through whom,' wrote Benjamin of Tudela, 'the Jews enjoy considerable alleviation of their oppression'. The Muslim world boasted doctors such as Maimonides, a Jewish philosopher who also treated the Fatimid Caliph and led Cairo's Jewish community; and Avenzoar, acclaimed by Averroes as the best physician since Galen, whose analysis of intestinal tuberculosis had a profound influence in the West.

Europe couldn't compete. Her physicians prescribed asses' dung to promote fertility; her sick swigged *teriaca* or overdosed on quacks' 'miracle' pills. When the Franks arrived in the Levant, the more perceptive among them, men like Raymond of Tripoli, quickly appreciated the advanced status of Eastern medicine. But Frankish physicians didn't lose heart: there were plenty of saps ready to sacrifice themselves to their eccentric techniques. Usamah Ibn Munqidh tells the story of Thabit, a Christian Arab physician in Syria. One day, Thabit presented a dietary cure for a mentally ill woman. Her recovery would have been assured, had it not been for a Frank with a razor. He cut a cruciform incision into her head, peeled the skin until the skull was exposed, and rubbed the wound with salt. The woman didn't fall ill again. She died.

It was during this period that the golden age of Arabic learning began to wane. In 1150, the Caliph of Baghdad had incinerated the works of Avicenna. Averroes' books met the same fate in 1194. Where once the peninsula had danced to a polyphony of Greek philosophy, Gnostic Christianity, Mazdekite Communism and Qu'ranic theology, the conflict with the West led to a stricter imposition of orthodox authority. Slowly the reed pens were put down, the books stopped being written, and the Arab world lost its mantle as international centre of intellectual activity. Its poets, who had once filled the streets as abundantly as its shoeshine boys do now, slipped into history: men like the bombastic al-Mutannabi; or al-Ma'ari, the tenth-century Syrian misanthrope who rejected animal foods and profit, preached that the best way for a father to show love to his sons was to 'leave them in your loins', and railed against the sheikhs who 'fill the mosque with terror when they preach'. But it was the sheikhs who won. Entertainments were frowned on, and the liberalism of the Abassid Age was replaced by a more literal emphasis on faith. I wondered if there were any traces in the modern Middle East of the poets or satirists or storytellers – the *hakawati*s – who filled the streets and drinking parlours with the first versions of *Scheherazade* and the *Fables* of Bidpai, and were still commonplace well into the twentieth century. In Aleppo, we had been told that the *hakawati*s had been replaced by the TV. I assumed that Damascus would be the same . . .

Behind the Umayyad Mosque, beyond the crashing traffic of the Street they call Straight, the road sagged under wooden planks and scaffolding, wheezed under medieval archways and flattened out beside a coffee house.

Men in shifts were sprawled across tin tables with glasses of tea and *nargileh*s, staring at a TV set. An octogenarian in tweeds was rocking on his stool, his pipe in his mouth. At one of the tables was a party of students in leather jackets, sipping Coke, flicking through trigonometry textbooks and fidgeting with mobile phones. Turbanned horse-riders and Hafez al-Assad stared from mahogany walls. It was the sort of place where the man next to you might sift through the folds of his *gelabiyya* and produce a magic lamp.

A little man, dressed in shalwar trousers, a striped waistcoat and a red fez, waddled into the café and nodded to the owner, who flicked a remote control to turn off the TV. The little man launched himself on to an ornamental chair and, off the edge of a makeshift dais, dangled the sort of curly-ended shoes that Master Philip would happily have worn. In his hands were a notepad, a brass platter and a sword. He sifted through the one, tapped the next, placed the third across his lap and started to hum. One of the students turned off his phone. Two older men leaned back from a mid-table conference, one of them placing his prayer beads in his pocket.

The hum turned into an incantation, slow and rhythmical, beating back and forth like the sea, until it was silenced by the rustle of the little man's notepad. Then he began to tell a story, the tale of a prince who lived long ago and fell in love with a virtuous beauty;* the same sort of tale that has been told in every city in every country for millennia. We had found our *hakawati*.

Everyone knew the plot. What captured the audience was the performance: the soft drawl of introductory details, the deep bass as the storyteller pumped up his pace, his voice rising faster, becoming furious, passionate, then slipping into the soft cadences of the hero's love, before flying into a powerful crescendo.

Then a mobile phone rang. All eyes turned from the

---

* The story was an episode in the *Qissat* of Antar, about a warrior of half-Ethiopian extraction, who fell in love with the luminous Abla and won her hand through a series of heroic feats.

hakawati and focused on the offending item. The offending item's owner did the same. Like everyone else, he sat in his chair and stared at it, as if its noise was a mystery attributable to the wonders of God. Slowly – very slowly – it dawned on him that he was expected to DO SOMETHING. So he picked it up (a good start) and stuffed it in his pocket (not so good). The phone continued to ring, but its owner lacked either the will or the ability to bring his ringtone to a stop. The *hakawati* tried to resume, but no one was listening: the spell had been broken.

He stressed every phoneme and rattled his sword on the platter. His audience clapped, trilled, laughed, slapped tabletops and thighs and issued well-worn responses. But they were performing as much as the storyteller. The older men beckoned the waiters for more tobacco. The younger men checked their text messages and whispered mathematical formulae. Then they left. The waiters, rushing with coal tongs and trays of coffee, were no longer tiptoeing. People walked in and hailed their friends. A woman (shock horror!) entered. She didn't stay long. When another phone went off and its black-bearded owner proceeded to lecture his caller at full throttle, the *hakawati* lost his patience. He shouted at Blackbeard, who shrugged, finished his conversation and casually, with delicious arrogance, placed his phone on the table. The *hakawati* whispered an incrimination. Blackbeard answered back. Neither could lose face. An old man screamed at a small boy for moving a chair. A tableload of *nargileh*-smokers bawled at Blackbeard. Blackbeard gave as good as he got. Then there was a thump on the table, a shaken fist, a righteous hand inclined towards the *hakawati* – 'My friends, respect for our storyteller.' The moral high ground had been assumed, with bald-faced gall, by the man whose phone had signalled the first interruption.

There being no ostensible public transport system in Syria,

the next morning we haggled for a taxi to Jordan. A Bedouin camel-driver, his black-and-white keffiyeh fluttering like a flag behind his head, preceded us outside Damascus, where the sand was mashed up with porphyry and basalt. Towns became scarce, and scarcer still as we entered Jordan; less common than goatskin Bedouin tents. The texture of the landscape had also changed: in Syria, it resembled an over-baked piecrust; in Jordan, it was more like lemon meringue.

Which would all have been perfectly pleasant, had it not been for our driver's refusal to close the windows. Now, I know that's not always a bad thing when it's hot – lets fresh air into the car. But it's not so great when the fresh air is carried by scalding dust-devils that sting your skin like something with big pincers that's been weaned in a volcano. Motor transport may protect the traveller from foot sores and the legendary Gruul, but it has its own irritations.

As we set about locating an Umayyad palace with a link to Prester John, I was feeling thoroughly groggy. This wasn't helped by the old lady on the bus from Zerqa, who bellowed like a hurricane, before the anguished O of her mouth twisted into a jolly U and she pattered down the aisle to collect payment for her singing. Nor did my spirits rise much when a gang of taxi-drivers invited us to join them for a meal of saffron rice and bread in Azraq, since the offer was made in lieu of a lift.

'We'd also like to get to this palace,' I explained.

'Please, meesta, some rice?'

'You wouldn't consider . . .'

'*Ya*, meesta! Today is difficult day.'

'Of course it is. But how about if we offer you . . .'

'It cost you too much.'

'Too much? How do you know? I might be a millionaire.'

'Meesta, if you millionaire, you buy for you trousers good.'

Mike was nowhere to be seen. Didn't he *want* to see this palace? I stood up, swiping the piranha flies off my dusty, torn flannel trousers. But, before I'd had a chance to look about,

I was collared by a call of 'Al-Jub!' There he was. And where exactly had he been? The clue was behind him: a young man in a shift, sitting in the driving seat of a four-wheel drive.

'So.' Mike's lips were parted in a triumphant grin. 'You want to see this palace – or not?'

A revving of engine, a wasteland of white sand and wiry broom bushes, from which an eggshell dome rose in front of a triple-humped sandstone compound. Smiling sheepishly, a teenage boy approached us, his key revolving around the cuff of his navy shift.

Inside the throne room, he sat on a stool, chewing a herbal stick and smiling dreamily. The room had the same atmosphere as his eyes – hazy and slightly high. Frescoes dripped down the sandy walls, fading in light, pastel-like colours. Angels, hawkers and dancers mingled with wild and mythological beasts and a monkey plucking something like a mandolin. In the steam room, astronomical imagery invited the bather to forget about the world and concentrate on the cosmos. There was a happy, hyper-real ambience – like a hippy mural. There were also, somewhat surprisingly—

'What on earth,' exclaimed Mike, 'are nudes doing in a Muslim hunting lodge?'

They danced in the antechambers, their modesty preserved only by the pallid texture and the coincidence of peeled paint. I'd never seen so many graven images in an Islamic building, and I'd certainly seen no nudes. It reminded me of ancient Greece – no coincidence, since the frescoes were painted for the Umayyads by Byzantine artists (another example, after the artisans employed for the Umayyad Mosque in Damascus, of the artistic links between pre-medieval Islam and Greece).*

Yet another nude stalked out of a pool in the throne room,

---

* The same link stimulated Arabic learning, as translations were churned out of Galen and Hippocrates, Ptolemy and Euclid, several centuries before they were rediscovered in the West, energizing the ideas of men like al-Kindi (who recast Greek philosophy in an Islamic mould) and al-Farabi (known as 'The Second Master' after Aristotle).

her posture evoking considerably more admiration for her curves from a huddle of voyeurs under an archway than she received from the six miserable kings beside her. But it was the kings and not the nudes who were the purpose of this visit. Alongside the Byzantine emperor, the Sassanian Shah of Persia, Roderic the Visigoth, the Chinese emperor and the prince of the Turcomen was the Abyssinian Negus. Robed in bejewelled Byzantine-style silk, he was distinguished by an Axumite headcloth. But it was significant that he was there at all: a sign of the importance attributed to Ethiopia in the pre-medieval world.

Homer imagined Ethiopia as a chill-out zone for the gods. The ancient Egyptians included it in Punt, a land of musk, myrrh and a fat-lipped ogre-like king. The Israelites called it Ophir, home to incense trees and gold. Alongside the exports of elephant ivory and salt from the Danakil depression, these became the PR images behind a mighty kingdom centred in Axum, whose quadruple-towered royal palace had been admired, not long before the frescoes were painted, by the sixth-century Greek geographer Kosmas Indicopleustes.

In the same period, the Prophet Muhammad described Ethiopia as 'a land of righteousness' (which evokes Prester John's boast that 'thieves and robbers are not found in our land; nor do we have adultery or avarice'). Indeed, Muhammad, several of whose followers had been granted refuge in Axum, warned Muslims to 'leave the Abyssinians in peace'. For nearly a millennium, they did. The fresco of Qusayr 'Amra snapshots the time when Ethiopia was still rubbing shoulders with Byzantium, but on the cusp of the isolation that would be accelerated by Muslim conquests around the Red Sea and concluded only by Portuguese sailors searching for Prester John in the sixteenth century. It was Islam's ascendancy – the ascendancy of the same authority who was depicted in Qusayr 'Amra, enthroned beside a fly-whisking slave – that plunged Ethiopia into the mystique from which it emerged as the empire of Prester John.

Inside the hazy-eyed keeper's tent, mint-flavoured tea chuckled into tiny glasses.

'May God multiply his blessings on you,' he said, beaming.

We needed transport. As Mike put it, 'Our Man in Amman's waiting' – Munther, a longstanding friend of 'the Knights', Mike's father's charity. The previous year, he had treated us on a brief hop over the Jordan to the spiciest, most expansive *meze* I had ever tasted, complete with sash-spinning, cane-twirling belly dancer and hubbly-bubblies on demand. Now that we were returning to Amman, Munther had insisted on looking after us.

There wasn't much traffic on the road, and what there was wasn't very friendly. Splashed with sand, coated in dust, our thumb muscles wilting, we were sinking in a quicksand of low morale.

'I hate lorries,' I grumbled.

'I hate the sun,' moaned Mike.

'Guys!' bawled the driver of a 4x4, with the frame of a cane toad and a bracelet that rattled on his wrist as he yanked his handbreak. 'What you are doing? This is danger road!'

'It is?'

'*Yaa*, people from al-Iraq want to steal and kill you. Get in.'

We could hardly refuse. Particularly when he revealed that he was heading to Amman.

'So where have *you* come from?' I asked.

'Al-Iraq.'

Our introduction to the capital of Jordan was a set of billboards proclaiming the benefits of Coke and satellite TV. There were Pizza Huts, Kentucky Fried Chickens, McDonald's. There was even a Wimpy. As for religion – well, there were a few minarets and some men twirled prayer beads, but mostly Islam was concealed. Blond hair flowered out of the black roots of women peroxided into the colour that had shocked the Arabs who confronted the Franks. For all the bombast about the Arab Nation, Amman didn't look like it belonged to an Arab nation. Built over a Roman city called Philadelphia, it looked now like it wanted to be another Philadelphia.

After the kindly cane toad dropped us at McDonald's, we were picked up by Munther. He was wearing a beige suit and brogues and his heart was definitely not in the Arab world.

'Howyadoin'?' he yelled, slapping our hands. 'Mike – how are your folks? You're gonna love your hotel!'

A minute by Merc, and we were blinded by glass and chrome and fake gold fittings.

'It's got air-con,' shouted Munther, 'and CNN, en-suite bath, minibar.'

'But it looks . . . rather pricey,' I mumbled.

'No way!' screamed Munther. 'You gotta stay here – I hadda bend a few arms to get you the room. You'll love it, guys!'

Oh, what martyrs we were. We fell on the sword of our bugless beds, suffered the thirty-six different TV channels, and sacrificed ourselves to the over-equipped bathroom. There were a dozen different types of soap, bottles of shampoo and shower gel, sachets of bath essence, cotton buds and face cloths. The bathroom spoke a completely different language from the accommodation we'd experienced throughout the Levant. I sat on my bed, fretting over the crippled state of my finances, and comforted myself with a look at the Master Map. We'd nearly completed the crescent of the question mark.

'Cheer up,' said Mike, emerging from a storm of soap suds and steam and smelling like the Body Shop. 'Could be worse.'

I looked around. At the telephone, the radiator, the remote-controlled blinds, the fresh, fluffy towels . . . and CNN's Gerald Kessel reporting the latest explosion in Israel.

It certainly could.

For a couple of days, we dragged our feet through the souks and mosques and shopped around for the cheapest cake deals. We breakfasted with Munther, fattening ourselves on the all-inclusive buffet, where the ingredients promoted by medieval Arabic cookbooks were replaced by processed cheese and those rubbery sausages that you find only in international hotels. We sipped coffee with another 'Knights' contact – the genial Bishop Selim Sayegh.

'We are squeezed.' He sighed, a resigned smile lighting his small, thin face. 'Before the Gulf War, eighty-five per cent of our economy depended on trade with Iraq and Palestine. Now the embargo against one, the lack of peace in the other – the country is a mess.'

His cup was rattling on its saucer.

'You must go to Jerusalem,' he said. 'I don't know when there will be peace. In Israel they say, "The Palestinians are your enemy" – on the TV, on public broadcast. From the Palestinians the same. They do not try to love each other.'

'Know what?' said Mike on our third afternoon, as the image of smoke on the hotel's TV screen was replaced by an aggressive politician's cachinnation. 'Let's y'allah al-Quds.'

'What? Go to Jerusalem?'

'Now. Get stuck in.'

'Right now? Well, I suppose . . .'

I was itching to see Jerusalem again: find out how old friends were coping, how things had changed in the last six months, throw myself back into that city's extraordinary frisson. But I was also apprehensive. In fact, I couldn't remember feeling this scared since, as a thirteen-year-old schoolboy, I had been ordered by a sinister sixth-former to steal jam sandwiches from the refectory and deliver them to his room on the Dragon Floor. There, on a corridor dedicated to fear and the stink of dirty rugby boots congealing on radiators, where an error of judgement could lead to the depilation of your eyebrows or your being whiplashed by a dozen wet, twisted towels, I had felt, as I made my presentation to a room filled with joss-stick smoke and most of the 1st XV rugby team, the same palpitations in my solar plexus that were afflicting me now.

'It's OK to be scared,' said Mike, gently.

'Are you?'

He considered for a moment.

'No.'

I sifted through the foreign papers. Like a sado-masochistic voyeur, I inflicted photos of bombsites and reports of Innocent Bystander Shot in Head on my already addled psyche. As we collected our backpacks and set off for the city that inspired the legend of Prester John, my head was a steampot of potential troubles.

Among which I hadn't included the act of getting there . . .

'Bus al-Quds finish,' said a porter, before adding, with apocalyptic emphasis: 'For ever.' But a taxi-driver called Ibrahim agreed to take us to the border for all our remaining Jordanian dinars. His rugged face was cowled in a red-and-white keffiyeh, and his eyes sparkled with the prospect of pecuniary gain. We asked him if the border would still be open. He was sure, inshallah, that it would. We reached the border in an hour. It was 'finish'. The security guard advised us to try the Sheikh Hussein Bridge, forty miles up the river Jordan.

Behind the wasp's nest of barbed wire, metal gates and machine guns that indicated our propinquity to Israel, Iraqi refugees in off-colour cotton were rubbing sticks outside their tents. We reached the Sheikh Hussein Bridge an hour later. It was 'finish'.

The sky had turned a sombre shade of indigo. Jerusalem would have to wait; in the meantime, we had the tricky challenge of getting back to Amman and finding a room without spending any money. It quickly became clear that Ibrahim wasn't going to help.

'We go back Amman,' he said. 'You pay double.'

'We haven't got double,' replied Mike.

Over the next half-hour, Ibrahim's hands became increasingly divorced from his steering wheel as the gesticulations necessary to a Levantine argument assumed precedence over driving. I was hoping that he would lecture us all the way to Amman. So I was disappointed when we pulled into the hard shoulder. I was puzzled when Ibrahim flagged down two cars. And, when a dozen Arabs bundled out and gathered round Ibrahim, waving their hands and gurgling together like a coven of witches, I was concerned. One of them was holding a stick. A man in a gingham shirt stepped forward. He had a gold tooth and the air of a Man in Control.

'There is problem?' he said.

'Yes,' boomed Mike. 'This bloke said the border would be open. Wasn't. His mistake. Now we need to go back to Amman. He's going there anyway, so he might as well take us.'

He stopped to absorb the response: the man with the stick was picking his nose; the Man in Control was tapping a suede shoe against the gravel; Ibrahim was spitting, snorting and doing a fine impression of an old-fashioned widow. The Man in Control patted him on the back, stuffed some banknotes into his hand and turned to us.

'You come with me,' he said.

I was of two minds. Maybe the Man in Control was very nice and would give us a lift to Amman. But maybe he was a psycho. He would take us hostage in this beautiful car of his, with its black leather upholstery and air-con and impenetrable instrument panel, and demand an enormous ransom, or put a couple of bullets in our heads and make us examples to any travellers who dared query the fundamental caveat of Middle Eastern transport – the driver is *always* right.

'Where are you from?' said the Man in Control, as we drove on to the highway.

'England,' I said; to which Mike gave me his 'You should have said Ireland' look.

'It rains in England,' said the Man in Control.

'That's very true.'

'Here – it never rains.' He passed round a packet of cigarettes. 'That's why we always have trouble.'

'Because it doesn't rain?'

'Yeah. If you have rain, you grow crops, you sell them, you have trade. If it doesn't rain, you have no crops, no jobs, so people are unemployed and they start fighting.'

Our accommodation, paid for in US dollars, was a broom cupboard with flies and the smell of detergent. That was nothing to the next morning's taxi, into which we squeezed with four Palestinians whose gowns and keffiyehs exuded a suggestion of much time spent among livestock. But the border was – hooray! – open. *Maftuh*. Ready for business. Once the bushy-browed official had finished his coffee. And read his newspaper. And scratched his equally bushy moustache.

'I look forward so much,' piped up the voice of the man behind us in the queue, 'to Israel.'

Wang-Li was a Buddhist from Hong Kong. He had travelled across the breadth of Asia, via Bangkok, Kathmandu, Esfahan, Aleppo – a slew of destinations, in none of which had he picked up the barest hint of the mayhem across the border.

'You're not nervous?' I asked. Why did no one share my trepidation? I was feeling like a real wimp.

'Why should I be nervous?' said Wang-Li.

'Perhaps,' suggested Mike, 'because of the intifada.'

'What is intifada?'

'It's a war.'

'This is interesting. Who is fighting?'

The innocent tone of his voice had a direct impact on the size of Mike's pupils. 'Haven't you heard about the fighting?'

Wang-Li shrugged. 'I have been travelling for many months. Is there a problem?'

'Problem?' Mike laughed. 'No, no problem. Just a few tanks, nail bombs, air-to-ground missile raids.'

'Wow.' Wang-Li looked genuinely intrigued. 'Why?'

'You've heard of the Palestinians?'

'They live *here*?'

'What?'

'There are Palestinians in Israel?'

'Yes. There are Palestinians in Israel. There are also Palestinians in Palestine. Which is where we're going right now.'

'You are? I'm going to Israel.'

'Mate,' said Mike softly, 'you're going to Palestine first. To get to Israel, gotta go through the West Bank. The *Palestinian* West Bank.'

'Ohhhh. I did not hear about this. So the war is between Palestinians and Israelis?'

'Uh-huh.'

'Has it been going on a while?'

'About fifty years.'

Wang-Li was incredibly disarming. I could imagine a Sufi poet stumbling across a Crusader battlefield, but I didn't expect to meet anyone so blithely innocent in the Information Age. In between having our passports stamped by the bushy-browed official, and denying any knowledge of Palestinians to his Israeli counterpart (hardly an act of disingenuity for Wang-Li), we discussed the ins and outs of the intifada, until Wang-Li knew who to address with 'Shalom' or '*Salam-u aleykum*', and understood a considerable amount more about the differences between Palestinians and Israelis than we did about Buddhism.

Rather less complicated, as it turned out, was our search for transport to Jerusalem.

'Michael!' called a man in a black dog-collar suit, with a large round face and a shock of silver hair.

'Don't believe it,' whispered Mike, turning towards Father Maroun, headmaster of the Latin Patriarchate's seminary in Beit Jala and another of the incredible coterie of Mike's parental contacts.

'You are going to Jerusalem?' he said. 'You must come with me.'

His white Volkswagen saloon glimmered in the car park and for half an hour, while Father Maroun sorted out 'some papers', we boiled in its leather acreage.

'Now remember,' said Mike to Wang-Li, 'Father Maroun is Palestinian, so no more mention of Israel, OK?'

As he collapsed into the driving seat, the priest's face was a waterfall of perspiration.

'You cannot,' he croaked, jabbing his key into the ignition, 'you cannot say the Israelis are not thorough.'

The engine roared and the complications of customs dissolved into a bare canvas of sand. Father Maroun asked where we were staying, and before we could answer he beeped the number of the Latin Patriarchate into his mobile phone.

'You will stay at the Knights' Palace,' he said, 'on us.'

I caught Mike's glance in the rear-view mirror. It was a majestic grin.

'How have things been?' I asked.

'*Yaa*,' said Maroun with a shrug, 'it doesn't get any better. A Palestinian blows himself up, kills some Israelis; the Israelis destroy a Palestinian village.'

'Are we in Israel now?' asked Wang-Li.

'No,' said Mike.

Pause.

'Now are we in Israel?'

'Not actually entering Israel,' snapped Mike. 'We're entering the Occupied Palestinian Territories, which are under Israeli military control but aren't legally part of Israel.'

'But,' mumbled Wang-Li, 'I thought Israel is one country.'

Father Maroun's eyes turned into dinner plates. 'Oh my God,' he muttered.

Under the chalky white of the hills, the door of a tent flapped aside, exposing a woman with a child at her breast. Her husband stood in the sand, chin resting on a crook, surveying the road. It was an uplifting scene that – but for the husband's white trainers – might have been played out since time immemorial.

'Now are we in Israel?' asked Wang-Li.

Within the hour, the dry, gorse-riddled hills were knotted into homesteads, then villages of sugar-cube houses, topped with satellite dishes. The highest of the hills supported the odd Jewish settlement, sharp-angled fortresses of concrete and barbed wire. Gradually, the hills covered themselves in detail: putting on asphalt and breeze-block houses, hotels, shops and traffic lights. A Muslim in *gelabiyya* crossed the road, passing an Orthodox monk in a black cassock. A Jewish couple pushed a pram up the steep slope that ran abreast of the Old City's northern wall. The streets were – in spite of everything – comforting. Although we'd been to Amman before, it was too featureless to be recognizable. It was here, coming back to Jerusalem after weeks of travel in unknown territory, that I felt the hug of familiarity. It was like a homecoming.

CHAPTER TEN

'IN URBE HABERE ECCLESIAM'

The Sixth Letter of Master Philip to
Roger of Salerno

PHILIP OF VENICE, by the Grace of God, to his beloved friend, Roger of Salerno, greetings and sincere affection.

Although in these times the treasures of Jerusalem are familiar throughout Christendom, for every town boasts at least one who has carried his pilgrim's scrip or knightly lance, now I wish to record my own humble impressions of the centre of the universe. For she is a small city, fortified by three walls. And they do much work to repair these walls, so that the saying will be fulfilled: 'Do good in thy good pleasure unto Zion: build thou the walls of Jerusalem.' And the langue d'oïl is the most common tongue. For it is spoken by the king and the officials of the High Court, and by the many Franks who were goldsmiths, carpenters or cooks in the West; and now are goldsmiths, carpenters, or cooks in the East. With them have tarried many prostitutes, cognizant of the revenue to be reaped from so great a store of men; and also the men's wives, cognizant of the prostitutes. But otherwise, there are more tongues in this city than anywhere I have visited, for in the marketplace my ears are assailed by the winds of Arabic, Armenian, Aramaic, German, Hungarian and Ruthenian, the language of the Bulgars, the speech of the Jacobites of Barsauma, and the Greeks from Byzantium, the Angles and the Bohemians, the tongues of the black people of Prester John, and the strange language of the Samaritans of Gerizim.

And even around the Church of Our Lord can be heard manifold voices. For outside this holy place, the heresies of Greek and Syrian, Copt and Nestorian, are enunciated at the same time as the True Message of the Latins is enunciated within. And great is the clamour, for all believe that the Lord will listen only to the loudest petition. And in this church is Calvary, where is a white rock stained with the Lord's blood, and under the mortise which held the Holy Cross is the head of Adam, for Christ died to redeem us from Adam's sin. And here are the places associated with the passion of Christ, for the Empress Helen located them through an old Jew. And when this happened, the earth trembled and breathed from her crannies aromatic odours. And over these places in recent years the Franks have built a fine church decorated with mosaics. You would think, dear Roger, that the sight of such things would inspire virtue and purity in the hearts of the people. But this is far from the truth. My own eyes have witnessed a burgess and his woman in the alcove of the Chapel of St Helen, engaged in the act of sin. For they believe that children begotten there will have good fortune.

And I was shown around the city by the Archbishop of Tyre, who is called William. And he showed me the hospital of the Knights of St John, where they treat the sick of all creeds and clothe the poor and look after orphans. And all patients are provided with cloaks and sandals and white bread. Dear Roger, this hospital is well stocked and they have great wealth to purchase Milanese fustian and felts from Constantinople.

And Archbishop William showed me many places. We visited the Church of St James, where the Armenians maintain a hospital, and the Church of St Anne, where lives a college of nuns; and I saw the finger of St John Chrysostom and a part of the skull of John the Baptist and the Temple of the Lord. This was formerly a Saracen shrine, and it is surfaced with gold, so that it flashes with the gleam of lightning.

Archbishop William was tutor to King Baldwin, and he took me to the High Court to meet him. But as we entered the grand hall, we saw a company of men gathered on opposing sides. Mightiest of the voices on one side was the Count of Tripoli, whom I have found previous cause to mention. And across the hall, in fierce disagreement to the count, were the Master of the Temple and the Lord of Oultrejourdain, a Frank of sturdy build whose name is Reynald de Chatillon. With great passion did this Lord condemn the pagans, and never did he speak of them but foul words erupted from his mouth. He wishes to launch an expedition against the Land of Makka, where is their holiest shrine, but the Count believes that such a venture would unite the pagans and render them as multitudinous as Gog and Magog. And so did the quarrel persist.

Apprehend, dear Roger, how they dispute in the Holy City! And in the High Court can be heard as great a discord as in the marketplace or in the Holy Church. For there is a rift, between those long settled in Outremer and those but recently arrived. Consider the story told by Usamah Son of Moonkeeth, who prayed once near the Temple of the Lord. A tempestuous Frank forced his face eastward, averring that this is the correct direction of prayer. And some Knights of the Temple expelled this man and apologized to Usamah, saying, 'This is a stranger who had only recently arrived from the land of the Franks.' For those who have lived long in these lands are accustomed to the errors of the Saracen.

And even greater was my concern when I set eyes on the king. For this man is a leper. Archbishop William was of tearful disposition when he spoke of the king's condition, for he says that the king is a lettered and lovable man. And the Archbishop told how he first identified this disease. Baldwin was playing one day with his companions of noble rank, when they began to pinch each other's arms. And Baldwin endured this with no pain. And at first the Archbishop considered this a sign of natural prowess, but on further inspection he gleaned that it was due to the terrible disease of leprosy. And he is curable neither by oil rub nor fomentation, as diseased as the Knights of Lazarus, who fill the infidel with terror not from fortitude but infirmity.

Praise the Queen of Heaven, dear Roger, for there is another most fortuitous detail that will, with God's grace, outweigh the misfortune of King Baldwin's leprosy. For among the many creeds in the church of Our Lord, I have renewed acquaintance with the Abyssines, that is to say those of India, which is to say of Prester John. There is a host of them, come in religious peregrination. Here many remain until recalled to their maker, but others return to their fatherland, and to one of these I have communicated a wish to join tracks. He is a strange little man, as black as midnight, with a fat belly and gigantic eyes, and as I watched him in his devotions, with a distortion of his body not unlike acrobats, I realized that there is much to teach these people. And their music is answerable for this, the instruments no other than snappers and round-bottomed drums, borne upon the back of one, and beaten upon by the followers. The Lord has blessed me, for Archbishop William provided me with catechismal books to replace those swallowed by the wild seas of Greece. And so shortly will I set out,

261

dear Roger, alongside this Indian called Ezekiel. I beg of you your prayers, for united with those that I have committed at the holiest of tombs, they will grant safety to my journey.

'Jerusalem the golden, with milk and honey blest,' sang the twelfth-century hymnist Bernard of Cluny. Medieval man's metaphor for heaven, the *speculatio* of biblical Zion – no city has ever been so idealized: by Israelites weeping on the river banks of Babylon, by medieval Christians slugging it out with Bedouin tribesmen and dysentery, by Palestinians in Lebanese refugee camps. Could any collection of stones and mortar ever live up to those utopian imaginings?

Yet the attention heaped from outside is hardly unmatched inside the Old City's Ottoman walls. All those ceramic bowls displaying the Church of the Holy Sepulchre, the King David's tomb T-shirts, the calendars in which the Dome of the Rock preens out of pastry-coloured masonry. How can anywhere else compete? Jerusalem is

THE MOST NARCISSISTIC CITY IN THE WORLD.

Which means two things. One: Jerusalem is stricken with self-loathing. Hence its citizens drive tanks down its streets or hurl rocks through its windows, so they can prove their love for the city whose sewage, water supply and infrastructure their rivalry has wrecked. And two: Jerusalem is incapable of thinking about anything but itself. If Jerusalem could talk, you wouldn't get a word in edgeways. It would be, 'You'd never guess what happened to *me* yesterday', and 'After all *I*'ve done for everyone', and 'Stop telling *me* about Bosnia and Baghdad. You think they've suffered? They can't hold a candle to *me*!'

But there are reasons for Jerusalem's monomania. It's all there (which is precisely the problem – if it wasn't, there'd be nothing to fight over: the tombs of King David and Christ;

the Temple Mount – site of Solomon's Temple – or Haram ash-Sharif – where Muhammad tethered his horse en route to heaven). In keeping with the city's schizophrenia, everything – even the name of the city itself – Al-Quds, Yerushalayim, Jerusalem – has at least two names.* But, when the muezzin's call, the church bells or the *chazzan*'s chant are drowned by the thrum of a gunship, Jerusalem doesn't feel very spiritual. You walk past the winking Jesus holograms and battery-lit menorahs, and you see external symbols, skinned from the ideological flesh and bones that they purport to represent.

Back in the tenth century, the Arab historian al-Mukaddasi, citing the Torah, compared Jerusalem to 'a golden basin full of scorpions'. So, not much has changed. But Jerusalem wasn't like that for most of the last millennium: it was a backstreet of the Ottoman empire, a pointillist's paradise for the younger sons of well-to-do European families. The establishment of Israel in 1948 took the region back to an earlier age. Not to the original Jewish state, but to a realm that was created more than a millennium later. It's no coincidence that many Arabs talk about modern Israel as 'the latest Western Crusade'.

When the Crusaders conquered Jerusalem in 1099, the city became a political milch cow. Christian leaders swarmed to 'the navel of the world', cloaking worldly pursuits in a mantle of spiritual piety. Holy Roman Emperor Barbarossa lost his life en route, Louis VII of France his marriage, the respect of his subjects and most of his army; and Conrad of Montferrat fell to the Assassins' daggers. But they kept coming.

---

* 'First,' according to a medieval guidebook, 'it was called Jebus, then Salem; from which two names it had its third name Jerusalem. It is also called Hierosolima, and Solima, and Luz, and Bethel. It was also called Ælia, from Ælius the Roman quaestor.' Add ancient Rushulimim and Urusalim, Byzantine Hagia Polis, Arabic variants like Beit al-Maqdis and al-Balat, and of course Israel's Zion, and you have the world's most named city.

Geography
Both Outremer and Israel are coastal strips tucked between the Mediterranean and the Arab desert, and built around Jerusalem. As local resident Dr David Wasserstein told me, 'The Crusader kingdom covered an area roughly the same size as modern-day Israel. But of course Israel is important not in terms of square mileage.'

Division between hawks, doves and locals
Those seeking accommodation (like Raymond of Tripoli or Shlomo ben Ami, the former Israeli foreign minister) are pitted against their less flexible co-religionists (such as Reynald of Chatillon or Binyamin Netanyahu). Their local fellow faithful who reject what they consider to be colonialism (the *haredim* of Mea She'arim or the medieval Orthodox Christians) are pitted against both.

Democracy
Israel can plausibly claim to be the only democratic state in the region; the Franks ran the only state in the region whose leader was elected (by the High Court).

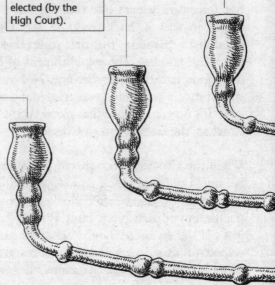

Figure 6: The menorah of Israel and Outremer.

Western origins
Theodore Herzl conceived Zionism in the coffee houses of Vienna; Pope Urban II conceived the First Crusade at Clermont. Both enterprises were funded (generously) by the West, and populated initially by pioneers from the West.

Old Testament
The Knights Templar saw themselves as modern-day Maccabees (and Crusader annals are peppered with references to the Israelites); Israel's declaration of independence described itself as a re-establishment of the Jewish state that existed two millennia earlier.

Dependence on Arabs
Arab labour has built the Jewish settlements, just as Arab labour was crucial for the construction of the Crusader castles; Arabs are employed by Israel, particularly for manual work, just as they were by the Franks.

Division between the newcomers and the long settled
Native Crusader barons wanting to enjoy the fruits of their labours resented the tensions exacerbated by newcomers seeking glory and new lands; settled Israelis tend to disdain the settlers, who consider themselves to be pioneers.

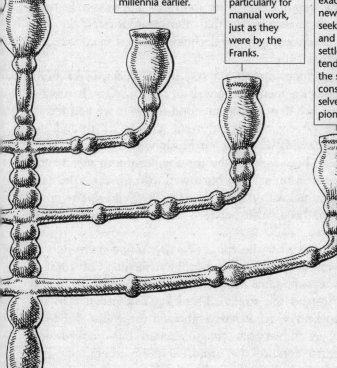

Prester John himself expressed his intention of visiting Jerusalem with his 'very great army'. Like so many before and since, the priest-king wished '*in urbe habere ecclesiam*' – to have a place of worship in the city. It was Jerusalem that inspired the Prester John legend. It was the priest-king's ostensible motivation for corresponding with European leaders; it also provided a spiritual, cultural and geographical meeting point. It was in Jerusalem that the worlds of East and West collided: a city administered by Western Christians, inhabited mostly by Eastern Christians, surrounded by Eastern Muslims. In order to maintain control, the Crusaders needed to contain the threat from the East with their own Eastern counter-attack. Prester John was supposed to be their linchpin. It makes sense that European interest in him declined in tandem with the decline of interest in conquering Jerusalem.

Most mornings during our stay in Jerusalem, Mike and I would scour the medieval bowels of the Old City. It was reassuring to see that Jerusalem stood much as we had left it. Men with olivewood nativities still chased us around the Tower of David, targeting our cash where Master Philip would have been targeted by the Frankish corn merchants. Padding near a tunnel that burrowed towards the Armenian quarter, a camel with a Bedu on its back would square up to a yellow taxi in a battle between ancient and modern transport systems.

Constructed over the ruins of a Byzantine martyrion to hold the relics of Christ's brother, the Armenian Cathedral of St James was the same picture of serenity I remembered. No gunfire; instead the strangled-bird squawk peculiar to the Armenian liturgy. *Khatchar*s embossed the walls of a forecourt where flowerpots conglomerated on crooked oak balconies to conjure the atmosphere of community life. Teenagers potted snooker balls in games rooms linked by foot-polished flagstones to vaulted medieval stables. Behind a leather blanket slapped across the portal of the church, grudging pearls of light gleamed from the brass lamps cob-webbed above our heads; *kutayha* tiles danced around us; and through a tortoiseshell doorway, a novice cawed the prayers in a balcony lodge. A more sombre reminder of past tragedies, Armenia's generous supply of martyrs shot plead-ing glances from the walls, as their heads were torn off and their bodies burned by turbanned Saracens or centurions with blood-tipped swords.

Death was less grim around the corner and through the Zion Gate, where wine-red velvet smothered a coffin big enough for Goliath but built for King David. The lions of Judah, emblems both of Israel and of Ethiopian emperors, primped under the crowns of the Torah. A *chazzan*'s nasal strains carried out to mingle with the birdsong in a cloistered garden where a plaque commemorated a diaspora yeshiva. Under candle-blackened vaulting and an archway guarded by an Ottoman inscription, steps lifted us up to the ice-grey Crusader cenotaph built in memory of the Last Supper.

Proceeding alongside a Palestinian peasant girl with a laundry basket on her head, the walls ran towards the Valley of Gehenna, named after hell and once the city's rubbish dump. The ruins of an Ayyubid tower nodded towards the Herodian cisterns; an early Byzantine church crumbled near the Tanners' Postern Gate, where cowhides used to be carried from a Crusader cattle market. Israeli soldiers bounded across the tiles and leaped inside the jeeps clattering uphill to the Western Wall. There, men in fur-trimmed hats slotted petitions into the cracks, while above them the dome that the Crusaders called Templum Domini hovered over the sensu-ous blue shoulders of its faienced drum like a vision of St John's New Jerusalem lowered from heaven.

Manning their checkpoint, gun-toting soldiers formed a barrier against the Arab children spitting at Jews darting into the vaulted shadows of their quarter. Ringlets dangling over their ear-lobes or hair tucked inside *sheitel* headscarves, they nudged their prams past the German Hospitaller hospice where schoolchildren turned the stumpy arches of a triapsidal church into goalposts. The hot smell of *challah* bread, first baked in medieval times, lured us towards candelabra and figurines of mystical Eastern European rabbis, and on to Hurva Square. There, the archway of the Rambam Synagogue (named after the man who established, in 1267, the first Jewish community in Jerusalem after the Crusades, anticipating Zionism by six centuries) cambered over the minaret of the disused mosque of Sidi Umar.

The remnants of Crusader shopfronts studded the street that bottle-necked into the Souk al-Lahmann, the Frankish Street of the Herbs, where the repose of the Jewish Quarter was knocked aside by the city's most exhaustive artery. Yelps looped above the crank of wheeled carts as a tangle of shoppers knotted us up in its suffocating sweat. Roman letters inscribed the walls, symbols of Frankish trade, and sunlight squeezed inside Crusader vaulting to beam golden gemstones on to butchers' knives. The Crusaders' Street of Bad Cooking pulsed into the Street of the Perfumes, where teenage pranksters tripped up chanting Italian nuns whose white veils were duplicated by the Muslim mothers marching satchel-swinging infant hordes through 'those triple or rather manifold streets which', wrote Master Philip's contemporary, the German pilgrim John of Würzburg, 'contain all manner of things for sale'. An Arab boy tinkled a tray of coffee glasses steaming under a brass handle, past Jacoub Badriyyah, a restaurateur whose family lived in Jerusalem in Master Philip's day ('And it's only now,' he mutters, 'that we make no profit!'). Christian armies – Copts in embroidered cowls, pointy-hooded Armenians, Ethiopians in skullcaps – marched between the shopkeepers who seesawed in and out of their stores to catch a buyer from the multitude squeezing towards Damascus Gate. Everywhere was the smell of paprika and sweat and the tremor of the marketplace.

Then, burrowing through the tunnels of the Khan az-Zeit, on one side the Franciscan library where I had first read Pope

Alexander's letter to Prester John, on the other a gang of boys heaving a rolled-up carpet like a battering ram into the tiny doorway of an Armenian souvenir shop, and into the Church of St Anne. At last, the 'vision of peace' that medieval churchmen identified with Jerusalem. Between a garden of palm trees and geraniums, and a pool where invalids used to await the daily visit of a healing angel, was the church that once housed Benedictine nuns and the abandoned wives of Crusader kings. Buttresses and half-square piers hugged a stately façade of milk-grey stone, decorated with acanthus moulding and an Arabic inscription that elegantly indicated Saladin's transformation of St Anne's into a madrasa. But inside, ribbed arches running towards Evangelical beasts, steps dipping towards the coin-cluttered spot where the Crusaders believed that Mary was born, the credo of Frankish Christianity received its most attractive expression.

Christian Outremer's most powerful ecclesiast was the Latin Patriarch. Master Philip would have met Amalric, 'an extremely simple man', wrote William of Tyre in one of his less charitable portraits, 'of practically no importance'. But, if he'd taken a couple more years to reach Jerusalem, Philip would have received Communion from one of the Patriarchate's most infamous incumbents. Heraclius is notorious for two things. One is his mistress, a draper's wife from Nablus who earned the nickname 'Madame la Patriarchesse'. The other is his departure from Jerusalem after Saladin's conquest in 1187. Heraclius fled the city in an enormous convoy. Not that there was space for his congregation, whose less fortunate members were valued at the price of a sandal in the slave markets of the Levant. Instead, he made sure that he didn't leave without his coffers of silver and gold.

In the forecourt of the neo-Gothic Patriarchate, dog-collared priests in smartly creased suits clicked the remote-control keys to their diplomat-plated saloons and jeeps. Computers and telephones pinged and brnnnged in the warren of offices, audience chambers and a long refectory where toasted cheese and ham sandwiches disappeared between clerical lips under the gaze of gilt-framed patriarchs. But, for all the affluence, Patriarch Michel Sabbah was the polar opposite of Heraclius. A Palestinian refugee clamouring for an 'end to occupation', he devoted his vast funds to a network of schools, hospitals and orphanages that were among the most distinguished local institutions of their kind; his voice to sermons condemning the 'Western' occupiers; and his feet to palm-bearing marches between Bethlehem and Jerusalem.

'The turbulence,' he boomed, lowering his broad, cassocked frame into his sofa-chair, 'is in the souls of the people.'

His face was round but solemn, his small eyes locked on something unseen a few inches above the glass coffee table.

'Blood today,' he continued, 'is crying to God, claiming justice and dignity. The Israelis are destroying houses and olive groves. In response, you can resign your human dignity, freedom, and sacrifice all human rights in order to have material benefits. But in order to have freedom you have violence. It is not justified, and when you are consistently faced with death and are being trampled underfoot, the Gospel is still the Gospel and speaks of love. But the perception is very different from when you are sitting in comfort.'

His formal exterior concealed a generous non-sectarianism that had made Patriarchate schools an invaluable educational resource for Muslim children in cities such as Ramallah and Gaza, and enabled him to embrace the multi-religious concerns that were anathema to the Franks.

'Jerusalem,' he said, 'is part of the human heritage – not only for Christians, Muslims and Jews but for all mankind. We can divide Jerusalem into two – one Palestinian, one Israeli; or we could keep Jerusalem undivided, unified, old and new, so that everyone is present in Jerusalem, and everyone would have Jerusalem as his capital.'

It was a sense of Jerusalem as a symbol, the idealized city of Revelation and medieval theology. But it was tinged, also, with the pragmatism of the biblical mother who won't let her child be dissected. Only through co-operation, the Patriarch believed, could the city properly function.

'What do you think will happen?' asked Mike.

The Patriarch stretched out his hands and glanced at the Madonna, reposing irenically in her frame.

'The future,' he said, 'like the past and the present, is in the hands of God.'

Goats tinkled their harness-bells as a Palestinian farmer guided them down the steps towards the Church of the Holy Sepulchre. Young boys with American logos on their T-shirts swapped Pokémon cards across the laps of their backgammon-playing grandfathers. The delicious smell of hot baklava perfumed this part of the Christian Quarter, reeling us towards the men with almond-dusted moustaches who swung blades of filo pastry, like windmill vanes, above their heads. We were summoned into deep chambers laid out like Oriental fantasies, where shopkeepers in keffiyehs presided over carpets, cushion covers and nacreous jewel boxes – in contrast to the darkness that crawled past the Mosque of Omar and scattered on what a medieval guidebook described as 'a very beautiful open space paved with marble'.

Inside a double gateway half shored up by Saladin is the shrine that Prester John 'made a vow to visit'. The Church of the Holy Sepulchre certainly isn't the most beautiful shrine in the world. Hunched over its flagstones, hemmed between the Greek Orthodox Patriarchate and a flank of souvenir shops, it lacks the monolithic grace of St Anne's. But it remains the Crusaders' greatest architectural legacy, uniting and breathing local significance into the sites of Christ's passion and resurrection. A head-shawled matriarch grimaces up the steps of Calvary and prostrates herself over the mortise that supported the Holy Cross. Two Ethiopian nuns kiss a limestone

271

slab marking Christ's pre-burial unction. Nearby, a local shopkeeper spends his tea break paying his respects to Adam's skull on a stone bench that once entombed the first Crusader king.

The Parting of the Raiment and Pilate Washing His Hands attract prayers to their shallow recesses as worshippers ring the ambulatory with their devotions, before pattering between the cross-scratched walls that tumble into the Armenian chapel of St Helena. There, characters from the Gospel are fitted out in anachronistic Armenian hoods. Strolling towards 'a certain window in the wall at the north side', where medieval guidebooks promise 'the shrieks of the souls in purgatory', or the stone pillars said to sweat by night and day, you reach the rotunda. A pale-pink kiosk, punctuated by portholes, is cushioned in scaffolding: the Tomb of Christ. In a cavity built into its rump, a bushy-bearded Copt invites the faithful to admire a piece of granite in exchange for a financial contribution. On the other side, a pot-bellied Greek monk plays Cerberus under a cusped arch, shaking a sack of loose change and herding the worshippers inside. If he decides that they're making too much noise, he charges in and (without a hint of irony) screams.

Not long after the first Crusaders started saddling their steeds, a German count called Ernich had a vision. He was, he discovered, the Last Emperor of St John's Revelation, destined to take on the Antichrist in Jerusalem (well, someone's got to), where he would be crowned victorious and spawn a thousand-year Reich. There was, he decided, only one way to celebrate such a dramatic boost to his career prospects: a massacre of the Jews in Worms and Mainz. One Crusade later, the Jews of Mainz were yet again targeted by a Christian of dubious mental health – a monk called Rudolf. But this time they'd had enough. 'When the children of the holy covenant saw that the heavenly decree of death had been issued,' wrote the chronicler Solomon bar Samson, 'then all of them . . . accepted as just the sentence of God.' But, rather than wait for Christianity's version of Genghis Khan's Mongols, they decided to do the Christians' work themselves:

> The women there girded their loins with strength and slew their sons and their daughters and then themselves. Many men, too, plucked up courage and killed their wives, their sons, their infants. The tender and delicate mother slaughtered the babe she had played with; all of them, men and women, arose and slaughtered one another.

Such mini-holocausts were common throughout the Crusader era, even in Isaiah's 'City of Yahweh', whose Jewish inhabitants were burned to death in their synagogue by the victorious army of the First Crusade. Yet, less than half a century later, the poet Judah Halevi tramped that way, dreaming of Zion's 'forests and meadows' and yearning to 'carry the pieces of my broken heart over your rugged mountains'. Like Nahmanides a century later, or Maimonides in Master Philip's day, Halevi dreamed of the 'exiles' return' and a New Israel. Zionism didn't erupt from an empty chasm: born in the prayers of the Torah, it was suckled by the persecutions that accompanied the Crusaders across Europe.

Master Philip would have encountered few Jews in Jerusalem. But, throughout his trip, he would have spotted the same communities that Benjamin of Tudela identified, working as dyers and doctors, shoemakers and scholars, as industrious as the Christians of the modern Middle East. Now, apart from a surprising encounter in Cairo, the only Jews that Mike and I met were in the Holy Land. But Count Ernich must be spinning in his coffin. The atrocities perpetrated by his ilk, snowballing through the Inquisition until they exploded in the twentieth century, empowered the Zionist argument and promoted the ultimate act of Jewish isolationism, the last step on a ladder whose first rung was built by the Crusaders. And there's no getting away from this. It was the Christian fanaticism of the Middle Ages that convinced Jewry that it would only ever be an unwelcome guest in Christendom. Palestinians may see Israel as a trespasser, but to the Zionist the Palestinians were only ever housesitters, keeping the place warm until the rightful owners reclaimed the keys. Israel isn't so much a Crusade as an anti-Crusade, an escape from Christendom, the final step of a parallel route that can be traced through the rack-workers of the Spanish Inquisition to nineteenth-century nationalists and, finally, the Nazi brownshirts.

'You Jewish?' asked the icicle-bearded rabbi, as he plonked himself between Mike and me outside the Armenian tavern. The atmosphere was hardly thrumming, but the end of Shabbat still unrolled a carpet of cigarette butts and spilt beer on to the pavements of West Jerusalem. The threat of suicide bombers had reduced the previous year's atmosphere to a flicker – I can still see shards of glass and hot metal on King David Street, around the hole that half an hour earlier had been a café, ultra-Orthodox Jewish paramedics sifting for loose flesh so that every last human trace could be laid to rest.

'They're my goy friends,' laughed Heavy D, reaching across to slap an elephant's thigh of arm across Mike's back. On his lap lay a guitar, the Ark around which his kooky entourage flocked, as his sweet melody contradicted both the subject matter of his self-penned compositions and the weight of a body that implied he wasn't the only inhabitant of his skin.

> *'I can't do-oo wid-out you-oo-oo,*
> *Less drink whiskeeee an' screw!'*

As *nargileh*-hiss and olive-squelch insinuated Oriental sounds into Heavy D's unique version of the Blues, his entourage turned to Mike and me and imprisoned us in the indefatigable self-confidence that is as common to Israelis as extraneous hand gestures are to Italians.

A girl called Shlomo ran multicoloured fingers through a cabbalistic puzzle of flame-coloured hair and ordered us to go on yeshiva. Resting his gun against Mike's leg, a flak-jacketed Shin Bet operative demanded an explanation for the *dossim*.

'*Dossim?*' frowned Mike.

'The Orthodox – make me sick! They're leeches – do no work, don't serve in the army, and it's us pay for them to study Torah.'

'Hey,' said the rabbi, 'there's nothing wrong with studying Torah.'

'Even when it puts our security at risk, huh?'

The Shin Bet op folded his arms in a huff, while the rabbi turned to me and extolled the glory of building giant fortress-settlements in the *shtachim*.

'The *shtachim*?' I asked.

'The Territories.'

'Oh. You mean the Occupied Territories?'

'They're not occupied – they're ours.'

Lecture overlapped with interrogation as I found myself sinking under the scrutiny of a vodka-shot-draining demagogue called Eyal. How could I be a Christian? Did I think God was some kind of sperm bank? OK, I muttered, it's not like I don't have any doubts about it.

'You got doubts?'

A spray of vodka wet my nose, and a stray globule sizzled on my cigarette.

'But you're in Jerusalem,' bawled Eyal. 'You don't get doubts in Jerusalem.'

'It's Jerusalem that gives me doubts.'

There was a sharp crack.

'You do that again,' screamed the waitress, 'you're outta hee-arr!'

275

A pool of beer was swimming across the table from the fount of Heavy D's overturned two-litre glass.

'Hey,' he moaned, as Mike tapped a consoling hand on his shoulder, 'I just tweaked her ass, that's all.'

Arguments, counter-arguments, shaking locks and slurred invective rolled around the table, while Heavy D expressed his intentions towards the waitress through the more acceptable medium of guitar strings and plectrum:

> *'Come on, babe, you never outta my sight,*
> *I'm thinkin' about yu all throo-ooo the night . . .'*

Slowly, the great troubadour's rallentando melted into wild theories that transformed Ehud Barak into Kafka's giant cockroach, merged left-wing 'peaceniks' with medieval hermaphrodites, and cast vodka glasses as the ancient tribes of Israel.

'Now Nebuchadnezzar comes to – Eretz Yisrael!'

Then the disaster. Eyal's arms swept across a five-centimetre-high plane that cut through the vodka-tribes and sent them not to Babylon or the Hindu Kush but – our eyes meeting in sobered recognition of the sound of breaking glass – to shatter on the pavement.

'He took all of Yisrael. But—'

The waitress's fingers rapping her hips.

'He could not take Yerushalayim!'

Eyal's heavy eyelids nodding as she held out a dustpan.

'Because Yerushalayim – for the Jews!'

The sound of shards clunking in the pan.

'So where are the tribes now?'

Eyal's breath running in a cloud of lemon-flavoured steam.

'All over the world. India. Europe. Africa. But now – this is something magic.'

Picking a fragment of glass off his elbow.

'The tribes –' his lips curling like the branches of a candelabra – 'are coming back.'

*

One of the literary sources that may have contributed to the Prester John letter was written by a wandering Jew called Eldad the Danite. He turned up in ninth-century Tunisia, claiming that he had come from the mythical land of Kush – the name used in ancient texts for the region stretching from Upper Egypt to Ethiopia. His adventures had carried him across the Arabian peninsula, thrown him into the clutches of a tribe of cannibals (who let him go because he was too skinny), and introduced him to the Lost Tribes of Israel, scattered across Africa and Asia. Among them, cut off from the outside world by the same river of sand and stones that would form a barrier to Prester John's Jewish enclave,* was the tribe of Levi. Their locale was 'the land of Havila', somewhere 'beyond the rivers of Ethiopia'.

'Eldad was effectively a raconteur,' insisted Dr David Wasserstein, a bespectacled historian whose flat was on the same street as that of Ariel Sharon. 'A lot of his stories were invented to curry interest among the citizens of Qayrawan.'

Mike and I had returned from a trip to the West Bank that afternoon, with minutes to spare before our respective appointments – he with a rabbi who represented Israel's Anti-Defamation League, I to have tea with Dr Wasserstein. My taxi-driver maintained an impressively impermeable expression as I wiped my sweat with my T-shirt and swapped it for a more respectable polo-shirt, before being ushered into a sitting room where the plush sofa, wall-to-wall carpet, *Complete Works* of Shakespeare and glass-faced cabinet of leather-bound books suggested the British background that was expressed in the professor's Oxford brogue. His kindly mother bustled about, plying me with milky cups of tea and slices of watermelon ('You must eat cold food,' she urged,

---

* The 'ten tribes of Jews, who, although they pretend to have their own kings, are nevertheless our servants and tributaries'.

'when you are in a place as hot as Israel!'), while the professor dispensed information about the mysterious Danite.

Eldad belonged, he suggested, to a tradition in which medieval Jewry was looking for its own land of Prester John – a magic kingdom free from the persecution of Christians like Count Ernich. The promise of thriving Jewish kingdoms in terra incognita provided imaginative relief that was translated to medieval Christian culture in the letter of Prester John. By which time, like Eldad's tribal system, it was already an anachronism.

'That,' explained the professor, 'is why Eldad brings this subject up. He says, "Not only do I have a tribal identity, but mine is different from yours. We've survived with a tribal system longer than you." '

But, in Jerusalem, tribalism would always thrive. It wasn't just Palestinians and Israelis who locked horns in the 'City of Peace'. Israelis themselves were lacerated by sectarianism. The differences between an ultra-Orthodox Jew in fur-trimmed busby and *peyot* sideburns and a sleeveless, knee-baring secular Jew were only the outer expression of the divisions that turned the Israeli parliament – the Knesset – into a tussle between nineteen parties, each forming its own tribal unit.

At the Western Wall during the festival of Tisha B'Av, Mike and I tried to identify the various filaments that comprised Israeli society.

'Got to be Russian,' said Mike, slapping the palm of his hand and pointing to a red-faced endomorph with a beard as bushy as the lining of his *shtreimel* hat. A soldier with cocoa-coloured skin and woolly hair told us that he had emigrated from near Gondar, in Ethiopia. He was a Falasha, tracing his faith to the time of King Solomon. A teenage girl with brown eyes and frosted lipstick was half-Yemeni. Her grandparents, who had grown up with the prophecy of redemption by a great white bird, had been flown out of Aden by Israeli transport planes in Operation Magic Carpet. While talking to her, we were interrupted by a swarthy-faced Moroccan whose first language was Berber. Another evening, I dined with a Polish-born Ashkenazi of Hungarian provenance. Every day brought us into contact with a different strand of Israeli society, and every one of them had a different political perspective. Indeed, so heterogeneous was Israeli politics that Roupen Shahakian, a Jerusalem-based Armenian historian, believed, 'If there is peace, Israel will disintegrate. It's the Palestinians that are keeping them together.'

But immigrant countries are always torn between multiple backgrounds – even a nation with Israel's spiritual and cultural bond. Jerusalem has as great a talent for infighting as any city on earth: Mike and I saw more animosity between the Christian sects in the Church of the Holy Sepulchre than between Christians and Muslims in the whole of Palestine. A similar problem was identified in Outremer by the thirteenth-century Bishop of Acre, Jacques de Vitry. 'As for those men from the noble cities of Genoa, Pisa and Venice, and from other parts of Italy,' he wrote, 'they would be very terrible to the Saracens if they would cease from their jealousy and avarice, and would not continually fight and quarrel with one another.' It was the internal divisions that de Vitry identified as the Crusader kingdom's most vulnerable faultline: 'A kingdom divided against itself,' he wrote, 'cannot stand.'

The threat appeared to be recreated in modern Jerusalem. Left-wing peaceniks distributed pamphlets outside Ariel Sharon's house, while at a roundabout down the street banner-raising hawks chanted, '*Maravat L'Aravim*' – 'Death to the Arabs' – and a recently repatriated ex-New Yorker, in a 'Behold the Lion of Judah' T-shirt, denounced the peaceniks:

'Fu-gedd-about these quislings,' he fumed. 'They got issues wid being Israeli.'

But what is it to be Israeli? A man who believes in the Pentateuch and can trace his origins to the House of Jacob?

Like Samir, who spoke Arabic and had the thick, hawk-nosed features of a middle-aged Palestinian, supported Palestinian resistance and lived near Nablus. He was a member of the Hebrew sect that Benjamin of Tudela met on Mount Gerizim. 'They know the law of Moses,' noted the rabbi; but in one of his less generous moments, he pointed out that 'Their alphabet lacks three letters, namely He, Heth, and Ain': the Samaritans.

Perhaps David Parsons, in that case? His support for Israel went so far that he even praised the controversial Jewish settlers. 'They endoored all this w'a lotta grace,' he drawled in confident Texan, before launching into a diatribe against 'the sugar-daddy' – Yassir Arafat:

'It's the bazaar mentalidee. It's not the qualidee o' yu product, it's whether yu can manipoolate the nations.'

His organization, which attributed the creation of modern Israel not to the British Foreign Office, the United Nations or Zionist lobby groups but to God, was often cited by Arabs as evidence that Israel was a Crusade. But the International Christian Embassy wasn't Israeli, and nor was Parsons: he was an Evangelical Christian.

Two more contradictions greeted me one evening when Yitzi, a Polish-born student, invited Mike and me along to supper in the Old City.

'No can do,' said Mike, whose diary was choc-a-bloc with seminars, appointments and conferences with NGO managers and Foreign Office spokespeople. He was in his element in the Holy Land. He'd enjoyed the trip so far, but it was here that his political sensibilities were best satisfied. 'Everything seems so relevant, so immediate,' he said one night in the Knights' Palace. On the evening that Yitzi suggested, Mike had already secured himself an appointment at the Greek Orthodox Patriarchate. He snapped the latch on his Dictaphone and swept past the mock-Crusader suit of armour in the hotel hallway.

Some minutes later I found myself in a cell on Mount Zion,

at the top of a flight of stone steps. Yitzi's bedsit was, literally, a bed, separated by a moth-eaten curtain from a communal kitchen overspilling with unwashed implements. Cardboard boxes filled the couple of feet his room had to spare, stacked with dusty books that ranged from a black leather-bound Bible to a Russian lexicon.

'Nick, you don't think I invite you to eat *here*?' He slapped my back with mercurial confidence. 'No way. When I invite my friends to eat I always take them somewhere nice.'

So, shooing me out of his hovel with both hands flapping, he directed me across Hurva Square to an establishment where we were divided from the women by a metal screen and our bowls were filled with salad, bread and lentil soup: a Hasidic soup kitchen.

'Nick,' said Yitzi, raising his arms to greet a new arrival, 'meet Hanna.'

A limp hand held mine as I looked into cherry-black eyes lintelled by a straight line of thick, black brow and set in a face the colour of buff leather.

'I am alone,' murmured Hanna. His plastic spoon hovered over the lumpy surface of his bowl.

'Why?' I asked.

'I am an Arab.'

An Arab in a Hasidic soup kitchen?

'And I am a Zionist,' he added.

A cabbage leaf plummeted down the wrong side of my mouth and landed with a splash in my soup.

'I am learning Hebrew,' he continued. 'And I study the Old Testament. It is clear to me that God gave the Holy Land to the Jews.'

Before I could pursue this subject, the report of a megaphonic throat-clearing directed our attention over a row of skullcapped heads to a tall man in a pinstriped suit, who ranted at us like a furious schoolmaster.

'Who is he?' I whispered, careful to keep my voice down lest I be ordered to stand in the corner.

281

'He's from Mea She'arim,' said Yitzi. 'They believe that Zionism is evil and the state of Israel is a blasphemy. They even blame Zionism for the Holocaust.'

'They have a great mistake.' Hanna's lips were quivering and he looked like he was about to cry. It was an extraordinary dynamic: the Zionist Arab taking issue against the anti-Zionist Jew.

When we stepped back on to Hurva Square, gentle winds were tugging at the branches of sycamores whose trunks were gummed with posters proclaiming the teachings of disputant rabbinical authorities.

'Does your family know about your beliefs?' I asked Hanna.

'I cannot tell them,' he said defensively. 'When I read Hebrew, I must do it in secret.'

At the top of King David Street, Arab money-changers flicked thick piles of banknotes on the site of the Frankish Exchange.

'If my family,' whispered Hanna, 'or anyone in my neighbourhood know what I believe, maybe they will report me. They will say I am a collaborator.'

He took hold of my hand, a typically Arab gesture, and leaned closer.

'And you know,' continued his sepulchral voice, 'what happens to collaborators.'

If an Arab could be a devotee of the Jewish state, then why shouldn't a Jew be its implacable opponent? The pinstriped anti-Zionist was intriguing and Mike and I determined to meet the figurehead of his movement, the Neturei Karta or 'Guardians of the City'. The next afternoon, we picked up a taxi for our appointment with Rabbi Moshe Hirsch. Ben Yehuda's neon arcades blinked as tall, tightly packed apartment blocks squeezed us into a neighbourhood whose strict legislation was underlined by the banner hanging over our heads like a speech bubble written by God:

LADIES PASSING THROUGH OUR NEIGHBOURHOOD! WE
BEG OF YOU WITH ALL OUR HEARTS PLEASE DO NOT PASS
THROUGH OUR NEIGHBOURHOOD IN IMMODEST
CLOTHES. MODEST CLOTHES INCLUDE: CLOSED BLOUSE
WITH LONG SLEEVES, LONG SKIRTS OR TROUSERS, NO
TIGHT-FITTING CLOTHES.

The *haredim* of Mea She'arim follow laws that would have
been familiar to Master Philip's Jewish contemporaries,
based as they are on the Mishnah Torah, written by the great
Jewish polymath Maimonides, Master Philip's Cairo-based
contemporary. They forbid the mixing of meat with dairy
products, wool with linen, or unmarried men with unmarried
women. They also time the day from dawn and refuse to pay
taxes to Israel, serve in her army or speak Hebrew, have their
own electricity board so that they won't be tainted by trans-
gressive 'secular' Jews, and stone anyone who drives through
their neighbourhood on Shabbat.

We squeezed between families dressed for eighteenth-century Europe, who shadowed the posters exposing recent
violators of the Torah. A little boy, with elf-locks and a skullcap clipped to his blond head by a shiny silver hairpin,
pecked the driver's window with an index finger and guided
us through the gateway of Moshe Hirsch's house.

In the forecourt, we could hear the hum of neighbouring
worshippers rocking to the rhythm of the Torah. The
wrought-iron staircase clank-clanked as it carried us inside
the house, where the rabbi greeted us in a room lined with
bound religious texts. His velvet skullcap and silver beard, its
length indicating the Levitical disdain for razors, suggested
the mystical hero of a medieval Hasidic folk tale.

'The state of Israel should vanish without bloodshed,' he
said calmly. 'Every Palestinian is affected by what Israel does.
Everything that Sharon does affects Jewish *blood*.'

He identified himself so closely with the Palestinians that Yassir Arafat had appointed him his minister for Jewish affairs. Zionism, he insisted, was 'challenging God. Because we sinned, we're in exile. God says: "I will take you back in my own time." But these people say, "Look here, God, this exile – it's not appealing." They exploit the Holy City, but d'you see them in the synagogue? *I* don't.'

His was a strict Judaism, lightened by jokes about the bonds between Muslims and Jews – 'I order kosher food on the flight to Tunis, this Palestinian turns to me, says, "Hey, *our* food's kosher too." ' Were he as warm towards secular Jewry as he was towards the other monotheistic creeds, he could have designed a blueprint for inter-faith relations.

'So you're hoping to see the establishment of a Palestinian state?' I said.

'Sure.' Then, smiling through his waterfall of beard, he added: 'But it won't last long.'

'Why not?' asked Mike.

'The coming of the Messiah is imminent.' He shrugged. 'The turmoil of what's taking place – it gives it more weight.'

28 July: Tisha B'Av is a glorious day-long carnival, focused on that most un-carnivalesque quality – self-control. From sundown to sundown, the faithful are not allowed to eat, drink, wash, shave, use cosmetics, smile, laugh, sit on decent chairs, have sex or wear leather shoes. Instead, for twenty-five hours they stand or sit cross-legged, in the posture of the shiva – the traditional period of mourning – and remember all the terrible things that have afflicted the nation of Israel on this day: the sin of the spies that condemned the Israelites to wander in the wilderness, the destruction of the first and second temples, the ploughing of Jerusalem with salt, the demolition of the last fortress to resist the Romans in AD 135, the expulsion of Jews from England and Spain, the start of the First World War and the deportations from the Warsaw Ghetto. No wonder some of the mourners' faces – streaming with tears, lips shivering and eyelids swelling; sobbing and squealing as they waved wet tissues and remembered events of two millennia ago – looked like they carried all the heartache of history.

On this particular occasion, the Temple Mount Faithful had decided to liven up proceedings: what better way to mourn the destruction of all those temples than by laying the cornerstone for a new one?* They chiselled four and a half tonnes of marble, filled out the necessary paperwork, and (despite the presence on the Temple Mount of such Muslim buildings as al-Aqsa Mosque and the Dome of the Rock), determined to begin construction of the Third Jewish Temple. And if they set a foot on the site, pledged the Islamic authorities, they would be exterminated.

As we strolled under Damascus Gate, fresh from a particularly pessimistic meeting with a journalist near the West Bank city of Hebron, the stage seemed set for a bloody showdown. Soldiers buzzed between the limestone walls on the Old City's cobbled streets and searched individuals on the plaza inside Jaffa Gate. Orthodox Jews marched home in knots of worsted and *peyot*, under the scowls of Palestinian youths and the Arab waiters wiping glasses in the gathering dusk.

A visit to the Wailing Wall reinforced the sense of Something about to Happen. Men in Al Capone fedoras delivered loudspeaker lectures at the Dung Gate, outside which thousands of Jews were marching in a chain that stretched from the Valley of Jehoshaphat and formed a second wall around the city, as if the population had been commandeered as a buttress.

'Isn't this,' I said to Mike, 'the sort of event that suicide bombers die for?'

We approached a soldier in a fur-trimmed jacket that

---

* And all Prester John wanted was a chapel: maybe he was humble, after all.

doubled as a rucksack, with special pockets for cartridges and walkie-talkies.

'What will happen if the Temple Mount Faithful get on to the Mount?' asked Mike.

'There'll be bloodshed,' the soldier replied.

On the esplanade in front of the Wall, shadow fell like a cloak across several hundred crossed legs: the Holy Day had arrived. Phylacteries swung from the necks of pious Jews as lizards scuttled around the petitions slotted into the wall. A stone's throw away, the low murmur of Islamic devotions emanated from the dome whose myriad aluminium eyes shot golden rays above the Arabs' Stone of Paradise. But, looking around the esplanade, I wasn't so much struck by the spiritual dimension of the festival as by the secularism of Israel. Many of the girls were wearing high-heeled leather shoes and plenty of lipstick. The boys seemed to have been more faithful to Deuteronomical regulations: no laughs or smiles as an army of Mr Bigs swaggered across the square in their tight T-shirts. But, if hair gel counts as a cosmetic, they too had defied the law.

Out of one group whose members certainly weren't defying the law – Orthodox yeshiva students with rigid backs and tiny skullcaps balanced on their heads like inverted saucers – a young man fizzed like a zealot.

'Either the Temple will be rebuilt by the Messiah,' he said, a corkscrew ringlet tilting across his cheek as he leaned towards Mike's Dictaphone, 'or the people will build it ourselves. The point is that we believe this place – the holiest place for the Jews – belongs to us. It doesn't mention Jerusalem in the Qu'ran, but the whole Bible is about Jerusalem. After thousands of years of being killed with the Holocaust and so on, Jews came to Israel and kissed the ground – they were so happy. And now after thousands of years we come to Israel and we want our Temple Mount.'

'But what about the Arabs?' I asked.

'Jews don't want war,' he said, scratching the hair under

his skullcap. 'We've had enough wars. Every Jew has lost someone in his family. But we've tried for peace for fifty years, we gave them Gaza and Ramallah – and they're still attacking us.'

Perspectives ricocheted across the esplanade. Two young ladies, rather less conservatively dressed than the Orthodox students, stood up, brushed dirt off their miniskirts and insisted that the Messiah's arrival was imminent.

'We're waiting for him every minute,' trilled one.

'If we pray hard enough,' added her friend, 'maybe he'll come.'

'Esau hates Jacob,' chimed another, the half-Yemeni whose grandparents had flown out of Aden. 'The Arabs are Esau.'

Before she could develop this point, the Berber-speaking Moroccan had made his incursion.

'Is so simple,' he explained. 'The Jewish temple was here first. We own the Temple Mount.'

'I thought,' said Mike, 'it's an Islamic *waqf*.'

'We bought it,' said the Moroccan.

'When did you buy it?'

'King David bought it. He paid fifty shekels.'

In a West Jerusalem backstreet, where a model of the Temple stood on a raised dais, the tap of a walking stick preceded us into the office of Rabbi Hirsch's fellow doomsayer – the leader of the Temple Mount Faithful.

'We are living,' said Yershon Salomon in his soft Lithuanian lilt, 'the last days.'

Brown eyes gleamed from a kindly face, as the lame ex-paratrooper, whose supporters included white supremacists and Christian Evangelicals, gently drew his picture of Armageddon.

It was all rather self-explanatory: Yassir Arafat clearly being Satan and Ariel Sharon 'closer to the godly ideals of Eezrayel than any prime minister in the past', the conclusion was inevitable. 'We have reached the end times of the prophets,' said Salomon, with the tone of a favourite uncle reading a bedtime story, 'and the coming of the Messiah.'

His belief was not without precedent. Medieval Christians, inspired by the Crusaders' conquest of Jerusalem, predicted that the Antichrist would appear in Jerusalem to wage the great wars of St John's Revelation.

'All nations will come to destroy Eezrayel,' explained Salomon, his soft lips wrapping his words in a mystical gentility, as if he was sucking a delicious fruit. 'The prophets are saying that God will fight to defeat and judge them not only for now but for all history.'

A saintly smile curled under his clipped moustache as he compared Israel to a lamb and the Arabs to wolves, and denied the existence of 'the so-called Palestinians'.

'There never existed a Palestinian state,' he explained, 'and like all foreigners who tried to occupy and control the land of Eezrayel – the Romans, Byzantines, Crusaders and the British – they will pass from history.'

The same belief has been circulating since Nahmanides, who interpreted the defeat of the Crusaders as evidence of Zion's faithfulness to the Children of Israel; a belief renewed by the Messianic fervour that followed Israel's capture of Old Jerusalem in 1967. Like the Messianic David Allroy, who led a rebellion in northern Persia in the mid-twelfth century, Salomon had been singled out by God. So much had become clear to him thirty-four years earlier, when his 'mission' was revealed.

'I was wounded in the Golan,' he explained. 'A Syrian tank drove over my body.'

'Right over you?' Mike frowned.

'My soldiers said I was dead and I felt I was no more living. But God spoke to me. He said, "Yershon, you will not die today. I have a task for you."'

'What happened?' I asked.

'I was taken to the hospital, and Dutch observers told me: "We spoke to the Syrians. They came from the mountains and surrounded you, but they did not shoot you. Instead they ran back to the mountains."'

'Why?'

'They had seen above me –' Salomon shrugged, with proud resignation – 'a flock of angels.'

The next day, a Jewish man was pushing a pram down the path towards the Wailing Wall. He reached a corner and stopped, handed the pram to his wife, moved forward a few steps, peered, then turned round and wheeled the pram back up the hill. The reason for this U-turn was revealed when Mike and I reached the corner and heard a loud bang. The Temple Mount Faithful might have been prevented by Israeli soldiers from laying their cornerstone, but they'd done enough to light the short collective fuse on the Haram ash-Sharif. Policemen, capped, shirted and flak-jacketed in different shades of blue, belted their pistols and rushed up the path to al-Aqsa. We ducked under a sergeant's armpits, and shuffled between elbows and hips and heads and hands.

'Anything happened?' Mike asked a soldier.

'The Arabs throw stones over the wall,' he said.

'Ouch! Must hurt.'

'Yes,' the soldier reflected, 'I think it hurt.' He stroked the aluminium stock of his M16, as a trail of security guards filtered through the green door leading on to the Haram and disappeared to the chug of rifle fire. 'But not so much as bullets, huh?'

Outside the Old City walls, golden frescoes glittered on Gethsemane and thistles crawled around the cubes of the Jewish cemetery. Between the grey columns of the Abbey of the Blessed Virgin, steps pitched past the sepulchres of Frankish aristocrats and a medieval darkness enfolded the kiosk where a candle flickered over the rock-cut grave marking Mary's Assumption to heaven. The Valley of Jehoshaphat gaped under a slope thumping to the clod of soldiers' boots. One of the soldiers, on the spot once dedicated to the decomposition of Crusader bones, was standing on a tombstone where Islamic calligraphy danced in the Arabs' 'belly of the wind'.

'You know it's dangerous, huh?' said a female officer.

'Don't worry about us, honey.' Mike patted her shoulder as he worked his way around a TV reporter under St Stephen's Gate, framed in a crowd of Palestinians as she did her piece to camera. Fizzing behind her, around the back gate to the Haram ash-Sharif, were journalists from more nations than turned up at Pentecost. They smoked and sipped cold drinks and slumped in the shade of a palm tree, jotting notes or refilling their cameras, speaking to the editor on their mobile phones or screaming, 'Where the 'ell's mah stringer?'

A sheikh, the hood of his burnous floating behind him, emerged from the Haram straight into a polyglot deluge of notepads and ballpoint pens, cameras, Dictaphones and microphones poked at him like fishing rods.

'I am from Hebron,' he boomed. 'Where are the Jews from? They are from America, Europe, Yemen. Sharon is from Russia. It is not their land. It is not theirs to build a temple on this land. They are not from Palestine!'

Before he had reached the gate, his place had been taken by another sheikh.

'The Jews are all the same,' he snapped. 'Peace with one hand, slap you with the other.'

He moved towards the gate, and a third sheikh emerged from the compound. The area had become a conveyor belt of angry sheikhs.

By the evening the tension had slackened, so that people could stream on to the Western Wall esplanade with only cursory glances from the soldiers. The diminution of light had a correlative effect on the jubilation in the crowd. A husband kissed his wife and patted his son on the head. His son looked up gleefully as his father raised, with great formality, a gold pocket-watch. He checked the time, unrolled a package of bread and taramasalata, and presented a piece to his son.

Suddenly, everyone was doing the same. Out of pockets, from baskets carried in their hands, from a sack held by an Orthodox rabbi standing in the doorway of a black saloon, or even from under a fur-trimmed *shtreimel* on somebody's head came crisps and bread loaves, plates of chicken drumsticks, bottles of cold drinks.

'It's turned into a picnic ground!' exclaimed Mike.

Men and women lunged at the fountains in the corner of the plaza, screwing their necks as if they were looking at Fra Mauro's Mappa Mundi. An old Sephardi with an enormous bird's nest of beard, like the man in Edward Lear's limerick, strolled contentedly across the esplanade with a cigarette between his lips. At the wall, people were still praying, but with less formality. They hugged around tables pyramided with Torahs, and slapped each other's hips in rings of solidarity. Mike had befriended an old woman whose eyes shone through hollow caves as she dished out bread buns filled with kosher chicken. We munched and smiled and watched a group of young men and women beating drums as they cantered across the esplanade. A white *gelabiyya* flowed down their leader's broad frame, and a black turban bound his curly brown locks. Their wild dance generated a barbaric racket and, inevitably, Orthodox opprobrium. Men with walking sticks only a little longer than their beards wielded them like spears, while the strafe of Levitical laws drowned the beat of the drums.

The dancers belonged to King David's Drummers' Army, and their ambition (as put by Iyal David, their curly-haired leader) was to 'change the energy and bring it for togetherness between all the people, like it's written in the prophets'.

Later that night, as Mike and I talked to Iyal David in an Arab café in East Jerusalem, his companions generated a barrage out of their drums, which drew applause from a nearby party of Palestinians.

'You know,' said Iyal David with a sigh, 'we want to make Jerusalem the spiritual capital of the world – we need the right vibes, not the stone, and drums are an old way to bring the energy. The Prophet Muhammad used to play the drums. Maybe we can all sing Allah Wallah together!'

Rival muezzins locked their chants in a staggered *azan* as the sun set over Moab. We had just two days before we would have to leave Jerusalem, but the luxury of the Knights' Palace had nurtured a lazy inclination towards further delays.

'Right, gotta push on.' Mike tucked his Dictaphone into his jacket and set off on his latest dalliance with Jerusalem's diplomatic community – today, the British ambassador. I turned towards David Street: I had a quest of my own.

One of my favourite reads in the weeks leading to the trip was an Ethiopian epic called the *Kebra Nagast* – 'The Glory of Kings'. In its central storyline, the court of King Solomon receives an unlikely guest, lured less by his legendary wealth (in her own kingdom, after all, 'gold and silver were held as cheaply as brass') than by his wisdom. Her name is Makeda – mainstream history's Queen of Sheba – a woman so beautiful that her host can barely take his eyes off her (although when he does, according to another Ethiopian legend, he has his way with her maid – of which more later). The chemistry between Solomon and Makeda reaches its inevitable climax at night-time. Solomon, swearing that he will not take the queen by force if she doesn't take by force any of his possessions, feeds his guest 'meats which would make her thirsty' and orders his servants to shut the doors and leave a water vessel by her bed. When she wakes up, her mouth 'dry with thirst', she grabs the water and attends to her needs. Solomon, employing his legendary wisdom in the service of his legendary libido, asserts the right to attend to his own needs.

The result is a half-caste love-child called Menelik, who grows up in Sheban Ethiopia, ignorant of his paternity until he is sent to Jerusalem in early adulthood. There, Solomon offers him the crown, but Menelik, good son that he is, insists on fulfilling a promise to return to his mother. Solomon, disappointed, dispatches the sons of the Elders of Zion to keep him company on his homeward trek. But he doesn't realize that the sons of the Elders of Zion have taken a keepsake. And it's not something replaceable, like a timbrel or one of the olivewood souvenirs they've been hawking in Jerusalem's markets since time immemorial. Oh no – the sons of the elders of Zion have taken the greatest keepsake of all.

When Solomon discovers that they have stolen nothing less than the Ark of the Covenant, he is understandably upset. Woe, wrath and general dissatisfaction ensues, until a cameo appearance from the Spirit of Prophecy: 'Zion hath not been given to an alien,' it consoles him, 'but to thy firstborn son who shall sit upon the throne of David thy Father.'And so, the story suggests, 'The people of Ethiopia were chosen [from] among idols and graven images, and the people of Israel were rejected, and the daughters of Ethiopia were honoured.'

The story of Solomon and Makeda was painted to life in a chapel on the rooftop of the Church of the Holy Sepulchre, where an Ethiopian priest rocked on the carved chin-rest of his wooden prayer stick. Above him, next to Evangelical beasts and thurifer-swinging high priests, Makeda marched to her encounter with Solomon, wild green hair-locks casting her as the barbaric ruler of an exotic fantasia suggested by camels, elephants' tusks and the feather headdresses of her spear-brandishing bodyguards. On the other side of the painting, Solomon sat enthroned between lion-headed armrests, high priests and hatted Orthodox Jews behind him.

The clarity of these Jewish details surprised me, since Christian art tends to fudge the association between Old and New Testament: Caravaggio's John the Baptist or Michelangelo's David are no more Jewish than the artists who depicted them. But Abba Solomon, a delightful Ethiopian priest whom I met on the esplanade outside the chapel, where one of his contemporaries had first whetted my interest in his country, had a different perspective. His round face beamed gently under a square black hat as a singsong drawl fluted out of his lips.

'We feel close with the Jews,' he explained. 'When Israel defeat the Arabs, we were happy. I don't know why, but when anything bad happen with the Jews, it touch my heart and I am sad.'

The most unusual member of Jerusalem's Ethiopian community was most conspicuous for the fact that she wasn't Ethiopian at all. Sister Abraham, her yellow fez bobbing above brown-tinted sunglasses, was the only white member of the Ethiopian Orthodox Church in Jerusalem: a Danish nun whose original name was Kirsten. She had ended up with the Ethiopians by accident. Shunned by a Greek Catholic priest on her arrival in Jerusalem in the 1960s (the priest was later, she recalled with a wry half-smile, 'arrested for arms smuggling'), she fell into the friendlier arms of the Ethiopians and 'became one of them'.

As Sister Abraham and I squeezed around the hardware, Tupperware and underwear sold outside Damascus Gate, slid down the ravine of foreign exchange merchants and boys pushing wheelbarrows on flat tyres, and snaked into an empty alleyway, we discussed the assorted legends attached to Ethiopia.

'I don't believe the Ark of the Covenant is in Axum,' she said, 'but the Ethiopians don't like me to say that.' As for the Lost Tribes: 'I'm sure they write very good books about it,' she muttered, 'but when they say they have found the Lost Tribe of this or that, I don't believe it.' There was, however, one legend to which she was prepared to give credit.

'Well,' she mused, 'the legend of Prester John is not as fanciful as one might think. The Ethiopian emperor was not a priest, but he was allowed to enter the sanctuary barefoot, so perhaps this was interpreted as his being a priest.'

Another topic that we discussed was the Ethiopian

monastery on the rooftop of the Church of the Holy Sepulchre – the Deir as-Sultan.

'It's a funny name,' said Sister Abraham, 'because it means Monastery of the Sultan, which seems to be a contradiction. Well, the Copts say it is theirs, but the Ethiopians insist it was granted to them by Solomon.'

'As in Suleiman – the Turkish emperor?' I asked.

'No – Solomon. The son of David.'

'But the monastery wasn't even built then.'

'So might you say. They believe it has only been restored.'

Although it is hard to prove a continued presence over three millennia, the Ethiopians were certainly well established in the city by the sixth century. A pilgrim from Piacenza 'saw men in the streets who came from the direction of Ethiopia, wearing shoes, having their nostrils and ears slit, and rings upon their fingers and their feet'.

Jerusalem also hosted – at least legendarily – Master Philip's most famous Ethiopian contemporary – a member of the Zagwe line spawned by Solomon's seduction of Makeda's maid. Prince Lalibela, fresh from surviving a bowl of poisoned beer that killed his dog, a deacon, and a 'great worm' in his body, was carried by the angel Gabriel to the Holy City, where he hid from the man who had sent him the contaminated brew – his half-brother, King Harbay. So deeply had Jerusalem impressed Lalibela that it became the blueprint for the monolithic churches that he built on his return to his homeland, the same churches that would take Lalibela's name and, a little later, would be critical to our mission.

The battle between Ethiopians and Copts for control of the Monastery of the Sultan was an issue with which I became increasingly familiar as I got to know Abba Solomon. Was I planning to visit Ethiopia? In that case, I must come with him. Firmans, colophons and governmental edicts stiffened my arms: it seemed that I had unwittingly agreed to help him launch legal action against the Copts.

'This is all the history,' he said. 'You must take this away please and put it in good English.'

His eyes narrowed as a tubby Copt padded into a mud-brick hovel across the esplanade.

'You see this man?' Pearly molars gleamed through Abba Solomon's scowl. 'He live in our Deir as-Sultan – he is Coptic guard. But we no want Coptic guard. Deir as-Sultan is us!'

The contest over Deir as-Sultan had become a kind of mini intifada. Although the Copts had the compound keys, control of a gate, a residence behind the Ethiopian houses for their guardian, and authority over repairs and religious ceremonies, it was the Ethiopians who lived there: squatting on steps where they pored through Ge'ez texts, or propped up on prayer sticks for their exhaustive services, like the four-hour prayer sessions conducted every morning during Lent.

But, as I compiled a precis of Abba Solomon's material, I discovered a heap of evidence in the Ethiopians' favour. An Amharic manuscript written in 1863 by Alaqa Walda Madhen Argawi, an Ethiopian living in Jerusalem, claimed that Deir as-Sultan was given to the Ethiopians not once but twice: first by Saladin and later, in 1390, by the Byzantine Emperor. Their occupation of the compound was confirmed by Ottoman firmans in the sixteenth, seventeenth and twice in the nineteenth centuries. But, after their community had been wiped out by a combination of plague and a manipula-tive Egyptian called Ibrahim al-Jawahiri, and their property incinerated by the Copts (who simply *had* to contain the pestilence), Ethiopia's Jerusalem branch appeared to be extinct. It was then that support seeped in from unusual quarters – a British consul, an Anglican bishop, a German cartographer – and in 1905 Emperor Menelik II secured par-tisan signatures from every Christian leader in Jerusalem. Except the Copts.

The establishment of Israel in 1948 hardly facilitated matters. Deir as-Sultan had become a pawn – an increasingly dilapidated one – swinging to the whims of Jerusalem's rulers. Ethiopian rights might have been affirmed by the Jordanians in 1961, but they were abrogated by order of Egypt's President Nasser. Surely Jewish control of the city would favour them? But after victory in the 1967 war, Israel's government insisted that the Ethiopian government must acknowledge Israeli rights over Jerusalem in order that they recognize the Ethiopians' rights to less than an acre of it. Since he was President of the Organization for African Unity, which included several Arab states, Emperor Haile Selassie's hands were tied. So, as Yassir Arafat was establishing the PLO in 1964, Copts were throwing stones at Ethiopian Palm Sunday processions; when Lebanon was bracing for civil war, the Copts were receiving the keys to the compound from the Israeli High Court; and, while Israelis and Palestinians were plunging into the latest intifada, Copts and Ethiopians were glaring at each other around the dome of the Chapel of St Helena.

Anba Abraham, the Coptic archbishop, blamed it on the usual source of Arab disgruntlement:

'It is the fault of Eezra'eel,' he insisted, the clarity of his words somewhat compromised by a pillow of beard and the fact that, when I met him, we were wedged between several demonstrators and an IDF mobile command post near Bethlehem. 'They are trying to get political advantage,' he said, 'so they get the Falashas from Ethiopia.'

But Abba Solomon, with equal consistency, blamed everything on the Copts. 'Is so unfair,' he whined. 'Until our ownership is confirmed we cannot even fix a toilet.'

Nor, he assured me, were Coptic crimes confined to present-day Jerusalem.

'We tried to make our own bishops in the twelfth century,' he said, 'but they refused because they needed us.'

'Did *you* not need *them*?' I asked.

'Well, this is true – otherwise we would be isolated from Oriental Christians. But in the past, when we had a problem with Egypt, the Ethiopian ruler always sent a message to

Egypt: "if you don't stop this we will stop the flow of the Blue Nile." '

A thrill went through me as he said this: the ability to stopper the Nile was one of Prester John's legendary attributes.

Abba Solomon's office was in the Ethiopian Patriarchate, down a street of loose piping and painted crosses where you'd have struggled to herd a pair of side-by-side mules. A budgie cage hung beside the compound's gate, above a relief that embodied Ethiopia in the figure of the Virgin Mary.

Inside, potted plants shaded snoring laymen and a bleary-eyed porter called Jimmi whispered into a telephone. I had arranged to meet the archbishop, just as Fra Alberto da Sarteano had done in his own fifteenth-century Prester Quest.

Dead archbishops watched us from their picture frames as Jimmi led me into their successor's office. He was rocking in his chair, a homespun *shemma* wrapped around his black cassock and a medallion of Mary and Child hanging over his breast. He raised the silver cross in his hands and gestured for me to sit on a small sofa covered with a threadbare throw. Each question merited a faint levitation of eyelids and a soft drawl, translated by Jimmi. The Ethiopian community in Jerusalem, explained Abba Qawstos, comprised sixty monks and twenty-five nuns, as well as a significant lay population that swelled to a thousand-strong at Easter time. The Ark of the Covenant, certainly, was in Axum; and the community fasted two hundred days of the year, 'for Jesus' fast in the wild, because our church retains the customs of Jesus' times'.

'Did the Christian Church develop out of the Jewish faith in Ethiopia?' I asked.

'We Christi-arn,' the archbishop replied, through Jimmi's translation, 'before Jesus Jewish, from Solo-man. Eetopyarn Church tree tow-san' year old.'

The conversation gradually wound down, but to my surprise, as I stood up to leave, the archbishop raised his gold-embroidered cuff.

'He has question for you,' said Jimmi.

I sat back down and smiled obediently. Something in the archbishop's creased forehead suggested that there were serious matters he wished to resolve.

'He want know,' said Jimmi, 'why in Englan' you has womans priesties.'

'Er . . .'

'Womans for cleanin' an' cookin', no priesties.'

'Well, I suppose some people have different—'

'You go back Englan', you speak your Referee Carey.'

'I don't think I can – I'm not even one of his—'

'Say for him womans priesties stupid.'

They wouldn't give it up, so I promised to do my best. The issue of womans priesties was very dear to Archbishop Qawstos.

After the meeting I wandered back to the rooftop, where I had arranged to meet Mike. One arm wobbling on a creaky banister, I gazed towards the old Frankish cloisters as he marched past the dome of St Helen's, patting the Dictaphone with which he'd recorded the British ambassador's thoughts.

'Awesome!' he said. 'Big man gave me tea and said being an ambassador's like being a priest – gotta look after your parish.'

A fat woman in rags was hanging laundry from a mulberry tree, humming nasally, like a Jewish *chazzan*.

'Not long now, al-Jub. Three days and we'll be in Alex. The home straight.'

I frowned. 'The three-and-a-half-thousand-kilometre home straight.'

'Yeah, but it's not as complicated as the Levant.'

'God, I hope not.'

A balloon-bellied Ethiopian priest padded out of a cross-daubed doorway, holding a mug rich with the scent of nutty coffee.

'We'll be on the stem of the question mark,' I said. 'You know – on the map.'

There, on the rooftop of the Church of the Holy Sepulchre, we could smell our destination.

But, before we venture into Sinai, to a nocturnal haggling session with a driver whose favourite direction was backwards, and a monastery where medieval monks still resided in a charnel house, we must stay put in the Holy Land a little longer, to explore the West Bank and the Gaza Strip.

CHAPTER ELEVEN

VISIONS OF HELL

ONE DAY IN THE winter of 1183, Reynald de Chatillon hosted a party. His stepson Humphrey de Toron had married the eleven-year-old sister of the King of Jerusalem, and the lords and ladies of Outremer had come along to celebrate. It was going to be a scream.

It really was a scream. Touring the battlements while he was still compos mentis, Reynald noticed a torrent of terrified shepherds sweeping their goats into the bailey. Saladin was about. He didn't have an invitation, but he did (thanks to Reynald's recent pillage of Muslim caravans heading to Mecca) have a grudge. A big one.

Not, decided the groom's mother, that anything so negligible as a few stone-hurling Saracen mangonels was going to ruin her son's day. Jugglers juggled and flautists fluted; guests clashed goblets of honey-flavoured wine and Saladin's siege engines clashed with the walls. But chivalric values dictated the groom's mother must offer a share of the feast to the party's most literal gatecrasher: an assortment of dishes was dispatched, and Saladin reciprocated appropriately, instructing his soldiers to slow the siege and leave the bridal suite intact. Sure, highly commendable from the perspective of twelfth-century Ps and Qs; less so when judged by the more brutal rules of successful military strategy. Within a fortnight of his arrival at Kerak, Saladin had been chased away by the arrival of King Baldwin IV's full-scale Frankish army.

The wedding party at Kerak is one of the grace notes tinkling through the protracted brawl of massacre and machinations that is the history of Outremer. Our correspondent in situ is Ibn Jubayr, for whom the mercantile situation was typical of the dichotomy of war: 'Long the siege lasted,' he wrote, 'but still the caravans passed successively . . . In the same way, the Muslims continuously journeyed from Damascus to Acre [through Frankish territory], and likewise not one of the Christian merchants was stopped or hindered [in Muslim territory].'

If only access to Jericho had been that easy.

'You want Jericho? You're crazy?'

In the Jerusalem suburb of Abu Dis, on the morning of the same day that I was hoping to visit Dr Wasserstein in West Jerusalem, a microbus driver expressed his opinion of our plan to visit Jericho by spitting on my shoes.

'Only Palestinians,' he said, 'go Jericho.'

The city most famous for the musicians who blew it down had, since the beginning of the intifada, been sealed by a trench. Palestinians spoke of a siege: supplies that couldn't be brought in; people who couldn't come out. Instead of Joshua's trumpeting warriors, the encirclers were Israeli soldiers with big black shades and big black machine guns. It was irresistible.

Over a shirt-dripping half-hour, Mike and I worked our way through most of Abu Dis's cab industry: we wouldn't be allowed in; we would be taken for spies and arrested. Individually, drivers snorted, laughed and performed the nodding gesture that in the Middle East means no; uniformly, they drove off. The only positive response – and he certainly doesn't deserve our thanks – was offered by the Snake.

'Twenty shekels,' he hissed, slithering his saurian neck through the window of his rust-coated rattletrap.

The urban sprawl of Jerusalem's Arab suburbs – tottering apartment blocks festooned in laundry – ran into the pudding-trolley texture of the desert: rocky hills like chocolate-spotted sponge cakes melting into vanilla-coloured sand or trifles of scrubland where Bedouin herdsmen guided camels with ice-lolly necks. The road hooped and a cliff climbed over a wadi. The Jordanian border squinted in the distance and, out of a brilliance of white rock, there emerged an oasis metropolis.

'So,' sibilated the Snake, 'as soon as we see sheckpoint, you step out of taxi.'

Moments later, he slid towards the door and salaamed us into a screen of sandbags where a soldier's green beret flickered inside a nest of camouflage netting. The crunch of his boots chimed against the gravel as he stepped towards us.

'You cannot enter,' he said.

'But we've come all the way from Jerusalem,' I whined.

'It is the rule.'

He tapped the proboscis of his light machine gun and showed us his back. We were miles from Jerusalem, inches from Jericho. It was hot. We were thirsty. With impeccable economy, Mike summed up the situation:

'Bugger.'

I crouched on a hump of sand and dropped my chin in my hands. Now that we were here, we *had* to couldn't not must absolutely damned well would get in. But how? There was no secret tunnel (the traditional route for illegal entry), no clandestine rope like the one dangled from Damascus for Nur ad-Din's soldiers in 1154; and neither of us had a trumpet. There was only a taxi (leaving rather than entering Jericho) and lots of sand.

'Where you want to go?' asked the driver of the taxi.

'Jericho,' I said.

'This is Jericho.'

303

'Yes, but they won't let us in.'

The man studied our hats, our pink faces, Mike's sleeveless jacket, my drenched T-shirt, Mike's white trousers with the multiple side-pockets, my cotton drawstrings, and typed his decision into his mobile phone. The result, not more than five minutes later, glided alongside us, beckoned us into a black Mercedes, and introduced himself as Muhammad.

'You know tourists aren't allowed in Jericho,' he said, as he drove past a highway sign apparently erected to shore up this observation:

```
        No tourists admitted.
        Prepare your documents
             for inspection.
```

We drove away from Jericho, across flat, barren desert, heading towards the Jordanian border.

'Oh God, no,' I groaned, and buried my sweaty head in my even sweatier hands. It was one thing not to be allowed into Jericho, but to be transported back to Jordan – no, this was too much. I glowered through the windscreen at a wasteland interrupted only by the peeling corpse of a bus, wedged into the sand with sunlight shooting through its empty windows. Then I saw an orange orchard.

'Muhammad,' I began, 'where exactly are . . .'

Several palm trees. A couple of flat-roofed houses, one of them gashed by a missile imprint the shape of the Star of David.

'OK,' said Muhammad, steering the car to standstill. 'Go across that trench and wait under the tree.'

We crossed a crater and stood under a solitary palm. The most striking local feature was a big metal frame that might once have been a house. Nearby, a flock of goats did the hokey-cokey around a silver car that was slewing through their field. Down wound its window and out popped the Cheshire Cat grin of a man who introduced himself as Muhammad's brother.

'Well-com,' he announced, 'in Jericho!'

After the ordeal of getting into the city, the experience of visiting it was somewhat anticlimactic, that being the inevitable result when the shops are shuttered, there are no cars on the road and the streets are deserted. Like Felix Fabri, the fifteenth-century Dominican friar from Ulm, we could say: 'This city was first destroyed by Joshua, secondly by the Romans, thirdly by the Tartars, and last of all by other people so that at this day it is a village, without walls or moats and with but few inhabitants.'*

One inevitable effect in a city under siege is that its site curators have lost the incentive to turn up to work. This wasn't a problem when it came to visiting the Umayyad hunting lodge of Hisham's Palace, whose sandstone walls were short enough to hurdle; but it was more complicated with the building we most wanted to visit.

The Monastery of the Temptation was founded by the Crusaders on the spot where Satan reputedly offered Jesus all the kingdoms of the world. From Joshua's Tell we could see, superimposed on to the cliff like a fake photo, a double-domed structure of baklava-coloured brick, reached by a white staircase of biblical extent. At the top, we threw ourselves against the door of the church and took it in turns to attack the knocker, panting and fretting about the thirst that would have left us vulnerable to the most basic of temptations:

'A cup of water I will give you, if you kneel down and worship me.'

'Er – OK.'

---

* The intifada wasn't the only culprit. Jericho hasn't been the same for about, oh – eight centuries. It was a rich city in Outremer, prospering from sugar mills, but after Saladin's annus mirabilis of 1187 it was unable to withstand the raids of local Bedouin. A brief revival occurred after the First World War and the city's casino became a major source of revenue, but the instability of the Israeli-Palestinian conflict had drained Jericho's wealth and left it an isolated desert outpost.

Mike knocked. I knocked. We knocked together.

'There must be somebody in there,' I moaned.

We banged on the door with our fists. We called through the keyhole. Mike sang a lullaby. We shouted: '*Min fadlak* – please.' We displayed our entire Greek vocabulary for the benefit of the Greek Orthodox monks supposedly interred inside: '*Kalimera*' (Hello). '*Epharisto*' (Thank you). '*Pou einai oh pleion?*' (Where is the ship?) We found another door, poked our heads through the cross-barred window, and screamed. And knocked. We stormed up and down the steps in search of life. Nothing. So we knocked. Here was Sod's Law in all its splendour – you penetrate the City to which Foreigners May Not Go, and the site you've come to see is shut. Whether the monks were having a day off or had simply abandoned the place, we didn't know. Perhaps they were on their siesta. I felt an empathy with the devil: I too had been frustrated on the Mount of Temptation.

We climbed back down the steps and sat on the rocks. No doubt an Arab shepherd or two had rested where I now slumped, or, for that matter, an Israeli soldier, placing his gun between his knees as he smoked a cigarette before heading back to his tank. My rock was perfectly formed to act as a seat – round, shaped like a stool, and the right height for a good leg-stretch. Had an Ottoman janissary once stopped here, I wondered, to tie the laces of his red boots? Before him, a Mamluke or a coifed Crusader? A procession of fellow sitters slouched in my mind's eye: a Persian prince sipping balsam juice to cure a headache, one of Mark Antony's toga-wrapped Romans, an Israelite shepherd with his crook across his lap. Enemies, most of them, united only by the passion of their leaders to control the rocks on which we were sitting.

Our visit to Jericho was one of several adventures out of Jerusalem, during which we followed the clank of Israeli tank-treads into the West Bank, where Master Philip's fellow

Christians dwelt in rich cities such as Jericho and Nablus, surrounded by a wasteland of Bedouin tribesmen. The Bedouin and the wasteland are still there; so are cities such as Jericho and Nablus – though you could hardly call them rich. Now, what affluence the West Bank contains is concentrated in the rectilinear, solar-panelled Jewish settlements – alien constructions among the unwieldy contours of the East, symbols of the Israeli occupation created by the Six Day War of 1967.

Stony hills peel back Jerusalem's suburbs as our bus rolls past villages where soldiers nestle into camouflage netting above eyries of animals and aluminium cooking pots. Around us, grannies with shopping bags and grandchildren, farmers with hessian sacks and businessmen with suitcases chain us to a padlock of big brown eyes. Ahead of us is the West Bank's alternative to traffic lights: a military checkpoint. At each stop, a trigger-tapping soldier scrutinizes our bus, engaging the most defiant passengers in staring contests.

'What are you doing?' he asks us.

The truth is that we're en route to meet Khalad Amayreh, a 'radical' Palestinian journalist living under self-styled 'town arrest' in the town of Dura, near Hebron.

'Tourism,' says Mike.

One passenger has an imaginative way of dealing with the hold-ups. A lint-haired soldier with a bloodshot eye has refused our bus permission to pass. In the back, impatient throat-clearing gives way to exasperated gasps. A pinstriped Palestinian tugs his tie and squeezes his head through his window.

'Look,' he says, in English (discussion between Israelis and Arabs tends to be conducted through a 'neutral' language), 'I am doctor and we have sick baby in here, she needs treatment. I implore you: let us through.'

To the soldier's low grunt, the doctor responds by squeezing his neck and shoulders through the window and conducting an inspection of the soldier's face.

'I see your eye is bad,' he continues. 'I work with St John's ophthalmic hospital. If you let us through, I can make your eye better.'

The soldier touches his eyelid with a gentleness that seems to affect his other hand's grip on his carbine. He blushes, looks round to check that his colleagues aren't watching, and leans forward to listen to the doctor.

'If you don't treat your eye, you could contract a disease,' explains the doctor. He pulls a strip of paper from his wallet – perhaps a ticket or a receipt – scribbles a prescription and hands it to the soldier, who nods, stuffs it in his pocket and mumbles, 'Move on,' to our driver.

Ibn Jubayr's remark that, during the Crusades, 'The soldiers engage themselves in their war, while the people are at peace' is an antidote to the perception of war as an absolute. In the monochrome image of conflict, as reductive as the green night-goggles of an Israeli sharpshooter, we forget about David Khoury, forced to pare down production at Taybeh, the only brewery in Palestine; or David's wife Maria, who hands out free bottles of beer to the checkpoint soldiers so they'll let her complete the school run; or Maria's colleague Maher al-Atrash, switching off his computer as another threat of missile strikes forces him to leave the Latin Patriarchate Schools' office in Ramallah; or Maher's three-year-old daughter Marina, who wakes up screaming in the middle of the night. Yet even Ibn Jubayr's comment is a simplification: as the eye doctor on the road to Hebron showed us, co-operation doesn't necessarily mean conviviality. Just because you serve a man hummus, scrub his toilets or weave the material for his flags, it doesn't mean you don't want him dead.

Between our first visit to the Holy Land the previous year and this return trip, relations between Israelis and Palestinians had become even less convivial. In Ramallah, blank-faced men who used to work for Israeli bosses now sank on to milk-crate stools, siphons hissing as tobacco pumped into their mouths like a hospital patient's drip-feed.

'The average salary,' said our friend Diala Sa'adeh, a Palestinian journalist, 'is twelve dollars a day, but most people aren't even getting a salary. In some of the homes you find two or three families together, with no food between them. Many of them used to work for Israeli companies, but now . . .'

'Their bosses sacked them?' suggested Mike, as we passed Ramallah's landmark – the bullet-scored marble lions frozen under a giant kalashnikov-wielding *fida'i*.

'They sacked 30,000 of them. But sometimes they quit because they don't want to work for Israelis any more.'

'Even if that's the only way to make any money?' I asked.

'Maybe for us,' said Diala, 'the land is more important than money.'

In order to understand the pull of Prester John for medieval Christians, one has to understand the pull of the Holy Land. The importance of the soil sanctified by the feet of their Messiah boosted the hope invested in an Oriental Christian redeemer who might fuse the royal and religious roles embodied in Christ the King. It is hard to empathize with this ideology in the mobile Western world, where land means real estate and few people can locate the homes of their great-grandparents. But the Middle East preserves many of the ideas associated with the Middle Ages. In a refugee camp near Nablus, Mike and I would meet an old paraplegic still pining for a house in Haifa that he hadn't seen in fifty years; a similar nostalgia had affected the refugee I met in Sidon, who longed for a city in which he had never set foot. Often we found such traditions still strong in the most surprising people: Muhammad, a hotelier in East Jerusalem, slouched in front of a late-night blue movie with a joint in one hand and a bottle of Taybeh beer in the other, was one Palestinian I didn't expect to weep over the loss of soil.

'My father he lived in a town in what is now West

Jerusalem,' he said, 'and the Eezra'eelees they throw him out. So I go there, I want to know where was the mosque and I find these Eezra'eelees – they use it as a house, and they climb up the minaret for a good view. It made me cry, I tell you this.'

Diala had reported on many similar examples: a mosque in Tiberias that had become a bar, another in Jaffa that was now a fish restaurant, a nearby cemetery-turned-park, and a church in al-Kassa.

'Now,' she hissed, 'it's a dump for the rubbish.'

Diala was one of several friends from our previous stint in the Holy Land. People like Father Ra'ed, the genial Chancellor of the Latin Patriarchate, the teachers we had worked with six months earlier, or Sandra, Caro and Salam, three students in Bir Zeit who dressed in tight trousers, wore jewellery and laughed about boys with the familiarity that I had assumed to be exclusive to women in the West:

'So maybe they won't let us smoke on the street,' Sandra chortled one evening, twiddling a coil of black hair, 'but we have our own ways of making the boys do what we want!'

Superficially, at least, their lives had the appearance of normality. One evening out on the town in Ramallah, Mike and I went to the cinema with Caro and Salam to watch the Hollywood film *There's Something about Mary*, and followed it up with Irish whiskies in a local bar. Salam, the most beautiful woman I had ever seen this side of a film screen, was radiant that evening: her generous hazelnut mane pitched wildly around her shoulders, and her flushed cheeks lifted up her freckles as she spoke. But the intifada always simmered close to the surface. Conversation inevitably drifted into politics, and Salam launched a passionate tirade against 'Eezra'eel', before announcing, 'I would rather die than leave Fa-la-steen.' She pronounced the word with pietistic care, as if it was controlled by a different vocal cord from the rest of her vocabulary. After that evening, whenever I heard the word 'Falasteen' – whether from a student called Ra'ed, demanding rights, passports and 'Falasteen' in Bethlehem University, or from the Fatah activist Marwan Barghouthi in his tower-block office in Ramallah, insisting that the intifada 'expresses the feelings of the people of Falasteen', or from a sheikh outside the Haram ash-Sharif in Jerusalem, assuring a crowd of reporters that 'They (the Israelis) are not from Falasteen!'– it reminded me of Salam.

Ultimately, it was impossible to escape the intifada in Palestine. It cropped up even on an innocuous afternoon with the family of one of my favourite Palestinian hosts, a mercurial middle-aged haberdasher called Ghassan. I had first met him among the coils of cigarette smoke and the clink of journalists' camera equipment in the American Colony Hotel in East Jerusalem. One evening I had found myself wedged between Mike and a young English nurse on whom he had made a rather favourable impression. It was a tête-à-tête in which I had become a painfully extraneous à. My eyes roved in search of a sanctuary to which I could excuse myself, and found it in the form of Ghassan's frosted beer glass, raised above his head in greeting.

'My friend, you drink with me!' He rapped his copper table. 'Tonight we musht drunky!'

This time Ghassan invited me to have lunch at his house on the outskirts of Jeruslaem, in Bethany, near a church founded by a Crusader queen to commemorate the anointing of Christ's feet. A triple-storeyed box of curd-white limestone towered over the olive groves and an elderly man waved from an iron balustrade.

'I share the house with my family,' said Ghassan.

And so it proved, as three generations emerged from the orchard to offer their greetings.

First came Ghassan's mother and three veiled sisters, whose religious beliefs prevented them from shaking my hand. Then, as we stepped on to a stone-paved forecourt, I met the younger generation. 'Pick!' commanded Ibrahim, not so much an eleven-year-old as a mischievous smirk with arms and legs. A wooden ladder moaned as I rested it against an olive tree. Then something pricked my head. Olives rained down on me, trickling off my shoulders and falling into the hijab folds of the veiled sisters who crawled across the forecourt. Between the silver arrowheads of the leaves, Ibrahim's eyes shone impishly. And on the other side of the tree, too. And on the – hang on! – there were four of them, an army of assailants to whom the tree was a climbing-frame and I – the one they addressed with orders of 'How Are You!' – the target of their artillery. Bruised and beaten, I sank into the warm embrace of a sofa, where I became the focus of a more benevolent siege. Offers of cushions, coffee and cigarettes were catapulted by Ghassan and his father, whose whiskers drew the letter W around his shining nose.

'He fought under the British – with Glubb Pasha,' said Ghassan.

'I also fought in '48,' snapped his father, smoothing down his *gelabiyya*. '*We* did not lose Jerusalem in '48. *They* lost her in '67.'

Ghassan's dark-eyed wife, Amina, laid an enormous dish on a glass-topped table and, picking a grain of rice off her wool-knit sweater, invited everyone to start.

'This is *mensaf*,' she explained, 'our traditional dish.'

Ripe lumps of lamb bouldered a mountain of rice where almonds and lentils peeked out like scree. I stabbed at my helping with the only available utensil – a spoon – but was quickly corrected.

'Use your hands,' snapped Ibrahim Sr. 'You wash them later.'

The meat dribbled over my self-conscious fingers, while Ghassan's children surrounded me with loudly munching jaws and wide, astonished eyes.

'You like the way we live?' asked Ghassan.

'Of course,' I said, eager to please. 'The Arab world is famous for its hospitality.'

Amina sneered: 'Sometimes this is a problem. You heard about Hatim?'

'Oh yes,' said Ibrahim Sr, 'you will tell him about Hatim.'

'He was a Bedouin,' said Amina, who clearly had every intention of doing so, 'and he had only one horse, because all the others he gave to his guests. He believed that if anyone came near his tent, he must offer them some food, so now he had only a little left. But his enemy came near the tent, and he prayed to Allah, "Please, please, do not let him pass my tent." But his enemy walked past, and Hatim looked at the horse and said to himself, "What should I do?" But he knew what was his obligation. So he ran out of the tent and fell on his knees and said to his enemy, "Please, you must come and eat." And he gave his enemy his last horse.'

Ghassan shook his head. 'A foolish man.'

'It is a principle,' his wife retorted.

'And a good story,' said Ibrahim Sr. 'You will have some more – you are a skinny boy!'

I was already stuffed. But something in his face, as formal as a figure in a Persian miniature, suggested that he was not one of Glubb Pasha's weaker underlings. A second helping slipped down my gullet, a third followed swiftly behind, succeeded by the morsels of a fourth, so that by the time we sank on puffy sofa-chairs in front of the TV my ribs were being suffocated and there was barely any air-space left in my windpipe.

Despite the images of *Pokémon* on the TV, and the giggles of the children sitting cross-legged inches from the screen, the atmosphere had turned sombre.

'You know,' sighed Ghassan, 'I don't think I have enjoyed one happy day in Palestine.'

He remembered his days as a student in San Francisco, where he'd driven a Buick and had the pick of the girls.

'Would you rather go back there?' I asked.

'How I can?' He watched his wife carry an enormous gilt-brass cafetière. 'I belong in Falasteen.'

313

He pressed the remote control and *Pokémon* was replaced by the local news. A woman, her black hijab perfectly suited to widows' weeds, spidered her arms over her husband's bier. Amina shook her head at the screen and tilted the cafetière over a cup.

'I wish I had a gun,' she muttered.

'We are an ingenious people,' exclaimed Father Ra'ed, one of our favourite guides in the Holy Land, a tall, lean man in his black cassock with a hive of matted hair and a nose like a buzzard's beak. 'And when we have our independent country,' he added, 'we say it will be the dawn after the long dark of the night.'

Father Ra'ed often drove Mike and me around the West Bank to inspect his latest projects – a chicken farm he had established to promote the local economy, a municipal park in Bethlehem, a Bedouin tent that had been transformed into a restaurant. Once, he took us to the studios of Nativity TV, from where the Latin Patriarch's Masses were beamed to Palestinian and Jordanian villages. 'If the people cannot come to Jerusalem,' he explained, as his film flickered on the small screen, 'then Jerusalem must come to them!'

That Father Ra'ed was ingenious was manifested by the extraordinary tactic he employed at the fortified roadblock outside Bethlehem.

'I will do something,' he said, hands rapping his steering wheel as we slowed towards the soldiers, 'that they cannot expect.'

A khaki elbow leaned on the lip of the passenger window and a pair of aviator shades appeared above it.

'Passports!' snapped the soldier.

Then Father Ra'ed did something startling.

He smiled.

'Good morning,' he burst out. 'Is it not a beautiful day?' He handed over our passports. 'So much sun! So much joy! So much—'

'OK,' snorted the soldier, and a light machine gun waved us through to Bethlehem.

After our tour of his projects, Father Ra'ed dropped us a short stroll from Manger Square. Mounds of coloured spices rose among olivewood crucifixes and models of the Church of the Nativity manned by men with expressions as empty as their tills. Flapping beside them, superimposed in front of the Dome of the Rock, were the heroes of the Occupied Territories, the suicide bombers. Forget the ornamented casket of the medieval martyr* – the vaporized *shahida* were remembered through the more up-to-date medium of the photo-poster.

The man who served our falafel sandwiches in a den of sawdust and spit near the Church of the Nativity in Bethlehem was a *shahida* expert. He stroked his toilet-mat beard and guided us through the iconography of martyrdom as dispassionately as if we were studying a Byzantine fresco cycle. 'This is Hasan al-'Abyad,' he said, pointing to a skinhead with a face as impenetrable as an anvil, a bandolier around his neck and arm muscles as developed as those of the Mamluke warriors who sliced lumps of clay a thousand times a day with their swords. He was one piece in a full-colour jigsaw puzzle that attributed such expressions as 'He is worth a thousand men' and 'He won his martyr's crown in Jenin' to operatives for Hamas, Islamic Jihad, the PFLP and Fatah; square-jawed and bandoliered, or delicately built, with metal-framed glasses, or heavily pomaded, leather-jacketed and black T-shirted like extras from *Grease*.

Mike and I had raised the subject of suicide bombers a few days earlier, during an interview with the Grand Mufti of Jerusalem, one of their most high-profile supporters.

* Typical of his time was Master Philip's German contemporary, John of Würzburg, who located, among other items, John the Baptist's forefinger, the head of St James, the body of St Chariton and the hair of Mary Magdalene.

'Do you think,' I had asked him, 'that Saladin would approve of the spilling of blood by suicide bombers?'

Saladin, accused of usurping Nur ad-Din's power, legitimized his own through the religious sanction of jihad. But, like the author of the contemporary *Sea of Precious Virtues*, a book that he was known to esteem, he believed that a warrior must not kill women or children.

'These young men,' said the Mufti, 'who explode themselves for Islamic and national purposes are greater than all others. They have sacrificed themselves for a great purpose.'

'Even if such sacrifice entails the sacrifice of seventeen Israeli teenagers in an Israeli nightclub?'

'Even if they kill all Israelis. Anyone who explodes himself in Israel is a great person. They are the most noble of men, and they are alive in heaven, in the highest form of paradise, and God is taking care of them.'

Father Maroun, when we discussed the bombers with him later that evening in Beit Jala, admitted that they troubled him.

'The Islamic fatwa,' he began, 'says if you die for your faith or your country then you go to heaven. This is the same for Christianity. To die for your cause is honourable. But in Islam, also to kill for your faith – they don't wash the people who kill themselves like this, because they say their blood must be on them. It's their passport to paradise.'

Many Arabs wanted to emigrate to America or Europe. In a world where heaven and hell were as real as for Master Philip's contemporaries, the *shahida* had the green card to a different sort of emigration.

But killing for your faith isn't exclusive to Islam. The military orders of the Crusades practised the same policy of indifference to the blood of the 'infidel' as that followed by the modern-day *shahida*. And that wasn't the only common ground. The Hospitallers, like the modern militant Islamic group Hamas, provided care for the sick and poor, squabbled with rival factions, clashed with their government and preached an equation between death (in battle) and heavenly salvation.

The same philosophy that had transformed the *shahida* into the Palestinian alternative to pop stars was being expounded in Manger Square. In front of the Mosque of Omar Ibn al-Khattab, boys sat in cross-legged intensity, ears cocked as a crackling loudspeaker fulminated against 'Eezra'eel'. Men leaned against the pillars of a shopping arcade, while their wives huddled like black crows behind them. Apart from the odd pop of a cashew nut, the crowd was hushed, united by the sermon and the intensity burning in their eyes. On the other side of the square, facing their backs, was the Church of the Nativity. Its emptiness underlined the tragedy of the indigenous Christians, in Master Philip's day the largest demographic group in the Holy Land, now shorn to less than 2 per cent. Even the shape of the church, hugging the forecourt maternally rather than thrusting into the sky, expressed a lack of the aggression necessary to survival in the Holy Land. We ducked under the Door of Humility, shortened to half the height of the arched Crusader entrance to deter Ottoman-era looting, and strolled under the bright golds and greens of the mosaics produced by a collaboration between Manuel Comnenos and King Amalric of Jerusalem. It was a beautiful, eccentric shrine, whose price the medieval pilgrim Burchard of Mount Sion deemed inestimable. Surprising features filled the nave, like the 'well of sweet and cold water into which it is said that the star fell which guides the three magi' or the jungle of pillars frescoed with images of holy has-beens like Cathal of Ireland and Olaf II Haraldsson of Norway. Their images were so faded that the details had melted into the ruddy limestone. Kings and saints might once have been famous, but without a bandolier the chances of modern Bethlehemite stardom are slim.

Mike was already back outside, watching the crowd in the square. I wanted to visit the birth-cave, now without the crowds that had filled it at Christmas. My footsteps thudded down the stairwell and overhead I heard the murmur of low-flying aircraft. I wasn't alone. There, flipping the lids to the candles around the star-shaped memorial to Christ's birth, was the chandler. His eyes greeted me with a businesslike twinkle. I knelt beside the star, kissing a spot venerated by the Franks.

I felt uncomfortable. Maher al-Atrash said that his family was saved from death because they had prayed at Mary's Well the day their house was bombarded. But as I pressed my lips to the memorial, I could still hear the thrumming of an Israeli gunship. And all I could feel was a plate of cold metal.

In the evening, Bethlehem was still visible from the windows of the Latin Patriarchate seminary, across the hill in Beit Jala, where Father Maroun had invited us to spend the night. A pair of wimpled nuns offered smiles and a delicious spread as they bustled out of a kitchen where the windows were pocked by bullet holes through which you could stick a small finger. The nuns' water-grey eyes communicated an unfussy benevolence that language could not. They plied us with *koubeh* dough balls and hummus in olive-oil rings, and smiled patiently when the air roared to the strafe of machine-gun fire, as if to say, 'Oh, those silly boys, when will they learn?'

Puht! went the guns. *Puht-puht-puht-puht-puht-puht.*

'Have an aubergine,' said Father Maroun.

KA-BOOOOOOOOM!

'What was that one?' exclaimed Mike.

'Ya,' said Father Maroun with a shrug, 'it's just the Eezra'eelee tanks.'

'Sounds close,' I said.

Father Maroun nodded. 'It is.'

That night, I kept my window open to temper the heat. It was hard to sleep. Mosquitoes embossed my skin with bites, while gunfire called out from the valley. I peered through the window, and barely had a flicker of tracer fire crossed the vista than Mike's voice hailed me from the window next door:

'Come on, al-Jub – adventure time!'

We dressed, tiptoed down the stairs and across the seminary's esplanade, and crawled through the shrubbery towards a wire fence. Through the diamond-shaped gaps, we could see men crouched behind wheelie-bins, peeking towards the nearby Jewish settlement of Gilo, built on land annexed by Israel in the 1967 war and separated from Beit Jala by a steep valley.

'Look!' Mike pressed a hand on my shoulder and pointed to the open-top truck growling past us. Men stood packed together, obscured by balaclavas and bobble hats, old Enfield rifles poking above their heads.

'That's the Tanzim,' said Mike, naming a group affiliated to Arafat's Fatah party. 'Gonna scrap with the Israelis. Wait for it – any moment now . . .'

No sooner had the truck disappeared than the men were pancaking themselves against the walls as the air belched puhts and kabooms and a crackle that sounded like someone was popping a sheet of bubble wrap. We scurried further along the fence, until we caught a glimpse across the valley. Gun-towers garrisoned prefabricated fibreglass and reinforced concrete in a circumvallation of steel wire. Gilo was precise, impenetrable, cold. Whereas Beit Jala, as we discovered in the morning, was tumbledown and chaotic and full of warmth.

The cadavers of burnt-out cars lay on streets laced with shrapnel and bullet casings and stinking of charred rubber. Planks had been nailed over ruptures and canvas had created makeshift doors and some walls had been so widely gashed that you could look in on televisions and sofas and dust-draped baths filled with slats and tiles, as if you were touring the world's worst furniture showroom. Some houses had been so comprehensively struck that you could make out only a few random remnants: the soot-stained seat of a wooden chair, a fire-blackened sofa arm, a girl's ballet shoes. I remembered a story told to us by Maher al-Atrash, whose family once lived in neighbouring Beit Sahour, until they were forced out in a gunfight between the Israeli army and Palestinian militants. One night, Maher heard the sound of gunfire and threw his children to the floor. The TV was shattered, the curtains perforated, and chunks bitten out of the armchairs.

'For three hours,' Maher said, 'I lied down my kids on the floor, and pushed them to stay calm. As soon as there was quiet, I decided to leave my house. To run, reach my car carrying three kids, and driving in this situation – these three hours were the longest in my life!'

The citizens of Beit Jala were mostly, like Maher, ordinary people; mostly Christians, whose town, Israelis argued, had been exploited by the Tanzim to attract the support of the Christian West.

'We're just regular,' said Tag, a young Palestinian who had returned to Beit Jala from her studies in Michigan to look after her ailing father. She and her brothers prayed to St George for her father's recovery and slaughtered a sheep in front of the Orthodox Church.

'We gave the meat to the poor,' she explained; 'that's our tradition. But when we were coming back from the church we were stopped at the checkpoint. The Israelis asked us lots of questions and by the time we got to the hospital it was too late. My father had died.'

There was no protection, she said, for ordinary people; nowhere to hide from the shootouts. Hence a boy whose scar ran down his forearm like an enormous blister.

'Some people,' said Tag, 'get stomach ulcers and cuts without even getting hit. I've got loads of scrapes on my knees – just from nerves.'

'Shooting all the night,' added the woman in whose house we were sitting, middle-aged Samira, speaking in fractured English. 'Family gone, too much, live here too hard.'

She had piled sandbags against her windows, but there was nothing she could do about the water tanks on her roof, already punctured with bullet holes. Her cheeks were tense as she carried over cups of coffee from her propane stove and told us about her children, who had been moved to safety with their father. Samira, like so many Palestinians, refused to move: the soil was too dear to her.

'We're the lucky ones,' said Tag. 'There's a boy across the road. He was playing in his garden one day. Now he only has one arm.' She placed her cup on the floor and turned to us, her face burning with intensity.

'If you lose a cousin or even a friend,' she said, 'you wanna do something. Most of the Palestinians who shoot aren't even from Beit Jala. They're Muslims, mostly refugees from outside. But it's the people here who suffer. I know a woman who had to give birth at a checkpoint because the soldiers wouldn't let her go to hospital. Her baby needed an incubator, but they wouldn't let her through, so the baby died. You see the house across the street? With no wall? This seventeen-year-old – he was watching TV when the shooting happened. The others went downstairs. They forgot about him. Then they came back up and found . . .'

She bit her lip.

'The walls had fallen in. His body was all ripped up.'

Soldiers with their war, people at peace. Ibn Jubayr's remark haunted me throughout Palestine. It's all right if you have a mighty army drawn from Egypt, Greater Syria and Anatolia and led by Saladin. But the Palestinians didn't have Saladin. They had Arafat.

'The intifada for the leaders!' screamed a builder called Hassan. In front of a worksite of concrete and scaffolding near the house of the Grand Mufti, his kettle was whistling on a Primus.

'Arafat say to Arab leaders, "Ya Allah! My people suffers!

Give me monies! One hundred million? Not enough!" Eez-ra-'eel say Amareeka, "We need weapons for defend from Arabs. Give us tank helicopter F-16!" The people not want fight. I have friends for Jewish, we all do, but it's the leaders. They want fight so they have good cars, much monies.'

The Mufti himself, an Arafat appointee and therefore a member of the leadership, put a more positive spin on the Palestinian President. He sat on a plump sofa with gold scatter cushions, his long gown and floppy hat casting him as a Victorian just out of bed. His words did not, as he assured us with a smile that he would never forgive the British for 'selling Palestine to the Jews'.

'Is it true,' I asked, 'that you called for a new Saladin?'

'Yes, yes,' he replied. 'Salah ad-Din was forced to use arms because he was facing arms from the Crusaders. We considered the Crusaders occupiers and now we consider the Jews occupiers. And the country behind the occupiers are occupiers also: so that is America. I am wishing from God like many Muslims that another leader will come like Salah ad-Din.'

In his milky eyes I saw the European desire for Prester John: a source of relief from present troubles.

'Is Arafat that leader?' asked Mike, leaning forward with his Dictaphone.

'Arafat is a resistance fighter. But Salah ad-Din . . . Salah ad-Din was like a prophet.'

I thought of the man we'd seen in Bethlehem the previous Christmas. The communal gasp as a cocoon of black coats cannonballed down the nave of the Church of the Nativity, then split. The click of a thousand cameras drowning out the psalms as we all feasted on the sight of 'Abu Ammar', for three decades the symbol of Palestine. A pot-bellied man whose military uniform was decorated with every imaginable epaulette, pip, badge and chevron, with a frog's eyes, a wasteland of carefully mismanaged stubble, and the height of a jockey. Not that one-eyed, red-faced Saladin was any pin-up.

But whereas Saladin's appearance belied his stature, Arafat's mirrored his politics: he looked like a second-hand-carpet dealer. Later, once guards with Palestinian eagles on their berets had allowed Mike and me up the stairwell of Arafat's al-Muqata compound in Ramallah, we squeezed behind a U-shaped conference table with bouquets of flowers behind each place, and waited to shake the small, damp hand that once held Yitzhak Rabin's on the White House lawn. I remember two Arafats. One, enormous eyes and smile, gleaming in front of a blow-up Dome of the Rock, was all charisma. The other was indistinct in the dimness of the vertical blinds, a contradiction – reputedly incorruptible, but surrounded by corruption; a dare-devil guerrilla turned indecisive politician; the Arab clown, 'tea-towel man', but also the most important Arab between President Nasser of Egypt and Osama Bin Laden. A Saladin for Generation Ambiguous.

Would he have given King Guy of Jerusalem a glass of sherbet and cut Reynald de Chatillon in twain? The man enamoured of marching bands, red carpets and motorcades, the man whose character was demolished by Dr Eyad as-Sarraj after we'd passed through the cinder-block chaos of the open-air prison popularly known as Gaza?

Horses bent under their bridles to nibble from mounds of detritus, while boys in scruffy shorts hoisted a Palestinian flag as a kite. The graffiti behind them splurged the mantras of rival militant factions and a cartoon depicted the execution of a Palestinian collaborator. Out of the maelstrom rose a tower of cream-coloured brick, its intercom-operated gate snapping shut as a butler showed us to bamboo-cane chairs while the doctor completed a game of chess. Elaborately tasselled loafers sounded softly against the irrigated grass and the first practising psychiatrist in Gaza offered his hand.

'A few days ago,' the doctor told us, 'a man in the security services was killed. He belonged to a family who killed a member of another family in the first intifada. He was killed in revenge. Now another man, a popular Fatah leader, has been killed in revenge for his killing. It's a return to tribal identification. And Arafat exploits these divisions – he's even appointed a Minister for Tribal Affairs. He selected a tribal elite. Today we have tribal division, tomorrow we'll have underground robbers and militias. This is the school of Arafat. They did it in Lebanon, now they're doing it here.'

But was disunity a fair accusation to level against Arafat? While Saladin united the disparate Muslim principalities, forging a consensus that embraced Outremer in a united Islamic crescent, Arafat had sewn together the squabbling factions of Palestine. Under his charismatic leadership in the late 1960s, Palestinian Christians united with Islamists, pro-Jordanians set aside their differences with Palestinian nationalists, George Habash's Marxists shook hands with the old aristocracy of Jerusalem. Yet . . . it was a pan-Palestinian unity, only a microcosm of Saladin's achievement. Arafat had failed to spool the rich resources of the Dar al-Islam around the bobbin of the PLO.

One surprising advocate of Arafat had turned up beside me at supper in the Latin Patriarchate Seminary in Beit Jala.

'Father Ayyad advises Arafat,' said Father Maroun, spooning rice and aubergines on to a plate for an old man with a tapering beard worthy of the early Church fathers. 'When he goes to Gaza, Mrs Arafat cooks him his favourite food. He was a founder of the PLO, you know?'

The old priest smiled and concentrated on his meal, but later he dwelt fondly on the association.

'In the 1960s,' he said, 'I was in a monastery in Lebanon when Arafat came over from Kuwait. It took him two days to find me. I listened and I felt he was wise, so I agreed to help. He still visits me. Ha! When he kisses the nuns on the hand, you should see their faces!'

The blessing that he had given to Arafat was for the armed struggle adopted by the PLO in the wake of the Arabs' defeat in the Six Day War. Father Ayyad, like Bernard of Clairvaux, the Cistercian monk who wrote the rule for the Crusading

Order of the Knights Templar, believed in the justice of Arafat's cause and therefore the use of arms.

The soldier who shot us was standing behind a wall of sandbags and a giant barbed-wire web in the Old City of Hebron. When he'd finished shooting us, he put down his camcorder and laughed. 'I make Hollywood film!'

His colleague, wearing what looked like a cushion-cover on his head, followed us through the more conventional scope of an Uzi. The lantern-lit street that we were walking down wasn't so much Hollywood as Eastern European arthouse. Once the 'dwelling-house of the giants' (at least to twelfth-century guidebooks), the old city of Hebron had been reduced to the diminutive of 'H2'. One or two heads peeked between the curtains of laundry strung across bay windows, but most Palestinians obeyed the curfew that allowed them out only for a couple of supervised hours a week. If they broke the rules, padding down tight alleyways where the walls swooped towards each other and bellied over our heads and all you could hear was the squeal of an infant who wouldn't be getting much to eat until some time next week; then, like the teenager snorting at the rifle that was sticking into his sternum, they were usually caught.

This particular teenager insisted that he was perfectly capable of looking after himself. He certainly looked more at ease than the people who were out and about legally – dressed in suits and ringlets or floral-print dresses, pushing prams or chatting at the street corner or simply taking their constitutional. But if you were one of a four-hundred-strong Jewish settler community living among 120,000 Palestinians, you'd probably be prone to anxiety yourself.

'Now is peaceful,' sighed an old man, 'but in the evening the Ay-rabs will shoot on us. Ev-ery night! When will this stop? We will *not* be scared!'

Behind them, the Arab market was reduced to a mess of

metal poles and canvas that looked like it had been tossed from the sky in a fit of celestial pique. Soldiers directed us to the (Jewish) Cave of Macpelah or the (Muslim) Ibrahimi Mosque – built by neither Jew nor Muslim, but rather by the Crusaders, to house the relics of the Old Testament patriarchs. Despite the labyrinthine street layout, the cave-mosque was easy to locate: every hundred metres was another pair of lookouts. They smiled genially and posed for our cameras, but they always kept one hand on the trigger. The military gauntlet twisted and turned and finally a flight of steps climbed to a sand-coloured fortress built from enormous blocks of ashlar stone, with a crenellated parapet. Considering that it holds worship for not one but two faiths (and was originally constructed by a third) the cave-mosque didn't look very religious: only the minarets contradicted the impression of a castle.

'You are Jewish?' said a soldier slouched on the verge, holding out his machine gun in front of our shins.

Mike and I glanced at each other, exchanging subtle fluctuations of our eyebrows as we tried to gauge which response a) would get us in, or b) we could get away with; and took far too long about it to carry off a credible untruth.

'It's closed,' said the soldier.

'We won't make any noise,' protested Mike.

'It's closed.'

'Ask him three times,' I said. 'That usually works.'

'Please,' said Mike.

'I said, "closed".'

'Please.'

'You heard me, huh?'

'Pleeeeeeeease.'

The soldier shook his head decisively and fiddled with his gun's forelock; which said plenty about something, but it didn't tell us much about early Crusader and Ayyubid architecture.

*

We had arrived in Hebron after an exhausting afternoon in the nearby town of Dura. In fact, we were already exhausted by the time we reached Dura. Negotiating the Occupied Territories' latticework of divided zones was not the most pleasurable activity we encountered in the Middle East.

Bald fields stroked the road, shorn of the olive trees that had been deemed 'cover' for 'terrorists'. But who were the terrorists? Each time the soldiers scanned the microbus, their eyes settled on the terrorists. Terrorist grandmothers, smocked and hijabed, with their terrorist shopping bags and terrorist grandchildren; terrorist farmers with their terrorist hessian sacks; terrorist businessmen with their terrorist suitcases.

'You take taxi from here,' said a fellow passenger, when a barrier forced us to change transport at Halhul, outside Hebron.

'Where are you going?' asked Mike.

'Hebron, inshallah.'

'So do you have to change whenever you go from Jerusalem to Hebron?'

'When I go anywhere. If you want to go A to B, you go through Zones A and B and probably C. No matter how near or far, always you taking all day.'

The Holy Land is like a Last Judgement where the Green Line divides the Israelis, with their shopping malls, multiplexes, duplexes and democracy, from the Palestinians, enduring the brimstone of checkpoints and lack of statutory rights. Palestine is, literally, hell on earth.

In Dura, a typical Palestinian town – green awnings and placards promoting Sprite, yellow Mercedes taxis and boxes of breeze-block – we immediately attracted attention. Women studied us with long-distance stares and boys beat each other out of the way for the best position from which to peer. Men leaped off stools where they looked like they'd spent the better part of the day. Cigarettes burned between their fingers and suspicion burned in their eyes. They ushered us into a mini-market where, in an attempt to relax the frown of the shop manager, we spluttered multiple *salam-u aleykum*s.

'We're looking for Khalad Amayreh,' I said.

'Are you Jewish?' asked the manager.

'No.'

He pulled out some stools and indicated that we should sit down. Chill gusted up our backs from the banks containing buckets of cow's cheese and tubs of sour cream.

'Where are you from?'

'Baritanya.'

What are your names?

What do you do?

What is your religion?

How do you know Khalad Amayreh?

You have proof you know Khalad Amayreh?

He stroked his beard and muttered to himself. He analysed our features like a scientist reading a seismogram. One of his children flicked a rubber band at my face. 'Yahoudi,' he cried – *Jews*.

'Hmm,' whispered Mike, 'starting to look pear-shaped. Any ideas?'

'Well – there is one.'

I had a letter, written by the former *Guardian* correspondent Michael Adams, to help us secure meetings with 'difficult people'. I leaned towards my leather day-bag and the Mini-market Family followed the movement of the zipper. I handed the letter to Mini-market Manager, who turned it about and furrowed his brows. It was in English: a peculiar, back-to-front script, with none of the elegant ligatures and fantastical flourishes of his own language. And, since he didn't understand a word of it, it could have been anything. It could have been a recipe for roast duck.

He handed it back, called over a teenage boy and gestured for us to follow him. Outside, silver olive branches craned around building-block cottages and the smell of crops seeped out of the fields. Where were we going? A farmer peered at us from his haystack. A woman scowled from her nest of crumbling breeze block. Outside a cream-coloured house stood a bald, bovine man in a marine-green T-shirt that was matched by the colour of his front door.

'Aha!' he cried, beaming over his moustacheless grey beard. '*Ahlain!*'– welcome.

Khalad Amayreh was an angry man. He had been living under 'town arrest' for twenty years. If the Israelis located him, he said, they would shoot him, 'because Israel's definition of a terrorist covers not just the bombers but the people who write about it'.

They had closed down his office, severed his telephone lines and threatened to kill him.

'Of course, they did it subtly,' he growled. 'They said, "you know what happened to this man who was killed?" If you're Palestinian, there's no way out.'

His office, plastered with photographs of children killed in the intifada and newspaper cuttings depicting more bloodshed, seemed to have been decorated in homage to his apocalyptic vision of the Holy Land.

'What do I see for the future?' he muttered, huge, hairy forearms crossing his chest. 'I see continued apartheid, occupation and annihilation.'

'And the peace process?' I asked.

'What peace process? The Israelis have removed the horizons of the Palestinians so that all they have left are suicidal bomb attacks or humiliating subjugation. In some places in Hebron, Jews and Arabs live under the same ceiling. You can't choose your neighbours, especially when they've got tanks and Uzis.'

The only solution, as far as he could see (and you could rule out any form of 'Western secular democracy' in a region where 'secularism means decadence, violation of human rights and promiscuity') was – wait for it –

'Islamic law.' Amayreh beamed. 'Islam believes in a civil society, and respects Judaism and Christianity. The constitution of Medina, drawn up in Muhammad's time, resembles a Western European constitution.'

'Well, I don't think that's gonna happen too soon,' said Mike. 'You know the Temple Mount Faithful are hoping to tear down al-Aqsa Mosque and replace it with a Jewish temple?'

That evening, the festival of Tisha B'Av would begin. In the morning, when we had left Jerusalem, the air had been thick with a tension inhaled by Arab shepherd and Israeli soldier alike.

'It's a genocidal ideology,' hissed Amayreh; 'they want to destroy al-Aqsa and induce bloodshed on an enormous scale.* Because in their ideology the coming of the redeemer must be preceded by turmoil and bloodshed. If they succeed, they will cause a fire so big, no Arab or Middle Eastern government will be able to put it out.'

Shortly after the First Crusade, the Damascene Qadi, al-Harawi, led Palestinian refugees on a furious bout of eating in the streets of Baghdad. It was Ramadan, and their offence to religious law seized the attention of the crowds.

'How can the eye sleep between the lids,' screamed al-Harawi, 'at a time of disasters that would waken any sleeper?'

At Qalandia, the dusty checkpoint ripping Jerusalem from Ramallah, we set about meeting modern-day refugees. The crowds were as tightly packed as the concrete plinths from which machine-gun-wielding soldiers herded them.

---

* As Dennis Michael Rohan tried to do in 1969, when he stuffed kerosene-doused cotton under a pulpit in al-Aqsa Mosque and took photos of the subsequent blaze. Fifteen years later, a settler called Yehuda Etzion led a conspiracy to blow up the Dome of the Rock, with twenty-six like-minded Messianic Jews. Their plot was thwarted by the Israeli police. But the idea of inspiring the Coming of the Messiah remains strong among some Jews, and had been particularly prominent during our stay in Jerusalem.

Businessmen held up their suitcases to be frisked; mothers cried out to children lost on the other side of razor wire; mobile-phone-tapping students pleaded that they were late for their lectures. On a rubble plain, boys slotted small rocks into their slingshots as they prepared to repeat David's arm-action against Goliath. High above the limestone quarry, a sharpshooter watched us through the scope of his gun.

When our Arab *servis* driver was satisfied that every last space was occupied, we channelled between dazzling white cliffs and green fields speckled with rocks. Houses squatted along the roadside, crumbling under metal spikes that gave them the unfinished feel characteristic of Palestinian build-ings. There was a practical reason for the spikes – they would enable future generations to build another floor for their swelling brood, so that the family could stay in its ancestral home. But they were also metaphors, for a country in limbo, still waiting for international law and peace accords to com-plete its emergence as a nation state. I remembered Father Maroun's comment on the road from Jordan: 'We are a coun-try experiencing the pains of birth,' he had said, 'and ours is proving to be a very difficult birth.'

The checkpoints weren't too tricky that day, so to reach Nablus, forty miles north of Jerusalem, took only three and a half hours, or four taxis and a hike over the mountains. Men marched towards us, some carrying mattocks, others suitcases, calling out to us with voices like bassoons. Master Philip might well have had a similar experience: near Nablus, his contemporary, Theoderich of Würzburg, was 'met by a multitude of Saracens, who were proceeding with bullocks and asses to plough up a great and beauteous plain, and who, by the hideous yells which they thundered forth, as is their wont whenever they set about any work, struck no small terror into us'.

On the cusp of a lush hill, spotted with flowers and cheese-coloured scree, a solicitor brushed dust off his pinstripe trousers. Students clinched textbooks, while multi-armed mothers gathered up their children. Across the hill, stalking out of the gun turret of his tank, his jaws moving stiffly inside the straps of his helmet, a soldier was shouting in Arabic.

'They say we must not move,' said a student called Daoud.

'What happens if we do?' asked Mike.

Daoud crushed the flint under his feet.

'When the Eezra'eelees say no move,' he muttered, 'we no move.'

But patience wasn't as staunch as the soldier.

The solicitor led a crocodile of crouchers scrambling into the valley, sharing schoolboyish sniggers as we jumped into a fourth taxi that crawled past sheep farms and hilltop villas, and swept into the sprawling, boiling metropolis of Nablus. At the edge of the city was a muddy, reeking compost of breeze block and *shahida* posters and mounds of rubble: the refugee camp of Balata.

Our escort was a short, pockmarked man called Bassam, whose acquaintances amounted to a cross-section of the walking wounded. There was the one with the burst ribcage, the one with the broken leg, and the one with the hole in his neck as if he'd undergone a bungled tracheotomy.

'A bullet go through his neck and out the other side,' said Bassam. 'He only throw stone at soldiers.'

'But why did he throw the stone?' asked Mike.

The man in question beamed a full set of metal teeth.

'Because,' he said, 'I know not someone who have the gun.'

As we wandered through the camp, Bassam told us about IDF incursions: how they cindered a blacksmith's forge because it looked dangerous, destroyed an old man's breathing apparatus because it looked dangerous, shot a 22-year-old woman leaning out of her window because she looked dangerous. Children cackled nearby, kicking tin cans or fighting with plastic bottles and sticks outside the bullet-riddled walls of their school. They were the same age as many of the students Mike and I had taught six months earlier. Classroom artwork flashed through my head: crayon drawings of stick men with stones and Kalashnikovs, toy-town houses gashed by gunships with four spokes radiating out of the base. As the children of Balata ran around us, chanting the mantra of a nationalist folk song, I remembered the words of Dr as-Sarraj in Gaza.

'Uncle Eyad,' his niece had asked him one morning, 'are we going to die today?'

'I said, "Why?"' Dr as-Sarraj explained. 'She said, "the bombs – we're all going to die – you, me, granny and grandpa." We're in a prison where everyone feels vulnerable. Children ask their fathers, "Why don't you have a gun? How can you protect me?" Their highest ideal is to be a martyr. If you're a child who's seen your father arrested and beaten, someone killed, you want revenge. You're told that God says if you die for Him you won't die, but you'll start a better life in Paradise.'

Rivulets of muddy water streaked down the defiles. Women leaned out of jagged or doorless doorways, holding tin pails or the hand of a child, brown eyes widening the nearer we came. Above them, lines of laundry or chains of small Palestinian flags linked opposing buildings that shared the sound of the season's number-one pop hit – 'I Hate Israel', by an Egyptian part-time ironer. There was no need to knock to enter a house – you simply climbed through the massive hole dynamited into its wall by the IDF. You had to be careful about the loose wires hanging over your head like jungle creepers, and the smell of animals or an unreliable water system enforced a certain co-ordination between hand and nose. And there was something disconcerting about the profusion of holes: not just in the walls – in windows, ceilings, floor tiles, refrigerators and cookers; even in a teddy bear. As if the texture of Swiss cheese had been superimposed on to the whole neighbourhood.

But the most striking features weren't the signs of destruction. I did a double take when we passed some young men playing table football. It seemed too normal an activity for refugees, as out of place as the porcelain vases and potted plants in some of the houses, or the geometric patterns inlaid into some of the ceilings.

The friendliness of the inhabitants was equally unexpected. There was an element of propagandizing, as they ran around pointing out Israeli graffiti and blown-up bedrooms. But there was also remarkable warmth. An old lady, in a red-and-white-striped dress with a white kerchief over a face as brown and notched as bark, boiled coffee on her stove as her family *ahlan wa sahlan*-ed us into what little they had of a home. The tradition of hospitality was one of their few remaining possessions.

Behind a floral bouquet that designated the home of a *shahid*, the floor tiles in one house were all chipped, cracked or missing. The only interior decoration was the gold-framed portrait of a young man in a leather jacket. In one hand was a picture of Arafat, in the other the gun that won him his 'martyrdom' and widowed the young woman whose chocolate eyes blinked curiously under her black cowl.

She was about the same age as Mike and me. Her infant child scrambled among the mint leaves that his grandmother was plucking on the floor, innocent of the reasons for his father's absence.

'When they killed him,' said the *shahid*'s brother, 'they forced us all into one room and wouldn't even let our mother cry. All we could hear were gunshots and laughter.'

Across the street, a high-pitched moan reeled us between the concrete walls and rubble mounds that claimed to represent a house. There was no furniture. A single bulb hung syrupy light around a grey shift laid across two plastic chairs. One end of the shift moved and through the opacity we could make out an old man's head.

'He is paralysed,' said Bassam. 'When the soldiers come, they pick him up and throw him on the street.'

'What's the key around his neck?' I asked.

'That is the key to his house.'

'His house?'

It didn't look like the sort of house you'd need a key for.

'His house in Haifa,' said Bassam.

The old man whispered.

'The Eezra'eelees throw him out of his house in 1948,' said Bassam. 'He want it back. He say it's a very beautiful house.'

Whereas al-Harawi's refugees called for jihad in the 1150s so that they could be restored to Nablus, this old man was calling on jihad so that he could leave Nablus. It was a jihad with which his teenage grandsons identified. They stood behind him, hands clasped to their chests. They were angry. It was an anger you could feel and smell. An anger you could taste.

The farmyard stench punched through my nostrils and pulled a cough from my throat. I glanced at the floor, where two children were wriggling on a foam mattress, saliva dribbling off their bottom lips. They didn't even flinch when – with the same effect on my spine as if he had slowly scraped a fork across a plate – the old man screamed.

'What is he saying?' asked Mike.

'He says how the Eezra'eelee took everything,' said Bassam. 'They burn everything.'

The grandsons glared imperviously.

'What about *them*?' I asked. 'What do *they* want to do?'

Bassam asked them. 'They want to be martyrs,' he said.

Their big brown eyes were branded on my memory long after the taxis and microbuses had relay-raced us back to Jerusalem. They were still glaring in the back of my head when a bus drove us through the Negev Desert to the Egyptian border; still clasping their hands to their chests as a taxi floated between the sapphire swimming pools and gleaming glass hotels of Sinai.

And I remember thinking: if I lived in Balata and they did that to my grandfather, and they took him away from his rose-tinted house in Haifa, and they killed my neighbours when they looked out of the window, and every day I had to wake up to that awful smell, and they kept telling me, kept telling me as if they weren't telling me at all but they were hammering it in, hammering it in like a six-inch nail bored into my skull – IT'S THEIR FAULT – and I knew someone who could get me a gun— and then we were in Nuweiba, and there were other matters to think about.

Chapter Twelve

THE CAMEL AND THE FLY

OUT OF ISRAEL and ... back to Haggle-land! Bliss! Forget the Holy Land's rock-solid price culture, where you pay what you're told by the label, bill or meter. Because in Haggle-land, you pay what you want.

You offer half of what you want to pay. Your opposite number offers his own price. You walk away. He offers less. You walk away. He offers less. Eventually, when you've hacked him down to double your original offer – the price you want to pay – you accept.

At least, that's The Rule.

But Samir, who (since we had reached Nuweiba after midnight) was our only prospect of a lift to the Monastery of St Katherine, wasn't very familiar with The Rule. Which is why Mike and I found ourselves laid out on a road the same colour as the sky, our backs impressed by asphalt goosebumps, at half-past one on a Wednesday morning.

'A hundred dinars,' I suggested, as we began our lie-down protest at Samir's refusal to lower his price.

'Four handrad the seventy-five,' he retorted.

'A hundred and fifty,' offered Mike.

'Easee beasee, meesta! Five handrad.'

'Dammit, Samir!' Mike pulled himself upright and slapped

his knees. '*You're* supposed to haggle *down*. You're Egyptian – you should know how haggling works.'

'No Eezyib-zyan.'

'So what are you?'

'Bedu. For us this Sinai. We under the occu-bation.'

'I thought,' I muttered, 'the Israelis left two decades ago.'

'Eezra'eel, Eezyibt – is same. We no want foreign ruler. We no Eezyibt, we Bedu. Meesta, you want for pay me five handrad dinar.'

Mike and I acknowledged each other's frowns in the darkness. No, Samir, we didn't want to pay you five hundred dinars. In fact, truth be told, what we wanted to do was to rip out the loose springs peeking out of the seats in your microbus, tangle you up in them, strap you to a seatbelt, steal your keys and drive to St Katherine's for nil dinar.

However, that would require lifting ourselves off our asphalt bed, which I was finding surprisingly comfortable. At least, until the growing pools of headlight and an engine's ferocious growl announced the proximity of an enormous long-distance dumper truck. Its owner had a face like an irate squirrel and fierce, arched eyebrows that suggested little rapport with his brakes.

'Damn you, Samir. Here's five hundred dinars. Let's go.'

The next few hours were a haze of springs biting our thighs through rubber seats and a mountain road that rocked us about like a dinghy in a storm. I remember a soldier slapping my face at a military checkpoint and shrieking for 'Pazaport!' I remember Samir's calls of 'Meesta! Meesta!' recurring throughout the night like a record player stuck in the same groove. I remember our 3 a.m. arrival at the foot of Jebal Mousa, the mountain where Moses received the Ten Commandments; Samir badgering us into leaving our luggage in his microbus, prior to the drive to Damietta in six hours' time. And I remember being pushed, bleary-eyed, on to a pitch-black uphill pathway where Bedouin boys' voices echoed in the same nighttime air that plucked at our jumpers.

The path incised the mountainside, twisting up the slope, flickering with the torches of tourists that looked like a poor draft for the sophisticated network sparkling in the sky. An unsuspecting rambler might trip on loose stones or stumble over invisible walls, sudden dips and 'Bedouin car parks' – where camels grumbled together, their forelegs tucked under their thighs. As one's hip brushed a dromedary's fuzz, the temptation was to stagger backwards and pitch oneself into a hundred-foot abyss.

The path became squigglier, the darkness paler, the huffing of our most frail companions more desperate. Then we reached the first of seven hundred steps laid out by a local monk.

'Must have been a penance,' said Mike.

I stared up the towering staircase. 'He must have done something terrible.'

We manoeuvred around couples negotiating each inch of crumbling sandstone and small children scrambling up and down the steps, as if to triple the penance.

'Well,' said Mike, 'at least we're not doing this by day – rather all this to being boiled.'

Slowly, painfully, the steps crawled, tottered, lurched – enormous boulders swelling across the sierra – until we were so high up we could have spat on the clouds. We had reached the summit, the same spot where the fifteenth-century Dominican pilgrim Felix Fabri entertained his friends to a picnic of hard-boiled eggs, smoked meat and wine. All we had was a bar of chocolate and a can of Coke, and instead of being accompanied by counts, knights and clergymen, we were surrounded by tourists with baseball caps and hi-tech cameras, nattering and Bible-reading in a poly-glut of languages that was suddenly snuffed out by a moment of magic.

All eyes to the east. To the white orb rising, as dramatically as Excalibur, from a sea of blue cloud.

'Get up here,' called Mike. 'It's amazing!'

I yanked my stomach up a brittle scarp. The sun was

tearing itself from the mountains, as shadows washed the colour of honey or amethyst across smooth bevels bristling with barbs like stalactites made out of *doldurma* ice cream. It was exactly the sort of place where you might bump into God.

'To this mountain,' wrote the thirteenth-century chronicler Ernoul, 'where the Law was given, the angels bore the body of St Katherine, when her head was cut off in Egypt. There she lies in the oil which comes from her body, and thereon is an abbey of Greek monks; but the chief abbey of that house is not there, but at the foot of the mountain.'

The path pitched towards that abbey, the monastery named after the evangelist who inspired the Katherine Wheel (for the implement on which, after she had converted the emperor's wife, he had her impaled). A chameleon scuttled around sinewy tufts that cannoned into each other and cushioned the granite cliffs. Their cool shoulders protected us until, suddenly, sharp rays stung through a cleft that framed a field of scrubland and a monastic fortress whose golden walls were clasped by a bulging round tower. Only its cross-capped dome belied its military veneer.

The militant appearance was deliberate. In the sixth century, the monks of St Katherine's could barely fill a pail of water without being harassed by the local Bedouin. So their grand protector, Emperor Justinian of Byzantium, dispatched a squadron of soldiers to guard them. I felt a certain empathy with the monks, as the track to the monastery became a firing range of Bedouin merchant-boys, shooting out from rocks and crevasses with offers of stuffed camels, mineral water and quartz.

'Please, meesta! Good price!'

There was no sign of Justinian's soldiers: the monastery was defended only by the palm trees that lanced the scrub and a trench stuffed with wastepaper and tins.

It was a beautiful place: a camel-coloured village where, among sacks of peat and water tanks, you could find the giant dreadlocks of shrubbery that marked the Burning Bush or the well where Moses met his wife. In the charnel house was a motley collection of medieval monks, the same men who escorted the Castilian Pero Tafur across the weed-tufted cobblestones in the fifteenth century. Admittedly, you shouldn't expect much from an interview with a skull – even a tumulus of them. So they couldn't tell us much about the caravan that stopped at St Katherine's during Pero's stay, accompanied by pearls and spices and (I quote Pero rather than the monks) 'so many camels with it that I cannot give an account of them'. Nor could any of them shed much light on Nicolo de' Conti, the great traveller who turned up in the caravan and claimed to have dined with Prester John.

De' Conti had Tafur entranced. The Castilian listened like a Dictaphone as exotic adventures rolled off the conveyor belt of the Venetian's tongue. After his forced conversion at Mecca, there were demons who excelled at weather forecasts, white elephants, cannibals and a multicoloured ass the size of a hound; beefcakes who, to demonstrate their manliness, used foot-operated shears to sever their heads, and even a marriage arranged for de' Conti by that Cilla Black of the East – Prester John himself.

Whether that had taken place in India or Ethiopia, however, was unclear. References to the Nile and 'Christians eating the raw flesh of animals' suggest Ethiopia, but Indian practices such as suttee (and the suicidal beefcakes) also spice Tafur's account. What is certain is that, in the fifteenth century, European imaginations were still drawn to the mighty potentate who lured Master Philip out of Italy.

The names of medieval knights, scrawled into the wooden gates of the church, preceded a narthex whose iconography ran the gamut of the medieval religious imagination: St George and a dragon, bones peeking out of its lacerated sides; a heavenly ladder, up which men tiptoed towards Christ, assailed by gargoyles with spears; a tetraptych of miniatures, depicting flagellation, immolation, decapitation, inhumation. Between us, Mike and I couldn't decide whether it was a tribute to martyrdom or a pictorial guide for trainee psychopaths.

Nearby, cracks rippled across antique book covers flayed from farmyard animals. Inside their brittle pages, Slavic and Semitic scripts (medieval Ethiopic among them) looped and coiled. Long-haired ascetics glowered joylessly from the nave, upstaged by candle-bearing lions or the eagles that swooped out of the arms of a golden cathedra. It seemed that, surrounded by the majestic barrenness of nature, the monks needed to celebrate their riches. There was a romance to St Katherine. It was a diamond in the desert, a meeting place for adventurers with fantastical tales to tell.

Samir's car-horn was on sustained duty as we rushed to the microbus a full twenty minutes late. He waved his arms, juggled his shoulders and screamed, before stamping on the accelerator and promising us 'Damietta no time, meesta!'

But God knows what happened to his brief flirtation with temporal precision. That day was one long parody of discomfort, hot, sweaty and cramped (thanks to a crockery set of passengers shaped like those wide-rimmed teacups that double as cereal bowls, with an extra pudge of belly instead of a handle). Not only were the conditions atrocious, but Samir had chosen an innovative method to secure as much profit as possible from as many nooks, crannies and roadside coffee houses as Sinai could provide. This method dawned on me when we passed the causeway castle of Salah ad-Din, near the Israeli border – and a checkpoint soldier patted my shoulder.

'Meesta, you like Egypt?' he said.

'Well, I would,' I replied, adding (social graces having been beaten out of me by my companions' brutal, if garrulous, thigh-slaps), 'but this man's the worst driver in the world – he's gone backwards!'

We did, belatedly, turn in the right direction. But, as the

sun was fading in a pool of molten copper and we found ourselves lifting the microbus out of a sand dune (with Samir
providing expert supervision from the top of the bank), we
were still barely halfway to Damietta. Mike's face, as his
attempts to secure four or five winks were repeatedly foiled
by his neighbours' elbows, was a study of stoical self-control
inches away from explosion. But anger wasn't feasible: our
companions, however efficiently their physiques conspired to
exacerbate the anguish, were some of the kindest men we had
met. One of them clasped our hands and filled them with
Smartie-shaped termis beans from a rolled-up newspaper,
another handed round a communal glass of tea, while my
nearest neighbour – whose beaked nose and enormous waist
connected him to that other distributor of small gifts, Lewis
Carroll's Dodo – produced a couple of broken biscuits from
the dusty pockets of his burnous and divided them between
those who wanted them, which turned out to be few enough
that no one went without.

The following afternoon, after a sweaty night among chip-
board furniture and cockroaches, we finally reached
Damietta. We had abandoned Samir the previous evening,
having discovered at Port Said that the destinations of his
other passengers prevented him from delivering us to ours,
and launched ourselves in the morning into a luxuriously un-
populated microbus. It was quickly invested, with a mighty
huff and an army of children, by Old Mother Hubbard.
Plastic bags whispered against leather upholstery as satsumas
rolled down the aisle and children clambered among the
rusty framework of the seats.

Damietta might have been one of William of Tyre's 'oldest
and most famous cities of Egypt'; but, despite the writing
desks, polished to the shine of a toffee-stick, the wardrobes
and wicker chairs, rocking chairs, sofa-chairs, cabinets, cupboards, kingsize beds, bunkbeds and a creaky-wheeled
wagon on which a small boy curled across the deep-buttoned
damask cushions of a lacquer-legged sofa; despite the high

street, where the whiff of varnish was more potent than the *nargileh* smoke from the coffee houses or the scent of mangoes and lemons churned inside glass barrels by fruit-juice vendors; despite all these, Damietta was as scruffy as the jackets of the men who drove the furniture, or the ears of the donkeys they were whipping, which looked like they'd been woven out of the same threadbare material. How could this possibly have been the great medieval port whose strategic position at the Nile's mouth lured a combined force of Franks and Byzantines in 1169 and foiled them, as the Bishop of Acre, Jacques de Vitry, put it, with 'hunger, cold, and exceeding great floods of water'?

The siege of Damietta had several crucial effects. One was to rule out any co-operation between the Crusaders and the Copts, the Middle East's most populous Christian sect. A missile from a seven-storey Crusader siege-tower struck the Church of the Holy Mother of God,* putting paid to any East-West pan-Christian alliance. The siege was also a signal of the increasing importance placed by the Franks on Egypt: so long as Egypt was an enemy of Syria (as it was until Saladin assumed control of Cairo in 1169), they realized that the survival of the Crusader kingdom was assured.

A later attempt to capture Damietta, in 1218, was not only equally disastrous, but one of the most irrational moments in Crusader strategy. The Sultan, Saladin's nephew Malik al-Kamil, offered to cede the Holy Land to the Crusaders if they left Egypt at once. But a twisted little Portuguese cardinal called Pelagius, swollen with an inflated belief in Crusader prowess, declared that there could be no deal unless the

---

* Such incidents left a nasty aftertaste among the Copts. When we mentioned the Crusades to Abouna Sama'an, a young monk with an extraordinary, bifurcated beard, from the monastery of St Paul, his eyes turned into gimlets. 'The Crusades?' He bridled. 'We consider this a political conquest. You will not find one Copt who supports the Crusades. It had nothing to do with religion.'

Saracens handed over Egypt as well. Eighteen months of squabbling ensued, at the end of which Pelagius made the inspired decision to march on Cairo during the season of the Nile floods. The Egyptians snipped the river's sluice gates and incarcerated the Crusader army on an island of mud, before carrying out a massacre from which Pelagius – there's justice for you – was one of the few survivors.

But Pelagius' reckless self-confidence did have some justification. While he was reigning in Damietta, Jacques de Vitry informed European leaders that 'A new and mighty protector of Christianity has arisen. He is called King David of India, who has taken the field of battle against the unbelievers at the head of an army of unparalleled size.' This was apparently the son or grandson of Prester John, who had defeated the Khwarizmians of Transoxiana, conquered Persia, and was now marching on Baghdad. Also in the pipeline was a conquest of Jerusalem, and a full refurbishment project for the recently ransacked Holy City. It wasn't just Christians who were thrilled. Two of de Vitry's letters contained a copying error: King David, rather than being described as 'rex indorum', King of the Indies, was 'rex iudaeorum', King of the Jews. A frisson of anticipation swept through the shtetls of Europe as anticipation of the Coming of the Jewish Messiah reached fever pitch.

They were all wrong. Although de Vitry's letters imply some apprehension of King David the Builder's achievements in Georgia, there is a more specific source – a mighty conqueror whose army had swept across the Central Asian kingdom of Kwarizm and made mounds out of its inhabitants' skulls. Like Prester John, he was a 'king of kings', but his sword had more eclectic tastes: it was nourished equally by Christian, Jewish or Muslim blood. His people would terrorize East and West for the next three decades, abandoning their conquest of Europe only when one of his successors fortuitously died. He was the great Mongol leader Genghis 'Nice Guy' Khan.

Dusk was falling as our microbus lurched out of a web of horse-carts and rolled between the cotton fields en route to Alexandria. Moorhens and geese messed about in the canals, while children slid under the dripping tentacles of willow trees. We arrived in Alexandria in the dark. Saad Zaghloul, the great twentieth-century politician, stood up, all marble and pomp, beside the Cecil Hotel, once haunt of Noël Coward and Somerset Maugham. Mike, who quite fancied himself as a British officer in 1920s Alexandria, 'like someone out of *The Alexandria Quartet*', would have been happy to stay there; I, more of a scrimp when it came to matters budgetary, suggested, 'How about somewhere more . . . in the thick of things?'

'Hmmm – meaning cheaper?'

The Corniche stretched out grandly alongside the eastern harbour, inside whose black folds ancient obelisks and doorjambs remain hidden like the features of a burka-clad woman. We put down our luggage in a crumbling art-deco hotel, where our balcony inclined vertically as well as horizontally towards the sea. A glimpse of the view entailed a coating in leprous plaster.

The aura of dilapidation followed us on to the backstreets, where guavas and peppers stuck to our shoes and steam smoked out of drippy paper bags stuffed with fried fish. It was a noisy place, thrumming to tram-truckle and hawker-holler and, spilling out of the Mosque of the Prophet Daniel, the shuffle of hundreds of feet. Inside the mosque, the most arresting noise wasn't from the cross-legged hummers whose turbans flopped about their heads; or the boys reciting rote-learned *surat* – a mnemonic technique like those practised in medieval European education. It was from an old greatcoated woman, who clambered around a vacuum cleaner, a couple of metal buckets, a filing cabinet and a row of broken chairs, hauled herself over a wooden fence and –

like a very earthy djinn returning to the underworld – plunged into a hole.

On closer inspection there appeared to be a ladder, but a low, painful moan cast doubt on its reliability. Mike treated the ladder like a slide; with somewhat less skill and a little more apprehension I followed him. At the bottom it was difficult to see but a fierce cluck drew our attention to the figure of female piety, kissing corners of cloth as she circled a hajji's tomb with the elongated sigh of a widow. I looked half-expectantly for the stray shin-bone of Alexander the Great, reputedly buried underneath the mosque, before clasping my hands in emulation of Mike and following our supervisor physically (though not vocally – her shrieks were enough for the three of us) around the tomb.

Outside, pedlars traded stereos, watches, cigarettes and ironing boards on the ancient Street of the Soma. The Mousseion – the great ancient library of 700,000 scrolls to which, according to Benjamin of Tudela, 'people from the whole world' came in Master Philip's day 'to study the wisdom of Aristotle the philosopher'* – had long disappeared, its legacy diluted into a couple of hundred feet of pavement covered in second-hand books. Titles ranged from Edgar Wallace's *The Three Oak Mystery* to *A Course in Basic Scientific English*. Where archivists with long white beards would once have lorded over ancient manuscripts, now their place was taken by grubby-looking salesmen, frog-like on their haunches as they laid out 'new' editions as dusty as the magazines they were replacing. Mike haggled for a *Newsweek* dedicated to Bill Clinton's 1996 re-election bid, while I sat on the marble steps outside a shop. An astrolabe and an inkpot shone from a shelf above me; nuts and ciga-

---

* Perhaps they included the translator of Aristotle's 'Secret of Secrets', the Tripolitanian Philip who the historian Lynn Thorndike (one of the few even to consider this question) suggested might be the same man as Master Philip.

rette butts decorated the steps. I could smell musty paper and stale tobacco. Slummy and scholarly: that seemed to suit Alexandria.

Another great building recorded in Alexandria by Benjamin of Tudela was the 450-foot lighthouse. Otherwise known as the Pharos, it still had a century and a half before it would be submerged by an earthquake, and was one of the most popular wonders of the early medieval world. What makes Benjamin's account of it particularly exciting, though, is the 'glass mirror' that he located on the Pharos, which bears a striking similarity to a motif of Prester John's letter. 'Any ships,' wrote the rabbi, 'that attempted to attack or molest the city, coming from the Western lands, could be seen by means of this mirror of glass at a distance of twenty days' journey, and the inhabitants could thereupon put themselves on their guard.' One of Prester John's favourite toys was a thirteen-storey tower where a magic mirror updated him on the activities of his enemies: a sort of medieval webcam. The author of the Prester John letter may have been influenced by the Pharos, which did have a mirror (to amplify the light for distant ships), but the concept of a magic mirror isn't (despite the magic mirror legendarily owned by Alexander himself) exclusive to Alexandria. The mirrors fashioned by Spenser's Merlin, legendarily erected by Socrates on a tower in Armenia to discover two poisonous dragons, inspected by the Arabian King Sauria in a tenth-century tale, invented by Reynard the Fox or found by Tariq Ibn Ziyad in a tower in the *Thousand and One Nights*, suggest a primordial source that is shared by fairy tales all over the world.

Despite the earthquake of 1303, there were still traces of the lighthouse: pieces of its red granite were amalgamated more than a century later into the fort built on the site by Sultan Qaitbey. In the morning, brackish waters were slapping its feet, fragments from the lighthouse were winking mysteriously from its walls, and displayed inside – for no fathomable reason – were the bones of a dinosaur, a couple of sea cows and a pike-nosed *istiophorus gladius*. Children leaped on their fathers' shoulders as they imagined themselves into the Paleolithic age, before splashing their parents and making wigs out of seaweed in the breakwater rock pools on the fort's windswept side.

It was a full-on loony asylum round there, where an old timer chirped, 'Hulloo hulloo!' as he waved a canvas above his head, wind-filled like a medieval flying-machine, and someone else turned his lungs into a trumpet as he fished an old shoe out of the sea. Me being, of course, entirely qualified to cast judgement. Nothing at all odd about my insistence on following the walls round as the path became a swamp of scuttling beetles and the waves, ricocheting against a bulging watchtower, immersed me, extracting plenty of laughter from the singing fisherman. Nor was I the only visitor on whom Alexandria was having a strange effect.

'You are friend of Alexander the Great?' asked a white-suited policeman when I ventured, my dripping shoulders ringing me in a magic circle of wet, on to the walkway above the watchtower.

'Course he is,' announced Mike. 'He's my travelling comrade.'

I'm not sure to what extent he'd convinced the policeman of his new ancient Macedonian identity; in any case, the policeman was more interested in subtly enquiring if we could help him arrange an emigration visa.

As, it turned out, were most of the people in the bus station. They might have been waiting for lifts to Cairo or Port Said, but they talked like they wanted the next flight to Heathrow. The English teacher behind me in the queue for Cairo asked if I liked his country, if I was planning to visit the temples in the south, and if I could sort out his visa to London. The two students either side of Mike and me in the bus wanted to test our Arabic, scribble down their addresses for us, and ask us to sort out their visas to London. And, when the desert and fellahin fields had been swallowed by the flyovers and skyscrapers of Cairo, the driver helped us put on our backpacks, wished us a good stay and asked us to sort out his visa to London.

The intimidating scale of suburban Cairo was overturned as we crossed the Nile. Crescents hooked out of cupolas and bedsheets flagged from tottering apartment blocks. Between donkey-carts and yellow taxis, children chased footballs that bounced under smoking braziers where vendors dispensed kebab-meat to the men stumbling out of the coffee houses. From the rooftop café of our hotel, we could see women emptying chamberpots from wrought-iron balconies and dogs cocking their legs against dilapidated walls. There was an energy, expressed in laughter, screams and the tense call of desperate bootblacks, that the suburbs couldn't match. The material richness of one was bettered by the atmospheric richness of the other: a hustle-and-bustle that filled the city with excitement.

We spent much of our time in Cairo on the Nile, 'that huge and famous one', to quote the fourteenth-century Franciscan Simon Fitzsimmons, 'of whose length there is no end; by which you ascend by water from the Mediterranean Sea to Upper India, in which is Prester John'. At Doq-Doq, where the tap of the plump boat-owner's feet repeated the name of the port, floral-print cushions drew us under the crinkly-skinned sails of a felucca. On the stern sat a bundle of wrinkles wrapped in a white shift, coaxing the rudder with his hips and gazing into the soupy waters like a haruspex at his entrails. Huge hotel complexes towered above us, lit up with cosmopolitan restaurants – Chinese noodle bars, Italian pizzerias, Indian curry houses – and surmounted by swimming pools that sparkled like crystal discs. Medieval mosques slipped by, their minarets banded in luminous green cords. Lovers stood on the banks, gazing into the depths where workmen were tipping their waste. A ferry spread the jazzed-up version of 'I Hate Israel' towards us, while panama hats peeped over the sterns of cruisers hired out from the Hilton, and a Chinese ferry glided past us like a dragon-headed cucumber.

One evening, sitting alone in our hotel's rooftop café, I found myself delivering an account of a search that Mike and I had made that afternoon, to Huwaida, the kohl-eyed waitress who had delivered my lemon juice. We had been looking for the Nilometer, the 'pillar of marble' that, in the 1170s, Benjamin of Tudela located on 'an island in the midst of the water' in Cairo. Once we'd broken through a wall of child footballers screaming 'What is my name!' between mounds of housing and blocks of garbage, and reached Rhoda – the island that corresponded with Benjamin's account – a soldier waved us away. We pleaded: we had come all the way from England to visit the Nilometer. How could he refuse such a request? Was his heart made from the same material as the pillar?

Nevertheless, he grunted, the Nilometer was '*maqful*'. Literal translation: closed. More in-the-spirit translation: if you want to get in, you will need baksheesh or shameless sycophancy. So, sacrificing pride for budget, we attributed to the soldier the might of Ramses (a repeated '*maqful*'), the glory of Tutankhamun (a nod, implying a breach) and the munificence of Saladin (a signal to his subordinate, who guided us into a dome at the edge of the island).

Huwaida cradled her hands together and exchanged a smile with the twinkle-eyed, academic-looking man at the table beside me. His nose was shaped like an onion and a curtain of silver hair dangled over his mouth.

'Always,' he said, beaming, 'this is the way in Egypt!'

The Nilometer sticks out of a dry pit, a granite tongue braced by a Kufic-inscribed bar. Medieval rulers used to perfume it with saffron and it was still functioning when Lord Curzon visited in the nineteenth century. But now it is a fossil, from a time before technology curbed the river's power. As we descended into its mouth, we counted fifteen cubits' worth of arm-length stubs – the necessary depth for the 'Plenitude of the Nile' described by Benjamin – and imagined the Qu'ranic recitals and Sufi dances that invigorated Cairo at such festivals.

'And do not forget,' the academic-looking figure at the next table added, 'that they all drank much alcohol and you know what is the consequence for that!'

'The Nile is the longest river in the world,' he exclaimed, his grey-marble eyes sparkling as he spoke of the magic of 'the Great River': the crocodiles that used to terrorize Egyptian fishermen and still haunt its southern banks, the turtles and hippopotami and 'the stork with the head of a whale' in the Sudanese swamps, the fireflies that illuminate the water at night, as 'the closer you are to the source, the more the people are naked!'

'We call it al-Bahar' – the Sea, he smiled, 'because it is too great to say this is a river.'

It was a perspective with which medieval Christians such as the Florentine Simone Sigoli would have agreed.

> *It is true that this Sultan* [of Egypt] *must every year ransom himself or pay homage to Prester John. This Prester John lives in India, and is a Christian and holds many lands of the Christians and also of the infidels. And the reason why the Sultan pays homage to him is this, that every time that this Prester John has a certain cataract of a river opened, Cairo and Alexandria and all that country is flooded; and it is said that this river is the Nile, which flows beside Cairo . . . Therefore, for this reason, namely fear, the Sultan sends him every year a gold ball surmounted by a cross, worth three thousand gold besants.*

'Of course, in this time the people fear the flood or the drought.' My new friend chuckled. 'But now we have the dam at Aswan.'

For three decades, Egypt had been able to regulate the river's eccentricities, through its reservoir in Aswan. Not, he added, that control was entirely theirs:

'You know the Amareekans, they threaten to bomb the dam if the government do not catch the terrorists!'

Aptly enough, the threat of Prester John, self-styled 'most glorious over all mortals' of his time, had been replaced by the Stars and Stripes.

My head cluttered with tales of medieval festival high jinks, and a paper napkin in my hand cluttered with Huwaida the Kohl-eyed Waitress's directions, the next morning I set off alone for Babylon. I spent a lot of time in Cairo alone. On our first night in the city, Mike and I had engaged in the verbal form of a medieval jousting match. Its inspiration wasn't so much royal decree or the whim of a damsel dangling her hanky as a combination of my thriftiness, bookishness and medieval obsessiveness, and Mike's singing. It was the only serious argument we had, which is probably a good hit rate. For now, we decided it would be best to spend some time apart.

Fez-makers dusted down their wares as they raced men with buckets of watermelons to the pitches of the Khan al-Khalili, shimmying through the crowds, as flexible as the belly dancers Mike and I had seen gyrating in a downtown nightclub.* It didn't take much imagination to strip the streets of their telegraph poles, swap the taxis for donkeys, add a street-corner *hakawati*, and visualize myself as Master Philip struggling along here eight centuries earlier.

---

* It wasn't just the belly dancers. The most rapturous applause was reserved for a woman in the audience, who joined the performers on stage, threading exotic shapes in the air as she hip-wiggled and shoulder-juggled, while tuxedoed waiters floated between the tables with trays of *meze*. What was strangest about this woman was that she was dressed top-to-toe in black hijab. She was a dancing silhouette.

The Seventh Letter of Master Philip to
Roger of Salerno

To THE DISTINGUISHED physician Roger of Salerno, Master Philip of Venice humbly sends greetings; it is better to have hope in the Lord than in man. Amen.

The city of Babylon, dear Roger, is a city of war. For here have terrible things happened to me. It is said that the city was built by Giauher the Caliph, and he ordered astronomers to observe when were the good stars for constructing the city. They ran a rope around the place with bells so that, when the time came, a strike of the rope would induce the bells to ring and the bells would induce the workmen to begin building. But a raven shook the rope and at this time Mars was in the ascendant. So Cairo is always at war, and the Franks have tried many times to take the city, for they know that Egypt holds a great store of men, so that her conquest would be of great boon for the retention of the Holy City. But each time God has summoned floods and fire and the inadequacies of man to curb the ambitions of Christendom.

We reached Babylon after a journey of many days across the desert of the Israelites. I write we, dear Roger, for I have travelled with Ezekiel, the Abyssine monk whom I encountered in Jerusalem. And much have I learned these past days, for he fares not forth on Saturday, saying this is the Holy Sabbath; and he reads to me from the Book of Enoch, the same that Jude mentions in his epistle, and he tells me of strange beasts that dwell in his land. For there are serpents fifty cubits long that can swallow a calf at once, and giant stags six cubits in height, with a hairy tail and a neck that reaches four cubits long.

But there is no need to go to the land of Prester John to meet strange beasts. For there are creatures of great wonderment in Babylon. There are monsters called cocodryllus that live in the great Nile river, and they fill the people with fear. They are like dragons, and they devour horses and men in the water, and do not refrain from devouring them on the bank. And their dung produces an ointment with which the wrinkled whore anoints her figure and makes herself beautiful again. But not only are the animals strange. For there are people skilled in black arts, who consult with demons, and men with sieves that they use to sift the sand and glean the future. And loud is the call of alms-beseechers and storytellers and tradesmen who waylay the visitor at every turn, and offer rock crystal and wood carvings and fabrics so fine that a robe can be drawn through a finger-ring. The city consists of mosques, which are their churches, and markets. And they shout from the steeples of the mosques so that it seems that a riot has erupted. And they shout too in the markets. There are markets for marquetry and strange fruits, silk and ink-stands and camels and slaves. And at the slave market, great was my despair at the spectacle of Christian captives, seized in battle. For they were tied to the backs of camels and surrounded by timbal and horn. And had I money I should have bought them their freedom. But I had not the resources, and Ezekiel warned me that I must not draw attention to myself, else the sultan shall prevent me from voyaging south of Cairo. For the sultan here is Saladin, and he rules the land of Egypt with a fist of iron.

As we walked through the markets, there was great turmoil. For some students were coming out of the school of Azhar, where are young men from all over the pagan world, who sit in the courtyards and recite their false doctrines. And one of these students perceived a cross around my neck. He screamed, and his friends pulled the cowl off my head, and they spat at me and threw dust in my face. And then they took hold of me and threw me against a wall outside the mosque of Husayn, and they cried out that I must renounce my faith and declare that Mahomet is the true messenger of God. And I refused, saying that nothing will cause me to embrace the devil. But this made my situation the more perilous, and I questioned to myself if I should do as bidden, for was not my mission of greater moment than my soul? And such thoughts flew about my head like the harpies, and I felt the knives close to my cloak and was awaiting the sting of death. But suddenly the knives and the crowd abated. For Ezekiel warned them that his master is Prester John and he has power of the Nile and they feared that they would provoke him to flood their country. So they fell back, and I hid away my cross.

Nor, dear Roger, was this an end to my troubles. For Ezekiel hired us mules, and we rode through the streets. But hard was it to control our steeds, for the air was black with dust and devils possessed our mules. They threw themselves about, and no help was volunteered by the barbaric creatures about us, who hurled stones at our heads and tried to trip up our steeds, and pulled the tail of my mule so tight that I was thrown towards the ground. But worse still, I did not hit the ground, for between myself and the earth was the toasting-fork of a pagan cook. Terrible was my howl, dear Roger, for I felt as if I had been flung into the darkest corner of hell. And I was carried into a tent-maker's shop, where I lay on a bed of camel-hair cushions, with blood pouring out of four holes in my belly, and it was not until later that I reflected on their likeness to the Lord's stigmata. One man passed an amulet across my face, and another uttered prayers from his holy book, and the tent-maker fed me salep juice, and Ezekiel ran in search of a physician . . .

That afternoon, Cairo emerged – towering, tooting and stinking of rotten fruit – as Saladin's city. You could dip into the ablutions fountain at the mosque built in his honour and stroll across the parade ground where a sage correctly predicted in 1182 that 'After tonight there will be no more ox-eyes' (less cryptically, 'Saladin ain't coming back'). From his castellated citadel,* you could gaze at the multicoloured tombstones linked by laundry lines on one side and, on the other, an urban jungle. Tangled up in a flux of shoppers, vendors in navy shifts unbuttoned over their vests guarded banks of second-hand clothes that seamed the walls of mosques and madrasas, licked by overhangs of laundry. Veiled grannies knitted on the doorsteps of houses where the doorways had no doors and the window panes no glass, while children spooled around them, their tummies bound in torn T-shirts. Flocks of black silhouettes were sucked into tunnels where dust danced around them like disco-lights. Intermittently, a shell of clear air swelled around a drinks-seller – suited, booted and befezzed like an Ottoman – or a whirlwind of a newspaper boy, as cacophonous as the poultry cages stacked beside a nearby shoe stall. He seemed to have six arms and at least as many tongues.

'You!' he screamed, pouncing through the puddles. Didn't I want a newspaper? Why not? How about a beautiful leather wallet? A packet of tissues? A carton of Cleopatra cigarettes? B'Allah! Was there no way I could be persuaded to part with my dinars? How about his sister? My endless string of negatives could mean only one thing: I was, he snorted, abandoning trade for religion, a 'Massihi', or Christian, so I was no good for his sister anyway. He swaggered away, as self-assured as the Artful Dodger, and slotted a paper inside the arm of a prayer-bead swinger, before bullying the old man into counting out his dinars. As he strutted about under the

---

* Built, according to Ibn Jubayr, by 'the foreign Rumi [i.e. Christian] prisoners whose numbers were beyond computation'.

Bab Zuweila, the spear-shaped gate of the medieval city, I wondered what it was like in the 1150s, watching the corpse of Nasr, former lover of the late caliph (whose own corpse had been discovered in a pit in Nasr's home), swinging from the gate after his mutilation by the caliph's furious wives. Because Cairo, at this time, had more plot lines than the newspaper boy could have fitted into a full year's supply of the local tabloid, *Al-Shaab*. There were illicit romances, like Nasr's with the caliph, and cloak-and-dagger murders (such as the strangulation of the caliph's brothers, in front of the five-year-old caliph-to-be). There were grand escapes ('Hot off the Press: Nasr's Trans-Sinai Flight Foiled by the Franj!') and grand marches ('Extra! Extra! Battle for Cairo – Nur ad-Din sends General Shirkuh and his nephew Saladin'). There was General Shirkuh's tragi-comic death by overeating, and the grand spectacle of the Nubian Palace Guardsmen burning in their barracks after a letter to the Crusaders was found in the Nubian confidential adviser's shoe. And from the nearby minaret of al-Azhar Mosque, the trill of a muezzin recalled the Iraqi divine who, in 1171, climbed up its pulpit and replaced the name of the Shiite Fatimid Caliph with his Sunni counterpart in Baghdad, confirming Sunni Saladin's pre-eminence in Egypt: 'Read all about it – Caliph dead! Saladin says al-Quds is next!'

His quota sold, the newspaper boy joked with a termiscone salesman – cackling hoarsely like a man three times his age – and vanished in a hotchpotch of medieval masonry, where an eye clinic could be found inside the same Mamluke mosque compound behind whose Gothic ribbed windows Pharaonic columns flanked an Ottoman fountain. Burrowed inside this patchwork, young men inserted mother-of-pearl on to wooden jewellery boxes, or pieces of camel bone on to a backgammon board, or needled gold Qu'ranic slogans on to black cloth.

Along al-Gamaliyya, the street 'so narrow a handcart would almost block it when passing by', past the Mosque of al-Husayn (whose head was carried there in a silk bag in 1153), the street angled between coffee houses and market stalls and tottered into its medieval heart. Giant lamps, pieces of calligraphy, pots and pans and Tupperware cluttered shop interiors and slipped into the street in poorly contained piles. At first the predominant smell was spice, or perfumes credited with the power to cure infertility. Gradually these were mashed up with, then replaced by, sewage. The road slimmed, reduced to a ribbon of sludge bridged by broken wooden planks. Young boys tripped over outsize *gelabiyyas* and picked themselves up from coffee-coloured puddles. Their peers cackled as they scratched the sores and scars that dribbled down their legs. Big men built like barrels bullied carts down needle-eye defiles. Horses stumbled ahead of groaning wheels that flicked up mud on to muddy little boys.

This was the childhood haunt of Naguib Mahfouz, the Nobel Laureate whose *Cairo Trilogy* had entertained me on bus journeys across the Levant. It was a sprawling saga, keeling from the bawdy adventures of Yasin, a wine-swigging womanizer with a penchant for large bottoms, to debates about Darwin's theory of Evolution or the tragedy of Aisha, a golden-haired beauty whose husband and two sons are killed by typhoid while her last child dies giving birth. The helter-skelter of life on al-Gamaliyya – where everyone lives on top of everyone else and births, marriages, scandals and death are shoved into each other's faces – expressed the trilogy's narrative logic: here any kind of story could unfold.

Later that afternoon, a taxi dropped me at a secret location in the suburbs where I hoped to meet the wisest man in the neighbourhood. Naguib Mahfouz had been scaling down his public appearances since 1994, when, because it was possible to interpret some characters in his novel *Children of the Alley* as personifications of Muhammad, Moses and Jesus, an acolyte of the militant group al-Gama'a al-Islamiyya had severed his carotid artery with a kitchen knife.

But I had it all planned. Thanks to my correspondence

with Raymond Stock, Mahfouz's American biographer, I knew where to go. Just needed to pass the two security checks and shake hands with the merry group of intellectuals encircling their guru like the members of a Byzantine salon. Keep laughing at their jokes, try and nudge myself a little closer to Mahfouz – might need to dislodge that man with the face of a walrus, the one currently bawling into Mahfouz's hearing aid. And the lady in a sheath of black silk, towards whom his stubbly chin was directed as they lamented the actress Suad Hosny's recent fatal fall from a balcony in London. Then – at last – I was able to join Naguib Bey, in his cloud of tobacco smoke, locking his wrinkle-fanned eyes on mine and drinking in his wisdom as if his mouth was a faucet through which he could dispense his knowledge like an elixir.

'You may ask,' said the walrus, 'one question.'

So I turned to the author and, like an Oliver Twist already aware of his limit, posed my question – about the *hakawati*s.

'They were a great part of my early life,' he said. 'I used to spend a lot of time in the coffee houses around the mosque of al-Husayn, and there was a *hakawati* who came along. I loved listening to him, and maybe this had an effect on my work. However,' he added, sighing mournfully, 'when the radio and the television came, the *hakawati* was finished.'

But Mahfouz, whose tales embraced every aspect of Egyptian culture, from Pharaonic sagas to a sequel to the *Thousand and One Nights*, had assumed the *hakawati*'s role; which made his treatment by Arab governments (all of which, except for Lebanon, initially banned *Children of the Alley*), as much as his attempted murder by fundamentalists, an expression of the same cultural malaise that had allowed the *hakawati* to be displaced by second-rate TV soap operas.

Reuniting with Mike that evening was a delight. We argued over who'd spent his time more productively (Mike had been conducting research into the Copts, for which he had attended an audience with the Coptic Pope), debated whether we should drink coffee or beer, and played a game of chess in a coffee house (the result of which I shall keep from you, because I was distracted by a man riding a unicycle with a steering wheel). Then we walked over to the Mosque of al-Mu'ayyad in the Old City, to attend that institutional champion of unity – a wedding.

This somewhat unwarranted honour had been offered earlier in the day when, during my ramble through the medieval city, I was welcomed into the home of Sherif, a Sudanese folk singer. Plied with pomegranate juice on a bedstead that doubled as a sofa, in a tiny garret surrounded by black-and-white photographs that traced Sherif's lineage through Sadat's Cairo to Nasserite Aswan to the Nubia of the Egyptian-British conglomerate, I had explained that we would be visiting Sudan. This struck his family as worthy of a good ten minutes' chuckling and, eventually, an invitation to meet the expat community. Like the Nubian guard who filled the corridors of Fatimid power, Sherif was part of a Cairene community from the Balad as-Sudan – the Land of the Blacks. It was the first of three glimpses of Sudan – betrothal, bureaucracy and beasts – that swelled our anticipation of the most mysterious country on our itinerary.

Up a sandstone staircase in a courtyard behind the Mosque of al-Mu'ayyad, men offered handshakes for the opposite sex, and kisses on both cheeks for their own. A rainbow of coloured bulbs swooped towards the stage, where bow-tied boys shook tambourines and pink-frocked girls with henna on their hands twirled painted sticks, before an army of teenagers in yellow pyjama-suits harried them off with a foot-thumping stampede.

An aisle dissected the audience: on one side, veiled mothers rocking their babies or ululululululululating the *zagharid*, small girls chattering and knotting their fingers in their hair, older sisters darting their eyes between their laps and the other side of the aisle; there, to a din of belly laughs, men with enormous smiles were shouting and shrieking and attacking each other's backs with the flat of their hands. High above the crowd, on their own makeshift pedestal in front of a pyramid of pink crepe, were the bride and groom. *He* waved to his friends, who tiptoed up to kiss his cheeks and shake hands with his wife; *she*, in white with floral lace and her hair trained into beautiful black ringlets, sat on her throne in saucer-eyed awe.

Bureaucracy was provided, with jaw-stiffening tedium, on a tree-lined avenue near the Nile. The first time we marched past the gun-bearing guards outside the Sudanese embassy, we had missed the late-morning deadline for the visa application process. In consolation, a bright-eyed man with an Eddie Murphy smile gave us forms to fill. The requirements included a letter of recommendation from the British consulate, which we visited the next morning. It was an ironic request, since the British consulate doesn't actually recommend going to Sudan. They make this quite clear by including it in their list of countries where 'British Nationals may be in danger'. In true British style, they extricate themselves from responsibility by issuing 'a general letter, not a recommendation', as the cut-glass clerk in the air-con lounge oh-so-tactfully explained, before she charged us half the price of the visa for a printed exchange of compliments from one consulate to another, which took so long that we missed the Sudanese embassy's deadline again. The next morning we finally got it right and handed over our forms without being asked any of the sinister questions we'd expected.

A few days later, the consulate was a sweating Sudanese stew: keffiyehs, turbans, coloured cotton caps and Afros. What did all these people want? Signatures, visas, encyclicals, extensions, references, work permits, residence permits, handouts, or just a morning's worth of BAWLING THEIR HEADS OFF? The one unifying factor was the skin colour, which made Mike and me stand out like Sufi hermits at the coronation of a Crusader king. And Karl from Norway, a phosphorus-haired Rutger Hauer lookalike. He grinned manically every time anyone spoke, screamed or breathed. He particularly enjoyed the elbow-jabbing.

'Ah, this is the life!' he enthused.

But Eddie Murphy wasn't smiling. He barked names like a major-general, producing a domino effect, as the person at the front of the queue turned round, called the name to the person behind him, who turned round and called to the person behind him, who turned round – all superfluous as the person whose name had been called was calling his own name, only to be drowned out by the sound of his name being called out by the people standing around him. Inevitably this dragged the process out, so that we must have been waiting there for at least an hour (and it felt like three), our hopes raised every time Eddie reached for another passport, only to be quashed when he held up another Sudanese lime-green.

It was an assertive woman with metallic silver fingernails who provided the process with the dynamo that it so desperately needed. She tapped the glass screen that pro-tected Eddie Murphy from the crowd and screamed with an intonation that hinted she might use her nails to slice through the screen and gouge out his eyes. It certainly had the desired effect: Eddie shuffled into a back room, returned with a large suitcase, and thrust out passports like pantomime sweets.

'I can see your passport,' yelped Mike. 'There's mine! Mine's first! I win!'

Finally, our passports had appeared. But Eddie's head was shaking, in a you-don't-seriously-think-it's-that-easy sort of way.

'I knew this would happen,' said Karl. 'I have a friend, it took four months for him to get his visa.'

Mike and I looked at Karl in horror. He was smiling.

Another hour, another chit and several dollars later, our passports were newly embossed with silver holograms.

'So, guys, see you in Sudan!'

Karl clasped our hands, beaming as brightly as the sun that

had forced more sweat out of us than you could fit in a water-cooler, and vanished in a blaze of pure satisfaction. It was time to relax with a spot of window shopping.

In a car park behind the Ramses Hilton, a boy ladled out coffee to bleary-eyed locals. Asphalt turned into mud as our microbus lurched into the rural land of the fellahin, where sickle-bearing farmers tucked their *gelabiyya*s into their pantaloons and voluptuous hour-glasses of calico balanced baked jugs on their heads. The mess of urban life was reassembled beside river banks apparently built out of crumpled tissue paper. Primary-coloured mud-brick cubes tottered over horse-drawn carts and barrows laden with sugar cane and grapes. It was a rumbustious district, where children roly-polied under shaggy-haired goats and fat men stuck their fingers into gruesome bowls of mushy beans.

Yellow mud-brick houses squeezed together on a carpet of hay, blocks of straw on their hoods and hieroglyphics on their walls. Between them, men with long canes were herding packs of bawling camels off Nissan pick-up trucks, one fore-leg bound to a thigh to prevent them from escaping. We had reached our Sudanese beasts: the Souq al-Gamal, or Camel Market.

Some were collapsed on their haunches, baking in the heat, mouths boiling with saliva. Others gobbled piles of creepers and *bersim* leaves. If a camel intruded uninvited on the feast, he was whipped. Men sat smoking *nargileh*s in the huts, their black skin crinkled by the Forty Days' Road from Sudan. They were imaginative and also practical men, who turned their sticks into seats, walking canes, feeding props, back-stretchers and whips; who could flog a beast and simultaneously admire its fleece. Smelling of Sudan – of its *fuul*, its sun and its limited laundry facilities – they were another enchanting sniff of the world to which Master Philip was sent.

As for the camels: their coats contained as many colours

as an Arabic cake shop – as light as the cheese in *helawat al-jibn*, as golden-brown as deep-fried *qata'if* pancakes, or as dark as a date cake; manes as flaky as shredded filo dough or as smooth as a streak of whipped cream. Some had hairy thighs, others were bald. Some had tall humps, rounded monticles or flat, fuzzy plateaux. Across the belly of the most beautiful beast – marble-white, like a Canova sculpture, his mane flowing towards a cupola-shaped hump – was torn a septic, blood-coloured band. They bore grazes, gashes, bruises, inch-deep incisions, careless cuts and mosquito-gifted pockmarks. Yet they still – and under the circumstances, there was something deeply heroic about this – maintained the hauteur for which the camel is famous, looking down on their keepers even when they were looking up, as if they wouldn't deign to spit on them.

'*Gamal gamila*,' said a young trader called Ahmad, stuffing creepers into an invalid's mouth, its huge head laid across his lap like a child, its pockmarked body sunk in a fly-infested swamp of its own excrement – 'camel beautiful'.

The similarity of those words, an expression of the Arabs' affection for their dromedaries, seemed to heighten the misery of the beasts' condition.*

Inside his hut, Ahmad boiled a pot on a stove and poured glasses of tea for Mike and me. A buzz of flies glowed in the sunlight with which they conspired to attack our arms. Burned and bitten, we waved the flies away.

'Don't reject them,' said Ahmad, chuckling, 'they are gifts from God.'

'And the camels?' asked Mike.

Outside, another trader raised his whip over a camel's rump. Ahmad shrugged, and passed the tea glasses.

'They fetch many guineas,' he said.

---

* And here lies a semantic trap. If you want to compliment someone or something in Arabic, you should describe it as '*gamila*' – beautiful. For example, '*al-bint gamila*' – the girl is beautiful. Not, as I inadvertently once said: '*al-bint gamal*' – the girl is a camel.

Religion was nice; just not when it got in the way of business. The balance between the two – between lucrative camels and sacred flies, market and mosque – seemed to be the juggling act that characterized Cairo.

But religion was about to take on a wild life all of its own.

CHAPTER THIRTEEN

THE HUNT FOR THE
HEAVENLY HOST

AS SHE SAUNTERED across the rooftop café with two lukewarm coffees and a plate of scrambled eggs the colour of a cockatoo's underside, Huwaida the Kohl-eyed Waitress trilled.

'I'm a good singer, no?'

She certainly had an impressive voice. And the fact that it was accompanied by a canopy of sleek black hair and eyelashes as long as spiders' legs didn't do any harm either. She plucked a napkin out of its box and a biro out of the breast pocket of her blouse and started sketching a map; because Huwaida's function wasn't simply to sing, be beautiful and serve your breakfast. This morning, while I waited for Mike to emerge from his shower, she was once more providing directions, as she did most mornings during our stay in Cairo. A cross appeared on the napkin, at the centre of a maze of arrows and circles: she was directing us to the Coptic Patriarchate in Abassiya.

'Excuse me!' she cooed.

I shook my dizzy head and gulped down the taste of rose-water. In front of me, laid across the space that had recently been occupied by my breakfast, was a wrist. A beautiful, pillow-soft wrist streaked by two light-blue veins with a cross tattooed in the centre.

'I am Cop-teek.' She smiled.

She waved the cartographic napkin like a belly-dancer's veil, and as she handed it over it felt like the ritual handkerchief passed between a lady and her knight.

'Well, it might do to *you*!'

Mike stopped laughing and offered a familiar look – a mixture of a frown, a protruding chin and a disbelieving smile – as we strolled through a warren of electricians' shops and fruit-juice stalls and a coffee house whose shut-eyed owner rested his head on the table-top while he twiddled the knob of a radio.

'Al-Jub,' said Mike, patting my shoulder, 'you should've been born eight hundred years ago. Can just see you in hose and curly-ended shoes.'

'What about you?' I shrugged. 'You want to live in Alexandria like Lawrence Durrell.'

'That's not what I said.'

'You said you'd like to be a British officer in 1920s Alexandria, like some character in *The Alexandria Quartet*.'

'Yeah, well, eighty years isn't exactly eight hundred.'

'In your top hat and tails, hobnobbing with some Greek magnate's feather-boa'd daughter.'

'Now that *would* be awesome!'

In the gatehouse of the Coptic Patriarchate, walkie-talkies crackled on the hips of the janitors. An elderly priest in a knitted skullcap was chatting to a large lady with buck teeth and flowers in her hat. They beckoned us over and scrutinized us with questions. From where? Gasp. Did we know Queen Elizabet? No? Not even Prince Zyarles? How about – Elton John? Where were we travelling to? Why? Prester who? *Ya salam!* What strange people these are.

Eventually, we managed to make some enquiries of our own. There were, the large lady explained, ten million Copts in Egypt – a sixth of the population. They were 'the original church', added the old priest.

'We stick to the fundamentals,' he said, 'and the same rites and religion practised in the original Apostolic Church.'

To underline this traditionalism, the large lady told us the tale of her favourite saint. He was called Jacob the Cut, after what happened to his limbs. He suffered multiple amputations and, deducing that this would be an inconvenience, begged God to forgive him for his inability to pray on his feet.

'But if you truly want to understand our religion,' added the priest, 'you should visit the monasteries.'

'We intend to,' said Mike.

After all, it was the Egyptian desert fathers who invented monasticism, to which we both owed our own boarding-school educations. Without the eccentric ascetics of early Christian Egypt – men who lived with snakes or she-wolves, buried themselves in sand or dwelt in caves and restricted their diets to the sap of the sycamore tree or bread with a dash of wild marjoram – I might never have learned how to survive in a food-fight, build an ashtray into a sofa-arm and hide a bottle of Cinzano down my trousers.

So, with the aim of getting in touch with the roots of our schooling, Mike and I crossed the courtyard to an office where framed cœnobites were depicted, mortifying their flesh, in brightly painted icons.

'You want to visit the monasteries?' Abouna Jamal winced through a sunken expression that suggested he'd recently endured the same experiences as the coenobites.

'We want to learn about the Coptic Church,' said Mike.

'Apparently the monasteries are Paradise,' I added.

Abouna Jamal looked us up and down, nodded, and let his head drop back on to his desk.

'Welcome any time,' he muttered.

'Really?' Mike stepped forward. 'We can just turn up?'

Abouna Jamal nodded.

'And,' added Mike, 'we can stay the night?'

Abouna Jamal was no longer nodding. His considerable

beard, which had previously been rising and falling over the stack of manuscripts on his desk, was now brushing the edges of the paper as it shook from side to side.

'You will need,' he said, 'permission.'

I plucked out a pen and paper. 'That's fine, Abouna, if you could just write—'

'From the Pope.'

Abouna Jamal pointed to a portrait of a venerable Copt with a forest of facial hair and several layers of crucifix chained to his neck.

'That's Pope Shenouda,' said Mike.

'Pope Anba Shenouda the Third,' expanded Abouna Jamal, 'the one hundred and seventeenth successor of St Mark.'

'Well,' Mike began, 'is he about?'

Abouna Jamal folded his arms across his cassock, then, 'Write!' he snapped. Mike grabbed my notepad and wrote down our names.

'No!' muttered Abouna Jamal. 'Write a letter. To Pope Shenouda.'

Mike wrote a clear, to-the-point letter.

'No! This is the Pope. How do you write to the Pope?'

'Your Holiness . . . ?'

The monk looked exasperated. 'Be polite,' he cried. 'You know – start by kissing his hand, greet him humbly.'

'But we haven't met him – ah!'

Mike nodded cannily. He knew what he had to do. He put his head down and scribbled:

To His Holiness Pope Shenouda III,

After kissing your hand in humble greeting, we introduce ourselves as seekers of the divine Truth of the Desert Fathers, who have travelled from the Far Corners of Christendom to learn about the Coptic Church of Egypt.

We would be extremely grateful and humble if we could visit the Coptic monasteries of Saints Bishoi

*and Paul, if Your Holiness would be magnanimous
enough to grant us permission.*

*We thank you for your kind and generous assis-
tance, Your Holiness, and remain your humble
servants.*

'Good,' said Abouna Jamal.

He read it through a couple of times, nodded whenever he
came across 'humble', and scribbled a message at the bottom.
'This is correct,' he said. 'This is how you address a pope.'

Our first overtures with the Copts suggested a considerably
more affluent sect than the anticipated cross-fire fixture in
the battle between Islamists and the government. In London,
expatriate Copts complained that their co-religionists were
restricted from high office and military and security jobs,
barred from studying gynaecology and obstetrics, and
denounced by fiery clerics on government-controlled TV, and
that the murderers of Copts weren't properly punished. This
last was a particularly sore point, because a lot of Copts had
been murdered. The most spectacular bloodbath occurred on
the eve of the millennium, when a dispute between a
Christian shopkeeper and a Muslim customer in al-Kosheh
erupted at the expense of twenty Christians, one Muslim and
two unidentified bodies. Ninety-six suspects were detained,
but no one was indicted. The Copts, it appeared, were no
better off than in the twelfth century, when they were barred
from the civil service and had to wear five-pound crosses
around their necks.

According to Abu Salih, the Arab-Armenian who travelled
in East Africa a few years after Master Philip, the prophet
Muhammad extolled the Copts as 'the noblest of foreigners;
the gentlest of them in action; the most excellent of them in
character, and the nearest of them in kinship to the Arabs
generally.' But he also recounted how 'the mob of Cairo' and
'the Ghuzz and the Kurds, who came with Yusuf Salah ad-

Din ibn Ayyub' (Saladin) burnt the church of St John in Fustat, and 'razed [it] to the ground like the other churches'. There were ameliorating factors: the church of St John was rebuilt by a Muslim Sheikh; Copts were found among the Sultan's retinue, including Saladin's private secretary; and they were free to build their own shrines.* Flicking forward eight centuries to Hosni Mubarak's National Democratic regime, which begrudgingly appointed a couple of Coptic ministers and did little to curb the Copticide that often antic- ipated more high-profile acts of violence,† it was difficult to distinguish the Copts' second-class status (especially when an Ottoman veto still restricted them from repairing even the toilets in their churches) from medieval *dhimmi*tude.

Tunnelling under the city, the Metro shuttled us towards Cairo's most identifiable Coptic district. The towers of Roman Babylon rolled alongside us, hieroglyphs hidden among their stone trunks. Goats peered from a construction site, ears cocked at the absurd state of affairs where visitors could be more interested in the dance of crosses and Seljuk- style stalactites on the gateway of al-Mu'allaqah – the Hanging Church – than in that rather delicious dish of last week's grilled corncob.

---

* It is indicative of the fertility of medieval Coptic culture that the Copts taught Muslims to stamp and print patterns on textiles with wooden blocks, a technique which, brought to Europe by the Franks, may have contributed to the development of printing.

† In June 1981, allegations that a Coptic church was being built on land reserved for a mosque fuelled tensions in the Cairo slum of Zawiya al- Hamra, and culminated in at least seventeen deaths. That September, President Sadat arrested 170 Coptic clergymen, as well as the Supreme Guide of the Muslim Brotherhood, and replaced Pope Shenouda with a committee of five bishops, headed by Bishop Samwil. A month later, Sadat was assassinated and Bishop Samwil was killed on the platform with him. In 1997, twelve Coptic students were gunned down in Abu Qirqas, a few months before the massacre of fifty-eight tourists and four locals in Luxor, by gunmen from al-Gama'a al-Islamiyya. 'It's OK if you munch on little Copts,' jibed the Coptic weekly *al-Watan*, 'but don't touch the tourists.'

Al-Mu'allaqah captures so much of the Coptic faith under its barrel-vaulted ceiling that it reads as a symbol for the creed itself. Indeed, it is symbolism that is its most pronounced feature. The pillars representing Noah's family and the Trinity, the Fatimid-era marble pulpit held up by pillared emblems of the disciples, the honeycomb on the iconostasis representing the words of Jesus ('because,' explained a Coptic student called Faby, whose dimples shone as brightly as the amulet hanging over her thorax, 'his words are as sweet as honey') – these and many other features express the figurative quality of a faith that traces God in even the tiniest shard of cedarwood.

This is hardly unique – Christianity, with its blood-wine, body-bread motifs, is particularly suited to symbolism, and medieval Christians' perception of all worldly objects as expressions of faith has more in common with modern Copticism than the less imaginative developments of many Western churches. One of the thrills of our exploration of Coptic Cairo was the sense that here (emotionally rather than doctrinally) was the faith to which Master Philip subscribed. As Abouna Sama'an, a monk at the monastery of St Paul, told us, 'We are keeping the beliefs and traditions of the first church, preserved by the blood of thousands of martyrs.'

Not only the symbols would have been comprehensible to Master Philip, but also the faith in miracles and the quasi-magical qualities attached to physical objects that give them the power of an amulet in Ariosto's *Orlando Furioso*. Down a cobbled palm-arched subterranean street, where the walls smelt of water and a blind woman rattled a begging bowl, a silver chain was passed around the nunnery of St George. This was no workaday chain, but the same chain – so explained an elderly Copt who had just strained his shoulders under its weight in the Coptic alternative to body-building – that was used to test the strength of St George.*

---

* Or, because there's always an alternative interpretation, the manacle from which the saint saved a slave-boy.

'It destroy my bad spirit,' explained the elderly Copt, sweat spilling over his nictitating eyelids.

It was a dusty, sun-parched tangle of Coptry, where miraculous artefacts or intricately decorated works of mother-of-pearl lurked at every corner. Although, at one corner – the most unexpected of all Coptic Cairo's treasures – was a man who was extraordinary for *not* being a Copt. This much was expressed not by his round face and leathery skin but by the blue-and-white knitted skullcap on his head.

'I am Natan Ibrahim,' he announced. 'I am the Jew of Cairo!'

His friends and family had emigrated to Israel, but he had no plans to follow.

'I live here,' he said. 'I work here. This is my home.'

Round the corner was a synagogue that recalled the dynamic local Jewish community of which Natan Ibrahim was the last remnant. In Master Philip's day, it was led by the great physician, philosopher and jurist Maimonides, whose Mishnah Torah inspired the Orthodox law still practised in Mea She'arim. Inside the synagogue, a hexagram decorated the double-sided marble pulpit, mother-of-pearl twisted itself into Hebrew letters and a Torah stand unfolded out of marble. The similarity of materials and textures to those found in the Coptic churches recalled the connection that was underlined by a well behind the synagogue. Through the din of JCB diggers, a security guard pointed out (once the customary baksheesh had been dispensed) the site where the pharaoh's daughter plucked Moses' reed basket out of the rushes. It looked like a pit in a construction site, but it was arguably the cradle of monotheism.

More magic assailed us back at al-Mu'allaqah. Through a hole at the back of the nave, Faby showed us a cathedral of air that filled the empty space between the two Roman towers on to which the church was built.

'You see,' she said, 'the church has no foundations – it is held up by God.'

Master Philip would have given more credit to this theory than Mike and I, brought up on the Western faith in material science that is practised even in monastic boarding schools. The fresco of Mary gazing beatifically from a pillar in al-Mu'allaqah was, Faby explained, also the subject of a miracle – albeit one from a little more than a thousand years ago.

'There was a time of persecution,' she told us, 'and the king said to the Christian people, "You say your faith can move a mountain, so I challenge you: either you move a mountain or I destroy all the Christians. If you move it, you can build all the churches you want." So the Christian peoples were sad and thought they were going to die, but this image of Mary spoke to the bishop and said, "Simeon will move the mountain at Muqattam." The people took their animals and children to Muqattam and prayed and fasted and Simeon was there and finally the mountain lifted in the air, so you could see the sun underneath it. And the Christian people were saved.'

It was a typically Coptic story, with the ingredients they love: fasting, the Virgin Mary and a miracle.

The Coptic culture of faith-through-miracle was also expressed at the Shajara Maryam, the Tree of Mary, which sheltered not only the Holy Family in their flight from Herod but also, over a millennium later, the Crusaders, as they prepared to attack Cairo in 1169. We found the Shajara in Materiya, a potholed suburb where barouches spat puddles at skips piled camel-high with everyday detritus and men shaped wood panels in sepulchral workshops. Inside the compound's gateway were three white-suited soldiers, their brows creased with determination to deter us.

'Got no choice,' boomed Mike, waving a copy of our letter from the Coptic Patriarchate. 'We're special ambassadors of Pope Shenouda.'

He marched in and, squeezing between two of the spindlier guards, I followed. The tree itself was a gnarled sycamore, sprawling and crutched up on wooden planks, a weak elderly relative of the elegant fig tree preening beside it. And it was the fig tree that an excitable man in a blue-collar jumpsuit credited with the compound's magic.

'MaryJesusJoseph-eat!' he screamed, stabbing the tree with a crooked pole so that it shed a basketload of fruit, then depositing these spoils in our laps. The figs certainly weren't sweet, but Mike's cunning ploy of hiding his portion in a flower bed had the not particularly welcome effect of convincing Jumpsuit that he had the appetite of a true saint, and inspiring him to set about the tree with renewed panache.

'Oh no no no,' groaned Mike, 'MaryJesusJoseph-NOeat!'

Relief arrived – miraculously enough – in the form of a woman in full hijab. As she circled the trees, she raised her arms and enunciated the sound that people make when they get their fingers caught in a door. Only, her hypothetical fingers remained caught in the door as she continued her circuit. There were tears in her eyes but no sign of a cross. Was she a Muslim, expressing the Islamic veneration of Mary? Her conservative wraps suggested so, but I couldn't be sure – Coptic dress code isn't generally as 'Western' as Maronite. The 'Islamic' headdress, after all, isn't Islamic, but associated with ideas about modesty – common throughout Master Philip's Christendom – that prevail among nuns. Regardless of her religious label, her consternation had the welcome effect of keeping our fig-feeder away from the figs and (because miracles do truly happen at the Shajara Maryam) the fate of my own provisions was unexpectedly resolved by a ravenous Alsatian with strings of spittle swinging off its mouth. Nostrils flaring and tongue beating flaccidly against its lower lip, it gobbled the figs off my lap before padding back to men in navy-blue suits and caps marked 'Cairo K-9 Unit'.

'Well, that really was a God-send,' I said.

'Hmm . . .' Mike nodded. 'Except you know what those dogs are for? They're looking for bombs.'

Out of the Cairo slums we drove, and out of the trickle of the Delta emerged moorhens and washerwomen. Jaundiced grass spiked mounds of sand in the area around Wadi Natrun. A truck squiggled to a military checkpoint, where we flashed our letter of humble servitude to His Holiness Pope Anba Shenouda III. The soldier borrowed a pen and wrote down our names and passport numbers on the palm of his hand.

A few yards up the road, we stood before the seventh-century monastery of St Bishoi. Like so many of the Coptic buildings, its stout encircling walls suggested a fortress, an impression that the checkpoint did little to dispute. But, beyond the thick sandstone gateway, the sprinkle of fruit and ponciana trees lightened the atmosphere around an elderly priest who offered us tea spiced with mint from the monastery gardens.

'You are well-com,' he said, 'but I must tell you I don't like England.'

We braced ourselves for the usual recriminations: no doubt he would recall the British occupation of Egypt that lasted for seventy years from 1882.

'I had a car accident in England,' he explained, fingering the wickerwork crucifix that hung from a chain around his neck, 'and I damaged my hip. Now I can travel no more – *all* because of England.'

As we offered our condolences, a group of boys settled under a ponciana tree. One of them, who had the figure of a twig and the bony, feline face of a pharaoh, introduced himself as Ibram. He was reading chemistry at Asyût University.

'I wish to discover,' he said, his face tilted with eagerness to please, 'the cure for the AIDS.'

The priest angrily tugged his crucifix. 'This is a bad idea! AIDS is expressing God's anger on his people. In the past, there were floods and destruction, now this is God's way to warn against sin.'

Ibram nodded, and bowed to us as formally as a Persian vizier in the *Arabian Nights*.

'I am here for your service,' he said. 'You like to come with me?'

In a vaulted mud-brick tunnel, cowled monks glancing out of icons reflected the faces of the living monks who burrowed into the chapel. Date palms and coloured flowers crowded around a blank-faced papier-mâché Holy Family and spread the smells of fertility. In the guest wing, mushy fava beans festered in tin bowls and bread the colour of a tombstone sat stiffly in a basket.

'We consider the monasteries very holy,' said Ibram, as we sat around a little wooden table. 'All the Copt love for serve in the monastery. Especially *this* monastery, for St Bishoi make many miracles.'

'What sort of miracles?' I asked.

'Last year,' said Ibram solemnly, 'I got full marks in my mathematic examination.'

'How is that a miracle?' said Mike.

'I am not good at mathematic.'

Ibram came from Asyût, the largest city in Upper Egypt, which was also distinguished by miracles.

'You must go there,' he said, 'on August the nineteenth.'

'Why?' asked Mike.

'For the Virgin Mary will be there. She appear every year for three month, between July and September.'

'Have you seen her?' I asked.

'Of course! She is very dignified, and she wear a long dress and a veil.'

His eyes glazed over as he sank into a haze of religious fervour that prevented him from considering any other subject for the rest of the evening. Mike and I got out the Master Map and filled in the route since Jerusalem. But, before going to bed, we asterisked Asyût. A visit to the Virgin Mary was just up Master Philip's street.

When we turned up to chapel at five in the morning, Ibram

tapped his watch fastidiously. We were an hour late. A priest thurifered the nave, and thick smoke plumes choked any inclination we might have had to emulate the acolytes. We decided to observe them from a detached distance. They prostrated themselves several times a minute, planted passionate kisses on a small silver cross and the hand of the celebrating priest, and responded to his blessings by moulding their hands down their faces. A thunder of Coptic liturgy wound across the chapel, husky and inflexible, all eyes searing through the incense as if in search of the Holy Spirit. They reminded me of how effortlessly Christianity had flowed into Egypt, adopting the pharaonic language and the name 'Qibt', for Egyptians, which became the name for the Christians. The crosses carved on to the iconostasis in front of us (in six different styles that intertwined so that every inch of the screen was part of a cross) replaced the similarly shaped ankh sign that can be seen on pharaonic tombs.

'The service will go on until eight.' Ibram, beaming, leaned towards Mike and me. '*Then* we will have Mass.'

It was too much. Even St Bishoi cheated – he used to tie his hair to hooks in the ceiling to keep himself upright during marathon services. Having neither enough hair nor the hooks, Mike and I fled for the fresh air outdoors. Wooden walkways jumped between mud-brick walls and an iron-plated door creaked towards the rooftop. Fortifications that looked like they'd been moulded out of marzipan encircled eggshell domes and vegetable patches where monks scuttled with trowels. Behind the monastery, wreathed in a moat of ponciana trees, white cloud gobbled up the hazy wasteland of the Skete Desert. It seemed suitably divorced from the ruckus of Cairo. Wadi Natrun was Coptic Egypt's great escape pad, the hideaway for Pope Shenouda after he fell foul of President Sadat in the 1970s just as it had been for Pope Kyrillos V, whose nationalistic proclamations incurred British wrath in the 1880s. Wadi Natrun was where Copts came to disappear.

A couple of days later, the bus darted out of Cairo's topsy-turvy slumland and made a run for the desert. Near Beni Suef, 120 kilometres south of the capital, we were dropped at a police checkpoint.

It was one o'clock, the hottest period of the day, and the sun was slurping up our energy like a little boy sucking every last drop of milkshake with his straw. Mike crashed on a mattress in a concrete kiosk, beside the striped barrels where a policeman sat, scooping out the flesh of a pomegranate with his fingers. Perhaps he was hoping the aphrodisiac qualities that made it a popular delicacy in Master Philip's day would enhance his next visit to the nightclubs of Cairo.

I watched out for a lift by the roadside, beside a Bedu who was picking his teeth with a mastic twig. His complexion had clearly lost its battle with the sun: he looked as old as Gilgamesh. He offered me cigarettes, filled up my water bottle and, when a jeep stopped ahead of us, he held it up while I woke Mike, and helped us to clamber into the back.

It was full of soldiers, with whom we squeezed on to wooden seats. One of them held his gun between his knees. Whenever the jeep bounced on a bump, its business end jolted towards my chin. I wanted to suggest that the soldier take greater care of his equipment, but I wasn't sure how to express this in a tactful way, and busy fending off the Bedu's offers of mouldy bread, his toothpick twig or, as we scrambled over the soldiers' knees and leaped into a dusty street, a supper invitation that we reluctantly refused: the boat to Sudan was leaving from Aswan in three days' time, and there wouldn't be another one for a week. His calloused hands gripped ours tightly and a valedictory wave was veiled by a burka of dust.

Clanking on its steel tracks, the steam locomotive to Asyût was a faithful recreation of an Egyptian souk. Once we'd fought our way in, leapfrogging the men slouched on the steps, fought to heave our backpacks up beside that dripping package of meat on the overhead ledge, and fought for somewhere to stand, we were jostled by men balancing trays of tulip-shaped tea glasses on one hand while they used the other to cleave the crowd; men carrying metal buckets full of cold drinks; bread salesmen, sandwich sellers, hawkers of plastic combs or Qu'ranic pamphlets, cigarette vendors and passengers looking for spaces to crouch. There was an almighty honk, a cheer from the platform, a jolt of chattering brackets and chugging engine as noisy as the babble of passengers tumbling together like dolls.

'*Parlez-vous français, monsieur?*'

In the dance of crushed bones that constituted the journey, my current partner in hip-crunching was a man called Michel, whose neat beige suit was matched by his neat David Niven moustache.

'*Vous êtes chrétien?*' he asked.

'*Oui, et vous?*'

'*Sans doute,*' he said, slyly unveiling the Coptic tattoo concealed under his sleeve.

He was, he grandly announced, an employee in the government's 'Département de Finance'. We were *bienvenus* at his *petite maison* in Minya. Why not stay for a few days? We would love to, I replied, but we had to push on to Asyût. Why the rush? Well, we're hoping to get to Ethiopia in a few weeks, and we've got to catch the next boat to Sudan.

'*Ça c'est un grand voyage!* Why do you travel so far?'

'We're following an Italian physician.'

'He is in Ethiopia? *Peut-être* I can be some help. I have a friend in Addis Ababa . . .'

'It's a bit trickier than that.'

'How?'

'He's dead.'

Through the grimy window, I could see the soles of several feet. The Nile chased the track, framed in lush greenery that crept along the banks. Hyacinths sank in the water, where women in coloured dresses wrung rags or scrubbed dishes or filled plastic flasks, their skirts floating around them like lily pads.

'I am very sorry to hear this,' said Michel. 'You are related to him?'

'No.'

'Then why do you follow him?'

'You know,' I said, as I turned back to the window, 'that is a very good question.'

Old men were leaning on sticks on the stoops of their trellised mud-brick houses. Their sons laid down their hoes and dribbled guava juice down their shifts. Their grand-children sprinted alongside us before turning back to conjure fun out of wooden crates or water buffaloes.

Even before we'd reached Asyût, the local obsession with the Virgin Mary had expressed itself. While I wedged my feet under a seat and lay in the aisle, causing women to raise their skirts, the tea-tray man to moonwalk his legs, and the cold-drinks vendor to decide I was an easy target and stoop to pitch me a Pepsi, Mike managed to charm his way on to a bench full of Copts.

'Ya salam!' exclaimed the Coptess beside him. 'Our Lady Mariam? Of course I have seen her – she is very beautiful and there is bright light and many birds.'

Across the bench, crucifixes were fingered and blessings heaped on our arrival in Asyût. Would we be assailed by a flock of alleluia-singing doves?

'You come with me.'

Would we see the red lights and silver baubles that were spotted alongside Mary in the town of Shentena al-Hagar in 1997?

'I said, you come with me.'

No. We'd be assailed by a policeman, who bundled us into his car and refused all efforts at communication as we rum-bled down a street named after Saladin.

'It's your trousers.' Mike squinted at a pair of grey flannels that are not my proudest possession: 'You look like a geography teacher.'

Plane trees crowded behind a tall iron gateway. The policeman ushered us out and from the shadows stepped another.

'What's the problem?' said Mike (between us, we'd asked that question at least – oh, umpteen times).

'No problem,' the policeman replied. 'This your hotel – please inside and no out before new day.'

Up a flight of cool metal steps, a pot-bellied porter scraped a key in a door and gestured us into a small room with vertical blinds and two narrow beds.

'Well, what did you think of all that?' I said, as Mike fell to the floor and started his sit-ups.

'It's the GIs, I guess.'

'GIs?' I lay down on a moth-eaten blanket. 'I thought they were American.'

'No, Nick. As in al-Gama'a al-Islamiyya.'

'Oh, the guys who tried to kill Naguib Mahfouz?'

'Carried out the Luxor massacre in '97, killed fifty-eight tourists and eight locals.'

'But we're miles from Luxor.'

'Nick, Asyût's their breeding ground. Three of the six guys who did Luxor were enrolled at Asyût Uni. For the last decade Asyût's been a hotbed – mass demos, students waving banners, men in balaclavas. President Mubarak, being a diplomatic kind of guy, sends in the police and takes out the students.'

He rested against the side of the bed and started massaging his neck. 'Seems calmer now,' he continued, 'but I don't think they're taking chances. Two dead tourists wouldn't do much for Upper Egypt's tourist industry.'

In the morning, we were immediately assigned a police escort. At least, that's what he said he was. His baggy trousers and the bemused countenance that beamed affectionately under his curly black locks and his habit of patting the hip that didn't hold his holstered pistol, then correcting himself, suggested less a career in security than the circus. But Gamal was an endearing guide. He nodded conscientiously while Mike explained that we were looking for the Virgin Mary, and promised to help. On the way to the Coptic Church of St Mark, he pointed out the chicken-cage turrets and the stalls selling mangoes, watermelons and bananas in the souk, and the colonial mansions and the mosques and the boys with charcoal-pincers who scrambled between *nargileh* clouds in the coffee houses. He didn't point out the gun-clinching soldiers who stood outside the souk and the colonial mansions and the mosques and the coffee houses.

At the church, the Coptic curator showed us a black-and-white photo in which 'Mariam' (at least, a foamy white form with the grainy imprecision of Nessie prints and the figure of the Egyptian Museum's marble Aphrodite) hovered over the church steeple, and screamed her name at least thirty times without supplying any clue as to where and when we would find her.

In fact, it was left to a Muslim to seal our quest for the mother of Christ.

Ahmad, the son of a local café owner, greeted us by squeezing our ribs and anointing himself 'at your service'.

'You want to see Mariam?' he said, as we dipped wonderfully hot slabs of pitta bread into a dish of spicy hummus. 'So we go to Dirunka.'

'*Ya*, you must go to Dirunka,' cooed his mother, a buxom lady in a floral-print kaftan, who spread a maternal scent of warm, fresh laundry as she leaned towards us. 'There is so much light! When you are in her presence, it is a feeling I will never forget. Go Dirunka – she is there at ten o'clock.'

Gamal the Police Escort was less keen on a trip to Dirunka, but he was too busy enjoying his hummus to notice that Ahmad had summoned a horse-drawn barouche. We weren't exactly planning to abscond without informing him: he just seemed so closely engaged in digging chickpea lumps out of his teeth, it would have been unforgivable to disturb him. So we escaped on to the most impractical vehicle a pair of escapees could possibly choose: an open-air conveyance whose potential speed was compromised by the mutual lethargy of its mastic-chewing master and a steed that apparently hadn't eaten for a week. About twenty clip-clops down the high street, a police car screeched to our left, the horse whinnied, another police car screeched to our right. The police captain had been alerted to our escape and he was not at all keen on our plans.

'What's he saying?' asked Mike, as first Ahmad monologued with rapid digital gesticulations, then the police captain surrounded himself with six taxi-drivers. He dismissed all but one of them, wrote down the chosen driver's licence-plate and ID number, registration and tax disc details, and Ahmad's name and address, before repeating the details into his walkie-talkie, and finally bundled us all into the taxi. We would – as the replacement of Asyût's streets by a canvas of limestone pockmarked with caves suggested – be going to Dirunka after all.

'Now is the army there,' explained Ahmad, pointing out the little white men peeking out of the caves, 'but a few years ago there was a thief there called al-Khot. He was a very clever thief and he stealed from all the people who went past, and killed some of them, and the whole town was scared for him.'

'What happened?' asked Mike.

'The police finded him and shooted him.'

Ahmad was something of a raconteur. He told us the tale of his mother's university education in Birmingham, the tale of the defrocked monk who had inspired the sensationalist tabloid headline 'Miracle Monk Has Sex With 5,000 Women', and the tale of the Muslim who threw stones at Christians:

'And one day the blessed Mariam appeared for him and she told him stop hurting the Christians and for show he was sorry, he must paint a cross on his house. So, he painted forty big crosses all over the walls of his house, and never hurted the Christians again.'

It was an example of the Islamic reverence for Mary that had greeted us in the enthusiasm of Ahmad's mother; although, as my reading of Coptic history had already warned me, there could only ever be one champion in the battle to be Mary's number-one fan:

'We hail you,' declared Cyril of Alexandria in AD 431:

> through whom the heavens exult; through whom the angels and archangels rejoice; through whom the demons are put to flight; through whom the tempter fell from heaven; through whom the fallen creation is raised to the heavens; through whom the whole world, held captive by idolatry, has come to know the truth; through whom holy baptism is given to those who believe, with 'the oil of gladness'; through whom churches have been founded throughout the world; through whom pagan nations have been led to conversion.

Pagan nations converted? By Mary? The *whole* world apprised of 'the truth'? And how did this meek Israelite cause the tempter to fall from heaven? As the 'vessel' through which Christ was born, Mary had been credited with the achievements of Christ.

But Coptic Mary-worship has an ancient source. Isis, mother of a divine son and impregnated, in one version of her story, by holy fire, was translated into the veiled God-bearer, raising her – up, up, another Assumption – to a status that she didn't enjoy in Europe until the engagement with the East that took place during the Crusades. In Egypt we had reached the heart of the Marian cult, the mini-faith tucked inside Christianity that inspired the fresco in al-Mu'allaqah and still entices pilgrims to buy Ave Maria-singing toilet roll in modern-day Mary-spots like Lourdes.

Considering it was about to host a personal appearance of the Virgin Inviolate, Dirunka didn't look very grand. Flies whined around dust-saddled donkeys tethered to the roadside, in front of crumbling mud-brick houses. It was as likely a setting for a divine appearance as – er – a stable.

'There was a fire here five years ago,' said Ahmad. 'So many of the houses were destroyed.'

I was expecting to hear a tale of sectarian violence, but, as Ahmad pointed out, 'Not every disaster in Egypt is for violence.' Dirunka had been visited by a misfortune that would destroy (or increase) many people's faith in the Virgin Mary. On 2 November 1994 there was a flash flood. A bridge collapsed over a military fuel complex, causing an explosion of fifteen thousand tonnes of fuel. More than six hundred people, mostly scalded with third-degree burns, were killed.

Towering over the town was the clifftop convent of al-Adhra, built over the cave that traditionally represents the southernmost point of the Holy Family's troglodytic flight through Egypt. Underneath a jam-packed crocodile of local pilgrims curling in pursuit of the Virgin Mary, a squat of policemen was sipping coffee on plastic chairs. One of them summoned a microbus, cocked his gun at its passengers and ordered them out. He turned to us and gestured inside: 'Wellcom in Dirunka.'

The horn blasted and we charged up the slope, scattering the crowd like snooker balls. Families of Copts leaped out of the way, screaming and shaking their fists. Children yammered as they held tight to their fathers' shoulders.

'Stupids,' said the policeman chuckling beside me.

We parked in front of the gates to the convent. A five-man police contingent linked hands with us and ploughed into the crowd, waving their pistols in the air, prodding pilgrims with the barrels of their guns. The pilgrims turned to watch us, their faces widened with awe or scrunched with resentment. A path was fissured through the crowd, who slipped against one another, elbows careening into ribs, arms flailing and necks jolting. A fat man was struggling to squeeze through the gate to the convent, his frame trapped between the iron posts. A policeman tapped the man's shoulder with his gun, and several tonnes of obesity wobbled into the forecourt. Women with mewling babies, old men raising messianic arms: all were jostled by the muscle power of the policemen. But as soon as we'd passed, their arms flew back where they'd been and their tongues resumed their impression of bells' clappers. The ritual unfolding from the cave's lip, where an icon of Mary was raised on a priest's stick, was both the inspiration for the outburst of ear-thumping energy and the discipline that prevented it from spilling over into a stampede.

People screamed as they perched on the branches of trees, ululated as they dangled their legs over the walls of the forecourt, trilled as they hunched on the metal gateway. Those on the forecourt itself were increasingly compressed, as the heat and density squeezed out the stench of body odour and the din (Arabic for religion) of crowd-amplified piety. They raised their arms and dabbed their sweaty foreheads with the sign of the cross, and squealed to the priests' incantations. The frisson was tremendous – a sense of power, of belonging to one massive monolith that, if held together, could destroy a police checkpoint or burn down a city. I wondered if this was how the Franks felt when Pope Urban preached the Crusade at Clermont.

The experience was dizzying. Panting beside a soft-drinks stall outside the gates, inhaling a slightly higher rate of oxygen, I couldn't remember if I'd been on the forecourt for ten minutes or an hour.

'Where's Mike?' said Ahmad.

Before I could look from one side to the other, we were in the thick of a full-blown crisis. A walkie-talkie-crackling, officer-screaming, officer-waving-pistol-through-the-crowd crisis. I thought somebody was going to be shot.

'Mike,' I began, 'is actually quite capable—'

But I realized no one was listening when Ahmad pinned me to the wall.

'I protect you, Nick,' he said softly. 'You are my friend.'

At first I was nonplussed. Mike could handle himself several times over. But, as the minutes ticked by, the crackle of the guard's walkie-talkie communicating an increasing panic and Ahmad's arms slowly turning into a vice, I started to wonder. What if there'd been an accident? What if he'd been abducted by al-Gama'a al-Islamiyya? They might be turning their kitchen knives on his carotid artery right now. My travelling companion had gone the way of the inspiration for our travels – like Master Philip, he'd disappeared.

'Hallo!'

A little boy tilted his head from side to side as he subjected me to the sort of examination that people conduct in Madame Tussaud's. I rolled my eyes and the boy touched my nose. His countenance was one of sceptical curiosity. His father, Jacoub, offered me his hand and welcomed me in his country.

'Why does Mary come here?' I asked.

'This,' said Jacoub, 'is the last place the Holy Family stay in Egypt before they go back to Palestine. You know there is many problem here in last many years – between the Coptic and the Muslim? So, maybe this is God's way for helping the people. For making them see how important is to be witness to Christ here.'

A smile arced his whiskers.

'You come all this way to see Mary?' he said. 'So this is wrong what they say about the West.'

'What do they say?'

'They say that you forget God.'

I looked at the crowd – raising icons, kissing crucifixes, chanting prayers. No chance of God being forgotten here. They were pulsing, louder and more unified, as if all the heartbeats in the vicinity had been linked through a loudspeaker: *ba-booom, ba-booom, ba-booom.*

'Will we see Mary?' I asked.

'Of course,' said Jacoub. 'But she comes in many forms. Last year it is very bright, like the lightning, sometimes it's a bird, sometimes with three angels for company just a few metres off the ground. It depends – if you have the faith.'

He looked at me. Judging me. *If you have the faith*. I imagined the appearance of the Virgin Mary like a sighting of Nessie. The chasm was growing between myself and Master Philip.

Why all these doubts? Apart from the odd self-conceal-ment under a dormitory bed to avoid Sunday Mass, I had barely resisted the Teaching of the True Church in my youth. But now, in the cradle of my religion, all the questions I'd never thought to ask were heaping up inside my head. I remembered Jihad's calf-like eyes sorrowing at the heresy of a fertile God in Tripoli; the Israeli gunship rumbling over Christ's birthplace in Bethlehem; the rebukes my avowed faith had received from Orhan in Konya or Eyal in West Jerusalem; the stories of Crusading knights committing mas-sacre in the name of the same denomination that I had been brought up to profess. Master Philip would never have allowed himself to be distracted by such thoughts.

'Look!' Ahmad was pinching my arm.

A jubilant cheer, rushing through the crowd, swelling as it goes, bouncing off the walls, thundering from the trees, shrieking through the windows above our heads; huge, unan-imous, stripping the entire forecourt of idiosyncrasy and rolling all the voices into one spectacular bawl. A bright light, about ten thousand lifted noses, twenty thousand arms raised like stalks. Ahmad pointing, to the sky, to the form floating towards us, floating over our heads, floating away behind a flap of wall.

A dove.

(Or a pigeon.)

'Is that it?' I moaned.

'You should have come last year,' said a man nearby. 'The Virgin's lights were much brighter.'

'And there were more doves,' added another.

'They are not doves!' snapped Jacoub. 'They are the heavenly host.'

One of the policemen, patting his heart and pointing, looked like he'd seen something too. To the cheers of several policemen, Mike was greeted with back-slaps and hand-wrestles, and his neck swallowed by Ahmad's arms.

'I just walked off,' he protested. 'It wasn't that hard.'

But afterwards the policemen reinforced their grip, so that it was unclear whether we were over-pampered guests or prisoners, and our forearms were returned to us only when we had been safely deposited on the train to Aswan.

'Did you see it?' I said, as Mike tossed his rucksack on to the luggage rack.

'See what?'

'The – heavenly host.'

His eyes were certainly dilated. Were those the flushed features of someone who's just looked into heaven?

'Don't be ridiculous,' he said. 'It's just a load of balls to get the pilgrims.'

This is the Upper Egypt I remember:

Papyrus quills falling off the wooden platform of a truck, a boy tripping over his shift as he ran round to pick them up.

A young woman, head to heel in red calico, sniffing the orange peel that she had rubbed into her wrists.

The bright lights of the riverboat restaurants on Aswan's Corniche, and the bright smiles of the Nubian salesmen who sold shoes and sunglasses and combs on old sheets laid across the pavements.

The old Nubian, his tar-black skin as wrinkled as his rowing boat, arms rotating to the soft splash of the river as he floated us towards the West Bank.

*

We had booked our tickets to Sudan. In one of Aswan's slenderest alleyways, a tubby clerk snatched our money and talked merrily about a 'wonder-boat'. He didn't have pictures of any wonder-boat, although he did show us a photograph of a metal rust-bucket tangled in tarpaulin and hawsers, its sides blistered like sunburnt skin. It was an alarming prospect, so we decided to seek refuge in Master Philip.

For the papal ambassador, Aswan would have been, as it was for Abu Salih, 'the last post of the Muslims'. The frontier between Nubian Christianity and the empire of Saladin was home to one of medieval Egypt's largest Christian strongholds: the seventh-century monastery of St Simeon. Three hundred brothers filled its sandstone walls on the West Bank of the Nile – at least, until Turin Shah trawled through Upper Egypt on his brother Saladin's behalf. It was the mark of a different Saladin: the Sultan of Egypt, a ruthless leader determined to brook no opposition, burning the Nubian Guard in Cairo, and ordering the destruction of southern Egyptian monasteries like Qasr Ibrim, where Turin Shah slaughtered the bishop, his monks and seven hundred pigs.

The old Nubian pulled away from Elephantine Island, named after the shapes of the boulders on its banks. Plum trees glistened on General Kitchener's Island and goats bleated as they dug their hooves into the tiny islets on which they had found themselves, like the Crusader army at Damietta, trapped. A clump of grey rock was our designated landing platform, behind it a piste of sand that slid into a party of camel herdsmen and a policeman whose pipe-shaped beard suggested that his barbering was inspired by Tutankhamun's face mask.

'The monastery is clos-ed,' he joyfully announced.

'But it's only four o'clock,' Mike protested.

'Clos-ed.'

'Why?'

'Clos-ed.'

'Why?'

'Clos-ed.'

'Oh, shut up.'

We marched up a stony slope that snaked between sleek bumps of sand, ignoring the camel-herder offering transport in exchange for all our remaining dinars. Behind us, Tutankhamun blew his whistle.

'If you want us,' Mike announced, 'come and get us.'

We knew they wouldn't. Our skin melted and our feet shrivelled as if, rather than putting on our shoes, we had accidentally stuck them inside ceramic kilns. Ahead of us, the monastery's ruins were growing. Its slim, tawny walls looked as flimsy as cardboard. Mike jumped on a ledge, hauled himself to the top of the wall, and hurdled over. I scrambled behind, sending bits of flint and sandstone flying, and panting as I dropped myself over the other side and tumbled down an ankle-sprainer of loose steps.

I climbed over an inner wall and jumped into the belly of the monastery, scurrying past an oval tunnel that was once an oven, past niches and flaps of sandstone, and the monastery's guardian – a beady-eyed sun-striped cat. Inside a wire-gauze door, wooden planks seesawed under my feet and must filled a corridor of sun-dried brick. The only light squeezed through tiny orifices and exposed the dust and flies in the side chambers. They seemed like disembodied components from the Arabic writing scratched and inked above a mastaba bed by Muslim hajji.

At the top of a Gothic spiral of cobwebs, I found Mike gazing across the desert. It billowed like a silk cloth embroidered with black rock and camel tracks as sumptuous as the Egyptian Museum's most lavish Canopic box. A caravan of camels floated along the track, accompanied by the whoops of their herders, ancient-looking men in *gelabiyya*s, with long black beards and leather whips.

'I bet,' I said, 'they'd be recognizable to any traveller in the last three millennia.'

Mike smiled. 'Sure, until you get close up and see they're wearing Adidas trainers.'

On the other side of the monastery, the desert was parried by trees and bushes that burst above the Nile. Tutankhamun was clambering into a ferry, his shift completed. We looked down into the monastery's network of hallways and corridors, dormitories and narrow cloisters composed from different sizes of bricks. Some were tiny, others as big as sandbags. They tumbled down to the church, which the sun turned a mellow shade of pink. In the open-air nave, vestments faded in apsidal frescoes and faceless figures sat like ghosts above a small hatch that illuminated the sanctuary. There was a haunting silence, disrupted only by the wind; a desolation reflected in the monastery's isolated setting and its crumbling walls.

But when a felucca full of teenage girls, peeking at us from behind the massive wall of their mother, delivered us on the other side of the river, St Simeon's hush exploded in a carnival of music.

Sudanese men swung great polythene sacks as they shuffled towards the wonder-boat. Others swaggered with soft-drink coolboxes, rapping spoons and swaying to their self-produced tunes. We were elbowed along the queue by a foot-tapping security guard, ticketed by a humming clerk, slip-swapped by his shoulder-juggling colleague, and numbered on to the clipboard of a man with a dancing pen.

Behind a wooden shack piled with sacks, crates and plastic buckets, the tetrachord of the ticket inspector's grunts ushered us inside a metal tureen that seemed to be held together by a membrane of rust. The floor chimed with each footstep as men and women filled a dim-lit vault with their sacks, marking out their territory and exchanging chit-chat and figs. Body odour and brine intensified their reek as the aisle filtered into the canteen, where a fat man presided over a cooler and plastic jugs of tea. These he dispensed on payment of silver discs provided by an old man in a turban who sat cross-legged on his bench, like a Buddha. On deck, turbanned men were cackling, their prayer beads rattling as they snatched at a pair of binoculars to magnify the view – the view, that is, of a nearby cruise-boat, where two pairs of quarter-concealed occidental breasts were being offered to the sun – '*Shuft! Shuft!*' – look, look!

But Mike, tapping my shoulder, was directing me to look at a sight much more extraordinary. Slumped against the peeling white paint of the engine room, his hair now hidden under a black and white keffiyeh, was a familiar figure. His eyes lit up with such joyful imitation of our own that we were quickly wrapped in the sort of embrace usually employed by ravenous boa constrictors. It was Karl from Norway, our old friend from the Sudanese embassy.

This is the relativism of travel: a Norwegian and two Englishmen share a bond in Africa that wouldn't exist in Europe. As we sat in the shade of a safety dinghy, watching the turbans and cotton caps and sacks and bins and cardboard boxes and buckets and haversacks all swimming into the hold and reappearing in tottering towers on deck, it felt like we really had known one another for ever.

We were joined by a couple of Nubians – Mustafa, a cheery soul with a swarthy Arab complexion, and his cocoa-coloured friend Malik, who laid down a rug to temper the heat of the metal deck. We showed them the map of our route. Mustafa giggled at the green dragons – 'Oh, the Protector!' – and identified his home town on a speckle near Dongola. Malik waved his arms up and down and prodded the map at the confluence of the Blue and White branches of the Nile: 'Nil al-Azraq! Nil al-Abyad!' Five minutes after we met them, we all exchanged addresses and assured one another of eternal friendship.

There was a community atmosphere on the boat. As I left Mike and Karl locked in a ginless game of gin rummy and wandered the deck, questions hit me with the frequency and intensity that arrows hit St Sebastian. Where I was from? Where I was going in Sudan? Was I visiting as tourist or business? Could I help with visa application to London? An old man with a set of Islamic prayer beads around his neck asked if I had brought light and blessings, wished me God's munificence, and enquired if I had any children. He looked decidedly unimpressed when I admitted that I hadn't. I protested that I was in my early twenties and didn't feel that I had lost all opportunity for procreation, but he clearly disagreed. He hobbled away, shaking his head at such a disgraceful waste of one's loins.

I leaned over the prow, enjoying the brush of fresh air and watching the sun hang a sky of pink silk over pyramidal silhouettes of rock. I had a strange welling in my stomach, a feeling of departure for which boats are eminently suitable. We would be leaving behind Ibn Jubayr and William of Tyre, Sir John Mandeville and Usamah Ibn Munqidh, even (apart from a tangential reference) Benjamin of Tudela. Only Abu Salih and the tenth-century Egyptian envoy Selim al-Aswany would be joining us in terra incognita, until the arrival of the Portuguese.

This, I think, was my happiest moment of the trip. Despite the boat's anarchic conditions, there was a sort of serenity, mixed with the exhilaration that is travel's most precious gift. We were heading to Africa – Ifriqiya! – not almost-Africa Eezyibt, but real, messy, raw Africa. We had entered Nubia (medieval castles! silky deserts!), otherwise known as Sudan (civil war! poverty!). The poverty and war would hit us later; for now, focused on the castles and deserts, I felt a thrilling surge of spirits.

Passengers were wrapping themselves in woollen blankets and lying down on benches in the hold. The workers in the canteen cleared out the buckets of gruel. Their clients packed up backgammon boards and playing cards. Mike located a torch, a chessboard and a willing victim, while I shrouded myself in an Aleppan cloth and joined Karl on deck.

It was an evening when nothing bothered. The insects eating our arms were amusing, the hassle we remembered in Cairo was charming, the prospect of Africa was exhilarating. Gradually, silent except for the moan of the engine, a whisper of wind and the gentle tug of Lake Nasser, the conversation and the Middle East slipped into sleep.

The Seventh Letter of Master Philip to Roger of Salerno (continued)

DEAR ROGER, I awoke to find a man of sturdy beard and gentle speech bandaging my wounds. He is the personal physician to the son of Saladin, and also the vizier, and he is also the Nagid, which means that he is chief of the Jews of Babylon. His name is Rabbi Moses ben Maimon, but his acquaintances know him as Rambam.

He has tended diligently to my wounds, despite the great crowd of theologians and bailiffs and patients that fill his chambers. And on his desk are towers of papers, like the granaries of Joseph that rise in the desert of Babylon, except that those are built of brick, while these are composed of petitions from Jews of all lands who solicit his advice on matters important to them. When I was recovered, we discussed our beliefs. For he has written a code of Jewish laws and he believes that the story of Eden is not the truth, but represents a different kind of truth; namely, that Adam is the active spirit and Eve is passive matter, and the root of all evil, and that the serpent represents the imagination. And he enquired of me about Rabbi Jechiel and the Jews of Rome and what is their condition under my master Lord Alexander. And he also asked Ezekiel with great interest about the Jews of his land, for Ezekiel says that his king is descended from Moses and that there are many tribes of Jews. And this is true, for Prester John explained in his letter that the Lost Tribes of Israel reside in his dominion.

And in this part of Babylon, there are many Christians. But they are heretics like Ezekiel, and they share the same beliefs, and they have authority of the Church of the Indians. For Ezekiel informed me that when they lack a bishop in his land, they must petition the leader of the Coptics (for this is their name) to send them a replacement. And they have many churches, but many have been destroyed by Saladin. I spoke with these priests, and they were learned men of pious inclination. Their holiest men live in monasteries, where they devote themselves to prayer and mortification of the flesh. But some hold strange beliefs and maintain that the Franks are not their friends, for they accuse the Franks of destroying their churches when they invaded Egypt.

Dear Roger, great is my debt to Rabbi Moses, for I have been able to ride out of Cairo, and Ezekiel is cognizant of the ways by which to avoid the Sultan's guard, for such knowledge enables his people to travel to Jerusalem for pilgrimage. And many weeks it took us to reach the city of Aswan, by which time we had changed our mules three times, and bought camels from the Nubian merchants who tarry in these parts. Here the land is like fire, respite obtainable only from the waters of the Nile and the fruits of the trees on its banks. We must beware of divers dangers, for there are cocodrylli in the water, and giant red spiders in the sand, and bandits who attack the Christians. And I must take care of my belly, for if my wounds open in the desert, there will be no physician to assist me, and I shall have to be my own nurse.

And so I submit myself to God at every opportunity, and I pray to him with great passion, for it is necessary that I reach the court of Prester John and convert him to the True Faith. And I worry that this task will be obdurate, for Ezekiel refuses to accept my teachings, no matter how many times I repeat them. One night, we held a fierce argument as we sat around our fire in the desert. I was explaining that Christ is both human and divine, but he was ignorant of this, for he claimed that God has one divine nature. And so passionate was he in his heresy that he spent the night on the other side of the valley, and for three days spoke not.

But his silence broke near Aswan. For on the cusp of the hill we saw a great army of men, all black and bearing great store of arrows. And great was my fright, and I suggested that we flee. But Ezekiel recognized these people as friends. And so they have proved, for they are Nubians, of the Empire of Makuria, and they are Christians, so I am able to wear again the cross that I concealed after the polytheists attacked me in Babylon. They have escorted us through the Province of Maris, whose lord goes by the title Lord of the Mountain.

Truly, Roger, theirs is a hot kingdom, for the sands are as cruel as ostriches in the wilderness. And the churches are small and poor, although they are decorated inside with beautiful murals. But the Nubians have some riches, for we have met many caravans carrying gold from near the sea, and this provides the king with great wealth. And their chief city has many churches (although great was my shock when I discovered that there is also a mosque in this city, for there is a treaty between the Great King and the Sultan of Egypt). And this king is suzerain to a multitude of princes, like Prester John, but there is a strange custom that when he dies his authority passes not to his son but to the son of his sisters. And there are other strange customs. For the liturgy is Greek, but the bishops are Egyptian. The titles of the courtiers are the same as in Constantinople, but the creed is the same heresy that is practised in Egypt. And in the country, the farmers raise crops and dates and in the towns they work with sandalwood and pottery and live in houses fashioned from mud. And they sell the strange horns of beasts who live in the empire of Prester John and they make perfumes from the sweat of cats. But they have few able physicians, dear Roger, and this is of concern to me, for my wounds multiply the burden of my journey. However, I am succoured by the knowledge that Abyssines live to the age of a hundred and fifty, and so I shall doubtless meet expert physicians at my journey's end.

Pray for me, dear Roger, if you receive this letter. It is being dispatched with a caravan to the sea, and it is my hope that it will be carried thence by Christian ships. Keep me in your prayers, for there is much difficulty to overcome before I shall seal the alliance of Prester John with the lands of Christendom.

III

TERRA INCOGNITA

CHAPTER FOURTEEN

A KINGDOM ON THE NILE

'*La Allah illah Allah w Muhammad resul Allah.*'
The worshippers rose independently, uncurling and stretching and flipping their blankets aside. They formed bands of crumpled *gelabiyya*s that honeycombed the deck. They stood together, chanted together and prostrated themselves together towards the rising sun as it glowed behind the black crenellations of the East Bank.

Down in the canteen, life was more prosaic. The Buddha was distributing silver discs, while the fat man was ladling out steel bowls of *fuul* and scooping lukewarm tea from a tub. It was the most disgusting meal I never ate. Before I could commit my lips to the grim sentence of grey boiled beans, I had been enveloped in a cloud of pantaloons and loose smocks.

'Meesta, you eat for us!'

Spreading out his gold-trimmed mantle like a peacock displaying its feathers, at least a foot above his underlings and with the aura of one of Prester John's barbarian vassal kings, was Babiker.

'I am,' he announced, 'Department for Commerce in the Government of Republic the Sudan.'

Not quite the position I'd expected him to hold.

But Babiker wasn't quite what I expected from the Sudanese. When I admitted my nationality, he hung an arm around my neck; not (although the strength of his arms did not initially suggest this conclusion) in aggression, but approval.

'In Sudan, England is good. They build the road and the railway!' He leaned close and whispered, 'They is better than the present government.'

'Thanks,' I said, both to Babiker's comment and to the slice of slate-grey bread that one of his minions presented to me. But Babiker considered this an outrage. He screamed at his underling, slammed a fist on the table, and magicked a plastic bag out of his mantle.

'Today,' he announced, pouring its contents on to the table, 'we eat like kings!'

There were two tomatoes and a ricepaper confection the size of a slice of Ryvita. Sure, it was hardly a banquet; but consider the context. Babiker crushed the confection in one visibly unwashed hand and sprinkled the crumbs on to his *fuul*, then tore the tomatoes to pieces and tossed them in too. The result, which he tasted, dipping some bread and pronouncing himself thoroughly satisfied, looked like it had recently lined the stomach of a camel from the *souq al-gamal* outside Cairo.

'You no eat!' he complained.

'I certainly have,' I lied. 'It was – very tasty.'

'Good,' he squealed, cuddling me like a teddy bear. 'If you like this you love Sudani food!'

'Oh, that's really . . . great.'

The fresh air on deck expunged the stench of the canteen. Mike was deep in round fourteen of a marathon chess match with Karl, whose latest move caused him, chin resting Rodin-like on wrist, to gaze across a phalanx of craggy golden bluffs. These ran, cutting the sky in fiercely tapering scarps, towards the distant speck that slowly grew into a wooden wharf. Soldiers in Sherwood-green suits folded their arms as their colleagues rowed out to search the ferry for contraband. The Nubian Desert spread behind them, a vast golden swatch shielding Africa – its heat, its animal-skin water bottles, its worst-roads-in-the-world – like the curtain of a stage.

'This is ridiculous!' fumed Mike. An official was wading through his luggage in the customs shed. 'Look,' he said sharply, 'I haven't hidden Semtex in my socks, all right?'

Kickboxer winds and eye-jabbing dust chased us towards Wadi Halfa, as if the weight of my backpack (oh why did I pack all those books?) wasn't enough. A trio of boys covered their faces as their donkey-cart clattered across the old British railway line and a stray hut seemingly made out of all the rubbish that had fallen off the train listed to one side.

Wadi Halfa doesn't emerge, like so many Arab cities, as a triumphant desert oasis. She peeps out of the sand, shyly revealing a sprinkle of single-storey adobe houses and walled courtyards where travelling tradesmen lie on metal bed-steads. It was only when the limestone hills started to win their daily height battle with the sun that anyone ventured outside. Men carried themselves like eighteenth-century French noblemen, stalking the giant shadows that shaded their children and converging on the town's premier nightspot – a tangle of metal tables under a bamboo canopy.

OK, it wasn't exactly an evening on the tiles, but it had all the ingredients for a great night out: food, drink and plenty of chat. The food, served in steel bowls, came in the form of delicious battered fish ('the principal food of the inhabitants', as Selim al-Aswany noted in the late tenth century). The drink, served by henna-handed women in colourful saris who sprinkled mysterious herbs into small steamy glasses, came in the soothing form of tea. And the chat – apart from Karl's rhapsody about the guitar riffs he'd located in Egypt's souks, which he hoped would enhance his activities as a DJ back in Oslo – was commandeered by a genial Nubian called Midhat.

His rust-blistered bicycle whined as he slammed an armful of books on our table. He was a typical Nubian: the halfway house between Arabia and Africa, sharing the physiognomy of the former and the pigmentation of the latter.

'This town,' he muttered darkly, as he pulled up a bottomless metal chair, 'verrry old.'

It didn't look very old. There was no mosque to speak of. The grid of concrete houses and the makeshift souk – all crates and coloured awnings – implied that Wadi Halfa was not the sort of place to look for anything more antique than Midhat's bicycle. But perspective is as shifty as an Aleppan carpet-seller: little did I know that, within a couple of days, I would remember Wadi Halfa as a haven of luxury.

'You see,' said Midhat, gently turning the pages, 'Wadi Halfa *is* old.'

There were photographs of flowering forecourts, decorated parapets and colonial-style hotels bulging with balconies and businessmen. There were beautiful painted doors, patterned with chequers and diamonds, populated with ceramic crocodiles and men made out of snail shells. The only decorated door in Wadi Halfa now was the aperture to Midhat's office, which he pointed out across the track. He had designed it specifically in homage to the past.

'All this until 1964,' he moaned, stroking a black-and-white river-steamer, 'then the Aswan Dam is builded for the Egyptians, this town is under of flood and all for the lose. The government, they say, "Nubian people, you go Sudan or you go Egypt, but your homes no more." So many people lose – this is cream.'

'I'm sorry?'

'Terrible, terrible cream!'

In 1964, fifty thousand Sudanese Nubians lost their homes in twenty-seven villages as well as Wadi Halfa and a series of historical sites. Slowly, agonizingly, out leaked the tragedy of Midhat's town: the day the railway station was submerged, the hospital collapsed, and the hugely popular Hotel an-Nil was transformed into an underwater pleasure park for amphibians and fish.*

From the historical perspective, the principal tragedy was the submersion of the relics of medieval Nubia: palaces, monasteries and churches had been lost throughout northern Sudan – a wholesale wipeout of Master Philip's epoch.

'What about the cathedral of Faras?' I asked.

'Gone,' muttered Midhat.

'The medieval town of Gebel Adda?'

'No more.'

'The monastery at Qasr al-Wizz?'

'There is,' said Midhat with a shrug, 'the necropolis of Nuri.'

'Medieval?' I leaned forward excitedly.

'Actually,' said Midhat, 'is from the pharaoh times, but is verrry nice.'

My heart was sinking at the rate of the Hotel an-Nil. The only other medieval site that I could think of was—

'Dongola?'

Midhat pursed his lips. 'The capital of the Kingdom of Makuria,' he said. 'Many beautiful buildings there.'

'But no more?'

Something sparkled briefly in his eyes. 'Maybe. There is a castle, I think. But I never go for Dongola.'

---

* The event was recorded by the last district commissioner of Wadi Halfa, Hassan Dafalla. His tapestry of detail – rats scuttling to higher ground with their young between their teeth, the thunderclap of collapsing buildings and the dotted islands of fallen debris – is an elegy to a lost city. Its most poignant episode is the gradual inundation of the district around the Tawfikiyya mosque, Wadi Halfa's greatest landmark (whose minaret Midhat had recreated in a papier-mâché model in his office). Dafalla's description lyrically evokes the ruthlessness of the river whose fury, once attributed to Prester John, still held a spiritual, as well as physical, power over its inhabitants. 'It was the beginning of the end of Wadi Halfa,' he wrote, 'an end that had not come with a bang but by the creeping rise of the blessed waters of the Nile, the sole life-giver, the source of prosperity and the origin of existence of the area and its people.'

I remembered reading about an expedition of Poles from the University of Warsaw, who had excavated in Dongola. Something about a castle.

Dongola was the grand super-mall of medieval Nubia, compared by Abu Salih in the early thirteenth century to Baghdad. It was from there that Prince Georgios ventured in AD 836 to negotiate a treaty with the Abassid caliph. Not two centuries earlier, the Christian Nubian kingdom, whose capital was located at Dongola, was threatened by the slinging-machines of its newly Islamized Egyptian neighbours. Valuing flunkies over fellow faithful, the Egyptians agreed to leave the Nubians for now, on agreement to a *baqt* that pledged an annual tribute of 360 Nubian slaves to Cairo. But, by the fourteenth century (even as Genoese travellers were returning with fabulous descriptions of the city), factionalism and petty fiefdoms had stripped Dongola of its resistance to Egypt. Its great cathedral was converted into a mosque in 1317, signalling the end of Nubian Christianity. Of all the Nubian cities, this was the one to which Master Philip would have been led. It was also in the right direction, about halfway down the Nile's 'S' trajectory to Khartoum.

But we couldn't set out for Dongola just yet. Nothing so straightforward in Sudan. Because first, in order to visit anywhere, we would have to acquire permission – written, signed, stamped and paid for at the local bureaucratic headquarters. In the morning, Mike, Karl and I trudged across a dusty courtyard of coloured walls and iron-roofed shacks to photocopy our passports. We also triplicated our personal details and a list of the places we intended to visit, so that a lady in red calico could shuffle several forms together, tussle with an industrial stapler, insert them into plastic dossiers and charge us for them. A man in a turban sold us stamps, a man in full military regalia who called himself 'the captain' checked our spelling and a man in a hut beside the photocopier beat the forms with a small wooden stamp-press. Then the woman in red calico duplicated a mangle of stamps, signatures, counter-stamps and confirmatory signatures, charged us again, and left us with one scrappy photocopied sheet of paper each.

It took us two cups of tea and a tasty breadcrumb dough-nut to recover. It was boiling. Jewels of sweat chased each other down the bridge of Mike's nose and tumbled into his tea.

'Gonna buy all the bottled water this town's got,' he said.

He and Karl marched into a minor sandstorm, while I set off for a hut smelling of woodrot and stale tobacco. There, the ticket-vendor managed to sell me three tickets without moving the face that was plastered to the grain of his wooden desk.

'You enjoy the journey, inshallah,' he slurred.

As I stepped out under the iron eaves of his hut, I heard a sly chuckle firing out of his throat.

'What's the odds of it going the distance?'

Mike was on full-frown alert as he stood beside Karl in front of a giant chest splurged in primary-coloured floral motifs: if the artist wasn't four feet high then he was certainly high. Bags, buckets and brown paper packages spilt over its roof, barely contained by gnarled rope, clinging like some crazy creature from the adventures of Sindbad. A scrawny teenager scuttled up the side with our luggage and deposited it on top. As the four wheels supporting the chest implied, this was our bus.

Inside was a confusion of bodies as pantaloons and *gelabiyya*s brushed against the vibrant colours of African womanhood: canary-yellow swishing into tufa-pink, melting with greengage and gold-embroidered peach, tussled by magenta taffeta. I found a seat near the back, in front of a bulge of luggage that was kept from smothering me by a single strand of string. Turning to greet my neighbour, I was confronted by another hazard.

'I am constipated,' he declared.

409

He waved a packet of pills, patted his girth, and introduced himself. Othman was, indubitably, the fattest passenger on the bus, leaving me with the merest sliver of a seat. But at least I had a seat. In the aisle, some of the more slender passengers had been relegated to a standard of travel that must have contravened the Geneva Convention on Human Rights. They squirmed on metal bars cushioned with strips of card, or on rolled-up carpets corrugated over boxes. They looked uncomfortable before the bus lurched into life. As they were subjected to the unrelenting shudder that comes when you forget to fit a shock absorber, I tried to work out how many hours they had before they would die. But there was a group of hangers-on ('passengers' is too fancy a name) whose circumstances were even worse. They were, literally, hanging on: clinging to the sides and rattling against the empty windows as we crashed into the sand dunes. As if adapted from a medieval morality play, their flapping bodies enacted a grotesque mime of the movements of the bus.

The journey started auspiciously enough. Women sprinkled us with tins of water – an old Sudanese custom. But their charms didn't stick. Within the hour, we stopped beside a lagoon framed in yellow grass and pinnacles of rock. Our driver urged us out and set about repairing a flat tyre. He hadn't a spare, so the only solution was a second cover. But he did have help: the young men who were being persecuted on the sides of the bus weren't simply there to chastise us for the luxury of seats. They dropped to the ground and threw themselves at the undercarriage, banging about with a toolbox, while we milled among the rocks.

It was a splendid setting. Some splashed in the water, dipping their feet or dousing each other. Some slouched on the rocks, which were like cushions compared with the seats on the bus. A seer-like figure with a big nose, called Muhammad, motioned to his troop of young men, and indicated the direction of prayer. They froze at even spaces across the shore, facing a far-off shepherd who guided his goats between schist-black peaks. In a chorus, they declared the tenets of Islam, and endorsed them with one synchronized movement that left them planting devout lips against the tangled fruit on the banks of the lagoon. I looked across the vast golden vista: it was a different world from the Middle East. Everywhere there was space, limitless tracts of it, recreating the scale suggested by depictions of Africa in medieval maps. Here was the unknown continent, the terra incognita of Prester John – a world of magic and mirages.

Prayers and repairs complete, we bounced across rutted tracks between swathes of small stones that looked like chain mail. We were in the Batn al-Hadjar, the 'womb of rocks'. But there was nothing maternal about this womb. If its rocks didn't repuncture our tyres, the sun burst them. Then the battery went flat and the carburettor died. And when these had all been fixed, and the bus was managing to move at the sort of pace that could be described as 'forward', the radiator started hosing rivulets on to the sand. In order to fix it, one of the boys asked Mike for his torch. A couple of hours later, he was handed several pieces of broken plastic and glass.

'Hmm,' he mused, 'these people have got our lives in their hands and they don't even know how to use a torch.'

As we stumbled off the bus at each stop, we became caricatures of pain, each time more haggard than the last. I began to wonder if those women with the water tins had cast the evil eye. But the delays did enable us to rest our bones and experience refreshments Sudanese-style. The radiator fracas introduced us to the local version of the Little Chef: a sandstone hut with a square hatch that ejected trays of tea and *durra* bread (described by the nineteenth-century explorer Johann Burckhardt, with some justification, as 'coarse, and nothing but absolute hunger could have tempted me to taste it'). Sackcloth rugs took the place of tables and chairs, and their informality encouraged cross-rug chatter. Othman laid out his vast pharmaceutical collection, poring solemnly over every bottle, packet or phial; while our long-nosed neighbour, whose "ayrick 'ead of 'air" had ginger tints, invited us to join him for 'a week or so' if we ever happened to be in his neck of the desert.

He was the first Beja we'd met, scion of Rudyard Kipling's 'Fuzzy-Wuzzy' who petrified Lord Kitchener's troops with 'the skill 'e's shown / In usin' of 'is long two-'anded swords'. This particular Beja, more pragmatic than his ancestors, worked for a railway company in Port Sudan and traded in cotton. Sadly, he didn't live in a rectangular goat-hair tent, as I had assumed of all decent Beja (although I should have been alerted by his lack of a cow-skin shield or poisonous arrows). Nor did any of his womenfolk live the warrior life of the Amazons, the subjects of Prester John linked to the Beja by the likes of Selim al-Aswany. The Beja bought their lances, suggested Selim, from women who 'have no intercourse with men, except with those who come to buy the lances'. If the children who naturally emerged from such transactions were male, the women killed them, 'saying that all men are a plague and a misfortune'. Such an early form of feminism, however odd its attribution to Sudan, wasn't necessarily unnatural in a country whose women everted their lips at us or laughed (not a Levantine giggle but an African cackle), their confident brown eyes defying us to meet their gaze.

The bus jittered through the night, like an epileptic psychopath who's eaten a bucketload of raw *fuul*. Metal bars poked our ribs and cut gashes in the boxes. Sharp stitches were lacerating my sides and Othman was looking decidedly unsettled: he was running out of pills. The final insult came, shortly before dawn, when he buried his head in the seat in front, at precisely the same time as the bus crashed into yet another dip. His head swung back and ricocheted against the metal backrest, inspiring the longest, lowest, most excruciating moan I've ever heard. Enough was enough: he crawled off at the next stop, never to be seen again.

At the same stop, Karl – the anti-Othman – bounced beside me on a hillock of sand and rearranged his keffiyeh.

'Ah!' He chuckled. 'This is real travel!'

It was a depressingly accurate diagnosis. The word 'travel' is derived from the Latin *trepalium*, an instrument of torture consisting of three hooks that rack the body and tear it apart.

By morning, I felt like I'd gone ten rounds with the Gruul. Sticky tar seeped across the flooring, smearing the air with its thick smell. It smothered my hat, and I spent one stop scrubbing at it unsuccessfully with the help of an earthenware water jug. A young woman in cherry-blossom taffeta snatched the hat from me and rendered it clean in less than a minute. Pressing my hat into my hands, she sauntered away with a sassy flick of her veiled head.

The next two days were a living nightmare; as if we had accidentally bought tickets for the Sufi poet Farid ud-Din Attar's Valley of Poverty and Nothingness, where 'you are lame and deaf, the mind has gone; / You enter an obscure oblivion.' When the bus wasn't torturing us with its technical inadequacies, its tar and its sticky seats, that honour was handed over to nature. There was the *haboob*, a storm that stung us with sharp pins of dust. Next up was the river, into which we were beckoned by a trio of boys impersonating waterwheels. The louder the engine roared, the more water swept through the flooring and filled the spaces hurriedly vacated by our feet. Not that it worried Muhammad and his protégés. They raised their hands and declared the oneness of God; the engine gurgled, the bus swayed, we reached dry land and Muhammad kissed his prayer beads. God, he explained, had shown his munificence.

But river and dust were mere foot soldiers to the grand champion: assailing us from its watch-post in the sky, the sun beamed triumphant. It extracted the moistness from our throats and lined our necks with flakes of skin. It intensified the reek of sticky bodies and dirty clothes. It turned breathing into a chore that demanded constant effort. It mocked us with the sweat that started to exceed our shrinking supplies of water. One by one, with operatic timing, the children

413

dissolved into uncontrollable tears. Their parents were too exhausted to comfort them.

'No worries,' said Karl.

My attempt to puncture his ear-to-ear smile had failed. As we stepped inside an adobe-brick hut, he brushed aside my reference to his lack of clean water.

'I just drink the local water.'

An old man lifted his kettle off a cluster of faggots and poured us cups of muddy coffee (emphasis on muddy). On a cot in his shack lay an old woman, wearing the tail-backed garment of the traditional Nubian lady, the ends of her head-shawl hanging over her shoulders.

'But won't that make you ill?' I asked Karl.

My head festered with a horde of anthropomorphized diseases: polio crouching over typhoid while bilharzia and hepatitis slobbered over the shoulders of malaria and gastroenteritis.

Karl laughed. 'They say the water here is wonderful!'

'They' were slumbering under a bamboo-cane canopy. Their teeth were as dirty and misshapen as the sprockets on the wheels of our bus. But Karl did have a venerable advocate. Master Philip's great Jewish contemporary, Benjamin of Tudela, gushed about the 'medicinal properties' of the Nile and suggested washing down the fish with a few slurps of river water. There was a distinct lack of food in this particular hamlet, so Karl just drained a bowl of soil-coloured sludge before strolling into the sunlight, leaving his keffiyeh behind. He was having a ball.

He was still smiling when we reached Massura, a colourful settlement of palm trees and doorways decorated with diamonds. Muhammad passed round bowls of dates* (and dishes of dirtwater for Karl). 'Y'allah!' he cried, with the roar

---

* This wasn't the only use for dates: they are, as they were when Selim al-Aswany came this way, one of Nubia's most versatile resources, turning up as dowries, animal feed, sponges and even fuel; and their leaves are woven into rugs.

of a warrior king dragging his cohorts to sack an ancient city. Goats peered at us through crooked-thorn pyramids, roasting in their scrubland inferno. Boats like copper bowls, bunged up with pieces of rag to stop them from sinking, sculled to the far bank, where Mike mustered every last ounce of his energy to play football with the local children. I watched him in awe: I imagined that if the ball came into contact with my boots, one of my feet would fall off. In this state of almost-out-of-body lethargy, I was grateful to be carried through a street of timber doorways and mud-brick walls by the more gentle company of a newlywed couple. They showed me their hands, decorated in henna patterns as extravagant as the doorways, where pebbles and pieces of china were designed to ward off the evil eye.

'We return!' exclaimed husband.

'Return from where?'

'From wedding holiday!'

'Your honeymoon? Congratulations. Where did you go?'

Husband palpitated excitedly, while wife clung shyly to his arm.

'Wadi Halfa!' he exclaimed.

He smiled blissfully, as if remembering terrestrial paradise. By now, I was missing it too.

Ahead of us, crags spiked out of a steep hill, as if it had been sown with dragons' teeth. As she lifted her skirts to negotiate the terrain, I noticed that the bride's legs were also decorated with henna – beautiful moons and stars in blue and red ink. I tried not to look, what with her new husband standing next to me. But I couldn't help it – my eyes were riveted to the inky cosmography of her chocolate-coloured calves.

'I know what you do!' The husband locked a hand round one of my arms.

'I – excuse me?'

'I know what you do,' he repeated, pulling me towards him.

I smiled meekly, trying to convey by my expression that I represented no threat to his no doubt extraordinary sexual authority.

'In your land,' he continued, 'the man he sleep with other man's wife.'

'He – sleep? Ah.'

I swallowed a laugh. There I was, guiltily admiring the erotic art of a newly married wife, when all her husband wanted to talk about was the great pornoland across the Med. And it wasn't only its sexual licence that perturbed him.

'Is true,' he added, 'the womans no purified?'

He was, I think, referring to infibulation – the female circumcision widely practised in the less developed parts of Africa.

'No,' I said, 'we don't really go in for that sort of thing.'

He winced. 'I want no wife from your land.'

On the far side of the hill, I collapsed in the sand, smelling the dry desert scent. The bus, wedged at least a foot deep, was doing much the same thing. The driver's lackeys slotted sheets of metal under the wheels while their master revved the engine and tapped the dashboard like a piano player. Women sat on their haunches beside the river, while their men peered into the bus and pontificated about remedies. Since they all had an opinion, this process had no discernible end. But an elfin man with leathery skin knew exactly what to do: scream. Rolling his huge white eyes and declaring the cure in a voice like a flock of geese, he stretched out a sorcerer's arm as the bus shot into the wasteland.

'Get up,' snapped Muhammad, offering me a hand. 'There is scorpione.'

I got up, as one does when surrounded by scorpione.

'They will not kill you,' said Muhammad, 'but if they bite you, you will be in bed for many weeks.'

I rubbed the sand clinging to my sweat-gummed back, and staggered beside him. He was a Midob. His tribe was traditionally nomadic and traded in camels. But he was a 'modern Midob'. He was hoping to make a 'business deal' in Kerma.

'What kind of business deal?' I asked.

'I sell the carpet.'

'What are they made out of?'

'Camel.'

Scorpione weren't the only fearsome creatures haunting this patch of the desert. Mike, thanks to his nightly press-up regime, had reached the bus ahead of everyone else, where he was discussing another dangerous animal with one of Muhammad's protégés.

'So if we stay here at night,' he asked, 'we'll die?'

'Of course. The debya will tear off your head.'

'But what is the debya?'

'In your language, I am not knowing. He have sharp teeth and he luff for us a lot.'

'He loves us?'

'Luff. Hee-hee ha-ha.'

Somewhere in the distance, we heard the cackle of a hyena.

I could still hear it when we staggered into a village square. We were surrounded by a ghost town of mud-brick walls, roofs made of acacia leaves and palm-woven mats, and a tribe of vicious mosquitoes.

'How much longer d'you think this journey will take?' asked Mike, groaning, as we checked the local vicinity for scorpions, before lying down on date-palm rugs.

'I don't know,' I mumbled. 'I think it's one of those journeys that just never ends.'

For the self-indulgence of travel, we were being subjected to the traveller's equivalent of the bottomless pit.

Which only widened Karl's smile. Dousing himself in river water and patting the side of the bus like a long-lost friend, he was as robust as the hero of a *chanson de geste*. He was also the reverse incarnation of my pain. My limbs ached, his didn't; my head throbbed, his didn't; I had no water, he drank from the Nile. At least Mike shared my ambivalence.

'If we don't get this bloody journey over with today,' he muttered through gritted teeth as the morning sun propelled us towards the bus, 'somebody will die.'

When we had regained our seats, the hyena-haunted wasteland turned schizophrenic: on one side, mud-brick mausolea sat on rocky mats and sheets of golden sand; on the other, streams curled sensually through lush forests of tamarisk. Children cantered beside us, shaking buckets of fish whose silver skins winked at the sun. We had reached Nubia's breadbasket, a region where Master Philip, like Selim al-Aswany before him, would have seen 'cities and villages, and islands, and cattle, and date-trees, and Mokel trees, and fields, and vine plantations'. In short, we had reached a miracle.

Its fullest expression, anticipated by a ferryboat river crossing and introduced by a Toyota pick-up, was as exotic as a camel in Marylebone Station. An asphalt road. Banks. Pylons. Shops selling bottled water. Baskets of satsumas. After three days in the desert, Dongola inspired the sort of wonder I remembered feeling when I first stepped inside Haghia Sophia.

Not that its treasures meant much to Karl. He seemed to have decided that hotels were for wimps. He disappeared, to sleep up a tree or live in the river, or some such thing, waving goodbye with a hearty chuckle that sounded like its owner had just spent a couple of weeks at a luxury health spa.

Or maybe he'd been turned away: the owner of the Haifa Hotel informed us that there was 'no room'. It was our first refusal since Florence. Behind him, Nubian merchants belched on metal cots surrounded by their merchandise. We dragged our surprised selves across the road, and checked into The Palace. Rarely has a hotel so deserved its name. OK, our room's plaster may have been peeling and its windows broken, but it boasted two (rugged) beds, a (barely functioning) ceiling fan and a (rusty and erratic) shower. We'd bought water and satsumas in a nearby shop, and Mike gulped down the liquid as if he was competing in a speed-drinking contest.

'That,' he said, as his empty bottle rattled on the floor, 'is the fastest two litres I've ever drunk.'

I mumbled agreement, pressing my own bottle against my forehead and squelching a satsuma. Stretched across my bed, like a Crusader on his tomb, I gazed deliriously at the whirl of the fan. It was heaven.

The fruit juice was a necessary consolation. Because, once we'd showered off our recently acquired skins of gunk, we made a terrible discovery. Yes, this was Dongola, explained the hotel owner. No, there was no castle around here. No, there were no old buildings at all. No, this was never the capital of a medieval kingdom. Yes, he had studied history at school.

Dongola was one of the most developed towns in Sudan. But it wasn't Old Dongola. That was another 109 kilometres upriver. I would have screamed at the discovery, or at least winced; but my tongue was rigid and my facial muscles had been temporarily paralysed. Old Dongola would have to wait: its place in the queue had been taken by the more primal instincts for food, drink and sleep.

Dongola comes back to me in my ears. I hear our feet slapping against dusty streets and the drumbeat of dough balls in a bakery and the fizz of apple juice as our throats are excavated in a street-side drinks stall. I hear the door creaking at the police station and the officer squealing, his boots rapping the floor as he points to a television set: 'Mancha Stawnitid! Roy Kin! Ryan Kiks!'

Slumped before a street-side feast of breadcrumbed, meat-filled rissoles, I hear the questions that we might have expected of the police officer, filtered through the mouth of a local giant called Salim. From where? And where come from today? And where go in Sudan? And where start journey? And—

419

'You start Italy? This is many days! Why do this?'

'We're following the route of a twelfth-century messenger.'

'Why?'

Like I hadn't asked myself that one in the last couple of days.

'Because,' said Mike, 'we enjoy travel.'

Salim shook his head. This was very odd.*

It was a reminder of what recent transport had tempted us to forget – that travel is a luxury. Medieval wayfarers were usually businessmen like Marco Polo, or missionaries like Friar William of Rubruck. In their day, you didn't just jump on the next boat because its destination sounded kinda cool. You jumped on because you had spices to buy or pagans to convert. The Sudanese, shielded by poverty and tradition from the more self-indulgent of modern pursuits, were of the same mind.

'Guys! I look everywhere for you, man.'

We had been located by Yassir.

If Dongola recalls to me one face, it is Yassir's: rugged and milky-brown as a Mamluke, with a tuft of crinkly hair tapering off his chin, supported by a *gelabiyya* that flooded to a pair of snakeskin shoes. He latched on to us as soon as we emerged from our hotel and escorted us to the police station. He popped up at a fruit-juice stall a couple of hours later and, as the ruckus of the afternoon markets dimmed into the tinkle of dinnertime, he pulled up a chair and sat beside us.

'Where are you staying?' he asked.

Mike pointed out our hotel.

'That is strange,' he said. 'So am I, man. And where do you go tomorrow?'

'We're hoping to see a castle in Old Dongola,' I said.

'A castle?' said Salim.

---

* To be fair to him, if you live with Sudanese 'roads' and 'buses', it must be very hard to understand why anyone might, for pure pleasure, wish to do something so back-breaking, bowel-churning and migraine-inducing as travel.

'Yes, do you know where it is?'

'Castle?'

Yassir and Salim shook their heads at each other. 'There is no castle.'

'There is. Old Dongola.'

Having survived the journey from Wadi Halfa, there had better be a castle.

Yassir patted my shoulder. 'I know Old Dongola, my family live near there. If there is this castle, I find it for you, man.'

Maybe he was a guardian angel.

'He's obviously a spy,' said Mike, as we slipped into our beds that night.

A knock rattled the door and the pipes clanked a reply.

'Leave your window open,' whispered Yassir. 'Is better for ventilation.'

I opened the window; but when I saw Yassir peering across the corridor, I bolted it shut.

In the morning, we sneaked out before Yassir could spot us, and took the ferry across the river.

'Meesta, you want Dongola Ayouz,' said a pick-up driver when we asked about the castle. He loaded our bags into the back of his short-bed Toyota and suggested we 'wait just some minutes'. We wandered towards a boy rattling coffee beans in a pan. Our bags were peeking out of the pick-up, but there was no need to worry about their safety. Nobody was going to steal in Sudan: 'Pilfering indeed,' wrote Burckhardt, 'is almost unknown amongst them, and any person convicted of such a crime would be expelled from his village by unanimous voice of its inhabitants.' I thought of Prester John's assertion that 'thieves and robbers are not found in our land'; and later, of a beggar's stump in Khartoum, a permanent mark of his failure to obey the strictures of sharia law, established in 1983 by Colonel al-Nimeiry, and reintroduced by General al-Bashir in 1989. Regardless of tradition, the Sudanese now had good reason not to pilfer.

'I seek you everywhere, man,' said a familiar voice behind us.

Yassir was looking hurt. We should have waited for him; he was our good friend; why had we abandoned him, man?

'Oh, DWI,' Mike retorted, and gathered the local youth for a game of football, with a rotten melon as their ball and the gap between the wheels of two pushcarts as their goal. Where on earth he found the energy was as mysterious as the location of the Holy Grail or the puzzle of how the local men, without washing machines and with such a dirty river, managed to keep their *gelabiyya*s so white. While the children cheered, their older relatives murmured the *qalimeh*, the opening verse of the Qu'ran, as Yassir, standing in front on a palm-woven mat, commandeered the seesaw of a couple of dozen *gelabiyya*-clad bottoms. Now, his pride lifted, he reinstated himself as our protector. We would find the castle in Ghada, he assured me, clicking his tongue at the pick-up driver, who shrugged and broke open a pomegranate.

'It will take just some minutes,' said Yassir.

Just some? In my tattered paperback, Herodotus had taught me to catch a crocodile, mummify a corpse and build a pyramid before the driver made any discernible sign of movement. I drifted from Herodotus' descriptions of the classical world to the scenes in front of me, where waves were playing ping-pong with wooden dinghies and stevedores were unloading grapefruit from a barge. Here, unlike in Egypt, the inhabitants were at the mercy of the river.

'Man, if there's a problem with the Nile,' Yassir said, 'there's a problem with us.'

'Are there problems now?' I asked.

'Oh, man!' He sighed. 'There is flooding.'

'Why?'

'It's the rains from Ethiopia. Whenever it rains in Ethiopia, we feel the effect of it.'

I thought of Prester John and the Egyptian fear that he could cut the Nile.

The shuffle of a pair of shoeless feet drew our attention to a blind beggar, hobbling from carpet to carpet with a cotton cap for alms. With his threadbare rags and the scalloped seashell of his face, he could have been lifted straight out of Herodotus.

Although we'd best not tell Yassir that. Because Yassir, it turned out, was not Herodotus' greatest fan. In fact, after he'd flicked through the maps at the front of my Herodotus paperback, he revealed himself to be the original travel writer's most bitter enemy.

'Nicholas,' he snapped, 'where is Sudan?'

Not a question I expected to have to answer, to a Sudanese citizen, in Sudan.

'Africa?' I suggested.

He thrust Herodotus in my face and stabbed its map of Africa with an accusing finger. The entire area between Aswan and the third cataract was labelled 'Ethiopic Kush'. Stifling an embarrassed gasp, I pointed out that the map was drawn about two and a half millennia ago. When that didn't appease him, I confined the blame to Herodotus. He was just some silly Greek who worshipped a mountain.

'Your book is wrong,' he barked. 'Sudan very big in old times. You did not know this? It covered Kenya, Rwanda, Uganda, Ethiopia, Somalia, most of Egypt.'

He stormed towards a toilet behind a bamboo-cane coffee stall, muttering furiously to himself. And, at the same time, the pick-up driver conveniently announced that his 'just some minutes' were up. Mike, who was showing some signs of human frailty in the face of the extraordinarily nimble limbs of African youth, sprawled in the pick-up, resting his head against a haversack. By the time Yassir returned, we were swerving out of the market, a bundle of dust-caked shifts and plastic boxes. In my last vision of him, Yassir was glaring under an apricot tree: he didn't look like he'd ever forgive me.

The Toyota swept on to rolling slopes as fine as cumin. A caravan of donkeys and camels overtook us, held together by small men with scrubby Afro hair – possibly Baqqara Arabs from the border with Chad. The old man beside me started talking early on in the journey, and didn't stop until we dropped him off an hour later. His chatter was as consistent as the breeze that scalded our cheeks.

Both were left behind in Ghada. Through the gnarled boughs of date palms, the sun was setting over paddy fields where oxen crawled around soughing waterwheels.* Dogs barked and boys played football with palm-tree stumps as goalposts. By the time the driver had pulled to a stop and asked where we wanted to be dropped, the sky had turned the colour of soy sauce.

'We want to visit the castle,' said Mike.

'It is dark now, praise be to God,' said one of the passengers. 'The castle is closed.'

'Ohhh . . .' I'd imagined – and rather fancied – resting in the castle's audience hall.

'You have a problem,' another one announced. 'Now the question you must ask is where will you stay.'

'Of course, the Poles always stay with Abdulrahman,' offered another.

'Oh yes,' added a spindly man with a thick white beard like a bib. 'But they are special visitors.'

'And Abdulrahman only looks after the Polish team,' said his neighbour, nodding.

'The Poles?' I said, as something lit up in my head. 'As in the archaeologists?'

'Yes,' said the man with the bib. 'Do you know them?'

Behind me I heard the familiar crack of knuckles against the palm of Mike's hand.

'Know them?' He beamed. 'Didn't you realize? We *are* the Poles!'

---

* According to legend, the sound made by these wooden contraptions dates back to the time of Alexander the Great, whose barber discovered that his most prestigious client had the ears of an ass. Unable to keep the secret, he told it to the waterwheels, who have been gossiping about it ever since.

Within minutes, we were sipping lemon juice on metal bedsteads in a courtyard of chest-high mud-brick walls.

'And Stefanos?' asked Abdulrahman excitedly. 'You know Stefanos?'

'Awesome bloke!' exclaimed Mike.

'And Wlodzimierz?'

'Vloddy-zee . . .' I mumbled.

'Wlodzimierz.'

Mike chuckled heartily. 'We call him Vlod – he's like a brother!'

The lack of light was a terrific ally, concealing our furrowed brows as Abdulrahman rattled through his catalogue of Polish contacts, tuned his radio to a Polish station, and showed us such conveniences as the toilet – a cockroach-infested crack in the ground screened by a white wall and guarded by two scraggly-bearded goats.

'Please, my friends.' He smiled. 'This Sudan, no Polandia. Well-com.'

I don't think Abdulrahman considered himself poor. He had a large plot of land, several animals and a radio. A vast network of rooms locked us in a square: a kitchen, a sheltered verandah, a goat-pen, a room for storing grain. There was even a *hammam* – a bathroom. There, as the sun was striding up the firmament in search of the best position from which to incinerate Nubia, Mike and I poured water over ourselves with a bucket and inspected our appearances in a shard of glass. Our toilette complete, Abdulrahman announced that we would visit 'the mosque'.

'What about the castle?' I asked.

He smiled enigmatically and led us past white walls and palm trees that sprouted from pot-bellied sands, a tall, aristocratic figure in his grey shift. Using shade like stepping stones to avoid the sun, we zigzagged towards a mud-brick house, where a man in a dirt-caked *gelabiyya* clicked his fingers for our passports and permits, and pointed out that we didn't have permission to visit Ghada. This was true: when we'd filled out our permit forms in Wadi Halfa, we'd assumed that the castle of Dongola would be in, or near, Dongola. Mike shot his most disarming smile. I tried to look like world peace hinged on our visit to the castle. And Abdulrahman had a few quiet words. Which of these methods worked, I can't say, but our host was soon striding into the heat of the desert, swinging the key to the castle on a piece of string.

The sands were pockmarked with camel dung and the odd bright white bone of a recently deceased beast. At a straw hut, Abdulrahman handed out dates and drank from a flask. To one side, we could see the banks of the Nile: fields submerged by the Ethiopian rains, revealed in strips between forests of palm trees. Ahead of us, across golden plains, beyond rocky ledges and dimples of sand, and up an incline like the apex of a tent, stood a giant sandcastle.

Abdulrahman inserted the key into a wire-gauze door and led us up a slither of steps paved in animal droppings. What kind of animals could possibly exist here in such abundance? We didn't have to wait long before they introduced themselves, squeaking through tiny fangs and flapping cusped black wings that rustled like the quires of a medieval manuscript.

'Bats!' yelled Mike, flinging his shirt across his face like a cape and springing up the steps.

The bats' aura of Gothic gloom was dispersed by the aching beauty on the second storey. Light burst through square windows at either end of the corridor. From one end was a panorama of sandhills and palm trees and the farmyards of Abdulrahman's village; from the other, something altogether more extraordinary. Battered, shattered walls of grey and golden rock rose above or peeked around convex sands. A bulging block like a fortress loomed over them. It seemed some ghost town half submerged in sand, framed between a forest of foliage creeping out of the river bank and golden domes spotted across the plains under a porcelain sky. Somewhere nearby, Abu Salih had stood a few years after Master Philip's mission.

'Here,' he informed his readers, 'is the throne of the king. It is a large city on the banks of the blessed Nile, and contains many churches and large houses and wide streets.'

There was little left of this, but an atmosphere of splendour still seeped through the smell of sandstone and the rotten-chocolate stench of bat dung.

Our exploration of the castle was restricted by Abdulrahman's wagging finger. He pointed out holes in the vestries and shook his head: the fragile floor had created its own booby traps. But we were able to step inside the Gate of Heaven to explore the dark sanctuary, decorated with four Ionic columns and a mihrab that replaced the eastern-orientated apse.* Bats flitted across the walls, inserting themselves into nooks like cartoon spies. Up a set of crumbling steps, an open-air walkway provided a post from which to scan the surroundings. I didn't feel very high up, and wondered whether this had been a castle at all. It didn't seem to correspond with Abu Salih's description. 'The king's house,' he wrote, 'is lofty, with several domes built of red-brick.' This building wasn't lofty. It was short and squat and none of its rooms was big enough to swing a camel. Abdulrahman had told us it was a mosque; hence the mihrab. But it had the feel of a fortress: not a fortified religious complex like the Coptic monasteries, but a building whose principal function was secular. It was square-shaped, with no apse; and the prayer hall was on the second floor, at the back of the building, not centrally set: an architectural conundrum.

The mystery was solved a few days later when Mike and I

---

* An orientation deriving from Graeco-Roman basilicas, and all too familiar to the Crusader knight who accosted Usamah Ibn Munqidh for not praying to the east outside the Dome of the Rock in Jerusalem.

visited the National Museum in Khartoum. Two small boys in outsized *gelabiyya*s tugged our shirtsleeves and begged us for baksheesh as we strolled between faience scarabs, pieces of gold from the Dongola Reach (proclaimed the richest region in ancient Kush) and a spoon shaped like a female nude. Our attempts to transfer their attention from our penurious pockets to the exhibits were unproductive: dead pharaohs don't give baksheesh. But in the upper gallery they seemed to disappear, as we were jolted into a dazzling world – the riches of medieval Nubia. Greek letters celebrated the life of a Nubian eparch, a wooden Crusader stamped on his prostrate foe and men in gold mantles raised the wings of the Archangel Michael, a cross and a spear-point poking from either end of his sceptre. Ingenious artists had produced a cross from the neck of a pigeon and united Father, Son and Holy Spirit to the same shoulders, like Siamese triplets. In my favourite fresco, a gold-crowned queen reclined on her divan amid a storm of angels, horse-riders and animals – giving us a multifaceted glimpse of an artistically dynamic, confident kingdom.

Among the items on display was a board about the Polish excavations, including a description of the 'mosque building', attached to a diagram that corresponded with the 'castle'. The caption read, 'The only Christian building of the ninth century completely preserved, it originally housed an audience hall of the Nubian kings on the upper floor. It was converted to a mosque in 1317.' So it *was* a mosque, as Abdulrahman had said. But, before its mihrab was carved, the prayer hall had been a royal audience hall. So it had also been a castle. It symbolized the fluidity of the medieval relationship between church and state, expressed by Abu Salih's claim that the Nubian kings, like Prester John, were also priests.

The shattered dwellings that surrounded the castle were so deeply embedded in sand that we entered them from above. Concealed inside their poky rooms and narrow corridors were shards of pottery, the odd earthenware vessel, a portable mud-brick oven shaped like a teapot. Double lashings of wind and sun flogged us like a barouche-driver's whip. Columns stalked out of sand so hot it sizzled our spit. We panted on cross-engraved capitals and wheezed towards the grey-brick stairwells peeking out of a dig still in the early stages of excavation. I could feel my hands shaking as I rested them against the craggy archway of a Nubian church. Need drink now. I could think of nothing else. And hadn't I been warned? Selim al-Aswany, from his ninth-century vantage point, had drawn attention to 'tracts where the traveller is liable to suffer from thirst'.

As soon as we'd hobbled through the timber doorway of Abdulrahman's house, I plunged into the shade, lay down, closed my eyes. Mike's high-decibel gasps thumped in my ears like echoes of my own.

'Think I'm finished, al-Jub.'

'Me too.'

We were no match for the flies, and the only thing we had the energy to produce was sweat. Goat hooves pattered down the courtyard and a mad cockerel stabbed the ground with its beak. My eyes opened briefly to see Abdulrahman's teenage daughter swinging her hips as she traipsed past us with a tray on her head. Another time it was a sack, or a pot, or a huge earthenware jug. Perhaps she was practising her deportment.

Two little boys drifted in and out, to gaze at our odd colouring, while I drifted in and out of sleep. I dreamed of an ice-cube castle where the sofas were made from satsumas. There were streams of mineral water and lemon-juice lagoons and an ice-cream gateway behind which shower-head chandeliers sprinkled citrus juice on to courtiers dressed in fruit-skins. At the head of the Great Hall, enthroned in a giant, elaborately carved apple, ruling over one of Prester John's seventy-two vassal states, with a crown made out of black grapes and a sceptre that looked suspiciously like a straw, was Master Philip. He called me over, embraced me and invited me to sit at his feet. But barely had we started talking before I was dragged back to Dongola Ayouz by the earthy scent of Abdulrahman's teeth. He was looking extremely anxious.

CHAPTER FIFTEEN

KHAWAYYA!

WHILE WE WERE sleeping, Abdulrahman had been visited by a horrifying thought. His cheeks were swollen, emphasizing the lines between his nose and his lips, and screwing his mouth into a tight ball. As I pulled myself upright, he used his hands and what we could translate of his dialect to explain his fear: that Mike and I would lie on his bedstead, waking only to deplete his stock of *fuul*, until Armageddon. There was only one solution.

Under a parasol of palm trees, three fat men were lying on metal bedsteads. Lethargic croaks succeeded Abdulrahman's questions. They had the air of Roman dandies, swapping toga and divan for *gelabiyya* and bedstead, and replacing goblets of wine with the otter-skin flasks that they emptied down their fronts. However, the conference appeared to have been a success, and Abdulrahman assured us that we would be setting off for Khartoum at the agreeable hour of five in the morning.

Now that he was certain of our departure, a flush of relief lightened the smooth texture of Abdulrahman's cheeks. He asked for our telephone numbers and, to our surprise, produced an address book in which we could write them. We guiltily admitted that we didn't actually live in Warsaw, but

431

if he was ever near London we'd be delighted to show him Big Ben. We could have a pub lunch on the Thames. He nodded: 'Inshallah.' In the morning, the whole family was up to see us off. They waved as we bundled into a Toyota pick-up and Abdulrahman's farmhouse receded behind a screen of palm trees.

The pick-up was typical: we squeezed on to rear benches, legroom arrogated by luggage, sacks of grain and cooking pots, forcing us to dig our elbows into our bellies and sit like prisoners in the stocks. Every so often, I felt the cool of a brass serpent jangling on the wrist of the schoolteacher to my left; or heard, in my right ear, the bellyache of a man who said, '*Tamam*' – OK. *Tamam* was my favourite word in Sudan. Everyone used it. What made this man Mr Tamam was the fact that he didn't say anything else. Which, considering that he looked like he was about to vomit, was an unfortunate linguistic handicap.

'Bahar!' shouted the driver.

The seesaw of the sand dunes was about to give way to the seesaw of 'the sea'. We parked on the lip of the river bank and waited for a ferry to take us to the other side. Under the animal-skin awning of a bamboo hut, a gathering of startling physical diversity was taking place on a sackcloth carpet. We had gatecrashed an inter-tribal tea party.

A fuzzy-haired Beja sat on a bedframe, his head sinking into his chest, like the 'headless race whose eyes and ears do grow beneath their shoulders' – Pliny's Blemmyes, later identified with the Beja and located in Prester John's empire. Nearby, an angular woman,)-shaped, like the Arabic aleph, rocked a baby in her arms. She looked like a Dinka. Behind the hut, a man with a coppery Arab complexion crouched beside two women in calico wraps. A gold bangle hung from one woman's nose, while three horizontal scars were incised in her neighbour's cheek. She glanced at us haughtily, as well she might, for scars were traditionally a sign of royal provenance.

The ferry itself was comparatively mundane – a black box with a horseshoe deck where pick-ups and land-cruisers embraced each other's bumpers. Their owners clunked up the gangplank and didn't slow down until the damage was done. Not that anyone minded: the drivers kissed each other's cheeks, pressed their hands to their chests and cackled as heartily as the crew in their upper-level forecastle. An owl-like hoot from the toque-shaped funnel announced a vibration that pulsed around the poop, and with a curving sweep we turned starboard. The bank receded momentarily in a regression of waterlogged fields and palm-tree forests, then leaped towards us, the castle-or-mosque peeking at the tip of a golden arc.

'*Ya*,' sighed the ship's mate, 'before now this was great kingdom.'

We tacked across coffee-coloured waters and unloaded beside a shack on the other side, where we were welcomed with cups of tea by men in bright white *gelabiyya*s that could have been an advert for washing powder.

The palm-tree forest was instantly gobbled up by a parched desert that gave life only to emaciated farmers and chickens imprisoned in stick-and-twine pens. This wasn't exactly Arcadia. No wonder Shams ad-Din Dawla, seeking a potential refuge for his brother Saladin when the latter's relationship with Nur ad-Din was at its diciest, reported that Nubia wasn't worth colonizing. But a more contemporary Islamic warrior had been less picky.

'Wish we'd hurry up,' muttered Mike.

As in those ridiculous moments in fantasy movies, or Greek tragedies, his wish was granted. Sand turned to metalled road and our speed multiplied tenfold. It was exhilarating. For two minutes. Like its patron, the contemporary Islamic warrior himself – Osama bin Laden – the road had its drawbacks. Wind battered our arms and faces, coated us in sand, and blew at loose appendages. Consequently, the Aleppan cloth that I'd tied around my head acquired the behavioural instincts of an angry cat – slap, flick, swipe went its tassles, as it strangled me and attacked Mr Tamam, until a wise old man in a turban instructed me in the art of headwear-winding.

Checkpoints provided welcome reprieves. At the first, we drank Mirinda orangeade and a policeman invited us to watch the football with him. At the second, on the outskirts of Khartoum, where the Sahara slowly turned into the scrubland of the Sahel, an officer swaggered out of a shack as bedraggled as his sweat-stained, never-ironed polo shirt, pulled up his flannels, and growled for our passports. He studied them solemnly, and bemusedly, because he was holding them upside-down. It probably didn't help that the clean-shaven white faces from our photographs had acquired beards and thick, crusty visors of dust.

'You have copies?' he said.

'No,' replied Mike, 'but you'll find plenty if you go to Wadi Halfa.'

'This is very serious,' replied the officer.

'Well, we could make copies in Khartoum and give them to the police there.'

'I need copies here.'

'You need baksheesh,' I muttered.

'What is this?'

'Nothing, officer. Don't mind me.'

'This is serious problem.' His breath was rapidly increasing in pressure, as was Mike's.

'I will keep your pazaports.'

The officer lunged towards me and snatched at my passport. But we couldn't hand over our passports to a strange policeman in an obscure checkpoint (we were familiar enough with tales of police corruption, and the odd anecdote about Western visitors beaten for baksheesh).

'You certainly won't,' snapped Mike. 'We'll make copies when we get to Khartoum. *Tamam?*'

First they glared at each other as if they were competing to see who could enlarge his eyes the most; then the officer clicked his fingers and barked at a young man scuttling out of the shack.

'You follow Zeke and make photocopy,' he said.

Since Zeke was clearly slotting a pistol inside the waist-band of his trousers, our range of possible responses was reduced to 'Yes.'

Zeke, as it turned out, was rather less threatening than his boss. He hoped 'is no problem' and smiled gently as he gestured with his pistol for us to burrow into a labyrinth of shoeshops in Khartoum's suburbs. Beyond a screen of croco-dile slippers, an old sage in a grey shift blew a sheet of dust off a photocopy machine, thumped it to life with his fists, and uttered long wise-sounding words. An incantation? Not unless such things are included in bubble-jet instruction man-uals. Our photocopies accomplished, we caught the next bus to the core of the elephant's trunk.

Khartoum, from *khurtum*: an elephant's proboscis; where the Blue and White branches of the Nile, having travelled solo from Ethiopia and Uganda, join forces and snout together towards Egypt. Although, given the crowds bustling about with perspex folders full of ref-erences from Amareeka and Oorop, filling the waiting rooms of Western consulates, a packing trunk would be a more appropriate analogy for the human entrepôt of East Africa.

In its nineteenth-century youth, you'd have been forgiven for confusing *khurtum* with tusk, so abundant were the ele-phant's most valuable components in Khartoum's markets. Later in the century, the city became the target of a siege. General Gordon – who, with a Victorian's sensitivity to indigenous feelings, had designed the city's boulevards in the shape of the Union Jack – had made himself unpopular with a man who claimed to be the Twelfth Imam of Islam, or

Mahdi.* The siege ended, after ten months, when Gordon was hacked to death outside his headquarters, two days before the British forces sent to relieve him finally arrived.

But that was only the beginning for the city itself. From General Abboud in 1958 to General al-Bashir in 1989, Khartoum has been the scene of, on average, a coup a decade. Add to that famine in the Christian and animist south, the difficulty of supplying relief, and the even greater difficulty of supplying relief when its citizens are being bombarded by governmental gunships, and you have one of the world's most dire humanitarian disasters and two million deaths. But for us, arriving in Khartoum after the barren Sahara, the city seemed full of life.

Horse-carts carried freshly varnished cabinets past the compost of mud-brick and iron-raftered lean-tos. Oil tankers bearing Sudan's most valuable resource raced them over a bridge that threw us back into hustle-bustle land. The clip-clop of hooves was drowned by honks and skids and curses hurled out of splintered windscreens. Giant bottles of Pepsi or Lipton Iced Tea towered over us. High-rise apartment blocks jostled with banks and a Hilton Hotel and a mosque with a ten-storey minaret, like children straining to prove themselves the tallest. We jumped out at United Nations Square and searched for a hotel, our ears ringing with the screams of cigarette vendors, taxi-drivers and shoe-shiners, the sizzle of burger bars, the clang of tills, the chatter and

* The Mahdi is a common theme in Islamic lore. Medieval Muslims associated him with the End of Days and the conquest of Constantinople that had been predicted by the prophet Muhammad in a Hadith. The founders of Fatimid Egypt and Almohadian North Africa, as well as the first Safavid shah of sixteenth-century Persia, were believed by their followers to be the Mahdi. After the Crusaders had been defeated at Damietta in 1221, the poet Ibn Unayn wrote to Sultan al-Kamil: 'If there is a Mahdi it is you.' The Dongolawi of nineteenth-century Sudan was only the latest in a sequence that tugs imperial British history back to the mysticism of medieval Islam.

laughter and the policemen's whistles, the clash of pop tunes outside the cassette shops. The smell of food – spicy burgers and shish kebab and plateloads of meat-fat – mixed with the dirt and the stench of muck-filled puddles. The bright colours of restaurants and shopfronts fused with ladies' *tob*s and men's caps (from embroidered filigree to American baseball). But, despite all the colour, from our hotel's wall-walk everything had the tint of an old sepia photograph. I watched women haggling over crocodile-skin purses and serpentine bangles, or fleet-footed giants tapping their feet outside the *muzika* emporia, all screened in the yellowed veneer caused by Khartoum's most prolific commodity: dust.

Our hotel had everything we wanted: a (semi-functioning) fan, beds with mattresses and a roof. So what if the drains were blocked, the electricity hardly ever worked and the doorknobs were allergic to human touch? Before I'd even checked my bed for cockroaches, Mike was fast asleep. Still thirsty, I set out for water, scything through a tangle of shoppers, salesmen and beggars in the tiled gangway outside the shopfronts, and bumping into an embodiment of Sudanese civility.

'Good afternoon,' he said, 'can I help you?'

Fatih's calf-like eyes gleamed in a face the colour of milky coffee. A satchel hung from one shoulder, containing papers from his engineering course at the Islamic University of Omdurman.

Taking my arm, he swept me towards the souk. Beggars lined the pavement, crammed together with an orderliness that defied their condition as they stretched out their tin cups or threadbare caps, waved cardboard placards, or displayed their sores and stumps and septic lumps. One of them tapped me on the shin. A gap-toothed smile strained from his crinkled, fly-eaten face.

'You must not give to this man,' said Fatih, tugging my elbow.

'Why?' I asked.

'I will show you.'

The souk was a riot of commerce and coiffures. Tapes by the popular singer Hamid excited fierce haggling from Afrohives and Beja ''ayricks'; pencils and notebooks from woolly coils and students' quiffs; bars of soap and mesh-like necklaces from luxuriant manes and rope-like plaits half hidden by mantillas or entirely hidden by burkas. Men were dressed in suits or *gelabiyya*s or leopard-print pyjama suits; most women were dressed conservatively, but the risqué flash of bare flesh managed to escape through the scandalously short sleeves of a blouse.

'You are my guest,' Fatih said firmly, as he paid for my water.

I couldn't push the issue but I felt guilty: we had trekked through ten minutes of mayhem so that he could save the equivalent of three pence.

There was a noticeable absentee when we returned through the misery-go-round of beggars: the one with the gap-toothed smile had disappeared.

'Where's he gone?' I wondered.

'Come,' said Fatih, pointing at a burger restaurant. 'We eat there.'

Lakes of muddy water forced us to leap, building up our speed as we threw ourselves into a hall where satchel-bearing, textbook-poring, burger-munching students were crammed around the tables. As soon as a party left, the remnants of their meals were scooped into the arms of waiting beggars – among them the one with the gap-toothed smile. With half a burger already packed into his throat, he watched a waiter marching down the aisle. The beggar's hands shovelled gherkins, chips and sachets of ketchup into the pockets of his threadbare trousers. Then he flitted into the crowd before the waiter could catch him.

We sat at a plastic table, crossing our legs on our seats as the waiters poured buckets of water across the floor, treating the local insects much as the Nile had treated the Nubian villages in 1964.

Fatih was a Nubian himself, from a village near Atbara, about three hundred miles north of Khartoum.

'I have four brothers and two sisters,' he said, 'but in Sudan this is common. We are big families, not like Europe. All my brothers and sisters are married. But I think first my education, then I have success in business life and transactions with foreign companies. Then I ask my father to find me a wife.'

'You wouldn't rather choose one yourself?' I asked.

'She would have to come from a good family. It is better if my family choose someone who they know is a good girl, otherwise you cannot be sure of –' his eyes had turned patriarchal – 'her sexual history.'

He munched on a chunk of red pepper. 'My village is small, but it is modern. We protect ourselves from the floods with sandbags. We are not like the people in Dongola. They leave things to the will of God. This is the old Sudan. But we also have traditions. Before I came to Khartoum, I did not speak with women. If I speak with them in my village, this is not good. But in Khartoum, you do not know where people are from. So it is better if my parents choose my wife.'

It was an old suspicion: the licence of the city; even a city strictly regulated by sharia law. For all his sophistication, Fatih was a country boy at heart.

When I returned to the hotel, I discovered that there had been a coup. The manager was no longer in control and his assistant, a young man whose dreadlocks caressed the shoulders of his Adidas T-shirt, was at the head of a procession of lackeys who were filing towards the establishment's new master. Dreadlocks held a tin tray with two cups of tea and a packet of Panadol; behind him came a little boy with enormous eyes and lips, bearing a couple of doughnuts and a packet of cookies; and at the rear, a stooped old man with a tool kit and the gait of a puppet.

'Sir,' said Dreadlocks, his chin lunging floorwards, 'you need this man.'

His new ruler lay sprawled across a scorchmarked blanket with a bottle of water balanced on his chest. Dreadlocks gestured to the stooped old man, who leaned creakily into the toilet and conjured squelchy sounds that were as disgusting as its smell.

'Good,' cawed King Mike. He brushed the bottle off his chest and accepted his tribute. The old talent for supervision that I knew all too well from my days on his student committee had been dusted down as the staff became 'water boy', 'medicine boy' and 'find-a-plumber-to-fix-the-loo boy'. Noticing me at the back of the procession, he ushered me inside with a megalomaniac's grin.

'And where d'you think *you*'ve been? You're just in time for tea.'

When I talked to Dreadlocks later, he told me his name was Simon. He was a member of the Nuer tribe and a Christian.

'What's it like being a Christian,' I asked, 'under sharia law?'

Simon waved a hand in front of his face, as if to ward off a fly.

'We have no problem here,' he said, separating the words like an automaton. 'Some country has problem with Muslim and Christian, but here is good.'

In the burger bar, Fatih had also suggested that the eighteen-year civil war wasn't as severe as I had assumed.

'Many people,' he said, 'lose if the war is over. The arms traders, the politicians, the smugglers, the soldiers. The war has been going on twenty years. When you get used to something for as long as this, you start to think – well, maybe it's not so bad.'

Fatih's words were a counterpoint to the tendency to perceive war as a grand theatre that asks only the fundamental questions – issues of race, religion, class – detached from the sawdust of ordinary life. Sitting opposite him in the burger bar, I remembered my apprehension as we had approached Sudan; yet there had been hardly a threatening moment since we'd arrived.

But for the Christians whom Mike and I met on the streets of Khartoum, refugees from their war-torn homesteads in the south, the war was a nightmare whose scars were as indelible as the caste marks of a tribal Nubian, and much deeper.

'We are persecuted,' whispered a fine-boned student called Jane, her plump cheeks glowing as she spoke. 'This government is Islamic Fundamentalist. Before them, twelve years ago, was not like this. We were free. But now, we are not allowed to express ourselves.'

She arranged several layers of frilly-hemmed skirt across a concrete step. A priest called John, whose office was indicated only by a small pectoral cross tucked inside his T-shirt, leaned on a whitewashed iron railing at the top of the steps.

'We are treated as *khawayya*s,' she continued. 'You know this word? It means "foreigner". If you are Christian, you cannot walk around in public with any sign that you are a Christian. You cannot become a manager of business, and from the ninth grade up every child has to be schooled in the sharia curriculum.'

'They have destroyed many churches and Christian villages,' added Father John, 'and arrested many priests. They send spies among us and we have to be careful when we speak about Christian matters.'

'What about the animists?' asked Mike.

The population of south Sudan is divided between Christians and animists. We wondered if, despite the political common ground in their animosity towards the Muslim north, the infighting that had struck us in the Holy Land was equally poisonous here.

'We have our problems,' said Jane, 'but we have good rapport.'

'And we dance and drink,' added Father John, 'so that makes us similar. We are all African, not like the Arabs.'

Here was Sudan's identity crisis: was it Arab or African? And were the two mutually exclusive? This was one of several subjects that Mike and I raised with Dr Yusuf Fadl Hasan, author of *The Arabs and Sudan* – one of the best accounts of the country's medieval history and also an insight into the demographic upheaval that anticipated the current conflict.

'Culturally, the people in the south are very different,' said the short, stout professor, as he distributed cups of tea in his office in Khartoum University. 'But if I meet a man from south Sudan when I am abroad we have something in common. We are not completely separate. Many people from the north have wives from the south. But this is a problem – because a Muslim from the north can marry a Christian wife from the south, but a Christian from the south cannot marry a Muslim wife from the north. The people in the south need to have a sense of being equal.'

'But do you think you can ever be fully united?' I asked.

'Perhaps not,' he said, placing his teacup on a glass table-top. 'This is our tragedy. We are the bridge between the Arab world and Greater Africa, but we cannot hold ourselves together.'

We had turned up late for our appointment with Dr Hasan: the inevitable result when one places one's faith in Khartoum's taxi industry. Sure, they look great on the outside – slightly battered yellow Mercs reminiscent of *Breakfast at Tiffany's* – 'cabs' rather than 'taxis'. It's inside that the problems begin: the inoperable windows; the eccentric ignitions that are usually bypassed by hotwiring the engine; the doors that don't open unless you kick; the forty-five-degree heat, as if you are being parboiled in some medieval cook's earthenware cooking pot. And, most of all, the drivers. With all these technical concerns, I suppose they should be forgiven for not knowing where anything is. Despite our directions to Dr

Hasan's office, written in Arabic by Simon from the hotel, this particular chauffeur first selected an electrician's store in the shoeshop suburbs, then a mosque on the Corniche. The only solution was to walk. In the leafy avenues where General Kitchener's banyan trees observed the marriage of the Niles, a string of aid agency offices underlined the proximity of war – the World Health Organization, Save the Children, the UN High Commission for Refugees – bureaucratic emblems of the dire plight of the famine-stricken south. Behind a warren of wooden lean-tos, down a tiled corridor, a handsome young secretary with an aristocratic bearing and the skin tone of school shoes led us to Dr Hasan's office.

'So you made it!' The professor bounced off a leather swivel chair behind a desk with a computer and two telephones, and warmly offered his hand. We sat on fluffy sofa-chairs beside a dark-stained bookshelf containing leather-bound volumes of the Turkish newspaper *Hurriyet*, part of the professor's research into Sudan's history under the Ottoman Turks.

Like many of his countrymen, Dr Hasan was eager to know what we thought of his homeland. We told him everyone was very hospitable and how much safer Sudan was than we'd been led to expect, and indulged in five minutes' uncritical praise of a country blacklisted as one of the world's pariah states. Travellers are supposed to applaud the hospitality they encounter in foreign lands (even if that hospitality amounts to a cup of tea from a carpet-seller slyly manoeuvring you into a position from which you can't leave without making a purchase). Not that Mike and I hadn't received wonderful hospitality – whether gifts of hummus from our microbus companions or the accommodation offered in Byblos, Jerusalem and Dongola Ayouz. But we had also been inundated with so many requests for baksheesh, especially in Syria and Egypt, that the stereotype of 'Arab hospitality' had long lost its sheen. Arab countries were hospitable, broadly speaking, compared with most European countries; less so compared with the wild boasts of hospitality that many Arabs made. But in Sudan, more than anywhere else, the hospitality and generosity, sparkling in the dirt of poverty, never seemed anything but transparent and sincere. And this, Dr Hasan believed, wasn't necessarily an Arab attribute.

'It is the hospitality in the desert,' he said, as he filled our teacups. 'But you won't find that as much in Arabia. It is about survival in the desert. Do you take sugar? People must offer hospitality, otherwise people will die. The Nubians are traditionally hospitable, and I think this is because of their environment.'

Of all the countries we had visited, Sudan appeared to bear the closest similarity to its twelfth-century incarnation – with its untrammelled deserts and medieval markets, and practices, from scarification to infibulation, that had died out in other countries. But, Dr Hasan pointed out, there was at least one huge difference since Master Philip's day: the Arabs.

'Long before the twelfth century they came for trade,' he said, 'especially slaves. But the main influx of Arabs was because Egypt was no longer hospitable to them. They were driven out by the Mamlukes in the fourteenth century. And when the Arabs came, Arabs and Islam became the mainstays of the culture. People were Arabized biologically, especially Nubians, and the language was Arabized. In Wadi Halfa you will still find people who speak Nubian, and there are 114 different languages in Sudan, but in the north and the centre Arabic is the lingua franca. Many of the oldest Arabic customs are still practised here – bracelets down a woman's arm, the women's hairstyle, tattoos on the female lips.'

'I thought these were tribal African features?' said Mike, as the secretary brought in a fresh pot of tea.

'Oh no, they are Arabic,' insisted Dr Hasan, 'but it is more complicated. For example, scars in the face are a Nubian tradition – a sign of kingship. There are inscriptions about the three marks on the face of the king. But now it is a sign of Arab origin, because Arabs married into the royalty and inherited the position of king. Another cup of tea? Of course, the Nubians are no longer fully Nubian anyway – they are whiter, because some are of Mamluke descent. Have a biscuit. Others have Hungarian or Bosnian blood from the Ottomans. And few people in Sudan are really Arabs. It is a sign of cultural identification. Our hair, nose, big bottoms – these are African. You saw the boy who brought in the tea? He is a Dinka. He looks African. But his only language is Arabic and if you go back many generations in his family, you will find that they only speak Arabic.'

The hospitality code, ingrained into the Sudanese desert communities long before the Arab immigration, would have succoured Master Philip through the wild terrain south of Egypt. Had he reached Sudan, Dr Hasan suggested that he would have been assisted by the Hadriba merchants who traded among the gold mines around the Red Sea.

'There was a lot of gold and emeralds in the eastern desert,' he said, 'so there was a lot of traffic. In the Middle Ages, the Sudan was one of the most important sources of gold bullion, and that gave a lot of information from that area. Gold and emeralds were exported from Nubia, and were one of the main sources of Islamic civilization. In fact, in the mid-ninth century there was a gold rush almost identical to the one in nineteenth-century America.'

He cited al-Umari, a medieval Jesse James, who established a renegade state in the Red Sea hills, manipulating the Beja tribes and living off the local gold mines.

'And he was not the only one,' said Dr Hasan. 'Even now, the government makes more money from gold than ever before.'

I thought of Prester John's boast that 'we are unequalled under heaven' in, among other things, gold.

It wasn't the only link between Nubia and Prester John: as Dr Hasan pointed out, the connections between Ethiopia and Nubia were so strong that if one was the 'home' of Prester John, the other was automatically implicated.

'They shared the same church authority,' he said. 'The Copts were an important influence in Nubia, as they were in Ethiopia. When the Ethiopians needed a new religious leader, they often contacted the Nubians for help. But Nubia by itself – well, it fought many battles and Saladin considered conquering this area, but he decided it was too poor, so I don't think Nubia really could be the kingdom of Prester John.'

'So where do you think it was?' I asked, leaning forward hopefully. The trajectory of our itinerary had long deprived me of impartiality on this issue.

'India,' said Dr Hasan slowly, teasingly, 'didn't have a strong tradition of Christians. But India is very famous, so if you were looking for anything at this time, you could say it will be in India. But there was a continuous Christian presence in Ethiopia for a long time and the kingdom of Ethiopia was very wealthy. So I think that – yes, that Ethiopia was the land of Prester John.'

Considering our planned destination, that was precisely what I wanted to hear. And, as Dr Hasan pointed out, that needn't exclude the Nubians: 'The reference to Ethiopia might have meant somewhere south of Egypt,' he said, 'so it might include Sudan as well.'*

Sudan and Ethiopia had, after all, plenty of mutual connections: so many, I thought – as Mike and I carried our backpacks out of the hotel and set off for the Ethiopian border – that they could run on a joint ticket as candidates for the empire of Prester John.

The crowd outside the Safsaf bus to Gedaref was pushing and poking and flailing about with its boxes, radiating around the ganglion of a small woman who sat on a wooden crate serving tea out of a tin. An arched hand perched on top of the tin, while the other clasped its side, granting to the vessel the same dignity as a butler would to a porcelain teapot.

---

* In other words, the Ethiopic Kush that provoked the umbrage of Yassir.

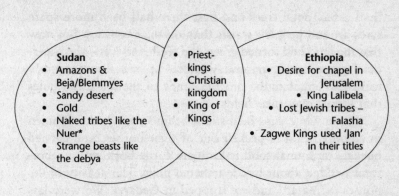

Figure 7: Sudan and Ethiopia's joint ticket.

The bus was remarkable. It left on time, took only five hours, on a bitumen road, arrived on time, and pampered us with an attentiveness that reminded me of Turkey. A TV showed Steven Seagal movies. The attendant strolled up the aisle with packets of biscuits, juice cartons, napkins and two different flavours of Mirinda, the local fizzy drink. There were no bumps, no leaking radiators, no fat men with packets of pills. If the journey to Dongola had been Hell, this was Seventh Heaven.

Even more startling than the bus was the scenery. After the endless sand dunes of recent weeks, it was a shock to see ploughed fields that washed into gentle green hillocks. Lime-coloured bushes and bamboo-cane houses with thatched conical roofs burst out of lush pampas grass. It was bucolic, but it was also bulimic: people were getting thinner. In the parched Sahara, where fertility didn't amount to much more

---

* Although we didn't meet any naked Sudanese ourselves, the tribes of the south were once famous for their minimalist dress sense. The great explorer Wilfred Thesiger, who worked as a district commissioner in 1930s Western Nuer, noted that one chief, wearing shorts to appease the British officers, found them too tight and consequently left his manhood hanging outside. Nakedness was also common in Prester John's empire; certainly according to Sir John Mandeville, who noted peoples who 'go all naked'.

than a few palm trees and figs, there had been more spare tyres around people's waists than on their vehicles. But now that the land had turned green and fresh and wet – the superficial trappings of natural wealth – it had simultaneously turned its inhabitants into the shape of the telegraph poles that lurked over their fields.

Men in white caps held sticks behind their backs. Women in coloured drapes peeked out of their houses, and carried buckets of animal food to troughs. Little boys with no bottoms padded about beside tethered bulls. The density of the houses increased, and we stopped in Gedaref. We were less than a hundred miles from the border. We'd travelled more than twice that distance from Khartoum. It was still morning. We would almost certainly be in Ethiopia by nightfall.

But that depended on two things: a metalled road and a reliable vehicle.

A great crowd of men was guarding an Isuzu pick-up. They wanted all our money. They tugged our shirts and talked about ridiculous sums that could have funded a food-drop in the Nuba Mountains. They pulled scary faces, revealing long, discoloured teeth that poked out at fantastic angles. They counted out the price by beating sticks against their hands or prodding our chests. We claimed destitution. Our claims (quite understandably – how can you travel if you're destitute?) washed over them. We were, explained a man with gloriously contorted bicuspids, 'khawayyas'– foreigners. We could therefore afford the moon. Eventually, we agreed to an extortionate sum that sent a dozen young men with marvellous teeth into the back of the Isuzu, hissing their indispensability to our progress.

Our driver was a young man called Iyman. He looked through us, stuck a handful of *qat* leaves in his mouth,* and

---

* *Qat* is the unprocessed and mildly narcotic leaf that shines like a green light in half the male mouths of Ethiopia, southern Sudan and Yemen, and is Ethiopia's fourth largest export product. Like the fertility of our surroundings, it was an augury of Ethiopia.

swaggered over to the Isuzu with all the self-assurance of a king. Flinging open the driver's door, he began his inspection. The gearstick was slightly stiff, but a few yanks sorted that out. He burrowed under the wheel and grappled with the clutch. He tried to wind up the window beside the passenger seat. It wouldn't rise, but he didn't consider that a problem. He summoned one of his lackeys to pour petrol into a canister under the passenger seat. Then he patted the side, had a few words with the mudflaps and proclaimed the Isuzu roadworthy.

We plunged out of Gedaref. Conical huts mushroomed the landscape, guarded by stacks of chopped logs and prowling goats. On carpets of rough straw, men prostrated themselves in prayer, after performing their ablutions with plastic jugs. The scenery flowed with freshness, lush meadows billowing into hills as velvet-smooth as Islamic coffins. From bushes and trees, blue-bellied rollers drifted into the air as if they were falling upside-down. Bulls strayed across the road, swaying to the saxophone that blew its taped melody out of the Isuzu, while a camel craned quizzically over a thatched fence.

The women in this district weren't veiled so much by hijab as by the pots and sacks that buried their heads. Less demure were the boys who kicked chunky stones across the fields – teams in next to nothing against teams in nothing. At one of our stops a similar group challenged Mike and me to a game of football. We were no match for their dazzling nimbleness, so Mike decided to teach them cricket. As he started designating the crease, I gratefully accepted an offer to join the men sipping tea outside a mud-brick hut. An old man with two teeth gargled excitedly, and a young woman sprinkled yellow grains of ginger into a tiny glass. As I sipped, the smell of the spice that Master Philip would have prescribed against colds, baldness and farting flowed through my nostrils.

Potholes and craters and lumpy tracks shaped like corrugated iron, only squidgier, shook us so aggressively that the periodic interruptions in conical-hut villages were a god-send. Boys hawked termis seeds in twists of newspaper and, at one stop, we sat on wooden benches hinged to wooden tables, like you find at English picnic sites, and tucked into strips of barbecued beef.

'Is nice, yeah?' beamed the man sitting beside me.

'It's delicious.'

'Go to Gedaref?' he asked.

'Just come from there,' said Mike. 'Off to Ethiopia.'

'*Ya!* Eetopya is wonderful place. You find *everything* there.'

'Like what?' I asked.

'Drink.'

That was a pleasant thought. I hadn't had an alcoholic drink since Cairo, thanks to a cocktail of Islamic restrictions and heat. That is, unless we include the lemon juice and Panadol mix-'n'-shaked by a student in a burger bar in Khartoum.

'When I mixing this with the juicies,' he had screeched, 'I am drunking!'

His smile looked so desperate it implied that this was the big thrill that restrained him from setting off a Kalashnikov inside his mouth.

The sky was charcoal-coloured as we descended bumpy terrain that forced the Isuzu to veer to the side like a drunk (or at least a man on lemon juice and Panadol). Why was it always the side that Mike and I were squeezed into? The movement tipped us against the open window, thrusting our faces towards the damp gorse and entertaining us with the chirping concerto of the local crickets. Iyman was unfazed. He spun the wheel, lurched back on track, and trundled us into a muddy canal. The lackeys in the back jumped out and buzzed around the sides, poking their heads under the chassis, screaming instructions and prodding each other's chests. Iyman had a more tranquil cure. With a shake of his wrists, he stood to the side, mumbled the *qalimeh* and knelt towards

Mecca. That did the trick. He jumped back inside, prompting everyone else to do the same, clamped his hands to the wheel and focused on the windscreen with the eyes of a rampant cat. We bounced in and out of trenches, ditches and chasms where the wildlife briefly popped through the window and stroked my face. We sank into a muddy swamp, where the wheels spun like roulette boards, before Iyman's sixth sense swept us down a brittle track that doused us in the strangely sweet smell of cow dung. We crashed into bushes and ricocheted off trees. We juddered into a drainage ditch. We skidded off a stray bullock. Then the heavens opened. It wasn't a pitter-patter or a splash or even a storm. It was a flash flood. Water went everywhere, spreading through the window and draping us in a thick blanket of wet. Ahead of us, sky and hills were mashed up in a melancholy swirl of wind and rain that turned white and black and white again. It was amazing.

Eventually, Iyman cottoned on to the message that was thumping around the jeep: LET'S FIND SOMEWHERE TO STOP! We pulled into a honeycomb of iron-roofed mud-shacks, and ducked inside to dry ourselves off. It was the police outpost of Doba. An officer sat behind a wooden desk in a small circular hut, and turned the pages of our passports as enthralled as the reader of a racy thriller. When, eventually, he directed us to a large thatched hut full of insects, it dawned on me that there was only one mosquito net that wasn't moth-eaten, and Mike was already inside it.

'Ha!' He beamed, rapping a palm with mischievous glee. 'Looks like al-Jub's sleeping with Mr Mosquito tonight!'

'It's not funny,' I whined, 'I might get malaria or something.'

'Well, boooo-hoooo.' His shoulders lifted to his ears as he convulsed with laughter, before he finally unveiled himself from the net. 'Go on then,' he said, generosity getting the better of traditional masculine distance. 'Why don't you – you know . . .'

So we slept top-to-tail, sheltered from the malarial hum and the crack of lightning outside.

Feet rustled and formless silhouettes were flickering in the dawn light.

'Meesta,' came Iyman's soft, small voice, 'we go three seconds.'

The engine was already growling when we leaped across a network of muddy isthmi and back into the Isuzu. The humid air was laced with the effect of last night's flood. So was the road (that word being a euphemism for anything that offered us a bat's hope in hell of getting through). Most of it wasn't even solid: the rain had turned it into a marsh. But these were all inconveniences to which we were now accustomed.

'The thing that really annoys me,' said Mike, 'is all this *khawayya* business.'

Being addressed as 'foreigner' isn't very nice. But the Bad Teeth Brigade didn't care. '*Khawayya*' was our name, and '*khawayya*' we would be called. '*Khawayya!* What time?' '*Khawayya*, give me cigarette!' '*Khawayya! Khawayya!* Ha ha ha! *Khawayya!*' Even Iyman, who seemed to consider conversation rather frivolous, called us '*khawayya*'. He pointed out another '*khawayya*' standing beside an upturned lorry. But he wasn't a '*khawayya*'. He was an albino. His ivory complexion and silver Afro lent him a ghostly aura. He wasn't one of us, and he wasn't one of them. He was in-between, always a dangerous thing to be. Throughout the morning, we were accosted with shouts of '*Khawayya!*', which became even more pronounced when, after a particularly sickly belch, the pick-up stopped moving.

'*Khawayya!*' screamed half a dozen of the Bad Teeth Brigade. They poured petrol into the canister under Mike's seat, soaked the engine with water and rattled the stock grill. Mike and I, sensing that something was expected of us, took turns to examine the engine, plucking our chins and nodding gravely, then stepped back to give everyone else a turn.

We heaved. We groaned. We bit the insides of our cheeks. An ancient blind man who happened to be passing this way pointed a crooked stick at the Isuzu, uttered an incantation, and looked deeply troubled when nothing happened. The driver of another pick-up tied a towrope around the front of his vehicle and linked it to the Isuzu's rear bumper, slanted and loose. He steered. The pick-up squelched back a full four inches. He accelerated again, and the rope snapped. We gave up on the rope and remobilized behind the pick-up. The blind man issued a message from another world. Iyman jangled his keys in the ignition. A sputter of mud and the pick-up jumped out of its trap. There was a mighty cheer as hugs and hand-slaps yielded to the inevitable calls of '*Khawayya!* Cigarette!'

Moments later, we drove into a watery ditch. This time, Iyman was unstoppable. The engine roared, as if to frighten the ditch, and we sloshed up an escarpment of sludge, past a lorry that forced us to curve through a field of cows, zigzag round a column of trees and weave between rival gangs of naked children. We stopped outside a police checkpoint at the end of a field of rickety, guitar-necked cows. A Sudanese flag sagged above a conical hut, where two children called out, '*Khawayya!*' and a couple of men on makeshift straw mattresses woke up to inspect our passports. Three check-points later we had reached Gallabat, the last town in Sudan. It had taken us nearly two days to travel less than a hundred miles.

But you don't get out that fast. How about one last dance? One final waltz with the Queen of Red Tape? The exit-tax collector rouses himself from his beauty sleep under a jasmine bush and rubs his dust-swollen eyes. The passport inspector cuts in, perched behind a desk in a conical hut, with a stern expression that doesn't really suit the wall-posters of fluffy animals and captions like 'I Love You Always'. But the card-playing cabal in a muddy alleyway sit this one out. A glance at our passports; a glance at the Ace of Diamonds. A passport can do a lot of things, but it can't win a game of poker.

'Go,' they said.

So, as sugar-grain stars sprinkled a sky like a vat of Turkish coffee, we went. After one last *fuul*, in a wooden hut whose loamy floor colonized our shoes and carried them up a craggy incline. Iron-roofed shacks broke the horizon, mired in wet, muddy lanes, where little boys dribbled flat cow-hide balls and young women with large, bright eyes padded through the sludge with babies poking out of their hoods.

'Are we in Ethiopia?' asked Mike.

'Of course,' exclaimed an old man in a pointed cotton cap. 'This is our sacred flag.'

Out of the customs hut fluttered a green, yellow and red tricolour – the colours of Ethiopia.

Finally, we had reached the land of Prester John.

CHAPTER SIXTEEN

DOES TERIACA WORK?

'YOU!' SCREAMED a little boy in half a *Titanic* T-shirt and a pair of rubber sandals.

Metemma's 'high street' – a muddy slope between conical *tukul* huts that claimed dubious functions like 'mini-market' and 'restaurant' – was fizzing with the *faranji* phenomenon. This involves a parade of extremely loud little children identifying the *faranji*, or Frank – the term applied to Westerners since the Crusades – and harrying him with the same monosyllabic declaration. Whether they were carrying wicker baskets or tin pails, wearing tattered rags, sweaters or dungarees, shod in sandals or scars, bare-necked or chained in amulets to deter nasty spirits and stomach aches, or even in one case exposing his particulars to the public – every single child in Metemma screamed: 'You!'

There was only one way to escape. We fled to a *talla-beit*, where we hid behind a bamboo-cane wall, kicked the mud off our shoes, and ordered our first beers since Egypt. It was a precarious refuge. Eyes peeped through the cracks, accompanied by squeals so shrill that they seemed to explain the town's lack of glass. 'You!' they shrieked when Mike unpacked his camera. Its digital images turned him into a sorcerer. Snotty-nosed screechers spilled over the threshold, to the consternation of the girl serving our drinks. They gawped across Mike's shoulder, sighing at an image of the Rialto as if it was a different world. Which it was. 'You! You! You!'

The girl was less interested in Mike's camera than in him. She stroked his knee and slid a finger across the tip of her tongue, but any further attention was postponed by the encroachments of the children. 'You!' they shouted, moaned, babbled and blustered, well-com-ing us in Ethiopia with incomprehensible gesticulations, cries of 'Faranji' and a hundred echoes of 'You!'

An authoritative boom, the pitter of dozens of footsteps, and they disappeared. In their place stood an extremely thin man who looked like he existed on a diet of wild berries. He upended his palms and declared:

'I wish you are hospitalized in Ethiopia!'

Not quite the sentiment I'd expected. At least, I hadn't expected such a sentiment to be expressed with such transparency. What would be the appropriate answer? Mike and I shuffled our feet awkwardly for a moment. Then, thrusting an arm forward and thanking him for his kindness, Mike said, 'You're offering us hospitality?'

The ascetic considered this rewording, then smiled.

'I very hospitally you! My name is Muna, it mean honey. You look like God.'

'What?'

He pointed to our beards.*

'I zank za lord for bring you to my town.' He pointed to the girl. 'You want sleep with her?'

---

* There were several arguments against shaving. One was articulated by Master Philip's Greek contemporary, Michael Choniates: 'Whoever puts off the manly hair of his chin has unconsciously transferred himself from a man into a woman.' Another was the inevitable reaction to sinks full of creepy-crawlies where, in order to accelerate a nauseating experience, we had given up on using our razors. The beards also made us feel like we were blending in – among people who, from Greek Orthodox metropolitans to Hasidic rabbis to Arab sheikhs – shared the same repulsion of razors that the dirty sinks had sown in us.

She was leaning against the corner of the café, knees crooked and hands running down her white pinafore as her thighs moved together and apart like a pair of scissors.

'It cost you fifty birr.* She is not special.'

'She's a prostitute?' asked Mike.

'All za girls here are a prostitute.'

'Look, I know it's a frontier town, but *all* of them?'

'Every one of zam.'

'How do you know?' I asked suspiciously, as Muna escorted us towards Metemma's 'best restaurant'.

'Za way zay walk,' he said, one arm waving sagely in front of him. 'Za hips, za look in za eyes. You see za girl in front of us? You see how she walk?'

It was unavoidable: her hips seemed to be swinging to a debate over which direction she should take.

'She is fifteen,' he informed us. 'She have slept for maybe a hundred men. She have sickness and she will die next year.'

The girl, apparently oblivious to her fate, rocked into a tiny hut, where a man in an unbuttoned shirt invited her to join him on the other side of a tatty curtain. But what choice did she have? Like thousands of young Ethiopian women, she had probably lost a parent, while the other was bedridden, her siblings suffering from AIDS or malaria, infants to look after, funds scarce. Crops are less reliable than men's libidos. Whether or not she had contracted HIV, the spread of the virus and the reluctance of Ethiopian men to use protection left her egg-timer very low on grains.†

---

* About four pounds.

† Most Ethiopian men have the same attitude to condoms as Lebanese drivers towards traffic lights: they are a slur on their manhood. Brothels and bars are plastered with posters to combat this attitude. Bikers in leather jackets are shown straddled by semi-naked beauties and surmounted by the slogan 'Value your life: Superior Protection', in English and Amharic. But it makes little difference. Prostitutes who don't use protection stand to make ten times as much money as those who do. Muna declared himself to be alone as a practitioner of safe sex. 'I only join with one friend,' he piously declared, 'and she only join with me.'

Under the wicker roof of Metemma's 'best restaurant', we had a splendid view of a mud-brick hut and an incontinent goat. Fading light and Muna's fingers left us little time to see our food. Which was just as well. We were eating *siga wat*, or goat stew, and *injara*, folded sheets of thick bread, like washing flannels. Neither agreed with me. While the girl serving our food juggled her shoulders in front of a screechy ghetto blaster that didn't sound much different from the local children, Muna shattered any last lingering expectations of paradise.

'When za rainy season ends,' he said, 'many in za village will die of malaria. Zis happen every year. Za rains stop, za mosquito come to za still water, za people are infected, and zay die.'

And if not malaria, they were killed by flash floods, Eritrean snipers or the government, which, in Muna's moribund vision of his country, was as unpleasant as everything else.

'We are not free to express ourself,' he hissed.

But the rest of his sentence was eaten by a strange growl, like a pack of dogs.

'Zere is regionalism in za government,' he continued.

So did the growl. It sounded close. It *felt* close.

'We are not in za right region,' he muttered, as something gurgled in my abdomen. 'We need to be Tigreans.'

I have a vague memory of croaking goodbye and clutching my belly as I ran to the hotel: an unlit hut in a sludgy dip. I needed a toilet. There was no sign of one. The owner's daughter watched me curiously as I searched the muddy courtyard for a suitable facility to satisfy the insistence of my bowels.

'*Ishee?*' she cooed – OK? A cross was tattooed on to her chin and her hair was divided into pixie plaits. It felt wrong to refer to my personal scatological circumstances. But, indifferent to my diffidence, my stomach made the request for me. A mighty belch sent her skittering across the courtyard, returning moments later with a steel potty.

'Ah,' I muttered, as it dawned on me that I would have to reacquaint myself with the practice of infancy, '*amesegënalo*' – thank you.

That night, Mike and I had the luxury of separate rooms (or sheds, to be precise). On a rock-hard mattress under a corrugated-iron roof supported by a large – and unstable – wooden beam, my stomach drumrolled the opening aria of a night out of hell. A trickle of rain, like the pitter of a finger-drum, replied. My stomach bawled. The rain responded in kind. Thunder followed – the full-on rumble of a hard-rock percussionist – with an almighty roar of rain lancing the roof and wobbling the beam. I knew that it was wobbling, because the lightning lit it up. If it fell, I reflected, it would either dissect my torso or suffocate me. The night turned into a spectacular sound-and-light show. The flicker of the sky was accompanied by a tattoo of thunder and the enthusias-tic, if tuneless, marching band in the amphitheatre of my bowels. I emerged in the morning with a splitting headache, a stiff back, creaking legs and tingling feet, the feeling that a dead animal was stuck in my intestines, and a severely restricted capacity to draw breath.

'Feeling good?' asked Mike.

'No.'

Even if I had been feeling well, the environment would have fleeced the *bon* from my *homie*. Everywhere was damp, muddy and grey, and smelt of excrement and ploughed earth. The dirty dumper-truck that offered the only exodus out of Metemma was so crammed that we had to squelch on its mud-cushioned roof. Men sat on their boxes and buckets; teenage girls clung to the sides, with babies in slings on their backs. Children chased us as we rolled towards Shehedi, swarming out of fields of long grass and cathedrals of drip-ping tropical trees, in various states of physical and mental disorder. Sure, a real pastoral, all green, wet and unsullied by modern technology. Ooh, see those women knee-deep in the stream wringing the laundry. And look at those men in their cow-hide rags. Oh, aren't those donkeys sweet – don't you just love the animal-skin water bottles on their backs? Well, you wouldn't exactly call it the empire of Prester John. 'For gold, silver, precious stones, beasts of every kind, and the number of our people, we believe that we are unequalled under heaven.' Not here you're not.

'I want to get out of here and go to Gondar,' said Mike; a perfectly natural response to Shehedi. Gondar was a major town whose basalt castles marked the culmination of Europe's flirtation with Prester John. Shehedi, on the other hand, was a warren of *tukul*s with thatched roofs ending in ponytail topknots, goats, stray dogs and children who responded to our lack of money, sweets and pencils with stones. Old men or malarial victims crouched on the leather straps that crossed their bedsteads, and an old crone roasted coffee-beans in her hovel. It was *not* somewhere you'd want to spend a few days.

'I take you Gondar, meesta.'

'Yes? Fantastic . . . Er, you'll need to stop playing cards . . .'

'Not now, meesta. Next Thursday.'

We were offered great deals to Gondar. For next week (maybe) or the day after the day after tomorrow (if you provide a deposit). Shehedi *was* somewhere we'd have to spend a few days.

Under a Lion of Judah tapestry, the old crone, skin stretched around her skull like a taut drumskin, beckoned us to watch the coffee-roasting ritual. Her hair shone with clarified butter and crosses tattooed her neck, an expression of faith even more emphatic than the Crusaders' cross-sewn uniforms. They cast her as a priestess, each element of her ritual – the tin-box altar, the water spilling out of a jerrycan (what, apart possibly from fire, is more ubiquitous in religious ritual than water?), the nut-flavoured incense of the brazier, the liturgical chant as she pestled her green beans into a thin powder – corresponding with an element of the Eucharist, and enhancing the mystical atmosphere that was fractured only by the 'You'-screaming boys in the doorway. They replied to her hisses by squealing, to which her response was a splash of the jerrycan. A man carrying a tin of millet beer stomped into the hovel and shoved along a groaning malaria victim who was taking up a bench.

'Holiday!'

Beer dribbled down the man's shirt as the thump of his bottom caused the malaria victim's head to leap several inches off the bench, before falling back with a smack. The spiritual atmosphere had been sundered and between squealing boys, splashing crone, slurping dipsomaniac and shrieking malaria victim the hovel had become as noisy as the bowels whose internal coup was powering me towards a goat-guarded, lice-invested toilet.

Now, so near our final destination, my body decided to avenge itself for every dodgy bus ride, falafel and bed to which it had been subjected. I retired to a stiff cot with a mosquito net, in a tin-roofed, mud-walled room off the local hotel's mud-floored courtyard. I exhausted my Immodium tablets, to no effect, while Mike patiently waited, reading and occasionally popping in to see how I was.

'Still no better?' he said, frowning at the torn pharmaceutical packets heaped up on the floor. Modern medicine had been conquered by the power of my bacilli.

I divided my time between the cot and the toilet. Day and night passed with little variation. Bed. Toilet. Bed. Toilet. Bed (now rendered as unpleasant as toilet). Toilet. Extended stay. Bed. Reprieve. Toilet. Bed. Toilet. In those countless and painful visits, I discovered why they call it a thunderbox. My most proactive excursion over the next twenty-four hours was a ten-minute tea break in the courtyard, which left me so tired I lay panting on my cot in a pool of sweat. Then I had to get up again for the toilet.

The great French author and Orientalist Gustave Flaubert thought there was nothing greater than the bowel movement of number two. 'At the end of the day,' he wrote, 'shit. With that mighty word, you can console yourself for all human miseries, so I enjoy repeating it: shit, shit.' Now, Gustave, I see where you're going. But you're wrong. Because in that rank-smelling shack, with my shrinking supply of tissues, the shitting and the human misery became inseparable. If you'd crouched like me, knees wobbling as another spurt cuts out of your insides, smearing your feet and immersing you in its hot, rancid stench, those would have been the last words to squeeze out of your pen.

For two more days, I went through a perpetual repetition of Flaubert's favourite activity. It felt like I was gradually emptying out my interior. As if I would soon pump out my liver or my lungs. When I went to the toilet, I could barely hold up my trousers. I would have been less alarmed if, like the man in the marginalia of a medieval devotional book, I'd started defecating edible eggs.

On the third night, as I staggered back from the toilet, clutching my trousers like an oversized towel, without the energy or the facilities to escape the acid smell that embalmed my body, I decided that it had to be tried. If it was good enough for medieval travellers, it was good enough for me. I reached into my backpack with hands still streaked in my shit, and grabbed the ampoule of *teriaca* that Jed had given me in Venice. I could hear the quickening thump of my heart as I lay with it on my lips. It was a miserly portion. Eucheurghhh! I felt my hand drop off the bed and heard the ampoule clack on the stone floor. Then I passed out.

Mike at least managed a sightseeing tour of Shehedi. He watched the local workers running home from the rain squalls, tools slung over their shoulders. He strolled down the streets, where he reported untethered donkeys, small shoeless 'You'-screaming boys and young women sent into fits by the sudden shrieks of Amharic pop cassettes.

'The music sounds like tirades against their menfolk,' he said, as he sat on the edge of my bed and held his nose.

'Tell you about the owner's daughter,' he continued. 'Pretty girl – big lips, oval face, complexion like the tastiest chocolate. Going about her daily chores – cleaning the bar, wiping the glasses – all very coy. Then someone turns on the tape player and she's arms in the air, legs akimbo like she's been possessed by a poltergeist. Wasn't sure whether to call a doctor or an exorcist.'

I tried to take it in, but I could hardly keep my eyes open. The only discernible impact of the *teriaca* was a shivering fit. I had tried to read Francisco Alvares' *True Account of the Land of Prester John of the Indies*, but the words merged into a smudge of watery black marks. The only thing I could concentrate on was my pain. So I tried to make the most of that. I imagined my pain as a red devil, a medieval allegory, with a forked tail and a trident. I surrounded him with imaginary warriors and sliced him to smithereens. Unfortunately, there were a lot of smithereens, and they each developed a tail, a pair of cloven hooves and a neat red goatee. They formed dense constellations inside my head, radiating around each other, recreating ever greater constellations of pain-devil, melding together and forming a giant pain-devil that thumped its feet inside my head, causing a red tidal-wave that washed out my brain—

'Nick!'

A shaft of white light unclasped my eyes. Inside it were two silhouettes.

'This is the doctor.'

A hand on my pulse. On my boiling forehead. On my glands. A face hanging over me like a lampshade. With big brown eyes and tussocks of black hair.

'Tell me about your bowel movements.'

Details frothed out of my mouth, an unexpurgated account of my lavatorial adventures. Grimaces lacerated the doctor's face.

'Thank you, that will do.' A hand hovering under the face. 'You have fever. You have lost a lot of fluid.' The voice more distant.

'Not malaria?' asks the other voice.

The rustle of pockets. The clink of pills in a plastic bottle.

'He must take two of these three times a day.'

'How much do we . . . ?'

'Sir, I ask no money. I don't often treat Westerners. I hope your friend recovers.'

Mike handing me a glass of water. Pills. Acid taste. Dry water. I can smell my sheets. Some of the cloven hooves have gone.

Note to medical historians: *teriaca* doesn't work; white pills in an unlabelled bottle from Shehedi's pharmacopoeia do.

The doctor's prescription made me feel marginally better. Which was a good thing, because the transport situation did not. While I'd been convalescing, Mike had attached himself to a pair of Addis Ababans also waiting for a lift to Gondar. They had smiled at his Amharic and promised to secure us seats on the next truck. Then they had zipped up their bags, dragged them to a truck, and driven into the dust.

Not that this was going to deter him. Arms swinging like a sergeant-major's, he marched his hobbling shadow of a travelling companion up the main street and bellowed, 'Awesome!' when a roofed pick-up truck pulled alongside us. It was heading to Gondar and its driver tossed our backpacks inside. Things were looking alarmingly easy.

The driver showed us three ten-birr notes. It didn't matter – we'd been warned that you only get a couple of chances a week to flee a border town like Shehedi: there was no way we were letting this one go.

'We have,' said Mike, as he counted out our combined funds, 'only twenty birr and an Israeli shekel.'

It's amazing how quickly such details register with the drivers of pick-up trucks. Our bags were dropped back on to the road and coated in a spray of mud from the departing wheels. 'We're going to spend the rest of our lives here!' I groaned.

'No, we are *not*!'

With a determined swagger, Mike propelled me up the street, past the malaria victims on their cots, the old men on their bedsteads, the small boy who hit my left ear with a stone.

'Ow!' I said.

'You!' he replied.

I wanted to get out of Shehedi – get out now, at once. It was the dirtiest, smelliest, horriblest town in the world. Only once in our three days there did I smile: at the top of the slope with my ear still stinging.

It wasn't exactly a bus. In fact, it was a wooden flatbed trailer attached to a tractor. And it was crowded, with at least a hundred locals, many of them missing a leg, a hand or an ear. But it was going two-thirds of the way to Gondar and it cost barely a birr.

It was a miracle.

I hauled myself on to the trailer and sat between my backpack and a muddy metal bucket, knees crushing my chest. Beside me sat a one-legged old man with one eye clamped by conjunctivitis. He smiled at me and I smiled at him. He made me feel better.

Driving in Ethiopia is a constant series of challenges. How will we avoid trampling that cortège of naked children or knocking the jar off that woman's head? How will we keep ourselves out of the ruts that have snared the vehicle in front, and how will we get round it without impaling ourselves on the horns of those oxen? And how will we get up that steep escarpment studded in jagged scree? Easy – everyone out and *push*! Right, we're at the top – everyone in – this is the best bit – downhill! Faster, faster – hey, driver! – just try to avoid that big sharp menhir – and the stray hump-backed cow – and the mother with two babies in her hood. And now we've reached the bottom – *plip*!

Did you feel *that*?

I held out my arms and welcomed the downpour. My sizzling forehead was cooled. But it continued to rain. The track turned into a slough, and if the water didn't hit me directly, it dripped off the limbs and clothes of the people packed around me, with legs over stomachs and toes poking into earholes. We had, with the same immaculate sense of timing that brought us to Sudan at the most boiling period of the year, arrived in Ethiopia at the heart of the rainy season.

Someone cleverly discovered a massive tarpaulin canvas, appropriately labelled 'United Nations Human Rights Commission'. Someone else, even more cleverly, produced a pannier of plums, so that a feast briefly took place in our newly established mobile marquee. It was strangely idyllic.

'It's hell.'

Mike was sitting at the edge of the cart, half covered by tarpaulin and half drenched by the wash that slipped off a man hooded in a plastic bag.

'Been waiting for weeks for rain,' he muttered, 'but now it's here, I want to go back to the desert.'

Steep hills rolled us on to broad plains. The mountains folded around us, crenellating in a Noah's Ark of convolutions. Brambles and acacia trees twisted into a humped camel with a crocodile's jaws, a polar bear with a fish on its back, a raven on an elephant. I gazed at the beautiful shapes and wondered what exactly *were* those pills?

The smell of damp wood welcomed us into a small village, where Mike and I shivered around burning coals and shared a damp mattress in a poky shack. Children's screams were replaced by the hustle of rats gnawing at a mouldy sack of maize. We bundled back on to the tractor in the morning, to be delivered after several more bone-crunching hours in another village. We ate *inkolala tibs* – scrambled eggs and bread – while the locals enquired after our origins.

'This Ingaland,' asked a fat man with an Afro-hive, 'is near Amreeka?'

'Near France,' said Mike.

'This is near Germany?'

'In Ingaland, do you use waterwheels,' asked another, 'or pumps?'

'Meesta,' added someone else, leaning close, suffocating me with the smell of millet beer, 'why are you so thin?'

We were in one of the world's poorest countries, and they called *me* thin? I looked for a mirror, and the Afro-hive presented me with a shard. Now, I may never (apart from a brief flirtation with fat as a baby) have had a very round figure, but the creature who gawped from that shard was a parody of emaciation. Since my last acquaintance with my reflection, in Khartoum, I had acquired the physique of a flute.

One of our inquisitors guided us on to a packed bus, where I met my first Ethiopian priest. He had a thick, biblical beard and an enormous stomach that suggested there weren't many goats left in his parish. He tapped me on the shoulder and flicked a hand, then tugged my shirt and lifted me out of my seat (a simple task, since I was currently as light as styrofoam).

'But I'm ill,' I moaned.

He shrugged. 'I am a priest, not a doctor.'

It was not an auspicious introduction to the Ethiopian clergy.

I squeezed on to a bench at the back, between an invalid who was coughing blood into his bandaged hand and an old man holding a live chicken by the neck. Mike, deterring wannabe seat-grabbers with orders to DWI, had maintained his rights over a seat near the front, where his principal foe was the blistering engine.

En route to Gondar, there was only one breakdown, when the engine overheated, and the driver fetched some water from a distant farmstead. The delay can't have lasted more than two hours. I spent it, crouched on a sharp cairn, hugging myself in my alpaca jumper, as far from my companions as I could muster the energy to be. I was surrounded by the most aching natural beauty. Flowers seamed soft downs you could have rolled around in. Above them, the foothills were carved into terraces that wriggled around each other indecisively, before soaring up harsh escarpments that turned blue and black and snapped at the clouds.

It should have cheered me up, but instead it inspired selfishness. The drizzle tipping over my head seemed laced with gloom, which stoked my frustration at my lack of energy and hatched a choking pessimism. Who on earth was this papal physician, anyway? I'd flattered myself over the preceding weeks that, by learning about the medieval world, I was learning about Master Philip. But the painful truth was that I still didn't know the first thing about him. Perhaps it was appropriate that, the very next day, I would be called upon to defend him.

Behind me, Mike was trying out his latest Amharic expressions on our fellow travellers. I admired his high spirits and was grateful that one of us, at least, was in full possession of his faculties. But there was also a darker part of me that envied him his health and even wished he'd be struck down by sickness too. It was an awful thing to feel, not to mention deeply unpragmatic, since I had depended very much on him in recent days. But before I had time to develop these thoughts, cutting off a nascent plot to tamper with his next bottle of St George beer, I felt a rough, gentle hand on my shoulder. The man with the live chicken was gesturing to the bus.

I remember the slow climb up the mountains, wind crawling down our spines and plucking our clothes, granite-laced dust dunking us, a living skeleton blessing us, mutant animals entwining in those strange mountain-top vivaria. And I remember the intense, fresh feeling of relief that breathed through my ribs when an origami cube of fields unfolded around the *wanzey* trees and stone huts and the oh-thank-you-God fruit stalls of Gondar.

There were telephone booths, buildings with more than one storey, and (most welcome of all, since it saved us from the prospect of picking teff for a few weeks) banks. At a hotel in the hills, we were as startled as the Venetian doge, presented with such implements along with a Byzantine bride, by the novelty of forks. Like a medieval ewerer, a red-coated waiter pitched water on to our hands before filling our frosted glasses with beer and serving steak and chips on china plates. But sophistication comes at a price, and in Gondar the price dressed itself in anoraks, baseball caps and a determination to see away with every birr we had.

They followed us to the bank, joined us inside the telephone booths, and sat in our hotel room watching us laying out our soggy clothes. They offered to book us a jeep for a mountain trek, or a table at a nearby restaurant, where the sawdust, wall-grime, stale-food-caked plates and lack of clientele suggested that such a precaution was unnecessary. When Mike waved them away, they became belligerent.

'We walk with you from bus! You think ziz free service?'

'Wasn't much fun for us either. Piss off.'

'I make for you trouble, meesta.'

'Yeah, I'm petrified, you four-foot-nothing midget. Out!'

'It's all talk,' insisted Sasha, the first traveller we'd met since Karl. We sat drinking St George beer with him, in front of an electric fire in a hilltop bar that overlooked King Fasilidas' seventeenth-century tufa and stone royal compound.

'So, they wanna know how I get about town on my own,' he explained. 'I say, "hey, easy," pull out my guidebook. You shoulda seen the look on this kid's face. He's stomping on the ground, frothing at the mouth. Says, "I wanna find their factory, burn it to the ground."'

The teenage vultures were running their own midget mafias, with reports of broken legs in the quest to lord it over the town's most profitable commodity.

'They all want a piece of us,' said Sasha, sneering at the skulking army on the other side of the window.

Sasha had done his fair share of travelling. At least, so suggested his passport, glowing with the insignia of some of the world's unlikeliest destinations. He'd danced with Ecuadorian shamans, trekked through the wasteland of Chad and supped with the cannibals of Vanuatu, who worshipped a crate left during the Second World War by an American GI. He was a modern-day John Mandeville, travelling to the ends of the earth in search of the most eccentric stamps to fill out his passport.

'See this one – the Republic of Somaliland. It's a break-away state, technically it doesn't exist. I just gotta go! Soon's I step over that line, I'm a nobody!'

But Sasha didn't have much sympathy with my own medieval nobody.

'Let me get this straight,' he said, stroking his goatee curiously. 'The Pope wrote a letter and sent it with someone who no one ever heard about, to someone who didn't exist, and no one knows if anything ever came of it?'

'Uh-huh.'

'So – why are you following him?'

'To complete his mission,' I said.

'But – what's so important about this mission?'

I tried to think of something factual.

'Well,' I said, 'I suppose if Philip had succeeded, he'd have become the first European to make a diplomatic alliance with sub-Saharan Africa since the Byzantines.'

'But,' said Sasha, 'you don't know he was going to Africa.'

Oops; forgot about that. He was eyeing me with the clinical detachment of a master debater.

'So why follow a mission,' he continued, 'when you don't know where it was going? I mean, I can understand why people would want to follow Marco Polo or Vasco da Gama – there's a historical validity. But this Philip guy – he's nobody.'

It was true. Ruthlessly true. But it was wrong and had to be combated. I arched my back, took a decisive sip of St George beer and cleared my throat as I prepared to launch

THE CASE FOR MASTER PHILIP.

'That's exactly why,' I declared. 'Philip was no one. No one's ever heard of him, no one cares who he was, no one's ever going to give him a statue or name a street after him.'

'Because he failed.' Sasha shrugged.

'Only in a way.'

'He never came back. Everyone forgot about him. Trust me – he failed.'

'Yes, but only in a – No! How could he fail if his mission was doomed from the start? The prospect of success was purely a matter of his own, and Pope Alexander's, perception. Think of it from Master Philip's point of view. If he'd succeeded – and for all he knew, Prester John was waiting for him at his emerald dining table – if he'd reached Prester John, enlisted his support and returned with the Fountain of Youth or some similar trophy – he would have been the greatest explorer the world had ever seen. He didn't know that there wasn't the slightest chance of such an occurrence. He set off on this incredibly ambitious, fatally impossible journey – and not only did he not return, but everyone forgot about him. I mean, doesn't your heart just bleed for the poor guy?'

To one side of me, Mike was smiling with the slightly embarrassed indulgence of habit; on the other was a countenance of unremitting blankness.

'Mmmm.' Sasha gently nodded his head, like you would to a child who's telling you about his meeting with the tooth fairy.

Gondar became famous in the seventeenth century, when King Fasilidas was advised by an angel to build his capital in a city beginning with 'g'. After trial runs at Guzara and

Gorgora, he selected the reputed paradise of Ezra and Enoch and stabled the nomadic royal court in Gondar.

Under a square tower, salt-cellar domes clasped the crenellated parapets of Fasilidas' castle. The thick brown stones conjured a feudal, Arthurian majesty, but the windows' tufa rimming emphasized the castle's indigenous character.

'This is not true,' said Getnet.

A self-proclaimed fount of local omniscience, he tramped through the long grasses of the compound with us. 'Za architecture,' he said, 'is too civilized. In zis time, za Eetopyans were barbaric, they could not build zis.'

'But Francisco Alvares described a rich court,' I protested, 'and the king had a beautiful gold crown.'

'He lived in a tent,' retorted Getnet. 'No, my mind is sure. It was built by za Portuguese.'

But it couldn't have been. Because the castles weren't built until after the Portuguese had left. Gondar represents a new Ethiopian era, which rejected the recent involvement of the 'Wolves of the West' while using Portuguese motifs in its architecture. Ever since 1493, when the Portuguese spy Pero da Covilham turned up in Ethiopia, the two countries had been intertwined. But in the 1630s Fasilidas broke off the relationship that had been inspired by the search for Prester John.

In 1487, da Covilham had been dispatched with four hundred ducats, a planisphere on which to mark the lands of Prester John, and the blessing of King João. When he reached Ethiopia, the Negus was reluctant to let him go. So he stayed, living the life of an Abyssinian nobleman, learning the language and entertaining the dowager Queen Helena with tales of Christendom.

He was still there in 1521, when Fra Francisco Alvares arrived with an official embassy sent in response to a letter written by Queen Helena and delivered by an irascible Armenian called Matthew. His irascibility was not unwarranted.

On his journey to Portugal, Matthew was imprisoned, robbed, had his beard plucked, his ears boxed, and his wife appropriated by his Portuguese companions. To complete his misery, he fell ill soon after his return to Ethiopia, and promptly died; leaving Alvares and his comrades to make their own way to the travelling court of King Lebna Dengel.

But they were well received. Nuns washed their feet and washed their own faces in the same water; they were fed wheaten loaves by local chieftains, who insisted on their drinking every horn of honey wine at their disposal. When finally they penetrated the maze of curtains in the royal tent, they experienced what Fra Francisco believed was the first meeting of the West and Prester John. 'The Prester was dressed in a rich mantle of brocade,' he wrote. 'From his knees downwards he had a rich cloth well spread out like a Bishop's apron, and he was sitting as they paint God the Father on the wall.' The Prester wasn't too happy with the embassy's gifts (he wanted more pepper and the Portuguese ambassador's breeches), but Fra Francisco's success in a snap theological quiz swayed him ('asking me to say all the books of the prophets, Apostles, and Evangelists of the Old and New Testaments') and he appointed the Franciscan as one of his bishops.

The increasingly close relations between Ethiopia and Portugal were strengthened in the 1540s, when Lebna Dengel appealed for Portuguese aid against the jihad of Ahmad Ibn Ibrahim, the Muslim Ghazi known as 'al-Gragn', or 'Lefty'. Having crushed the Ethiopian army and conquered most of the country, al-Gragn was currently top dog in the Horn; at least, until a contingent of Portuguese musketeers led by Vasco da Gama's son, Christovão, pushed him back. Christovão himself was unable to enjoy his triumph. Captured in battle, he had his face beaten with slaves' sandals, his beard set alight and his head cut off. By the time al-Gragn had been killed and Abyssinia restored to the

Solomonic dynasty, da Gama Jr was well en route to the pantheon of Portuguese folklore.

Portugal was now Abyssinia's official favourite ally. Indeed, so warm were the Negus's feelings towards these Iberian Catholics that, when the Jesuit Pero Paes turned up in the early seventeenth century, King Susenyos converted to Catholicism. It was the beginning of the end: Ethiopian traditions were trampled underfoot – pig farms were established, royal polygamy abandoned (like Prester John, the Negus traditionally had a full harem), and Orthodox lands transferred to the Portuguese. But demonstrations broke out, sixty monks threw themselves off a rock, and internecine battles bled the country dry. Only Susenyos' abdication could end the nightmare. The crown went to his son Fasilidas, while the Portuguese received their marching orders.* Prester John, it turned out, didn't want them after all: there would be no serious attempt to locate the priest-king again.

'We have little time,' whispered a man in a green coat as he wrapped us in the motherly clinch of his arms, 'then they will be everywhere!'

Gondar's bus station was under siege. As the crowds slanted the fence, his eyes widened in proportion to their noise. He herded us on to the bus, glancing over his shoulder as if he was awaiting the eruption of Gog and Magog.

'Quick! They come!'

And come they did, dragging children, poultry and all their worldly possessions, filling every conceivable inch of seating and flooding the aisle. Beside the door of the bus, an official (you could tell he was an official because he wore a green blanket around his shoulders) beat the pushiest passengers with a knobbly stick. Not that it deterred them: they splurged

* Although, as late as the nineteenth century, a Galla Harrar tribe would be found worshipping a sixteenth-century Portuguese sword.

into the carriage as if this was the last ride to heaven and made the sort of noises that are (so the medieval accounts assure us) more commonly to be found in hell.

Despite the scarcity of oxygen, the journey to Lake Tana was sublime. Gondar's amenities had revived us, and I was at last able to enjoy the rugged beauty of the land – its millet and maize fields tussled by the wind; its pools of wild flowers humbled by towering massifs. The road's pebbly granite allowed us to sit still for periods of up to fifteen seconds, and the prospect of Lake Tana's monasteries, where monks were reputed to live in the style of medieval hermits, had refreshed my historical appetite. I waved at the farmers with wide-brimmed hats tramping through the pampas, goggled at the roadside shrine where a man in sackcloth showed off a pair of rotten teeth like shards of wood, and shared my neighbour's stick of *qat*, the narcotic I had first seen Iyman use on the journey out of Gedaref.

When a posse of teenage touts leaped out from a column of jacaranda trees on our arrival in Bahir Dar, we resisted their offers of 'cheap price' rooms in hotels with jolly names like 'Ha-Ho', and the almost equally aggressive entreaties of the ladies who raised the hems of their white lab-style coats a few inches above what a medieval belle like Maenz of Martignac would have deemed appropriate.

'NCD,' boomed Mike. 'Going straight to the lake.'

Gentle gusts followed our diesel-engined dinghy across Lake Tana, billowing through khaki-coloured teff and yellow cornfields. Nearby was the source of the Blue Nile, which the Scottish explorer James Bruce discovered in 1770. There was no sign of the hippopotami that he noted in Lake Tana; our only company was a papyrus *tankwa*, coffee and lemon laid across its prow, its two-man crew dipping their oars into the murky water. A crowd of wide-eyed children heckled us as Yohannes, our treacle-skinned helmsman, coaxed the stuttering engine towards an angular, shrub-scaled spit basking in the water like a dozy crocodile. Egrets padded sulkily in the reeds, as if outraged by their noise. The children's tatty rags and presents of papaya fruit suggested a different era from their requests for cigarettes, razor blades and 'eyeglass'. They panhandled, interrogated and scrambled between our legs, their requests drowning the birdsong and following us up the muddy path that squiggled through a tropical spinney and broke upon a woodland glen.

There, in the middle of the green, stood a round hut fenced in bamboo cane: the church of Uri Kedane. The air was crisp and earthy and felt like a setting from Chrétien de Troyes. A man in a sackcloth suit, dressed like a fairytale woodcutter, followed Mike and me around a gallery of charcoal sketches that circled the church. Inside, all was dark except for the cubed *mak'das* encasing the Holy of Holies, panelled in the bright and clearly demarcated images of saints, kings and biblical villains. St George speared a blue-headed dragon. Jesus held a needle in front of a camel. Apostles were crucified, decapitated and amputated. A huge blue devil shook the red chains that melted into his seat of flames, while underneath him a horde of little blue devils set about clobbering miserable blue sinners with crimson clubs. They were like a cross between Hieronymus Bosch and the Smurfs.

Many of the scenes were irreconcilable with the Bible that I knew. Remember the bit where a dragon swallows a troop of spear-wielding soldiers in front of Mary and Jesus? My ignorance of this incident inspired the woodcutter's jaws to slacken and his eyes to gaze at me in disgust. Maybe Mike was doing a better job of representing the *faranji*.

'Here are the wise men. You know what were their gifts?' The priest pointed him to a lavishly painted panel.

'Gold, frankincense and myrrh, of course,' said Mike.

The priest frowned. 'This is a very bad mistake. As everyone knows, their gifts were gold, frankincense and candles.'

'Candles?' asked Mike, incredulously.

'Candles,' repeated the priest, with equal incredulity, as if such ignorance was inconceivable.

This quirky vitality made the *mak'das* fascinating. Many of the most exciting moments in travel are those that fuse the familiar with the unknown – like a Bedouin tribesman in an internet café. The *mak'das* captured that quality, and filled it with Christianity's narrative warmth – a feature that the Middle East's religious mayhem had almost made me forget.

Outside a small hut across the glen, an old anchorite drained a tin of Tella beer that looked like it had been scooped out of the lake, and unlocked a wooden door to show us a spoon. It was, he insisted, 'za spoon zat Jesus Christ use at za Last Supper!' He asked us for a financial contribution, as did the woodcutter, the monk and the children, who danced between our legs, banging drums and shaking arms full of semi-saleable goods. With Mike safely tucking into a papaya on the boat, I was trapped in a jungle of squeals. When I offered one birr to a girl with a sweet smile, it was snatched from her hands by a little fingersmith with a highwayman's grin, who was subsequently pounded in an arm-wrestle involving most of his peers.

'Meesta,' he moaned, with a contrite tap of my shoulder, 'sorry!'

We shook hands with all the solemnity of a couple of colonial Englishmen carving up an African kingdom.

If Uri Kedane had captured the individuality of the Ethiopian Church, the learning that gave authority to that individuality lay halfway back across the lake. The sun was starting to set, tanning the water the colour of copper as the red tip of a monastery peeked over a slipper-shaped mass of thick scrubby trees.

'For za boyses,' said Yohannes, steering towards a strip of shale: like the islands of gender segregation that Friar Jordanus of Severac, among others, located in Prester John's empire, the island of Kebran Gabriel allowed for no intercourse between the sexes.

A tunnel had been hacked through the rising forest to an

iron-roofed circular church that stood in a web of fishnets erected to keep out bats.

'Well-com,' said a monk, tapping a stone slab with a pebble. 'I summon za keeper of za key.'

It was a title that reeked of learning and antiquity, an impression hardly compromised by the emergence of an old priest whose eyes had more cataracts than the Nile. He wheezed through the wet elephant grass to his library of 174 manuscripts – a tiny mud-brick shack bolted by a wooden beam. When I mentioned Master Philip, he produced a leather-bound Bible.

'This book,' he explained, 'contains all the knowledge any man may need. We call it the Old Testament and the New, and also the Book of Law and how we measure the stars and the sky.'

Its jaundiced pages were exotic grids of Ge'ez, the language of sacred Ethiopic texts, framed in illustrations of winged birds and tea-coloured saints. Among the contents were some of the apocryphal texts that are unique and integral to the Ethiopian Orthodox canon, such as the Book of Enoch, which incorporates a vision of world history and was lost to Western Christendom until James Bruce stole several copies in the eighteenth century.

As I listened to the priest's gentle recitation under the gathering storm-clouds, surrounded by wooden clappers 'because of the policemen who slapped Jesus on the face' and King Amda Seyon's incense-darkened fourteenth-century crown, my pulse raced to an unfamiliar form of Christianity. It would have appalled Pope Alexander III; but Mike and I, more susceptible to the romance of mysterious texts, were enthralled. The richness of the books was all the more conspicuous for the poverty of the monks' lifestyles: as if only the Holy Word warranted a dip into the ecclesiastical coffers.

'It is a very hard life,' said the priest, as we strolled back to the church. 'But this is the honour, and this is a sacred place.'

'Would monks have been here in the twelfth century?' I asked.

'No,' he said, 'then there were no Christians in Lake Tana.'

'But I thought Frumentius preached in Ethiopia in the fourth century?'

'Yes, but in this area there were no Christians until the thirteenth century. People here worshipped a dragon. Or the eye of the sun.* Lake Tana is very holy, but it is not our most sacred place.'

For that, we must shuttle forward a few days, to the final destination of our trip. With only one day left before our return to England, Mike and I arrived in the holy city of Axum. The hills bucked past burnt-out tanks, and rusty ground-to-air missile systems poked out like rolling pins as we approached a dishevelled, beaten city on the edge of the country, leaning into Eritrea.

'This,' the keeper of the key had said, 'is where we have the Ark of the Covenant.'

A woolly-haired teenager called Melchisedech, whose sole occupation (as Fra Francisco Alvares remarked of a pair of sixteenth-century Abyssinians) was scratching his head, bundled us into a *garis* – a wooden trap bound to an emaciated horse. It shared its owner's habit of leaning forward with his mouth wide open, but not his sense of humour. As we drove away from the ramshackle stone foundations where the Queen of Sheba's reputed palace slept under a blanket of yellow meskal flowers, he burst into a startling strafe of laughter. Mike and I glanced quizzically at each other. Seeing we were having trouble grasping the joke, the driver pointed at the rainclouds gathering over the jagged shoulder pads of the mountains. Ah! It was about to rain – now we get it! Mud puddles splashed our faces, raindrops like dead bullets smacked our heads and the driver giggled even more. But he

---

* This sounds like the belief in Wak, a supreme being whose eye is the sun, traditionally held by the Oromo people, who represent modern Ethiopia's largest ethnic group.

stopped giggling when, as we splattered across the mud-swamp town centre, a wide-eyed giant claiming to be his boss grabbed the side of the *garis*, then the driver's ear, flung him into the street and left him gawping in a puddle-bath.

'What's going on?' I asked, as the big man took the driver's place and thunderclapped a whip against the horse's back.

'Ark of Covenant,' he said cheerfully.

A bulbous monstrosity towered over us, pierced by an obelisk-shaped belltower. Behind it, capped in a copper-green dome and locked inside barbed iron palisades, was a granite box, otherwise known as the Church of St Mary of Sion, locally acknowledged home of the Ark. Its wizened, *shemma*-clad guardian did pop his head through the door, and even squeaked at us, but he was unlikely to agree to Mike's request, however bright the smile with which it was delivered.

'Oh, come on,' called Mike. 'Just want a peek at your holiest treasure – we're not going to steal it!'

It was only a few years after Master Philip's mission that Abu Salih, the Arab-Armenian traveller, first announced the Ark's presence in Ethiopia. 'The Abyssinians,' he wrote, 'possess also the Ark of the Covenant, in which are the two tables of stone, inscribed by the finger of God with the commandments which he ordained for the children of Israel.' As this was written so soon after Prester John was first announced to the world, I wondered if there was a link: could rumour of the Ark have seeped out a few years before its first recording by Abu Salih, and been translated into the Fountain of Youth with which Prester John was popularly associated? I was distracted by a fierce shriek. Behind us, rocking under a creeper-choked tamarind tree, was an old priest in a yellow shawl. Framed in the crenellated parapets of the seventeenth-century fortress-church of Fasil, he was like a vision from another world. He seemed to belong to the atmosphere of the artwork inside the church – the egg-dyed images of Abba Arezawi, an almond-eyed monk clinging to a snake that carried him up a clifftop to found the monastery of Debre Damo; or St Yared, the great cantor of Ethiopia, whose rendition of 'May you be blessed, O Israel' so mesmerized King Gebre Meskel in the sixth century that he dropped his spear on the saint's foot. Like Yared, the priest under the tamarind tree looked so absorbed in his sacred verses that such an occurrence might have passed him by.

The great granite obelisks erected, according to tradition, by the force of the Holy Ark were lying outside the church compound, the largest of them broken like Ozymandias' face mask. A trio of young boys, exhibiting trinkets and diseases, whined like mosquitoes; but our *garis* rolled past them. We climbed around the slippery escarpment above the Queen of Sheba's pleasure pool, where women were filling clay jars from the muddy pit, and marched off on our final pilgrimage.

Mud squelched as we climbed towards the castle of the sixth-century King Kaleb. A miasma of bats' breath assailed us in the underground granite vaults where the Axumite kings once kept their treasure. Through the must, the light of Melchisedech's torch gilded a *croix-pattée* on a stone coffer – an unexplained signature of the white man in Ethiopia – possibly Abu Salih's bearers of the ark, 'who are white and red in complexion, with red hair'. Only a few years after Master Philip, Europeans had, apparently, penetrated Ethiopia.

Behind the castle, cactus trees filed round the fields. Looming above us was Francisco Alvares' 'peak which is slender at its base, and appears to mount up to the sky', and above it 'a very elegant small church of great sanctity'– the Church of King Kaleb's military adviser, Abba Pantaleon, an arch-ascetic renowned for a forty-five-year stand-up prayer session during which his skin stuck to his bones and his eyelashes were worn away by his tears.

The church was guarded by a pair of ancient priests, who cried like egrets as they hoisted their hands for alms. Ethiopia's poor communications systems (scotching any effective distribution of funds) and the ease with which men could be ordained (ballooning the priestly population) reduced many of its clergymen to mendicants. As for medieval Europeans, the ordination of at least one member of the family leavened financial difficulties; but for us, it was strange to be introduced to five teenage boys who looked like acolytes but answered to the title of 'abba', as fully ordained priests. Like so many of their contemporaries throughout our travels, they asked us for pens and performed five grateful bows as Mike emptied out his pockets.

Behind them, an older priest donned ceremonial robes (once he'd secured his fee), clasped Abba Pantaleon's personal cross with a knitted scarf, and raised a gospel that he claimed was as old as the saint. Its images – the pink eagle perched beside St John, the big-nosed gnome with St Mark – glowed with extraordinary brightness in calligraphic pages that declared the exuberant piety of an earlier age.

'We pray to Abba Pantaleon,' whispered Melchisedech.

Steps climbed up the perpendicular slope, tightening our chests until Melchisedech pirouetted at a granite demarcation.

'Take off your shoes,' he said, his eyes filled with holy fear. 'If you don't, bad things for you.'

There was no light inside the church. The boy priests held candles while their leader pointed out the brightly painted frescoes of archangels, monarchs and St Pantaleon in a cave. The candles sizzled as wax dropped on their bearers' fingers. The sun was setting, and when the candles sputtered out we were left in the dark. Outside, a spread of every conceivable shade of green melted into an explosion of black rock that tussled with the cirrus clouds. It was a tremendous, spine-chilling sight – our last highland vision of Prester John's empire.

And now back a few days. Back, past the perpendicular summit, the ancient gospel reverting to its hut and the egret-priests' hands falling back to their sides. Then back some more, as a white-cloaked priest called Abba Ecsaza closes a truffle-coloured curtain. One 4x4 reverses through an alfalfa field, another arrives back from Dessie, while a clapped-out bus stays still and a pick-up driver called Gideon pulls back his fist, volte-faces into his Isuzu, and starts liking us again.

'Za singer I love for!'

The singer sounded like she was giving birth to one of the more outlandish creatures on the *mak'das* of Uri Kedane: 'Aaaaaaarghhh-raaaa-hahahaaagnyauuuwaaa!' But Gideon, with his coffee-coloured eyes and the swagger that was built into his shiny leather zip-up jacket, was irresistible. As soon as he'd counted out our banknotes, he patted down our seats, beamed a mouthful of *qat*, and stop-started out of Bahir Dar on the road to Addis Ababa.

Early morning mists were rising over a mattress of brightly flowered fields. Under a cranky wooden bridge thrown over the Abay river, brown waves like liquid pyramids pulsed towards the Nile. On the roadside, families hustled to market: women bearing sacks on their heads; their husbands jogging with clay vessels strapped to their backs or herding raucous bands of fat-tailed sheep; old men carrying sticks over their shoulders, possessions knotted into Dick Whittington handkerchiefs. We stopped for breakfast in a market town, where blind beggars sat cross-legged on the ground, hands nonchalantly outstretched like ascetics trying to see how long they could keep their arms straight, while women with babies on their backs bustled past young boys shaking wicker baskets full of bitter green oranges.

Whenever we stopped, the streets smelt loamy and the air had the crispness of recent rain. Under posters advertising condoms or *Titanic*, we nibbled meat-fat and inhaled the nutty smell of Ethiopian coffee in dingy cafés where girls in white lab coats waited to provide some pit-stop entertainment to the truck-drivers. We'd done this several times when Mike pointed out that we had been on the road for eight hours.

'Are we ever going to reach Addis?' he asked.

Gideon checked his watch. 'Two o'clock.'

'But it's two o'clock now.'

'Two thirty.'

'That's impossible. Got at least three hundred kilometres to go.'

'Three o'clock.'

Rather than improving, things rapidly became worse. We emerged from a *tukul* coffee shop to discover that the Isuzu had acquired, strapped to its rump, a Mini – with six passengers inside.

'I don't think this is going to speed us up,' I suggested. Gideon smiled and offered me *qat*.

The easy part was over. Now, on a road that had doffed granite for mud, the increasingly perilous conditions received dramatic expression. Perched on a precipice was an upturned lorry. Perched on the lorry, legs swinging childlike over the ravine, was an old man waving an empty liquor bottle. His predicament was the inevitable consequence of a crocodile of children hawking bottles of Highland Eagle Blended Scotch Whisky. One of them also carried a brightly painted icon of a local saint, and held out both items as if they were of identical significance. Well, I thought, at least Gideon hasn't shown any interest in a tipple.

The bone-crunching was briefly disrupted by our arrival in Debra Markos, a tidy grid of *tukul*s that marked the halfway point to Addis Ababa.

'Meesta,' exclaimed a young man, popping his head through the passenger window, 'as God is my witness, I study accounting at Bahir Dar University. Now I must visit my muzza for za New Year festival. In two days, if God is willing, we will enter za year nineteen-ninety-four.'

When Europe switched to the Gregorian Calendar in 1582, Ethiopia had maintained the Julian Calendar – the same time system that was common in Master Philip's Europe.

'In your land, meesta, you are seven years fast.'

'That,' said Mike, 'is relative.'

'You also make za wrong time,' added the accountant-to-be, with a theatrical tap of his watch.

'I make it about four o'clock,' I said.

'Zank za Lord is za false. It is ten o'clock.'

'But it's not even dark.'

'Meesta, I think your watch make problem.'

We'd forgotten the time difference. In Ethiopia the day begins at daybreak, so that noon is six o'clock and twelve o'clock occurs around teatime.* Gideon was right.

As the light abandoned our helter-skelter of a road, the enclosured quilt of the hills tumbled into a veil of purple irises that mirrored the sunset. Woodsmoke drifted from *tukul* chimneys, diaphanous ribbons that seemed to dance to the distant drumbeat. The drummer himself was hunched outside a roadside café, eyes drained of expression by *qat*. Or perhaps he'd spent too long debating his nation's history with the man who accosted me in what, strictly speaking, was a swamp, but for the sake of clarity I shall describe as a toilet.

'What is your purpose of visiting Eetopyar?' he asked as he squelched into the urinal third from my left.

'I'm trying to find out about the kingdom of Prester John.'

He moved one urinal closer.

'Who is Prester John?'

'He was the most powerful king in the world, and he was believed to rule in Ethiopia.'

'Is true,' he said, moving up another urinal. 'Eetopyar was very powerful. You know Haile Selassie was descended from Solomon? He was very powerful. He weared Solomon's ring.'

'Haile Selassie had Solomon's ring?'

'Of course. But Mengistu stole it to have his power. You should read about Mengistu. He stopped all the kings.'

This was true. Mengistu smothered Haile Selassie with a

---

* The same system maintained by medieval Jews and sustained in Mea She'arim, Jerusalem.

pillow and buried him in the royal lavatory. Which only made this man's proximity creepier. If he moved any closer, we'd be sharing more than historical information.

'And you know who helped him?' he said, in a stage whisper. 'It was the CIA.'

'The CIA helped install a Communist regime?'

'Of course.'

Outside it was getting cold. We drove along the ridge of a sheer escarpment under which there was no sign of a valley. We did manage to see the Blue Nile gorge, lit up by a flash of blue lightning that brought its usual comrades, rain and thunder; hence sludgy roads, slower and more dangerous progress, and a general sensation of gloom. The route really didn't need any more danger: we were driving along steep, unstable terrain in the dark with a driver who'd had thirty minutes' rest in the previous sixteen hours. He'd refused to drink coffee at the last stop, insisting that he was kept awake by his cassette. A fair point: with that hysterical chanteuse thumping out her stomach-churning diatribe, you'd be less likely to nod off than suffer a heart attack. But I didn't much fancy our chances as we bounced out of potholes and swerved unpredictably across a stalk of unmetalled road. I suggested that we stop at the next town and resume in the morning. Gideon would have none of it. In order to shut me up, he offered me his *qat*. It tasted disappointingly like lettuce. I gazed out of the window, and watched the mountains plunge towards the jagged floor of mica rock that presumably represented our imminent grave.

But – and whatever happened later, I must give him credit for this – Gideon knew what he was doing. I don't remember the ring of eucalyptus trees that famously encircle Addis Ababa, or the stone-walled palace built by Emperor Menelik II after his consort had founded the city in 1886; I just remember concrete buildings, a roundabout, and the feeling of extreme cold that comes with building a capital eight thousand feet above sea level.

The room that we were shown in the Baro Hotel (once we'd dragged the blanket-wrapped manager out of his shack) was dingy and airless, and smelt like it had preserved the odours of all its previous occupants. Oh, and the bedsheets were streaked with blood. It would do. First, we had to sort out Gideon's bill. We'd paid him at the start of the journey, but he insisted that this was for 'the car only'.

'You've got gall,' said Mike. 'You said we'd get to Addis in ten hours. It's taken eighteen.'

'Give me money.'

'No,' I said, 'we've already paid you.'

'Give me money.'

'No.'

'Give me—'

'No!'

Then Gideon lost it. He lunged at us, before the hotel guard wrestled him against a wall. Suddenly, our fellow passengers were upon us, pointing their fingers in disgust. We had betrayed Gideon's trust. We made them sick. If we just paid him much-more-monies, we might be forgiven.

Mike threw back his head. 'We paid him enough at the start.'

The manager suggested a compromise.

'We can't afford to pay any more,' I whined.

We rotated around the room – Mike, me, Gideon, the manager, the guard and five passengers, all shouting at one another, listening to no one, and following each other in a badly co-ordinated carousel. Then we were joined by two gun-wielding policemen. Mike explained our point of view with poise and panache, while Gideon impersonated his favourite chanteuse. But the policemen, fiddling with their rifles, weren't swayed either way; and the manager wondered if we had a contract.

'What do you *think*?' snapped Mike.

'Big trouble for you,' hissed Gideon.

Finally we reached a deal. It involved us paying a small

sum to get rid of Gideon, in exchange for a reduced bill from the hotel: hardly an unmitigated triumph, but we felt we'd saved face (which, having spent so long in the Middle East, was important). Crucially, it enabled us to crawl into our beds, shivering under three layers of blankets, and sleep.

Addis Ababa may mean 'new flower', but its petals are made out of tin, mud and scrap metal, and its pistil is a steamy compost where flies hover over hummocks of turmeric or black *kurarina* grains, flee the sandalwood incense sticks and buzz towards testicles apparently snipped by the Afar tribesmen of the Danakil Desert. Taxi-drivers in third-generation cagoules rubbed their mud-caked hands and whispered the prices for ganja, while scowling wool-wrapped girls threatened to show us a good time. Boys in ripped togas cooled their hands over portable Primuses where slivers of *siga* meat fried in geysers of rancid butter. They danced around us, their feet tapping to the reggae beats that drifted out of the *tallabeit*s where dirty men drained bottles of St George beer and beckoned over the barmaids, a quick fumble for a handful of birr.

'Meesta and meesta, please – you join us!'

Two young deacons were beating forks against their dishes of *injara*. We pulled up stools, while an Azmari beat artist plucked a *mesenko* fiddle and incorporated references to our 'San Giyorgis' beer and our assumed 'Amareeka' nationality into his song.* Later in the evening, its masculine drumbeat had melted into the syrupy femininity of a lounge singer, hyacinthine hair coiling between her shoulder blades. Her breathy voice oozed the most melodic Amharic I'd heard through a noirish honky-tonk where the smoky darkness was coloured by a posse of finger-wetting, strap-fiddling sex

---

* The Azmari beat artists are the Ethiopian minstrels, the local troubadours, who still ply their ancient trade while their Western counterparts have long since died out.

488

kittens. Armed with stiletto heels and figure-hugging outfits that crawled up their thighs when they wiggled their hips, these latter-day odalisques shot the perfumed promise of sex right up our nostrils.

'You like me?' one of them whispered, nudging me on to the dance floor and pressing the huge, sensuous sideways 8 of her mouth against my ear. How could I not like her? Mother-of-pearl eyes lit up her Tigrean moon-face, where the colour of cocoa lightened across her cheeks, glistening in the spray of electric light. Bare shoulders swung back as a bodice the colour of passion tautened to breaking point across her chest.

'Like fucky-love?' she whispered, juggling her breasts with a disturbingly childlike glee – as if she'd only just discovered that she had them.

'Er, no,' I croaked, '*amesegënalo* – thank you.'

Her lips seemed to dry in front of my eyes, before she swivelled towards the bar and the more receptive arms of a grey-bearded sugar-daddy.

*

We couldn't hang about in Addis Ababa indefinitely. We had booked our tickets back to England for four days' time, as late as we could reasonably leave before Mike's job began. Lying at the bottom of my backpack, smeared with the accumulated dirt of Africa, was Pope Alexander's letter to Prester John. We were hoping to deliver it in Lalibela, the royal medieval city, about 350 kilometres away as the lammergeyer flies. But Ethiopians, quite sensibly, don't calculate a journey in kilometres. Because there are many different kinds of kilometre. There are metalled kilometres (rare), sludge kilometres (more common), rutted-track-on-windy-mountain-precipice kilometres (very common). Instead, they calculate the journey by dividing in two (at least) the number of days it will take.

'For Gott sake,' muttered Karen, a miserable German staying at the Baro, 'chust stay avay from ze bus.'

But we had no choice. We couldn't afford private hire. We

had exhausted our overdrafts by booking our transport from Lalibela to Axum, so that we could fit in Ethiopia's holiest city the day before our departure for England. This left us just three days to reach Lalibela and deliver Master Philip's letter. We booked our tickets to Woldia, halfway to Lalibela, and owned up on our last night in Addis.

'Ze route to Lalibela is fery dangerous,' said Karen. 'Zere is bandits ant prezipiz and it vill take many days. You must try to sit near ze mittle. Zen you may surwive ven it goes off ze cliff.'

Her Teutonic monotone droned gloomily for the rest of the evening, but it only enhanced the prospect of Lalibela, the Fisher King's castle of our adventure. In the morning, as we scuttled to the bus stop under pinpricks of rain, I felt a thrill of anticipation.

The Eighth Letter of Master Philip to Roger of Salerno

TO ROGER, BY the grace of God, his dear friend, Master Philip, ambassador of my Lord Alexander, sends greetings.

The way to the land of Prester John is perilous, for the desert from Egypt commands a crossing of fifty days, and it is scattered with multitudes of beasts and wild tribes. But God has preserved me this far and now I write from the Empire of Prester John, the glorious king to whose faith it is my privilege to administer improvement. And when we reached the first town of the Indians, great joy greeted us, for the nuns threw water on our feet and a woman wearing nothing but a hawk's bell over her privates invited us to the repast, for she desired to prove herself the ablest in housekeeping. And she supplied us five wheaten loaves and a sticky concoction. Men surrounded us and expressed great curiosity for the colour of my skin, for in these parts the folk are as black as ink. And the priest of this village threw up his hands and made strange gyrations of his body. This, said Ezekiel, was an act of celebration, for the priest held it as a prophecy that the Franks from the end of the earth would come to join with the Abyssines and together they would destroy the tomb of Mahomet at Makka. And this I took for a sign of the likely success of my mission.

But the land that I have seen is not the same that glistens in my prayers. For the roofs of the temples are not made of emerald but mud, and no sacred balms emanate from the trees. And this, dear Roger, is because the Empire of Prester John is made of many different provinces, and what I have yet witnessed is but the poorest part. For does not the Emperor write: 'Seventy-two provinces obey us'? And even this province is richer than the eye can see, for now is the season of rain, and this endures one month, and at its end they tell me that the earth is softened and the land is spread in a mattress of gold.

The folk here are clad in two kinds: some wear linen and cotton; and others wear nothing but a few beads (though in their hair, some place the horn of a unicorn). And there are women with breasts down to their waists and no concern for their modesty. I tell you, Roger, it is a peculiarity of this province, that whereas we marry ignorant of what is inside, these people marry knowing everything quite certain. And these people dwell in houses of mud, and they trade in gold and sugar cane (for there are infinite quantities of sugar cane) and the giant teeth of creatures with large ears like cloth. And they worship in churches with roofs of straw and silk curtains and stone bells. They remove their shoes and receive the body of Christ in the hand and they do this every day or not at all. And no women are permitted in these churches. And though I esteem these people strange, they tell me there are stranger. For there are pagans who live underground and worship a dragon, and there are women who ride on cows and dry up their left breast so that they can wield the bow; for these are the Amazons.

And we were invited to the tent of the Ras, which is the king of this province. And he drinks wine with honey and beer made from wheat and he does nothing else. For even when the priests read from the mysteries that escaped the flood he continues to drink. And he offered me a horn of honey wine, and no sooner had I taken the first sip, than he had already finished his horn, and ordered another. And I asked if what is told of his king was true, and if he was the most powerful man in the world, and he assured me that this was so. And I would have asked him many questions more, but through the potency of the wine Ezekiel was unable to make sense of his speech.

Dear Roger, you must not be concerned for the drops of my blood that you find on this sheet, for here parchment is scarce and otherwise I would start again. But the light was lost to me last night, and I must hurry to complete this letter, for I have only a small supply of wax and soon it will be dark. And I will be able to fare forward, I believe that this is God's will, for else he would have struck me down at an earlier stage in my journey. And today, I have survived a fright of such greatness that it assures me of God's protection. For we have travelled by boat, and this is because the horses in this land are weak. And though there are cocodrylli in the river, they are powerless against divine clemency. And so too is the mighty beast that assailed us in the Great Lake of this land. For our boat was attacked by a sea-horse as mighty as Job's behemoth, and Ezekiel says that these beasts are many, and they fill the fishermen with fear. And so close was this beast that had I been carrying my stylus I could have stabbed its eyes. Its stench was as foul as if it had been sent out of hell. It took our helmsman in its maw, and were it not for Ezekiel's able steering, our bodies should not have reached the shore intact with our souls. But as we lay on the banks, I felt that the wounds of my stomach had been ruptured, and I cried out for the assistance of a physician, though I feared that Asclepius himself could not cure me. And an old fisherman assured me that I suffered from the yellow jaundice and applied a hot burning iron to my stomach, laying a cotton upon the wound and saying that this way the humour would issue forth. I thanked him, though my pain had not decreased. And though I have suffered the loss of great quantities of blood, I take solace in St Paul, who also suffered shipwreck before he completed his mission.

Dear Roger, when you receive this message, the union of Prester John with the True Catholic Doctrine will be complete. I am too tired to write more, but hark to this, that when your eyes are united with my history, long shall I have stood in the great castle of the Indies, where will be thirty thousand men at a table of precious emerald, and at their head the king who will be the sword of Christendom. And I will deliver to him the letter of my Lord Alexander and he will understand its wisdom.

CHAPTER SEVENTEEN

SECRET SOIL

SO THIS WAS WHAT we'd been waiting for: delivery time. Although, judging from the hour-long lack of movement on the bus to Woldia, we had plenty of waiting yet.

'*Chigger yellem*' – no problem – said the plump man behind us.

Which was rubbish. There was clearly a problem, else the ticket inspector wouldn't have pattered up the steps, snorted at the empty seats and ordered us off with a brief but comprehensive 'No bus.'

'They sell not enough tickets,' said our plump companion, as rainclouds vented their disgust on half a dozen immobilized vehicles, 'so they think it's not worth the effort.'

Fortunately, another bus *had* sold enough tickets. Although its destination was Dessie rather than Woldia, it was heading in the right direction, and it was the only bus in the station that looked like leaving today. But the gain in forward movement had an inevitable payback. Passengers weren't just fighting for seats, swinging blanket-loads of all their worldly possessions; they were fighting for oxygen too. So much for sitting in the middle, Karen: we couldn't sit at all.

Mike was constricting his gut between a pair of nuns. With

494

a little more air, I was gummed to the plump man. He introduced himself to me, as you do when somebody else's hipbone is nudging the groove of your hindquarters. His name was Fisseha and he was an automobile expert.

'Za cars are very bad here,' he said with a sigh, 'but we have four-wheel drive from Jarmany and Amareeka. I don't think zere is so many cars from Brit-an. Za Volvo is Fransh, Renault is Fransh, BeeEmWa is Jarman. You have single carriages in Brit-an bus?'

Addis Ababa's cardboard slums were gobbled up by plasticine-green hills. The sky flickered with the black-and-blue crosses of a skein of starlings. Underneath them, farmers worked crescent-horned oxen with wooden ploughs shaped like wishbones. We were leaving Shawa, the heartland of the Christian state that Francisco Alvares encountered, for the fulcrum of the medieval kingdom. The scenes in the marketplace of Debra Berhan – where men and women raced about with baskets, boxes and sticks – could have been seen through the eyes of Master Philip. A cripple – all stumps and crutches – was selling dung patties to a woman with a rattling basket of maize, and a tiny boy was trying to load faggots of firewood on to the back of a donkey.

The bus growled up the terraced ridges of Wallo and plunged into an extraordinary sea of cloud, which dissolved the houses and hills and enclosed us like a protective shell, disrupted only by the black fumes spurting from the exhaust pipe. The effect was infinite space: an eternity of whiteness, like TV impressions of heaven. Then the shell was cracked by trees and bushes and the thatched roofs of *tukul*-houses. Down the canyon, clouds bubbled over a town (at least, a fricassee of tin shacks) as if it was a vision in a witch's cauldron. Like a falling buzzard, the bus spiralled down and round, round and down, until it was rocking to the rhythm of panhandlers and tradesmen beating its sides, their fingertips pecking at the windows. A stream of knitted hats and papaya fruit, roasted barley and plums, swept us up, and we were washed outside on the mendicant surf. Fisseha punched a pre-pubescent mohair-sock-seller in the nose, and pressed one hand against the cavernous face of a crone, whose pot unleashed a yellow geyser of lumpy honey. At the nearest restaurant, he boomed at the waiter and treated us to atar peas and chunks of raw goat (a.k.a. 'hello tapeworm') generously sprinkled with pepper.

'In Eetopyar,' he said, 'we have a tradition. If there is a visitor, we put ourselves out for zam, and we put zam first because we are pleased to see za white man here.'

It was an awkward hospitality. At several restaurants the maître d's bent double as they escorted us to our seats, beating the staff and purging local clients from their tables. Francisco Alvares, in his sixteenth-century journey, also remarked on the warm reception of the Abyssinians. But sometimes it was refreshing to receive unadulterated contempt. An earth mother with an enormous bottom sat beside me on the bus (now thankfully pared to seatability) and made liberal use of her elbows. Whenever I frowned in response to another clip on the nose, she shook her head heavenwards and burst out laughing. It was very odd.

Time moved with rather more consistency than the bus. First the wheels developed an addiction to axle-deep ruts as persistent as the local fondness for *qat*. On another occasion the engine overheated and we spent a pleasant hour picking trumpet-flowers the orange of an Oromo lady's headdress, while the driver's lackey fetched a gourd of water from a nearby village. Mike and I gazed overhead at a lammergeyer, the bearded vulture unique to Ethiopia, before Fisseha reclaimed our attention as he laboriously listed each species of plant. He was soon interrupted again, this time not by a vulture but someone with an equally aggressive attitude to the dead – an Evangelical born-again Christian.

'There are six religions,' he boomed, thumping a massive leather-bound Bible like a drum, 'zat are hostile to Jesus Christ za Redeemer. And zese people will go to hell.'

'Like who?' asked Mike.

'Za Buddhists.'

'And what did the Buddhists do?'

'Zay fail to accept Jesus Christ.'

'I don't think he's really their thing.'

'Then zay are damned.'

If anything was damned, it was our bus. There was only one consolation to its penchant for breakdowns: it's easy to write in one's diary on a bus that isn't moving.

4.00   Lime-green valleys spotted with yellow meskal flowers. It's boiling hot, but the locals refuse to open the windows. They believe that allowing hot and fresh air to mix is a catalyst for plague. The air is thick and sticky, and a couple of chickens are squawking by my feet. The bus stops and Fisseha chases a boy with a basket full of Pepsi bottles, while Mike and I listen to a lecture on Christian supremacy.

4.20   We're off.

4.22   We stop.

5.20   We set off again. At a pace that is unequal to a man on a mule.

5.25   There was a point when stopping was a welcome opportunity to catch some of the bracing upland air. Now, stopping is simply What We Do. An atmosphere of pessimism has crept into the bus, expressed in scowls, spitting and mid-aisle disputes. I think a couple of marriages have broken down. The driver buries his head against the wheel, whilst his optimistic one-eyed assistant rushes about with a spanner. The more enterprising passengers are already on the road, their hitchhiking thumbs out. It's dawned on us all that we've landed a dud.

6.05   We've moved. One and a half triumphant kilometres. Outside an iron-roofed wooden hut, a young girl scythes sticks of sugar-cane and glances dreamily at our bus.

6.10 No progress. I'm starting to wonder if we'll reach Lalibela in time. The hills are losing their charm.

6.20 These are the facts. The bus won't get us to Dessie tonight. If we don't get to Dessie tonight, we've no chance of making the early morning bus to Woldia. If we don't get to Woldia early tomorrow, we'll miss the bus to Lalibela. If we miss the bus to Lalibela, we'll lose a day, and we won't be able to get to Lalibela and back in time for the flight to London. Which, considering that Lalibela is the destination of the entire trip, would be annoying. It isn't helped by the din of children, chickens and fully grown adults, or the driver's perpetually frustrated efforts to rev the engine.

Just as its occupants prepared to bid the bus a fair '*dehna senbetu*' (that's goodbye, in case you suspected something a little stronger), its engine managed one last two-kilometre-long roar, diminishing to a whimper at the edge of a small town. The driver and his assistant made a valiant attempt to escape but they were somewhat hampered by the fact that the earth mother was holding them by the hair.

'This driver is so stupid!' squealed Fisseha.

'Indeed,' I said, 'but does –' crack! – 'that mean –' the driver was lying on the ground with a bleeding nose – 'that they have –' his assistant was covering his one functioning eye as half a dozen former passengers attempted to remove his legs – 'to die?'

Cigarettes were waved like ceremonial torches to a torrent of cheers.

'But I suppose it's more satisfying than filling in those complaint forms you get on the Tube,' I added, turning to Mike; at least, the space where he had been.

'Er, Fisseha – have you seen Mike?'

Maybe the mob's attentions had moved to the *faranji*.

'He's over there,' said Fisseha.

While bedlam was exploding around the bus, Mike had

498

buttonholed the driver of a Land Cruiser. A driver on his way to Dessie.

'Sure, I can take you,' he said. 'Two of you.'

This was Fisseha's kamikaze moment, and he knew exactly what to do. He clasped our hands, then ran a handkerchief across his brow like he was auditioning for Glyndebourne.

'Please,' he said with the voice of a choking martyr, 'go – without me.'

Several dozen jealous scowls, and Fisseha's handkerchief, saw us on to the road. The sky had turned the colour of peppercorn, and suited the mood of our driver. Tekle was a pug-faced man with a gash across one cheek. He was as positive as a subtraction.

'The economy disaster!' he barked. 'Corruption in politics, the leaders they take the money . . . If you are Tigrean you have everything – the best jobs . . . But if you are not – the human rights so poor they arrest journalists who criticize and students too . . .'

One of the villages we passed through belonged to the Oromo, the people who came to Ethiopia with Ahmad al-Gragn, the Left-handed, in the sixteenth century. Barefoot Oromo children staggered through the dusk, baskets of firewood on their frizzy heads.

'Is because of the Portuguese that these people come,' snarled Tekle.

It wasn't true – the Portuguese helped to drive them out. But it was typical of an Ethiopian to blame unwanted issues on foreigners. I remembered Abba Tekle in Rome explaining that 'the Ethiopians are suspicious of foreigners', and the reluctance of Emperor Haile Selassie to ask for foreign help when famine ravaged his country (and led to his demise) in the 1970s; and the same reluctance from the man who deposed him, Mengistu. The Ethiopians, we had been warned, were 'proud'. Sometimes 'proud' means withdrawn, sometimes in-your-face. Pride can inspire a man to kill, but it can also inspire a man to treat perfect strangers to raw goat and atar peas. As a national trait, it would have made Ethiopia a fabulous land when experienced only through the reports of medieval Ethiopian pilgrims – the paradise of Prester John.

There was nothing proud about Woolly Blanket Man. The receptionist at our hotel in Dessie told us that the bus to Woldia would depart at six o'clock the next morning. At a minute to six, Mike and I leaped out of our beds, grabbed our gear, and sprinted to the bus stop just in time to glimpse the disappearing rump of our bus.

'Where you wan' go?' asked Woolly Blanket Man.

'Woldia,' we said.

Zip! Woolly Blanket Man became a whirl-spool of wool that rocketed to the bus, where his fingers did to the windows what woodpeckers do to trees.

As we waved thankfully from the squash of the back seat, it was impossible to overlook the fact that under his woolly blanket all he wore was a pair of red underpants.

And now – the modern trappings of a bus journey in Ethiopia: the plastic fruit and 'Love You' stickers above the dashboard, the windcheaters and Eagles baseball caps of our companions, the tiny boys who swagger down the aisle peddling keyrings and condoms, and the beggar with a Mickey Mouse thong on his sandal. But against that we must balance the keffiyehs and turbans, the tattooed crosses on girls' foreheads, the truncheons of sugar cane in their hands, the beggar's ancient blubber and the rugged mountain walls glissading into foot-shaped formations or golden maize fields protected by brushwood fences. Like all Ethiopian buses, this one was trapped between ancient and modern. It had fuel and (apparently) such modern attributes as an engine, but it sounded and acted like an old, undomesticated camel, and consequently when it delivered us in Woldia—

'The bus left half a minute ago,' said a man in an anorak. 'You like private hire?'

'How much?'

'Fifteen handrad.'

'Ridiculous.'

We marched to a café, informing the anorak that we would be available there for negotiations. In the meantime, we would be eating omelettes.

'Think this is gonna take a while,' said Mike.

I opened up Evelyn Waugh's *Black Mischief* and read the bit where the hero accidentally eats his mistress.

'One zousand!'

'Nine handrad!'

'One zousand fee-handrad-and-za-fifty!'

Every time we rejected their offers, they cackled.

'What?' snapped Mike. 'D'you think we're made of money?'

They eyed him greedily, like they were ogling a bar of gold. Rather like, I imagine, medieval European adventurers would have eyed the vast gold reserves putatively located in Prester John's empire. In Florence, Fra Livio had commented on the reversal since medieval times in terms of vocations: more priests now came to Europe from the continent to which missionaries like Fra Alberto da Sarteano had been sent. But there had been another reversal: whereas medieval and Renaissance-era Europeans saw in Africa the gold of their wildest dreams, that was what many of the Africans now saw in us. We might have been looking for transport, but they had their eyes on something much greater – the beginning of untold wealth.

Consequently, it was only after Mike had threatened the town with a pasting in a well-known guidebook (for which he installed us temporarily as contributing editors – 'We will tell them Woldians are evil and no tourists will come here!') that we were offered a decent price with a driver called Noah. It still took a ride on a horse-and-cart, another haggling session, and the temporary conversion of our 4x4 into a local bus service that drove up and down Woldia's high street for a couple of hours (which gave us a tour of several dozen tin huts, blue-leafed eucalypti, a dead horse and a window through which two boys were spying on a prostitute's boudoir) before we started making progress towards Lalibela. Even then . . .

When Noah's assistant's brother wanted some lunch, we stopped in a village a couple of kilometres outside Woldia. A young man poked his head through the window, in front of an army of locals whose T-shirts all bore the fake likeness of Leonardo di Caprio.

'You want to buy something?' he asked.

'Nope,' said Mike, 'we want to go to Lalibela.'

'You are here for work or tourist?'

'We're here on an errand.'

'From the Pope,' I added.

The young man looked unconvinced, so Mike took a deep breath.

'We,' he declaimed, in the same orator's baritone that he used when he was delivering speeches as president of the Junior Common Room, 'have travelled to the ends of the earth. Through desert, rain, flood, through areas of civil conflict and strife and nations inflicted with UN sanctions, so we can deliver a letter to King Lalibela, in his tomb.'

The young man nodded appreciatively. 'You want sugar cane?'

Noah's assistant's brother returned, and we drove into the Lasta Hills. Brass hills swam with blue mountains incised with shelves of road. Thatched *tukul* huts perched on the slopes. A cluster of gelada baboons scampered around the edge of a cliff and dispersed at the sight of our car, their chestnut manes vanishing over the edge, only to peep back at us as we rode past. We followed the granite arabesque through villages of wattle-and-grass houses and the skeletal frames of wooden huts. Air gusted through the half-open windows and glazed the scenery, as if I'd just polished my glasses. Children waved, pointed us out to their owl-eyed friends, lifted up their shirts to show us their genitals, threw stones at us or even stuck up a couple of fingers. One little boy slapped the leathery cheeks of his bottom and ushered us into a golden wheatfield.

'Roha,' said Noah.

Al-Roha: the Arabic name for Edessa, the city identified by medieval writers like Joannes de Hese as Prester John's capital.

Injara-coloured mountain walls flashed gilded ribbons of meskal flowers. Cowherds whipped beasts several times their size to the side of the road, spun round with bright smiles and waved us on. We passed families carrying sacks and baskets and received a friendly wave from a couple of men with sharp-pointed spears.

'Look,' said Noah, 'Laleebela!'

On the horizon, blue hills beat together and subsided in waves beneath a black fort-shaped silhouette. It was a spectacle of doom and thunder. One hundred and twelve days after our arrival in Venice, on the afternoon of 11 September 2001, we were approaching our target.

Lalibela is a surprisingly small settlement of farmsteads and (unusually in Ethiopia) circular stone thatched houses, many of them double-storeyed. Juniper and aloe flowers spruce up the characterless grids of shops and hotels. As we arrived, young men touting their tour-guide credentials made acrobatic assaults on the 4x4 – 'Meesta, I know every church and total history cheap price good tour!' One of them, Joseph, carried our bags into the Asheton Hotel. Neglected by an Australian, an Englishman and a girl from New Zealand swapping travellers' tales in the bar, he insisted that, without his services, we hadn't a chance of procuring entrance tickets for the medieval site, and as for Lalibela's tomb . . .

'We need someone who knows the history,' I said.

'For this me.'

He pulled himself up to his full six and a half feet, as proud as an Abyssinian *fitaurari*. But, since he had no idea who was king in 1177 (admittedly a tricky question) Joseph's self-styled status as a local sage was looking tenuous.

'We need the wisest man in town,' I said. 'Someone who knows lots of history.'

Visibly shrinking as he realized that this wasn't him, Joseph led us to the aptly named Solomon.

He didn't look very impressive when we found him: a slim figure filled out by a navy-blue windcheater, fiddling with a Pepsi bottle in a den of nutty coffee and straw. He had a long, serious face with small black eyes, and a beautiful smile – an enormous oval of white teeth breaking out of his smooth caramel complexion.

'There is a problem with your mission,' he said, as we dipped pieces of bread into honey mead. 'You see, we do not know who was king at this time.'

'What about Lalibela?' I asked.

'Maybe he was king. But maybe he was in Jerusalem when Philip had his mission. He was in Jerusalem when angels told him that his brother Harbay would abdicate in his favour. You know what year this was? 1177.'

'So it *was* Lalibela!' exclaimed Mike, thumping a triumphant hand on the rickety table-top.

'Not necessarily,' said Solomon. 'The Ethiopian calendar is eight years behind the Gregorian calendar. So it was 1185. And this is only according to the hagiography, which was written by the monks two centuries later.'

'And I thought the Holy Land was confusing,' muttered Mike.

The lack of written evidence prior to the *Kebra Nagast* (the great epic about the Ark of the Covenant's journey to Ethiopia), the burial or destruction of manuscripts when Ahmad al-Gragn invaded in the sixteenth century, the refusal of priests to reveal many of the manuscripts still in their possession and the reluctance of the government to fund excavations since the 1970s had masked the Zagwe period in secrecy and ambivalence.

'You know,' said Solomon, 'when I was a child they found in St Mary's church here some precious treasures – crosses and a pot. They used charcoal and ash and buried the pot in water and discovered it had honey. But now they don't try to find anything. There is a pillar in the same church, it is covered in a veil, but no one is allowed to remove the veil. Not even the Patriarch of the Church.'

'What's behind it?' I asked.

'Maybe,' he mused, 'the name of God, or the history of King Lalibela. Who knows?'

Impractical as it was, this obfuscation suited the enigmatic atmosphere of Prester John. We arranged to meet Solomon the next day, to visit the churches and continue our discussion. Back at the hotel, I started writing up a neat copy of Alexander III's letter to Prester John, in preparation for its imminent delivery. Two Ethiopian men sat down noisily at the table next to us, chattering excitedly.

'Excuse me,' stammered one of them, leaning across, 'you hear za breaking news?'

'News?' said Mike.

'You haven't heard?'

'What?'

'You did not hear?' The man gasped and, leaning further across, clutched Mike by the wrist. 'Amareeka,' he announced, 'under za attack!'

I imagined there had been an incident at Addis Ababa's US embassy.

'Maybe a million dead,' he exclaimed. 'Za World Trade Centa is destroyed!'

I put away Pope Alexander's letter while Mike grabbed a radio and fiddled furiously with the knobs. An American spokesperson crackled on the BBC.

'Thousands of lives have been lost,' he announced. 'The world will never be the same again.'

*

The next morning, Mike and I breakfasted in a coffee house that boasted Lalibela's only functioning television. On the screen were world leaders and pundits and New Yorkers with crumpled faces like discarded shoeboxes. Everybody gasped at the planes and the bubbles of flame that billowed out of the skyscrapers. People grabbed our sleeves and asked us if we had lost anyone close. But when we climbed downhill to the eleven medieval churches, the tragedy was lost somewhere among the censer fumes and the beat of *kebero* drums.

Turbanned priests in bright ragged strips shook crosses forged from beaten gold and nuns in yellow fezzes bent to kiss the steps. Above them towered a pink wall a hundred feet long, hewn out of volcanic tufa and gashed with keyhole-shaped windows: the church of Medhane Alem. Watching them from tufa shelves, we discussed the history of the Zagwe dynasty that ruled Ethiopia at the time of Master Philip's mission.

Two centuries earlier, the Axumite kingdom had been battered by Ethiopia's version of Boudicea – a fierce warrior queen called Yudit. Royal power had drifted from the Solomonic line to the Agaw of the central highlands. Without claiming descent from the Queen of Sheba, they didn't stray too far: legend linked them either to the queen's maid or to Moses' Abyssinian wife. With such impressive PR, Ethiopia's most enigmatic dynasty was able to hold the throne until the late thirteenth century. But one more detail considerably increased its influence – like Prester John, its rulers were priest-kings.

'If the Church didn't ordain you,' said Solomon, 'you could not have the crown.'

'So by Lalibela's time the kings were priests?' I asked.

'Certainly. Lalibela and Harbay were very religious and they are saints in the Church.'

Could this, I wondered as we passed a sludge-filled baptismal font, double as Prester John's capital? It wouldn't

506

need vast reserves of amethyst or a gate inlaid with the horn of a mythical serpent. But it would need an atmosphere that could have been Chinese-whispered into the Prester John legend. That the Zagwe kings could be called 'presters' was a start.

A reedy voice whined out of a scoop of rock: draped in a yellow shawl, a beggar held a Ge'ez manuscript in one hand and shuffled the fingers of the other. Through the walls facing him, inscribed and embossed with escutcheons and crosses, sunlight bladed into a jungle of thirty-six pillars* that sliced the church into a sequence of vignettes: a priest squatting between icons and flowers, working through a wad of tickets with the diligence of an accountant; the burial spaces dug into the ground that were named after the Old Testament patriarchs ('I think,' suggested Solomon, 'they were for the original architects'); the pilgrim gripping a cross stained black by smoke as he lay in a sunlit vault by the doorway; the hole in which the Lalibela Cross used to be secreted.† The church, like the kingdom that I was trying to conjure out of its shadows, was occlusive and mysterious.

Now I had to get my shoes back on, which was proving difficult because a little boy was holding on to them. My shoes, please? Ah, you want to put them on for me? For a

---

* There were also thirty-six pillars outside, contributing to an aggregate of seventy-two, that magic biblical number that also accounted for the number of kings under Prester John's suzerainty.

† Until this richly decorated gold artefact was stolen one night in 1997, when its two guards were, respectively, asleep and ill. Eventually, after a police panic that saw forty priests to jail, a bizarre story emerged. The cross was believed to have healing powers. A man whose daughter was sick had asked a priest to use the cross to heal her. One night, the priest stole the cross and used it to bless the sick girl. The father plied him with alcohol and, in the morning, the priest found himself back in the church, without the cross. It later transpired that the father's brother had sold the cross to an antique dealer in Dessie, who sold it on to a colleague in Addis Ababa, who sold it on to a Belgian art collector. It was eventually returned, in 1999, after a $25,000 remuneration, and is now back in Bet Medhane Alem.

small fee, no doubt? Each time we arrived at a church, a little boy called Dawit helped us untie our laces, kept guard over our footwear, and helped us reinsert our feet when we came out. With button eyes gleaming under a crop of woolly hair and around his legs a piece of cloth ingeniously tied in the form of trousers, he was a part of Lalibela's magic.

It was a magic that whispered through the lichen-streaked subterranean passageways and cavernous chambers smudged by pilgrims' fingerprints. This was a city where the burden of sin was believed to sink a chasm-straddling bridge, and magic grains of soil could cure disease. In the church of Emanuel (its rosebud walls pockmarked by Italian bullets because, the priest angrily informed us, one of Mussolini's generals had been 'jealous of Lalibela'), a cross was pressed three times against a pilgrim's face to enhance his wife's chances of conception. Elsewhere, priests ran their fingers over goatskin-bound manuscripts that mingled orb-faced saints with the Zagwe kings. Lalibela certainly held the right ambience for Prester John's capital. Although its myths were very much its own, it wasn't inconceivable that European scribes could have translated them into the stories with which they were familiar.

Even within Lalibela, myths mutated. Yesterday, the pillar in St Mary's had held the name of God or the history of the king; today, as I ran my fingers down the white cloth that veiled the pillar, and on to a spangly gold band stamped with a badge of Mary and Child, Solomon proposed that it represented 'Jacob's ladder. When Lalibela began building the church he wasn't sure where to begin, but a light fell on the pillar, so he started construction.'

Like the legend of Prester John itself, morphing through successive generations, the secret pillar was versatile.

The symbolism that crowded Coptic Cairo and filled the Gothic churches of medieval Europe was manifest. Swirling around the secret pillar were bulls waging the battle of good and evil, a rooster crowing the denial of Peter and the seraphim and cherubim of a two-headed eagle. Equally cryptic were St Mary's external walls: keyholes and up-and-down arrows representing the virgin's womb and Christ's trips to heaven and hell were carved alongside what Solomon described as 'the most perfect cross of all' – the swastika.

'You don't realize it is a cross,' he said, 'so it is good to avoid persecution.'

It also hinted, through its replication of the Brahminic cosmic symbol for the four-fold principle of divinity, at an engagement between India and Ethiopia, the two nations most commonly associated with Prester John.

Outside St Mary's, an orchestra of priests rattled clappers, shook staffs and jingled *sistra*. Anchorites with possessed white eyes rapped the cowskin lids of their drums while the *debtara*s raised their shrill voices. Their chant, like the manuscripts or the *mak'das* of Lake Tana, expressed the idiosyncrasy of a Christian culture estranged from medieval Christendom. They could have staged quite a contest with the beggars outside St George's, slumped under a tamarisk tree, unleashing shrivelled arms and agonized appeals like an organum of the undead. Here was an emphatic contradiction of a literal association with Prester John, who claimed that 'there are no poor among us.' If Lalibela had ever been Prester John's city, her hermits and pilgrims were now in the dumps.

But their presence in Lalibela was part of another Presterological link. One man, huddled outside St Mary's, had travelled four hundred kilometres from Adigrat by foot. He had very few teeth and one eye was bubbling in a septic blood-bag. He wanted to visit the Holy Land, but it was too far and he had his family to think of. In Jerusalem I had met an Ethiopian woman called Asib, who had travelled as a pilgrim and stayed for seven years. Ethiopians couldn't simply jet in and out, so they had a choice: visit the Holy Land and stay, or visit Lalibela instead, which, according to the *Acts of Lalibela*, is equivalent to seeing the face of Christ. Lalibela is a Jerusalem in Ethiopia. Between churches like St Mary's (or 'Gethsemane') and Beta Golgotha (or 'the Holy Sepulchre') runs a river called the Jordan (which is believed to connect directly with Jerusalem), recalling the Holy Land for those unable to visit the real thing. Lalibela expressed the importance of Jerusalem to its founder: an importance that was shared by Prester John, who had himself 'made a vow to visit the Sepulchre of our Lord'.

But what sort of a man was this founder?

'When he was born,' said Solomon, 'Lalibela was surrounded by bees, which we consider as the Holy Spirit. There were many prophecies about his greatness and his mother called him "Lalibela", which means "the bees know his sovereignty".'

It took time for that sovereignty to be conferred. His half-brother Harbay's attempt to poison him threw him into a mortal sleep in which angels carried him to heaven, where God instructed him to build the eleven rock-hewn churches. Which wasn't as tough an assignment as it sounds: Lalibela and his masons only had to build by day; the night shift was carried out by angels. Like Prester John, the heroes of the contemporary *chansons de geste* and Karl from Norway, Lalibela was superhuman.

You have to feel sorry for Harbay – when he flogged his brother, Lalibela felt no pain; when he cast him into the desert, Lalibela's dinner turned up via God's version of a dumb waiter. Poor Harbay was as hapless as Dick Dastardly. Add to that Lalibela's pin-up looks – cheeks like pomegranates and eyes like the morning star – and it's little wonder Harbay felt a certain fraternal envy.

Which is all well and good; what it doesn't confirm is when Lalibela actually ruled. Speculation spans most of the twelfth century, and much of the thirteenth. The hagiography enthroned him in the late twelfth century; in the 1920s, the British historian C. F. Rey nudged him forward a decade or two; Ethiopia's most respected modern historians, such as

Tekle Tsadak and Sergew Hable-Selassie, dragged him back again. He was almost certainly in power in the last two decades of the twelfth century. But whether his coronation (accompanied by a hail of fire, trumpets and flutes, and cries of 'O blessed O King of Israel') occurred two or three years earlier, and coincided with Master Philip, is – and will probably remain – as murky as the baptismal font that we'd passed outside Medhane Alem. What is certain is that Lalibela, clothed in the fabulous stories that legends must wear, was worthy of identification with Prester John.

The only concrete (or tufa, to be precise) evidence of his greatness is represented by the churches themselves. Intricately designed, each church different from its neighbours, they are a match for Prester John's palace: filled, instead of precious stones, with the scent of beeswax and the idiosyncrasies of Ethiopian lore, they achieve their most majestic expression in St George's. Although it was the last of the churches to be built, it was a sacred commission: just as he was about to lay down his toolbox, Lalibela was startled by a haloed horseman. St George, finding that no church had been dedicated to him and imbued with the vanity normally associated with Mount Olympus, had decided to express his anger in person. The monolith that rises, lichen-streaked, from its gorge more than makes amends, sunlight slipping through ogival windows hewn under myrtle-shaped lintels. It is the most visually arresting building in one of Africa's most visually arresting countries and underlines the mystery of this miracle-city, making it as magical a place as any of the fictions of Prester John's letter.

There was still one church that we hadn't visited.

'You are sure,' said Solomon, tracing a cross in the ground with his foot, 'that Lalibela is the right king?'

We had been tussling with this question all morning: should we deliver Master Philip's letter to Lalibela or Harbay? I wanted it to be Lalibela: he deserved it. A king who had spent twenty-five years in Jerusalem, and had built

511

a new Jerusalem, was appropriate to a mission that was born in Jerusalem, and never left its shadow. And in Lalibela (in the land where midnight is teatime and 1177 can be 1185, and people are still furious with sixteenth-century Iberians), a few years here or there didn't seem terribly significant. Harbay, on the other hand, flogged his brother and attempted to poison him, and made a hash of discarding the Coptic yoke that culminated in famine and plague.

Harbay	Lalibela
The first-born	Born in a prophetic swarm of bees
Threatened to stop the Nile	Visited heaven in a dream
Failed to secure independence from the Copts	Sent embassy to Saladin's brother, with a gold crown, an elephant, a lion, a giraffe and a zebra
Tried to poison his brother	Built Ethiopian Jerusalem
Flogged his brother	The greatest of all Ethiopian kings

I put it to Dawit, who was picking Solomon's cross with a twig.

'Harbay or Lalibela?' I said.

He looked up, swaying his head from side to side, then jumped on the cracked earth.

'Lalibela,' he screamed, 'LalibelaLalibelaLalibela!'

We just had to find Lalibela. His tomb is in the church of Golgotha (which Francisco Alvares compared to 'the sepulchre of Christ in Jerusalem'), near the 'Tomb of Christ', creating a connection between monarch and Messiah of which Prester John would be proud. Spindly twigs were the décor in a corridor of rock walls, patinated green by lichen. A cross had been gouged over a doorway at the top of a short set of steps. Sunlight brushed the tufa glacis behind this brief corridor and stroked the gaunt façade of Golgotha. From its thick wooden door, cold and forbidding, hung a metal padlock.

'Maybe,' said Solomon, 'if you come back this afternoon—'

'Maybe?' I burst out. 'Will it definitely be open this afternoon?'

'Maybe.'

'But – what if it isn't?'

'And we need *you*,' said Mike. 'Otherwise we'll have no chance explaining what we want.'

'What exactly,' Solomon asked, '*do* you want?'

'Well,' I said, 'we – we want the priest to understand that we've come all the way from Italy, with a letter, and we'd like to give it to King Lalibela.'

Solomon raised an eyebrow. He needed to sit down.

'You think we're mad, don't you?' I said, slumping on the ledge beside him.

Solomon hesitated: an incriminatory pause. 'I think,' he eventually mumbled, 'is very good you do this journey.'

'Ha!' Mike chuckled, reviving the knuckle-palm slap that I hadn't seen for a while. 'The man thinks we're mad.'

But when, moments later, a stately white-cloaked figure floated up the steps to the door, that didn't matter. Abba Ecsaza, Guardian of Golgotha, produced an iron key from his vestments, inserted it in the padlock, and pattered through to the back of the church.

Behind a pillared nave, carved saints (including our old friends George and John) peered across at us from porticoes in a secreted chapel, 'so well done', wrote Francisco Alvares, 'that they seem alive'. The chamber was cold and cavernous and its walls were damp. It was like being inside the belly of a whale. Abba Ecsaza crouched on a ledge that lipped out of the wall and exchanged some words with Solomon, before sweeping back a truffle-coloured curtain to reveal a domed memorial draped in red-and-gold cloth and pinnacled with crosses. I stepped towards it, but he held out an arm.

513

'You cannot pass the curtain,' said Solomon. 'It is forbidden to all except the Guardian.'

Now Abba Ecsaza was hovering over a hole behind the curtain, holding his staff. He inserted it into the hole to indicate its depth.

'That,' said Solomon, 'is where Lalibela is buried.'

I gazed at the hole like a child: like one of those Ethiopian children enchanted by the sight of *faranji*. Abba Ecsaza, perhaps in response, closed the curtain and blotted out that tiny chasm that led, like Alice's rabbit-hole, to something unknown and mysterious.

'Now,' said Solomon, as the priest regained his watch-post on the ledge, 'he will answer your questions.'

We asked him, through Solomon, about Lalibela's importance to Ethiopians.

'Lalibela,' he said, 'made these churches which could speak the Bible in stone. He was a good man, a man of God. Christianity was preached all over Ethiopia during his time. He could speak with God, and even after his death there is the soil from his grave which is able to heal the sick, and his prayers which help our people to cultivate the land.'

'How do the prayers help?' I asked.

'This land is barren,' he explained. 'It should not be possible to grow crops here, but through Lalibela we do.'

In Abba Ecsaza's intense speech, Lalibela seemed to live. It reminded me of the Arab attachment to Saladin. He told us about a Greek scientist, who had stolen some of the soil to investigate its properties. When he arrived in Greece, the soil had disappeared. But, a year later, he returned to Ethiopia, opened his luggage and found the soil again. Fearing supernatural activity, he grovelled to Abba Ecsaza, who remembered the incident with a flicker of a smile.

'When I am sick,' he said, 'I never go to the hospital or the doctor. I take the holy soil and I am healed.'

I thought of St John's tomb in Selçuk, where medieval

visitors like Abbot Daniel of Russia attributed similar properties to the dust.

'Lalibela,' continued the priest, 'is all in all for me. He was the holiest and greatest of all Ethiopian kings. I believe that God has sent a lot of messengers, but King Lalibela was the best. Not alone for me – for all Ethiopians.'

It was incontestable. How could Harbay, whose most famous exploit was his failed attempt to poison Lalibela, compete with Lalibela himself? Who better to combat the mighty armies of Saladin? If Ethiopia was the kingdom of Prester John, it had produced no sovereign worthier than this architect-king, artist, carpenter, priest and healer.

'Go on,' whispered Mike. 'Now's the time.'

I held out a crumpled scroll of paper with my most ambassadorial expression.

'Could we present –' I began, my stomach tightening at the excitement of the occasion, 'we'd like to . . . to present this – letter – to King Lalibela.'

The priest creased his forehead and mumbled to Solomon.

'He says,' Solomon explained, 'no one can touch the tomb.'

'Right. But could we put the letter by the tomb?'

The priest swung his head like a thurible.

'He says no one can go beyond the curtain.'

This was turning out to be trickier than I had expected.

'Perhaps,' I suggested, 'as he's the guardian of the tomb, we could give *him* the letter – in Lalibela's – um . . . absence?'

I flashed the scrolled Latin copy and translation of Alexander III's epistle, and with as much ceremony as the rather intimate occasion allowed me, unrolled them. Solomon and Abba Ecsaza conferred. The priest's face had stabilized. At least, it had grown more rigid.

'He says he doesn't read Latin,' said Solomon.

'It's a gift,' I pleaded, smiling like a sycophant.

Solomon looked rather embarrassed. 'He says how he

knows it contains nothing insulting to the Ethiopian Church?'

Mike and I exchanged a frown. This had become a serious problem.

'Look,' I explained, 'we *have* to deliver the letter. He doesn't have to *do* anything with it. He can throw it away. He can burn it. Once we've left, he can do whatever he likes with it. Just let us deliver the letter.'

More conferring.

'No,' Solomon shrugged. 'He won't take it.'

'Wait a minute,' said Mike. 'Haven't you got the pennant?'

Aha! Our secret weapon. The almond-shaped piece of tin that Johnny had given us in Rome. I brandished it in triumph.

'This,' I announced, 'is from the Pope.'

Abba Ecsaza reached out, snatched the pennant and twisted it between his fingers.

'That's Mary,' said Mike. 'She's holy to both our churches.'

Abba Ecsaza nodded. Then he handed it back.

'He says this is a fraud,' explained Solomon.

'What?'

'When Mary is represented in the Ethiopian Church, the angels Gabriel and Michael are always standing behind her.'

'Well,' said Mike, 'our traditions are slightly different.'

The priest didn't flinch.

'But,' I pleaded, my voice dwindling to a whimper, 'if you don't accept our letter . . .'

And, as Solomon nudged us towards the door, the grim truth struck my back like a sudden chill.

'. . . we've failed.'

The pennant felt cold in my hand. We had come all this way, only to be turned back at the final test. It seemed bitterly cruel.

Inkolala tibs may have some merit (it preserves people from total starvation, for example) but it isn't much good as comfort food. We'd failedfailedfailedfailedfailed. Slumped in the café, I was angry, inconsolable and desperate for a cake to cheer me up. But cakes aren't Ethiopia's thing. I flicked despondently through my notebooks. Was a visit enough? Was there some way to round off the trip, underline it, give it some order?

Two often mentioned motivations for travel are to see another world and to disappear. In that sense, a journey in the footsteps of someone who disappeared in search of another world was the perfect journey. But disappearing – slinking off to dissolve in a weft of natives – isn't as easy now as it was for the great Victorian gentlemen explorers like Sir Richard Burton. Every day, the world where Master Philip could vanish without a trace – with its old-fashioned cooking methods, folkloric medicines, magic amulets – sinks in a swamp of Starbucks coffee, SIM cards and ISPs. Yet . . .

We had drunk miraculous waters, eaten medieval recipes, attended the apparition of the Virgin Mary. We had been shown a monk in a coffee cup, a Nubian castle barely touched since its rulers were ousted, a secret pillar in an underground church. A Greek had raged against Turks and Crusaders, Arabs had raged against Jews and Crusaders, Ethiopians had addressed us as Franks. Master Philip and Prester John might have remained elusive, but their world had become visible and solid.

We had come across several Prester Johns: the idealization of Barbarossa's attempt to fuse the secular and the spiritual; the reincarnation of St John the Divine; the parody of Manuel Comnenos; the counterpart to the Fisher King; the Christian rival to Saladin; the exaggeration of fabulous leaders in Georgia, Nubia and Ethiopia – a Jack of All Traditions. When we first set out, I didn't understand who Prester John was, or why Europe believed in him. Now, I felt I did. Just as Palestinian refugees remembered their old houses in Haifa, with the rose-tinted vision of distant memory, so the 'Arab nation' remembered Saladin as the archetype of their perfect leader. Saladin was no longer a real historical character. He was an ideal. Prester John provided a Christendom that lacked great leaders (however many strong characters it boasted) with its own ideal.

But in subsequent centuries, less obsessed with the Holy Land, the priest-king's significance changed. In Jerusalem, Dr Wasserstein had suggested that Prester John's principal importance lay in the voyages of discovery.

'He encouraged popes and political leaders to explore the possibilities that might exist,' said the professor. 'Prester John fits into ideas about the edges of the world and offers material about them. If the edges of the world are populated by people who eat their children or have heads down here' (he tipped his head towards his teacup, at chest height), 'that's interesting, but it's not relevant. But if *Prester John* lives at the end of the world – a rich, powerful ruler – then the end of the world suddenly becomes significant.'

And nowhere were we closer to him than in Ethiopia. Historians have often puzzled over the medieval Ethiopian pilgrims' tendency to agree with Europeans who designated them as subjects of Prester John. Dr Steven Kaplan in Jerusalem had interpreted their agreement as a white lie to gain acceptance among their Italian hosts. But there was another answer: they actually *believed* that Prester John was their king. Because Solomon certainly did.

'But the letter wasn't *really* written by Prester John,' I had said, in the café the previous evening.

'It *was*,' he protested.

'With the Elixir of Life and the Tower of Babel?'

'Of course.'

Solomon believed that Harbay was Prester John. And so was Lalibela. And so were all the Ethiopian kings. Because in Ethiopia so many features of the Prester John legend, an uncanny number, were brought together:

- The Lost Tribes of Israel — The Ethiopian Falashas
- The Priest-King — All Ethiopian kings had to be anointed
- 'Heretical' Christian culture — Prohibition of pork, apocryphal texts like the Book of Enoch
- Fountain of Youth — Ark of the Covenant
- Edessa or Edissa — Roha
- The King of 72 Kings — The Negus of Neguses, ruler of the Rases
- The name John — The honorary title of Jan
- Request for chapel in Jerusalem — Granted to the Ethiopians by Saladin or one of his successors
- Diverse pagan beliefs — Oromo belief in Waq, among many other animist, totemist and Judaeo-pagan sects
- Strange beasts — Like the *gomara*s or seahorses that Francisco Alvares spotted in Lake Tana – the hippopotami

Here was the kingdom of Prester John. *Here* was where Master Philip should have delivered his letter.

'We've got to deliver this letter,' I said, turning to Mike.

He was leaning forward, across the table, towards the TV. There, reporters' cameras lit up the mayor of New York like a strobe light.

I felt a flush of shame. Here was the most important global event of our lives, and still I couldn't shake off my obsession with Master Philip. In hindsight, the resentment towards the West that had chased us across the 'Arab world' – from the men in the restaurant in Aleppo to the Hizbollah taxi-driver in Beirut or the refugees on the West Bank – seemed some tiny warning of the madness that had unfolded on the screen.

During the flight back to London, Mike and I would discuss the dozens of examples of 'anti-Western' attitudes, but none of their exponents seemed capable of anything as emphatic as had happened in New York (though nor, I imagine, did any of its perpetrators). We also thought of the parallels, the connections between the Crusades and the twenty-first century's 'East–West conflict'. The greatest difference seemed to be the scale of destruction that could now be caused in one blow.

'Let's just watch this report,' said Mike.

'Yes, but we've only got an hour till the chapel closes.'

'Nick, it's the biggest event we've ever lived through.'

'I know. But . . .'

So obsessed had I become with Master Philip's letter that I simply couldn't bear the thought of going home without delivering it.

I suppose it took me a little longer to realize what Mike already knew. Whether panting alongside Abdulrahman as we had approached the castle-mosque of Dongola Ayouz, crossing the trench to sneak into Jericho, marching either side of Father Tekle as we penetrated Vatican City, these experiences – the cumulation rather than the conclusion – were as precious as the delivery of Master Philip's letter. But the delivery of the letter, at that moment, still seemed more important in my own world than the tragedy that, at the same time, was reverberating across the wider world outside. Because hindsight is all well and good, but I didn't just think (oh no, it was nothing as flexible as thought), I knew – I really *knew* – that there was nothing – absolutely *nothing* – quite as essential on 12 September 2001 as the successful delivery of Master Philip's letter.

According to legend, when he was still a novice St Yared considered packing up his *sistra*. He changed his mind only when he saw a caterpillar climbing up a tree. Three times it fell, until finally it reached a bough and began its metamorphosis into a butterfly.

There was less than an hour to go before the church would

be padlocked for the night. Joseph, the young tout from our hotel, led us through a rock-cut canal where we squeezed around monks with burning eyes and heavy crucifixes. Inside Golgotha, the atmosphere was different. Before, it had been intimate and brooding. Now, it was crowded and noisy. The Englishman, Australian and New Zealander from our hotel were in Lalibela's chapel. Mike and I sat on a ledge facing the tomb and watched the circus. Abba Ecsaza stood in the centre of the chapel, solemnly dressed in his ceremonial robes. He clasped a twelfth-century cross while the Englishman, the Australian and the New Zealander took photos: Abba Ecsaza with cross, Abba Ecsaza without cross, Abba Ecsaza with Australian, Abba Ecsaza with Englishman. I felt rather indignant. Here we were, on the threshold of completing our mission, only to be delayed by a guided tour.

The session ended, and the Australian placed several birr notes in a wicker basket. Abba Ecsaza watched the notes carefully, counting with his eyes. I looked at him. I looked at Joseph, staring blankly at the back of the chapel. I looked at Mike.

'Not gonna have much opportunity,' he whispered. 'Make sure you take it when it comes.'

'So,' said the approaching Australian, 'this is where your physician came?'

'Well, not here exactly.'

'You seen the tomb?'

'Oh, you can't see the tomb,' said the Englishman. 'See that hole there – that's it.'

He stepped forward to point at the hole. I glimpsed Abba Ecsaza's yellow cloak fading into the sanctuary.

'Yeah, you can't actually go past the curtain,' continued the Englishman, 'but you can see it from here.'

'What?' I said breezily. 'That hole there?'

I stepped towards the curtain. I could see no sign of Abba Ecsaza. I edged forward. I felt the Englishman's hand at my elbow.

'Yeah, he stopped me,' he said. 'Only priests allowed.'

I was past the curtain, hovering over the hole, gazing into the black emptiness believed to contain the body of Ethiopia's holiest son. I gripped the slab of letters-and-pennant tucked inside my sleeve.

'No, you can't actually—' The Englishman gripped my arm, pulling me back. 'It's not actually allowed,' he said.

'Shhh!' His voice was replaced by Mike. 'Go on!' he whispered.

I looked at the hole. A flash of Abba Ecsaza's yellow cloak shone in the corner of my eye. The little black hole. The letter. The yellow cloak. I could feel myself hesitating, held back not by the Englishman but by my own awe of the moment.

'Nick!' Mike's voice was firmer. 'Go on!'

And then, it happened.

Inside, it was nerves, excitement, the pump-pump-pump of adrenalin. Outside, it was a little black hole and the letter and the yellow cloak and the letter slipping – *Master Philip's letter* – rocking against the edge of the hole, so that for one moment there was no hole, only Master Philip's letter, and then—

Gone.

In the centre of the chapel, Abba Ecsaza was holding another cross and watching the banknotes in the wicker basket. When I shook his hand, trying to tell from his eyes if he knew, I saw nothing. The cold fetters of his gaze became the cavernous chapel became a dark tunnel became a field where light splashed wildly over the Lasta Hills.

'We've done it!' Mike was laughing. 'We've done it!'

We ran across a stubble field and clambered over the shiny grey boulders that staggered the route to a summit overlooking Lalibela. Master Philip almost certainly never made it to Prester John's land, and Ethiopia probably wasn't Prester John's land: not because there was an alternative, but because it was a kingdom created out of chapbooks and the quill of an imaginative twelfth-century scribe. But, standing on the top of that hill, gazing across the vista of green and blue and brown that rolled around the thatched huts and the tufa peaks of the rock-hewn churches, the empire of Prester John and the world of Master Philip didn't seem much further away than the lammergeyer that flew over our heads as it swept towards the hills and disappeared in a nimbus of cloud.

APPENDIX I

PRESTER JOHN'S LETTER TO MANUEL COMNENOS

No twelfth-century copies of Prester John's original letter are extant. However, in the nineteenth century Friedrich Zarncke reconstructed the 'original', given below, on the basis of his comprehensive study of the available manuscripts.

John the Presbyter, by the grace of God and the strength of our Lord Jesus Christ, king of kings and lord of lords, to his friend Manuel, Governor of the Byzantines, greetings, wishing him health and the continued enjoyment of the divine blessing.

Our Majesty has been informed that you hold our Excellency in esteem, and that knowledge of our greatness has reached you. Furthermore we have heard from our secretary that it was your wish to send us some objects of art and interest, for our pleasure. Since we are but human we take this in good part, and through our secretary we forward to you some of our articles. Now it is our desire to know whether you hold the true faith, and adhere in all things to our Lord Jesus Christ; for while we know that we are mortal, your little Greeks regard you as a god; still we know that you are mortal, and subject to human weaknesses.

If you should wish to come here to our kingdom, we will place you in the highest and most exalted position in our household, and you may freely partake of all that we possess. Should you desire to return, you shall go laden with treasures.

If indeed you wish to know wherein consists our great power, then believe without doubting that I, Prester John, who reign supreme, exceed in riches, virtue and power all creatures who dwell under heaven. Seventy-two kings pay tribute to me. I am a devout Christian and everywhere protect the Christians of our empire, nourishing them with alms. We have made a vow to visit the sepulchre of our Lord with a very great army, as befits the glory of our Majesty, to wage war against and chastise the enemies of the cross of Christ, and to exalt his sacred name.

Our magnificence dominates the Three Indias, and extends to Farther India, where the body of St Thomas the Apostle rests. It reaches through the desert valley towards the place of the rising of the sun, and continues through the valley of deserted Babylon close by the Tower of Babel. Seventy-two provinces obey us, a few of which are Christian provinces; and each has its own king. And all their kings are our tributaries.

In our territories are found elephants, dromedaries and camels, and almost every kind of beast that is under heaven. Honey flows in our land, and milk everywhere abounds. In one of our territories no poison can do harm and no noisy frog croaks, no scorpions are there, and no serpents creep through the grass. No venomous reptiles can exist there or use their deadly power.

In one of the heathen provinces flows a river called the Physon, which, emerging from Paradise, winds and wanders through the entire province; and in it are found emeralds, sapphires, carbuncles, topazes, chrysolites, onyxes, beryls, sardonyxes and many other precious stones.

There is also a sandy sea without water. For the sand moves and swells into waves like the sea and is never still. It is not possible to navigate this sea or cross it by any means, and what sort of country lies beyond is unknown. And though it lacks water, yet there are found, close to the shore on our side, many kinds of fish which are most pleasant and delicious for eating, the like of which is not seen in other lands.

Three days' journey from this sea there are mountains from which descends a waterless river of stones, which flows through our country to the sandy sea. Three days in the week it flows and casts up stones both great and small, and carries with it also wood to the sandy sea. When the river reaches the sea the stones and wood disappear and are not seen again. While the sea is in motion it is impossible to cross it. On the other four days it can be crossed.

Between the sandy sea and the mountains we have mentioned is a desert. Underground there flows a rivulet, to which there appears to be no access; and this rivulet falls into a river of greater size, wherein men of our dominions enter, and take therefrom a great abundance of precious stones. Beyond this river are ten tribes of Jews, who, although they pretend to have their own kings, are nevertheless our servants and tributaries. In another of our provinces, near the torrid zone, are worms, which in our tongue are called salamanders. These worms can live only in fire, and make a skin around them as the silkworm does. This skin is carefully spun by the ladies of the palace, and from it we have cloth for our common use. When we wish to wash the garments made of this cloth, we put them into fire, and they come forth fresh and clean.

In a plain lying between the sandy sea and the mountains is a stone of incredible medical virtue, which cures Christians or would-be Christians of whatever ailments afflict them, in this fashion. There is in the stone a cavity of the shape of a mussel, in which the water is always four inches deep, and this is kept by two holy and reverend old men. These ask the newcomers whether they are Christians, or do desire to be so, and then if they desire the healing of the entire body, and if the answer is satisfactory they lay aside their clothes and get into the shell; then if their faith is sincere, the water begins to increase and rises over their heads; when this has taken place three times, the water returns to its usual height. Thus everyone who enters, leaves it cured of whatsoever disease he had.

For gold, silver, precious stones, beasts of every kind and the number of our people, we believe that we are unequalled under heaven. There are no poor among us; we receive all strangers and pilgrims; thieves and robbers are not found in our land, nor do we have adultery or avarice.

When we ride forth to war, our troops are preceded by thirteen huge and lofty crosses made of gold and ornamented with precious stones, instead of banners, and each of these is followed by ten thousand mounted soldiers and one hundred thousand infantrymen, not counting those who have charge of the baggage and provisions.

Flattery finds no place in our land; there is no strife among us; our people have an abundance of wealth; our horses, however, are few and wretched. We believe that there is none to equal us in wealth and numbers of people.

When we go out on horseback on ordinary occasions, there is borne before us a wooden cross, without decoration or gold or jewels, so that we may be reminded of the passion of our Lord Jesus Christ, and also a single golden vase full of earth to remind us that our flesh must one day return to its original substance, the earth. But in addition there is also carried before us a silver bowl full of gold, that all may know that we are lord of lords. Our magnificence surpasses all the wealth which is in the world.

There are no liars among us, nor does anyone dare to tell an untruth, for he who speaks a lie dies forthwith, or is regarded by us as dead. His name is not mentioned, nor is he honoured among us. It is our pleasure to follow truth and to delight therein.

The palace in which our sublimity dwells is built after the pattern of that which the apostle Thomas erected for King Gundafor, and resembles it in its offices and the rest of its structure. The ceilings, pillars and architraves are of *shittim*-wood. The roof is of ebony, which cannot be injured by fire.

At the extremities, above the gables, are two golden apples, set in each of which are two carbuncles, so that the gold shines by day and the carbuncles shine by night. The greater gates of the palace are of sardonyx inlaid with the horn of the serpent called *cerastes*, so that none may enter with poison; the lesser gates are of ebony; the windows are of crystal. The tables at which our court dines are some of gold and some of amethyst; the columns supporting them are of ivory. In front of the palace is the square where we watch the judicial contests of the trial by combat: the square is paved with onyx, in order that the courage of the fighters may be increased by the virtue of the stone. In our palace there is no light burning, except what is fed by balsam. The chamber in which our sublimity reposes is marvellously bedecked with gold and all manner of precious stones. But whenever an onyx is used for ornament, four cornelians are set about it, so that the evil virtue of the onyx may be tempered. Balsam burns perpetually in our chamber. Our bed is of sapphire, because of its virtue of chastity. We possess the most beautiful women, but they approach us only four times in the year and then solely for the procreation of sons, and when they have been sanctified by us, as Bathsheba was by David, each one returns to her place.

We feed daily at our table 30,000 men, besides casual guests; and all of these receive daily sums from our treasury, to nourish their horses and for other expenses. This table is made of precious emerald, with four columns of amethyst supporting it; the virtue of this stone is that no one sitting at the table can fall into drunkenness.

During each month we are served at our table by seven kings, each in his turn, by sixty-two dukes, and by three hundred and sixty-five counts, aside from those who carry out various tasks on our account. In our hall there dine daily, on our right hand, twelve archbishops, and on our left twenty bishops, and also the Patriarch of St Thomas, the Protopapas of Samarkand and the Archprotopapas of Susa. Each of them returns to his dwelling every month in his turn; otherwise no one departs from our side. Abbots, in the same number as the number of days in the year, minister to us in our chapel.

If you ask us how it is that the Creator of all things, having made us the most supreme and the most glorious over all mortals, does not give us a higher title than that of *presbyter*, 'priest', let not your wisdom be surprised on this account, for here is the reason. At our court we have many ministers who are of higher dinity than ourselves in the Church, and of greater standing in divine office. For our household steward is a patriarch and a king, our marshal is a king and an archbishop, our chief cook is a king and an abbot. And therefore it does not seem proper to our Majesty to assume those names, or to be distinguished by those titles with which our palace overflows. Therefore, to show our great humility, we choose to be called by a lesser name and to assume an inferior rank. If you can count the stars of the sky and the sands of the sea, you will be able to judge thereby the vastness of our realm and our power.

APPENDIX II

POPE ALEXANDER III'S LETTER TO THE KING OF THE INDIES

Alexander the bishop, servant of the servants of God, to my dearest son in Christ, the illustrious and magnificent king of the Indies, health and the apostolic blessing.

The apostolic see over which, though unworthy, we preside, is the head and mistress of all believers in Christ. The Lord attests this, for he said to blessed Peter (to whom, though unworthy, we are the successor), 'You are Peter, and on this rock I shall build my Church' (Matt. 16). Christ wished this rock to be the foundation of the Church, foretelling that it would not be shaken by any whirlwinds or tempests. And therefore not undeservedly did blessed Peter, on whom he founded the Church, receive in a special and outstanding way among the apostles the power of binding and loosing. For to him it was said by the Lord, 'I will give you the keys of the kingdom of heaven and the gates of the underworld will not prevail against it. And whatever you bind on earth will be bound in heaven, and whatever you loose on earth will be loosed in heaven' (ibid.).

We had indeed long heard, from many sources, and from common knowledge, how, since you came to profess the name of Christ, you have devoted yourself ceaselessly to good works and have concentrated on what is pleasing and acceptable to God. Furthermore, our dear son Master Philip, our doctor and member of our household, informs us that he has spoken in those parts with great and honourable men of your kingdom, about your pious intention and purpose. Being a far-sighted and discreet man, circumspect and prudent, he has frequently told us that he has clearly heard from them about your wish and proposal to be instructed in the catholic and apostolic teaching, and that it is your fervent concern that you and the land entrusted to your Highness should never be seen in any respect to diverge from or clash with what is held by the faith of the apostolic see. Consequently we fully share our joy with you, as with a very dear son, and give heartfelt thanks to him from whom all gifts come, joining our intentions and prayers to yours. May he who caused you to adopt the name of Christian inspire your mind with his ineffable love, that you may desire to know fully what the Christian religion should hold about all the articles of faith. No one who fails to accord in word and deed with the Christian profession can hope for salvation from that profession. It is not sufficient to bear the name of Christian while holding other personal views than those of the catholic and apostolic teaching, since Jesus says in the gospel, 'Not everyone who says to me "Lord, Lord" will enter the kingdom of heaven, but only one who does the will of my Father who is in heaven' (Matt. 7).

Further commendation of your virtue comes from the desire which the trustworthy Master Philip avers to have heard from your household, that you earnestly desire to have a church in Rome and some shrine in Jerusalem where trustworthy members of your kingdom can dwell and receive fuller instruction in the apostolic teaching, so that you and your subjects may subsequently receive and hold this same teaching. Placed, albeit unworthily, in the see of St Peter, according to the Apostle (Romans 1) we recognize our debt to wise and foolish, rich and poor. We feel the greatest concern for the wellbeing of yourself and your people, and, in accordance with ministry of the office we have undertaken, we earnestly wish to recall you from those articles in which you are departing from the Christian and catholic faith, since the Lord himself said to blessed Peter, whom he made head of all the apostles, 'And you in your turn must strengthen your brothers' (Luke 22). Although it may seem excessively burdensome and laborious among so many labours, various journeys and changes of location in distant and unknown lands, to appoint to you a delegate from our side, nevertheless, in consideration of the duties of our office, and having carefully weighed your proposal and intention, we are sending to your Majesty this same Philip, doctor and member of our household, a person in every way discreet, circumspect and prudent, confident in the mercy of Jesus Christ, that if you wish to continue in the proposal and intention which we understand you have conceived by the Lord's inspiration, once you have been instructed by the mercy of God about those articles of Christian faith in which you and your people seem to diverge from us, you will soon have no need to fear anything from the error which might impede the salvation of yourself and your people or obscure the name of Christianity among you.

And so, your illustrious Majesty, we encourage and exhort you in the Lord, as far as this Philip is concerned, as you revere blessed Peter and ourselves, receive him with kindness and treat him with due warmth, as an honourable person, discreet and far-sighted, and sent to you from our side. And if it is your wish and intention, as it certainly should be, that you should be instructed in the apostolic teaching on those matters which Philip puts forward on our behalf, listen to him carefully and diligently. Send to us with him honourable persons and letters sealed with your seal, by which we may know fully your intentions and your wishes. The greater and more elevated you seem, and less puffed up by wealth and power, the more willingly will we accept and the more effectively grant your petitions both for the grant of a church in Rome and of shrines in the church of blessed Peter and Paul and in the church of the Holy Sepulchre in Jerusalem and your other reasonable requests, since we wish to satisfy your very laudable desires in every way that God allows, and to gain for the Lord your soul and the souls of your people.

Given at Venice in the Rialto, 5th of the Kalends of October
[1177]

GLOSSARY

ahlan wa sahlan	'welcome' (Arabic)
ankh	ancient Egyptian symbol representing everlasting life (its shape provokes comparisons with the Christian cross)
azan	Muslim call to prayer (see muezzin)
baldachin	canopy on columns, usually placed over altar of a church
barouche	four-wheeled horse-drawn carriage with rear fold-up hood and two facing interior seats
burka	Muslim woman's (substantial) body covering
caravanserai	resthouse for merchants
cavehane	Turkish coffee house, where men watch TV, drink and play cards
çay	tea (Turkish)
çayhane	Turkish tea house
challah	Jewish braided bread, baked without milk so it can be eaten with meat in a Kosher diet, and eaten on the Sabbath; the recipe originates in fifteenth-century Eastern Europe

chansons de geste	'songs of great deeds', heroic epics popular in eleventh- and twelfth-century France. Their heroes, usually drawn from the court of Charlemagne, tend to stress loyalty and physical valour, and eschew romance, eliciting comparisons with the Western
chazzan	Jewish cantor
chetés	irregulars or guerrillas used by the Ottoman Empire during and immediately after the First World War
debtara	Ethiopian cantor or scribe
deisis	depiction of Jesus, Mary and John the Baptist side by side
dolmuş	literally 'stuffed': Turkish taxi service that leaves only when full
faranji	foreigner
Fatah	leading Palestinian political party and erstwhile guerrilla movement founded by Yassir Arafat and Khalil al-Wazir in the 1950s; means 'conquest' in Arabic, and is an acronym for 'Palestine National Liberation Movement' backwards
fellahin	land labourers, especially in Egypt (Arabic)
fida'i, fedayeen	'the faithful' (Arabic), originally used to describe initiated members of the Assassins; Arab guerrillas
fitaurari	'commander of the spearhead' (Amharic); officer in Ethiopian imperial army
fleur-de-lis	'flower of the lily'; heraldic symbol of French royalty and the Virgin Mary
Franj	Arabic term for the Crusaders
fuul	staple Sudanese and Upper Egyptian dish made from cooked fava beans

garis	Ethiopian horse-drawn carriage
Ge'ez	language of sacred Ethiopic texts
gelabiyya	long Arab gown worn by men only
ghazis	holy Muslim warriors, usually working on a mercenary basis
Hadith	collection of laws and stories, apparently related by Muhammad to his followers and providing explanations for the Qu'ran
hajji	Muslim pilgrim who has been, or is going, to Mecca
hakawati	traditional Arab storyteller, particularly common in coffee houses before radio and TV
hammam	bathhouse
Haram ash-Sharif	'the Noble Sanctuary', Arabic term for the esplanade that contains al-Aqsa Mosque and the Dome of the Rock in Jerusalem
haredim	ultra-Orthodox Sephardic Jews, often associated in Israel with anti-Zionism
hetoimasia	area dividing heaven and hell in depictions of Last Judgement
hijab	Muslim woman's body covering
Hizbollah	Shiite Islamic resistance movement based in Lebanon
hoja	old man (often of holy disposition)
iconostasis	altar screen, particularly prominent in Orthodox churches
ikat	tie-dyed woven silk fabric
inshallah	God willing (Arabic)
intifada	'shaking off' (Arabic); refers to the Palestinian uprising against Israeli occupation in 1987–93 and the conflict that erupted in September 2000
iwan	open-fronted hall in mosque

jihad	Muslim Arabic term for both Holy War and an individual's internal spiritual conflict
kebabhane	Turkish kebab restaurant
kebero	Ethiopian processional hand-drum, usually made from a hollowed-out log covered with oxhide
keffiyeh	Arab man's headdress
khan	resthouse for merchants
khatchar	intricately carved Armenian cross-slab
kiblah	direction of prayer, also used to describe wall of mosque corresponding to that direction
madrasa	Islamic theological school
mak'das	walled central enclosure surrounding the Holy of Holies in an Ethiopian church
mastaba	stone ledge protruding from a wall, usually to form a bed
menorah	Jewish candlestick, used in Hanukkah festival
mesenko	single-stringed Ethiopian instrument, usually played by minstrels
meze	selection of Arabic dishes, usually served as starters
mihrab	niche in a mosque, signifying the direction of Mecca
mimbar	Muslim pulpit
Mishnah Torah	commentaries on the Torah
muezzin	Muslim prayer leader, who issues the call to prayer (usually from a minaret) unless he is able to delegate that task to a cassette player
nymphaeum	ancient Greek or Roman sanctuary consecrated to water nymphs
omphalion	square of floor inlaid with marble in the centre of an Orthodox church

oneiricriticon	interpretation of dreams (Greek)
panaghia	'All Holy', a Greek title often applied to Mary
peyot	Orthodox Jewish ringlets
pittakion	authorized document (Greek)
qalimeh	opening verse of the Qu'ran
Qu'ran	holy book of Islam, dictated to the Prophet Muhammad by God
saz	Middle Eastern stringed instrument, similar to a lute
sephardi	term used to describe Jews and their descendants from the Iberian peninsula, parts of the Middle East and Yemen
servis	taxi (Arabic), follows the same rules as a *dolmuş*
shabbat	sabbath (Hebrew)
shahida	martyr (Arabic, literally 'witness')
shalwar	baggy trousers, like pyjama bottoms, popular in Turkey
sharia	Muslim legal system based partly on Qu'ran (although other influences, including pre-Islamic Bedouin and ancient Jewish laws, are also included)
sheitel	Jewish woman's headscarf
shemma	Ethiopian shawl worn by priests
shtreimel	fur hat worn by Hasidic Jews
sikke	felt hat worn by Sufis
sistra	metal rattles played in Ethiopian religious ceremonies
souk	Middle Eastern market
surat	verses from the Qu'ran
tabbouleh	Arabic mixed salad
talla-beit	Ethiopian beer hall
tankwa	Ethiopian reed boat
terra incognita	'unknown land' (Latin)

tetraptych	painting on four joined wooden panels
tetromorph	apocalyptic creature with four heads
tob	wide sewn garment worn by African women
Torah	central text in Judaism: the first five books of the Old Testament
tukul	thatched hut (Amharic)
vaporetto	Italian ferry boat, particularly common in Venice
walima	Muslim wedding feast
waqf	Islamic theological endowment
wefa	ceremony to celebrate rising of the Nile
yeshiva	Jewish theological school
zagharid	women's cries of joy, usually made communally (Arabic)

A NOTE ON THE ILLUSTRATIONS

For Part I, Christendom, the illustration is based on an eleventh-century icon of St Michael, in the treasury of St Mark's, Venice. Part II, Orient, features an Arab astrolabe, used by astronomers for measuring the altitudes of heavenly bodies. The illustration for Part III, Terra Incognita, shows a twelfth-century Ethiopian cross.

BIBLIOGRAPHY

Abu Salih, *The Churches and Monasteries of Egypt and Some Neighbouring Countries*, ed. and trans. T. A. Evetts (Oxford, Clarendon Press, 1895)

William Y. Adams, *Nubia Corridor to Africa* (London, Allen Lane, 1977)

Ayla Algar, *The Complete Book of Turkish Cooking* (London, Kegan Paul International, 1985)

Francisco Alvares, *The Prester John of the Indies; a true relation of the lands of the Prester John, being the narrative of the Portuguese embassy in Ethiopia in 1520* (trans. Lord Stanley of Alderley, 1881) (Cambridge, Hakluyt Society/University Press, 1961)

Michael Angold, *The Byzantine Empire 1025–1204* (London, Longman, 1984)

Karen Armstrong, *Holy War – the Crusades and Their Impact on Today's World* (London, Macmillan, 1988)

Aziz S. Atiya, *A History of Eastern Christianity* (London, Methuen & Co. Ltd, 1968)

Farid ud-Din Attar, *The Conference of the Birds*, trans. Afkham Darbandi and Dick Davis (Harmondsworth, Penguin, 1984)

Baha al-Din Yusuf ibn Rafi, *The Rare and Excellent History of Saladin*, trans. D. S. Richards (Aldershot, Ashgate, 2001)

Marshall Whithead Baldwin, *Raymond III of Tripolis and the Fall of Jerusalem (1140–87)* (Princeton, Princeton University Press, 1936)

C. F. Beckingham, *The Achievement of Prester John* (London, University of London/School of Oriental and African Studies, 1966)

C. F. Beckingham and Bernard Hamilton (eds), *Prester John, the Mongols and the Ten Lost Tribes* (Aldershot, Variorum, 1996)

T. S. R. Boase, *Castles and Churches of the Crusading Kingdom* (London, Oxford University Press, 1967)

Alain de Botton, *The Art of Travel* (London, Hamish Hamilton, 2002)

Poggio Bracciolini and Ludovico de Varthema, *Travelers in Disguise, narratives of eastern travel,* trans. John Winter Jones, rev. and introd. Lincoln Davis Hammond (Cambridge, Mass., Harvard University Press, 1963)

E. A. Wallis Budge, *A History of Ethiopia, Nubia and Abyssinia* (London, Methuen, 1928)

E. A. Wallis Budge (trans.), *The Queen of Sheba & her only son Menyelek (A complete translation of the Kebra Nagast)* (London, Medici Society, 1922)

John Bulloch, *No Friends but the Mountains: the tragic history of the Kurds* (London, Viking, 1992)

Burchard of Mount Sion, *The Library of the Palestine Pilgrims' Text Society, Vol. XII* (London, 1897)

Johann Burckhardt, *Travels in Nubia* (London, John Murray, 1819)

Claude Cahen, *Pre-Ottoman Turkey* (London, Sidgwick & Jackson, 1968)

Christian Cannuyer, *Coptic Egypt, the Christians of the Nile* (London, Thames & Hudson, 2001)

T. Carmi (ed.), *The Penguin Book of Hebrew Verse* (Harmondsworth, Penguin, 1981)

Penny J. Cole, *Approaching Jerusalem: the Legacy of the Crusades in the 21st Century* (Regina, Saskatchewan, Campion College at the University of Regina, 2000)

Anna Comnena, *The Alexiad*, trans. Elizabeth A. S. Dawes (London, Routledge, Kegan & Paul, 1928)

Erica Cruikshank Dodd, *The Frescoes of Mar Musa al-Habashi: a study in medieval painting in Syria* (Toronto, Pontifical Institute of Medieval Studies, 2001)

Curzon, Robert Baron Zouche, *Visit to Monasteries in the Levant* (London, John Murray, 1849)

Hassan Dafalla, *The Nubian Exodus* (London, C. Hurst & Co., in association with the Scandinavian Institute of African Studies, Uppsala, 1975)

Andrew Dalby, *Siren Feasts: a history of food and gastronomy in Greece* (London, Routledge, 1996)

Joseph P. Donovan, *Pelagius and the Fifth Crusade* (Philadelphia, University of Pennsylvania Press, 1950)

Georges Duby, *Women of the Twelfth Century: Vol. 1; Eleanor of Aquitaine and six others* (Oxford, Polity Press, 1997)

Will Durant, *The Story of Civilization: the Age of Faith* (New York, Simon & Schuster, 1950)

Lawrence Durrell, *Mountolive* (London, Faber & Faber, 1961)

Umberto Eco, *Serendipities* (London, Weidenfeld & Nicolson, 1999)

Amos Elon, *Jerusalem: City of Mirrors* (London, Weidenfeld & Nicolson, 1990)

Ernoul, *The Library of the Palestine Pilgrims' Text Society, Vol. VI* (London, 1897)

Wolfram von Eschenbach, *Parzival*, trans. A. T. Hatto (London, Penguin Classics, 1980)

Richard Ettinghausen and Oleg Grabar, *The Art and Architecture of Islam, 650–1250* (Harmondsworth, Penguin, 1987)

Felix Fabri, *The Library of the Palestine Pilgrims' Text*

Society, Vol. VII (London, 1897)

Robert Fisk, *Pity the Nation* (Oxford, Oxford University Press, 2001)

John Freely, *Istanbul: Imperial City* (London, Viking Press, 1997)

Otto of Freising, *The Two Cities: A Chronicle of universal history to the year 1146 AD*, trans. Charles Christopher Mierow (New York, Columbia University Press, 1928)

Adalbert Hamman, *How to Read the Church Fathers* (London, SCM Press, 1993)

Graham Hancock, *The Sign and the Seal* (London, Arrow, 1997)

Alan Hart, *Arafat* (London, Sidgwick & Jackson, 1987)

Yusuf Fadl Hasan, *The Arabs and the Sudan* (Edinburgh, Edinburgh University Press, 1967)

Paul Hetherington, *Medieval Rome: a portrait of the city and its life* (London, Rubicon, 1994)

Christopher Hibbert, *Venice: the biography of a city* (London, Grafton, 1988)

John of Hildesheim, *The Three Kings of Cologne*, ed. C. Horstmann (London, Early English Text Society, 1886)

Philip Hitti (trans.), *An Arab-Syrian Gentleman and Warrior in the Period of the Crusades – Memoirs of Usamah Ibn Munqidh* (New York, Columbia University Press, 1929)

Ibn Jubayr, *The Travels of Ibn Jubayr*, trans. R. J. C. Broadhurst (London, Jonathan Cape, 1952)

John Kinnamos, *Deeds of John and Manuel Comnenus*, trans. Charles M. Brand (New York, Columbia University Press, 1976)

Rudyard Kipling, *Barrack-Room Ballads, Vol. I* (London, Methuen & Co., 1892)

Laurence Kirwan, *Studies on the History of Late Antique and Christian Nubia* (Aldershot, Ashgate Variorum, 2002)

Manuel Komroff, *Contemporaries of Marco Polo: William of Rubruck, John of Plano de Carpini, Friar Odoric of Pordenone, Rabbi Benjamin of Tudela* (London, Jonathan Cape, 1928)

T. E. Lawrence, *Crusader Castles* (London, Golden Cockerel Press, 1936)

Bernard Lewis, *The Assassins: a radical sect in Islam* (London, Weidenfeld & Nicolson, 1967)

Jeronimo Lobo, *A short relation of the River Nile, of its source and current; of its overflowing the campagnia of Egypt, till it runs into the Mediterranean; and of other curiosities. With a new preface. Written by an eye witness, who lived many years in the chief kingdoms of the Abyssine empire*, trans. Sir Peter Wyche (London, Lackington, Allen & Co., 1798)

Amin Maalouf, *The Crusades Through Arab Eyes*, trans. Jon Rothschild (London, Al Saqi, 1984)

Paul Magdalino, *The Empire of Manuel I. Komnenos 1143–80* (Cambridge, Cambridge University Press, 1992)

Henry Maguire (ed.), *Byzantine Court Culture from 829 to 1204* (Washington DC, Dumbarton Oaks Research Library and Collection, 1997)

Sir John Mandeville, *Mandeville's Travels*, ed. P. Hamelius (London, Trübner & Co/Oxford University Press, 1919)

Jacob Rader Marcus, *The Jew in the Medieval World, a source book 315–1791* (Cincinnati, Hebrew Union College Press, 1999)

John Matthews, *The Grail: Quest for the Eternal* (London, Thames and Hudson, 1981)

J. S. Meisami (trans.), *The Sea of Precious Virtues: a medieval Islamic mirror for princes* (Salt Lake City, University of Utah Press, 1991)

James Morris, *Venice* (London, Faber & Faber, 1983)

Mukaddasi, *The Library of the Palestine Pilgrims' Text Society, Vol. III* (London, 1897)

Arthur P. Newton (ed.), *Travel and Travellers of the Middle Ages* (London, Kegan Paul & Co., 1926)

John Julius Norwich, *A History of Venice* (London, Allen Lane, 1982)

Richard Pankhurst, *The Ethiopians* (Oxford, Blackwell, 1998)

Richard Pankhurst, *History of Ethiopian Towns, from the Middle Ages to the early 19th century* (Wiesbaden, Steiner, 1982)

Richard Pankhurst (ed.), *Travellers in Ethiopia* (London, Oxford University Press, 1965)

Edward Peters (ed.), *The First Crusade: the Chronicle of Fulcher of Chartres and other source materials* (Philadelphia, University of Pennsylvania Press, 1971)

His Holiness Abuna Philippos, Ethiopian Archbishop, *Know Jerusalem* (Jerusalem, 1962)

Joshua Prawer, *The World of the Crusaders* (London, Weidenfeld & Nicolson, 1972)

Odile Redon, Françoise Sabban, Silvano Serventi, trans. Edward Schneider, *The Medieval Kitchen, recipes from France and Italy* (Chicago, University of Chicago Press, 1998)

Thomas Renna, *Jerusalem in Medieval Thought – 400–1300* (New York, Edwin Mellen Press, 2002)

C. F. Rey, *In the Country of the Blue Nile* (London, Duckworth, 1927)

Jonathan Riley-Smith, *Hospitallers, the history of the order of Saint John* (London, Hambledon, 1999)

Jonathan Riley-Smith, *The Oxford History of the Crusades* (Oxford, Oxford University Press, 1999)

Lyn Rodley, *Byzantine Art and Architecture: An Introduction* (Cambridge, Cambridge University Press, 1994)

Francis M. Rogers, *The Quest for Eastern Christians: Travels and rumor in the age of discovery* (Minneapolis, University of Minnesota Press, 1962)

Francis M. Rogers (trans.), *The Travels of the Infante Dom*

Pedro of Portugal (Cambridge, Mass., Harvard University Press, 1961)

Steven Runciman, *A History of the Crusades, Vol. II: The Kingdom of Jerusalem 1100–87* (Cambridge University Press, 1952)

Kalistrat Salia, *History of the Georgian Nation* (Paris, Edition N. Salia, 1983)

Kamal S. Salibi, *Maronite Historians of Medieval Lebanon* (Beirut, American University of Beirut, 1959)

Elaine Sanceau, *Portugal in Quest of Prester John* (London, Hutchinson & Co., 1943)

Friar Jordanus of Severac, *Mirabilia descripta, the Wonders of the East*, ed. Peter B. Lobo (Nagpur, Dominican Publications, 1993)

Boaz Shoshan, *Popular Culture in Medieval Cairo* (Cambridge, Cambridge University Press, 1993)

Simone Sigoli, *Visit to the Holy Places of Egypt, Sinai, Palestine and Syria in 1384*, trans. Fr T. Bellorini and Fr E. Hoade OFM (Jerusalem, Studium Biblicum Franciscanum, 1948)

Robert Silverberg, *The Realm of Prester John* (Athens, Ohio, Ohio University Press, 1999)

T. A. Sinclair, *Eastern Turkey: An Archaeological Survey* (London, Pindar, 1987)

Deborah Sinnreich-Levi and Ian S. Laurie (eds), *Dictionary of Literary Biography, Vol. 208: Literature of the French and Occitan Middle Ages: Eleventh to Fifteenth Centuries* (Detroit/Washington, DC/London, The Gale Group, 1999)

Vsevolod Slessarev, *Prester John: the Letter and the Legend* (Minneapolis, University of Minnesota Press, 1959)

Joseph R. Strayer (editor-in-chief), *Dictionary of the Middle Ages* (New York, Charles Scribner's Sons, 1985)

R. N. Swanson, *The Twelfth-Century Renaissance* (Manchester University Press, 1999)

Pero Tafur, *Travels and Adventures*, trans. and ed. Malcolm

Letts (London, Routledge & Son, 1926)

Tamara Talbot Rice, *Everyday Life in Byzantium* (London, B. T. Batsford, 1967)

Tamara Talbot Rice, *The Seljuks in Asia Minor* (London, Thames & Hudson, 1961)

Lynn Thorndike, *A History of Magic and Experimental Science during the first thirteen centuries of our era* (New York, Macmillan & Co., 1923–58)

Colin Thubron, *Mirror to Damascus* (London, Century, 1986)

Chrétien de Troyes, *Li Contes del Graal, or Perceval*, trans. William W. Kibler (New York, Garland, 1990)

Benjamin of Tudela, *The Itinerary of Rabbi Benjamin of Tudela*, trans. Marcus N. Adler (London, Henry Frowde, 1907)

Dr Erkan Türkmen, *Rumi and Christ* (Konya, Damla Mataacilikve Ticaret, 1992)

Mark Twain, *A Tramp Abroad* (London, Chatto & Windus, 1880)

William of Tyre, *A History of Deeds Done Beyond the Sea*, trans. Emily Atwater Babcock and A. C. Krey (New York, Columbia University Press, 1943)

J. P. A. van der Vin, *Travellers to Greece and Constantinople: Ancient Monuments and Old Traditions in Medieval Travellers' Tales* (Leiden, Nederlands Instituut voor het Nabije Oosten, PIHANS 49, 1980)

Jan van Gelder, *Of Dishes and Discourse* (Richmond, Curzon, 2000)

Alexander A. Vasiliev, *Prester John: Legend and History* (Washington, DC, Dumbarton Oaks Research Library and Collection, 1953; with thanks to Professor B. Hamilton for kindly loaning a transcript of this text)

Jacques de Vitry, *The Library of the Palestine Pilgrims' Text Society, Vol. XI* (London, 1897)

Margaret Wade Labarge, *Medieval Travellers, the rich and restless* (London, Hamish Hamilton, 1982)

John Kirtland Wright, *The Geographical Lore of the Time of the Crusades* (New York, American Geographical Society, 1925)

John of Würzburg, *The Library of the Palestine Pilgrims' Text Society, Vol. V* (London, 1897)

Sir Henry Yule, *Cathay and the Way Thither* (London, Hakluyt Society, 1866)

INDEX

Abboud, General, 436
Abdulrahman (in Ghada), 424–30, 431–2, 520
Abgar, King of Edessa, 141, 146, 149
Abraham, 147–8, 153
Abraham, Anba, Coptic archbishop, 297
Abraham, Sister, 294–5
Abu al-Faraj, 141, 147
Abu Dis, 302
Abu Ibrahim, 182–4
Abu Nuwas, 218
Abu Salih: on Ark of Covenant, 31, 480, 481; on Aswan, 392; on Copts, 371; on Dongola, 408, 427; on Nubian kings, 428; travels, 396
al-'Abyad, Hasan, 315
Achrafieh, 216–18
Acre, 82
Adams, Michael, 328
Addis Ababa: arrival, 486–7; Baro Hotel, 487; departure, 494–5; journey to, 483–4; street scenes, 488–9
Ahmad (camel trader, 365
Ahmad (guide to Dirunka), 384–91
Ahmet (in Diyarbakir), 142–3
Ahmet (in şanliurfa), 148, 152–3, 154
Akasheh, Khaled, 61–2
Ala ad-Din, Sultan, 114
Alawites, 158, 164

Alberto da Sarteano, Fra, 23, 53–6, 298, 501
Aleppo: arrival, 164; citadel, 173–4; Great Mosque, 164; Greek Catholic Church, 173; journey to, 163; souk, 164, 170–2; storytellers, 243; street scenes, 167–9; taxi-drivers, 166–7
Alexander III, Pope (Orlando Bandinelli): care of triptych, 65; career, 40–2; influence, 28, 126; letter to Prester John, 20, 23–5, 489, 505; monument, 63; policy towards Hospitallers, 81; relationship with Philip, 25, 31–2, 78, 126, 397; text of letter, 530–3
Alexander the Great, 46n, 75, 173n, 347, 349, 424n
Alexandria: *Alexandria Quartet*, 346, 368; arrival, 346; Cecil Hotel, 346; Corniche, 346; library, 347; lighthouse, 59, 348; Mosque of the Prophet Daniel, 346; Street of the Soma, 347–8
Alexios Comnenos, 98
Allroy, David, 288
Alvares, Francisco: on Abyssinian hospitality, 496; on church of Golgotha, 512, 513; description of mountain, 481; description of Prester John's court, 472, 473, 479; on hippopotamus, 519;

549